Artists and Artisans in Delft

ARTISTS and ARTISANS
in DELFT

A Socio-Economic Study of the
Seventeenth Century

JOHN MICHAEL MONTIAS

Princeton University Press
Princeton, New Jersey

To my mother,
GISELLE DE LA MAISONEUVE, *who first kindled,*
then guided my interest in art

Contents

Illustrations

Tables

Preface

This book had two patrons and mentors, both leaders in the field of Dutch art history: Egbert Haverkamp-Begemann and Albert Blankert. Without Begemann's encouragement and guidance, my research might never have gotten started or proceeded very far; without Blankert's, the study might have lost its momentum: it was largely thanks to him that the Vermeer Foundation awarded me the Vermeer Prize for 1978 which sustained my efforts and helped to keep me going. I am deeply beholden to both for their direct assistance and for what I have learned from them, through their writings and in conversation.

In the last stages of my six-year journey through seventeenth-century Delft, the art historian Svetlana Alpers and the economic historian of the Netherlands Jan de Vries helped me to bring the project to completion: they read my manuscript for Princeton University Press and suggested many improvements that I have incorporated in the final version of the book. I am also in their debt.

The relation between theory and "learning by doing" in the area of technology transfer is on a par with that between intellectual stimulation from historians and the apprenticeship necessary to do successful research in Dutch archives. With regard to the latter, I profited enormously from the friendly counseling throughout my project of Mr. H. W. van Leeuwen of the Delft Municipal Archives. My ability to read seventeenth-century handwriting—starting more or less from scratch—and to interpret manuscripts in old Dutch depended critically on his help. I am also grateful to numerous other Dutch archivists in Delft, The Hague, and elsewhere who contributed to my education in epigraphy and language. Professor J. L. van der Gouw was kind enough to allow me to use his transcription of the accounts of the headmen of Delft's Guild of St. Lucas in the sixteenth century. Since many of the early entries are written in a semiliterate manner and are very difficult to decipher, the Van der Gouw transcription was of great help to me.

Money is an essential ingredient of research, and my project has benefited from the generosity of several institutions. I am grateful to the American Council on Learned Societies (and to Dr. Gordon Turner in particular) for supporting my first application for funds at a time when the only qualification—beyond enthusiasm and curiosity—that I brought to my project consisted in a background in the economics of central planning and comparative economic systems. Other financial help came later: from the Griswold Fund of Yale University, from which I received small grants toward the beginning and the end of my project; and from the Netherlands Institute for Advanced Research in the Social and Human Sciences (N.I.A.S.), a nonprofit organization financed by the Dutch Government, which paid for my leave in the year 1977-1978 and allowed me to make progress on my book in a pleasant and stimulating environment. Here I cannot omit to recall the friendly reception and assistance of Mevrouw Elisabeth van Loon, the vice-director of N.I.A.S.

Parts of Chapters 3 through 6 were previously published in *Simiolus.*

I owe a very special debt to Marilyn Campbell for her extraordinarily careful editing of this lengthy manuscript. My friend and colleague Truus Koopmans kindly checked through the proofs for errors in modern Dutch and German.

Several secretaries typed parts of this manuscript. I am grateful to them all. But none of them had as rough a job as my wife who typed all my drafts from yellow pages—Dutch citations and all. Her epigraphic achievement dwarfs mine.

Now a few words about the book itself, which is aimed at two possible sets of readers: Art historians with an interest in the socio-economic background of Dutch art and economic historians with an interest in art. Because the standards of the two fields differ appreciably, I could not always appeal to both sets of readers simultaneously. Thus some parts of Chapters 5 and 8 may be too technical for art historians and the abundance of details and anecdotes strewn throughout the book is sure to tax the patience of economic historians. I also had in mind a third set of readers overlapping with the other two: these are individuals with a knowledge of seventeenth-century Dutch, including archivists, who are likely to demand the maximum possible accuracy in the reading of original manuscripts and in the interpretation of original texts. It was mainly for these readers that, in an earlier draft, I frequently inserted in parentheses citations from the original Dutch manuscripts so that they could verify my translation; but I eventually limited myself to citing in

Dutch only words or passages that might reasonably raise questions as to whether I had read the original or translated it correctly. A special problem that my editor at the Press and I had to deal with was the lack of consistency in the spelling of both common and proper names in Old Dutch. In general wherever I cited a Dutch document directly I used the original spelling: this applies both to citations from notarial depositions and to lists of names culled from guild records. For example, a glance at the list of headmen of the Guild of St. Lucas in Appendix C will reveal that the spelling of names varies from year to year (e.g. Antoni Palamedes in 1658, Anthonij Pallemedes in 1663). (The consistency of names in today's world is an essential requirement of a well-policed society and an orderly social-security system.) However, whenever I referred—without direct citation—to an artist known to historians (such as Johannes Vermeer or Leonaert Bramer), I always used the "standard spelling" of art historical dictionaries and texts. Even if an individual was not so well-known (the faienciers Hans de Wint or de Windt and Gysbrecht Kruyck, Cruyck, or Cruck), I still tried to maintain the same spelling throughout (De Wint, Kruyck). Readers encountering problems should consult the index where most of the variants of names used are listed next to the main entry. With respect to common names, I also imposed some consistency on the material. Thus I write *plateelbacker* for faiencier or maker of delftware faience (literally, dish-baker) which is the most common variant of a word that may range from *plattielbakker* to *betielbacker*. In Appendix B, where the regulations of the Guild of St. Lucas in Delft are given in full translation, I have made an effort to be extra precise, both in citing original Dutch expressions in parentheses and in providing literal translations (e.g. clay-baker for *geleybacker* to distinguish it from *porceleinbacker* when in fact the text clearly refers to faienciers in general). I hope that this precision will have obviated the need for supplying a full transcription of these important regulations.

There is a fourth category of readers that may possibly have an interest in this book to whom I should address a few words. These are connoisseurs—collectors, highly specialized art historians—who may want to look up the names of obscure painters who were active in the sixteenth or seventeenth century in Delft. I have little to offer them beyond scraps of biographical information about individual artists and a few illustrations of works by painters who are largely forgotten today but played an important role in Delft's artistic development (Willem van den Bundel, Hans Jordaens, Pieter van Asch). These illustrations are not meant to show the peaks of Delft art but to give an idea of the typical pictures that hung in burghers' homes in seventeenth-century Delft. Paintings by Johannes Vermeer and Pieter de Hooch are also reproduced to suggest the full range of Delft's artistic accomplishments.

Institution for Social and Policy Studies, Yale University
New Haven
March, 1981

Money Equivalents

One (Carolus) gulden = twenty stuivers

One Flemish pound (*pont vlaems*) = six gulden

One schelling = six stuivers

One groot = one-half stuiver

One rijcksdaelder = 2.5 gulden

One duit = one-eighth stuiver

Artists and Artisans in Delft

Introduction

When I began my research for this book, I intended to write a comparative study of artists' guilds in the Netherlands in the seventeenth century. The decision to start my project in Delft was largely fortuitous. The first set of guild documents published in 1877 by F.D.O. Obreen in his basic archive of Netherlandish art history consisted of the masterbooks and the register of new inscriptions of the Guild of St. Lucas in Delft, 1613-1714.[1] This seemed as good a starting point as any for a comparative study of the range of occupations encompassed by Dutch guilds. But Delft also offered a special opportunity: the sixteenth-century guild accounts, which had been lost for over one hundred years, turned up in the sales catalogue of an American bookseller in the early 1970s and were bought by the Municipal Archives of Delft.[2] From these accounts and from the Obreen archive, I was able to compile a list of guild members from about 1560 to 1714. The question I could not resolve without further study was how exhaustive this list really was. By the time I had collected enough material to answer this question, I had given up any notion of including other towns besides Delft in my investigation.

According to the 1611 rules of the Guild of St. Lucas, "all those earning their living here with the art of painting ... in oil or watercolors, glassmakers, glass-sellers, faienciers, tapestry-makers, embroiderers, engravers, sculptors ..., scabbard-makers, art-printers, booksellers, and sellers of prints and paintings, of whatever kind they may be" were supposed to be members of the guild. Only masters in the guild could sell the goods or perform the services encompassed by these occupations.

My first task, as I saw it, was to draw up as complete a roster as possible of the individuals engaged in all these crafts and to check the names against the lists of seventeenth-century masters published by Obreen. My initial roster of artists and artisans was compiled from the registers of real-estate taxes of 1620 and 1632. I extracted more

[3]

names from the records of real-estate transactions for the years 1598 to 1644. By then I had many names of craftspeople who were not inscribed in the master lists. Were they apprentices or journeymen, or were they independent artists and artisans who simply had never joined the guild? To answer this question, I built up a sample of recorded transactions (sales of objects, bills for services rendered) that, according to the guild letter, could only be effected by members. This necessitated a search through the expenditure accounts of the Old and the New Churches, the city treasurer, and the Camer van Charitate, Delft's charitable foundation. These various records provided information on the economic circumstances of guild members that was at least as important and interesting as the matter of compliance with guild regulations.

I soon found that enough material was available for a study of the economic status of guild members. In addition to the data I had already collected on the taxes paid on houses owned by masters in the guild and their employees, and on the sales prices of the houses they had bought and sold, I came across records of their death donations to the Camer van Charitate that provided another indicator of their economic status. The real-estate records and the death donation books, incidentally, had never been exploited by historians of the arts, the economy, or any other aspect of Dutch society. They contained new information about Johannes Vermeer—the price of the house his father bought as an inn in 1641, the failure to make a donation at his death in 1675—which encouraged me to look for other documents on Delft's most famous painter.[3] To this end and to gather supplementary material on the activities of other guild members, I had to work my way through the notarial archives consisting of over six hundred volumes of handwritten documents for the period on which I chose to concentrate (1600 to 1680).[a] I first searched these volumes for any information I could uncover about members of the guild or their "servants" (apprentices and journeymen), including testaments, apprenticeship contracts, sales and transfers of movable and immovable property, debt instruments, and depositions concerning events that they witnessed. I kept notes also on the signatures and illiterate marks of these individuals, which appeared on documents they witnessed, since this evidence could be used to pin down the years

[a]At any one time there were about twenty notaries active in Delft whose papers have, in part or in whole, been preserved. A complete list of notaries whose papers were consulted is contained in the Bibliography.

during which they were active in Delft. Later I explored the estate papers of the Orphan Chamber of Delft, noting all references to debts owed by or to members of the community of artists and artisans that I was investigating. Finally I made a systematic record of the titles, prices, and attributions of the paintings and other art objects in about twelve hundred inventories culled from notarial records and from the estate papers (*boedels*) of the Orphan Chamber.

The research on guild members and their apprentices formed the basis for Chapters 4 (on guild membership), 5 (on the economic status of artists and artisans) and 6 (on painters in Delft). Chapter 7 on the art market—city commissions, lotteries, art dealers—drew on the accounts of the city treasurer and on notarial archives. My analysis of estate papers provided the data for Chapter 8 (collections of artworks in Delft). For Chapter 9 on the printing trades, the tapestry manufactures, and the delftware ceramic industry, I used notarial archival records, the handwritten notes of A.H.H. van der Burgh (who collected information on faienciers for thirty years), tax registers, and miscellaneous published studies on the minor arts in Delft.

The more research I did in the notarial and Orphan Chamber archives, the more fluent I became in deciphering the manuscripts and the higher became the proportion of grain to chaff in the raw material I sifted.

It was not long after I had begun my project that I realized Delft was of an ideal size and importance for a comprehensive survey of an artistic community. With its population of twenty-five to thirty thousand inhabitants in the middle of the seventeenth century, Delft was large enough to host a significant school of painting, of which Vermeer, Pieter de Hooch, and Carel Fabritius are only the best known representatives; it had a thriving faience industry with hundreds of apprentices and journeymen whose economic status could be statistically compared to that of the masters in the guild; yet it was not so large that its archival materials could not be exploited within a reasonable period of time. In a period of five years of intermittent research, I was able to go through most of the notarial archives at least once (about half of them twice)[b] and to scan the estate papers left by the overwhelming majority of burghers. I could

---

[b]I concentrated on notarial records containing depositions, debt acknowledgments, insinuations, powers of attorney, inventories of assets, and sales of real estate; I only skimmed the volumes containing exclusively testaments and marriage contracts that yielded little useful material.

only have made a dent during this period in the Amsterdam notarial archives, the capacity of which is measured in hundreds of meters of shelf space.

Delft being of moderate size, its guild regulations could be enforced far more effectively than those of a much larger city such as Amsterdam, where many independent artists and artisans failed to register as masters, and where those that did could more easily escape the headmen's surveillance. On the basis of admittedly slim evidence gathered in occasional forays in other archives, I concluded that the membership of Delft's St. Lucas Guild was fairly typical of a medium-sized artistic community under effective guild control

Besides a greater degree of compliance with guild regulations, Delft may also have differed from larger commercial and manufacturing centers such as Amsterdam and Leyden (and perhaps even Haarlem) in the near-absence of really wealthy families. My research in death inventories very seldom turned up any individual whose movable possessions (furniture, clothing, works of art, jewelry) exceeded 10,000 gulden (modern Dutch, guilders). Estates with movable possessions valued in excess of that sum are much more frequently encountered in the larger cities. I suspect, therefore, that there were fewer potential patrons of the arts in Delft—people who could easily pay 500 gulden or more for a painting or 1,500 gulden for a tapestry—than there were in Amsterdam or Leyden. This means in turn that the Delft art market was more anonymous, less oriented toward a few wealthy Maecenases than the market in larger cities.

On the other hand, Delft had one serious drawback for my project. Because virtually no work has been done on its economic history, in contrast to the numerous studies on Amsterdam and Leyden,[c] I had no basic data to compare my community of artists and artisans either with the city's population as a whole or with any crafts, professions, or other socio-economic groups. No vital statistics were available for the city, except a 1622 population count of 22,769. To arrive at a rough estimate of the population in 1600 and 1650, I had to make the very

---

[c]Among the most important of these specialized studies are Violet Barbour's *Capitalism in Amsterdam in the 17th Century* (Ann Arbor: University of Michigan Press, Ann Arbor Paper Books, 1963); Johannes G. van Dillen's *Van rijkdom en regenten; handboek tot de economische en sociale geschiedenis van Nederland tijdens de Republiek* (The Hague: M. Nijhoff, 1970), and N. W. Posthumus's *De geschiedenis van de Leidsche lakenindustrie*, 3 vols. (The Hague: M. Nijhoff, 1908-1939). Delft is only mentioned a few times in Jan de Vries's excellent study of Dutch agriculture, *The Dutch Rural Economy in the Golden Age* (New Haven: Yale University Press, 1974).

approximate assumption that the population changed over time more or less in proportion to the number of deaths and marriages. Nor were there data on hand about the regulations of other craft guilds that would have offered adequate comparative material. When I wanted to match the real-estate taxes paid by artists and artisans against the taxes paid by ordinary craftsmen such as carpenters or masons, I was obliged to gather the samples myself (even though I could not make the essential distinction in the data at my disposal between masters in these crafts and their apprentices, which a more systematic study probably could have brought to light). No data on prices of consumer goods and services or wages have ever been collected in Delft. To get some impression of trends in prices and wages, I had to consult N. W. Posthumus's series for other cities in the Netherlands[4] and extrapolate from small samples of Delft prices and wages based on scattered quotations in notarial documents. All these lacunae limit the extent to which economic historians will be able to use the material in this book for purposes of their own. One part of my study that I think may be useful for general historical purposes, however, is the statistical analysis of the appraised value of movable possessions in inventories of 461 estates, recorded between 1610 and 1680. Out of 1,224 inventories I collected, 617 contained information on the value of the artworks they listed. Of this number, 156 had to be discarded because they did not provide a total value of all movable possessions or because they were otherwise incomplete. To supply a firmer basis for my conclusions, I made a systematic effort to estimate the extent of the biases in these inventory data due to the incompleteness of the extant records and to sampling errors in their selection.

Just as I did not work up my statistical data primarily for the benefit of economic historians, so my analysis of economic phenomena is not focused on meeting the demands of professional economists. I aimed only at making reasonable inferences from the facts I collected, without trying to squeeze all the implications that a more systematic use of theory might have yielded. I tried, for example, to show that the parents of young men who wanted to become painters had to incur, in addition to significant money expenditures for their apprenticeship, the opportunity costs of the earnings foregone by the young artists during their six-year training. I made a rough estimate of the total costs involved and compared the result to the price of a moderately expensive house. I am aware that I should have discounted costs incurred in future years, but I saw no point to a refinement that could not possibly affect my conclusion. (For the benefit of the skeptical

[7]

reader, I may mention that interest rates were low in Holland in the seventeenth century—typically 3.5 to 6 percent on personal loans, despite a significant risk of default.) In general, I chose to introduce economic reasoning here and there in small, inconspicuous doses for the purpose of suggesting possible implications or conjectures, without any pretense of deriving tightly reasoned hypotheses.

These theoretical observations aside, the bulk of the material in the present book consists of more or less solidly documented facts about Delft's community of artists and artisans, the art market, art collections, and the city's art industries—faience, tapestry, and printing. Many of these facts are adduced here for the sake of completeness or because they just seemed interesting to me. The presentation of crude facts is no doubt bad social science, at least as rigorous (puritan?) social science is generally conceived.[d] But I can comfort myself with the thought that this multitude of facts may still be capable of satisfying a potential demand from readers who may some day wish to make use of them. Thus my miniature study of literacy among master faienciers and their apprentices in Chapter 5, while it does not add much to my estimates of the relative earnings and wealth of faienciers, will, I hope, add to the store of detailed information about the occupational basis of literacy in seventeenth-century Holland.

One question specialists in Dutch art will surely ask is how new all the facts presented in this study really are. Didn't Abraham Bredius explore these archives between 1880 and 1930, searching for documents on Delft's painters? Didn't A.H.H. van der Burgh comb through them for documents on the delftware industry? They did, of course, and many a notarial deposition about painters and faienciers that I stumbled upon turned out to have been discovered earlier by one or the other of these great scholars. J. Soutendam and D. P. Oosterbaan, both former archivists of Delft, also picked out many precious bits of information about guild members from the tax books, the expenditure registers of the city, and other sources. I have tried to give all previous researchers their due by citing their published discoveries[e] as well as their manuscript notes[f] wherever I became

[d]For a less "uptight," antipuritanical approach to economics, I recommend Tibor Scitovsky's *The Joyless Economy: An Inquiry into Human Satisfaction and Consumer Dissatisfaction* (London: Oxford University Press, 1976).

[e]Especially, of course, Abraham Bredius's invaluable *Künstler-inventare: Urkunden zur Geschichte der Holländischen Kunst des XVI[ten], XVII[ten], und XVIII[ten] Jahrhunderts*, 7 vols. (The Hague, 1915-1921).

[f]The handwritten notes of Abraham Bredius are preserved in the Rijksbureau voor Kunsthistorische Documentatie in The Hague, those of A.H.H. van der Burgh in the Delft Municipal Archives.

aware that my findings were not new. In some cases, however, I may have inadvertently cited original documents, not realizing that they had already been published or that they had been referred to in manuscript notes. I trust, however, that the bulk of the notarial records directly cited in this study are new findings.

As to what art historians may hope to learn from the book, I am hesitant to speculate since I am only an eavesdropper on the profession. Around 1900, socio-economic studies of artists' communities appealed to many historians of Northern art.[g] But in the last couple of generations, the material, palpable, visible product of the artist, the object in isolation of its social context, became the dominant concern of the profession, just as the analysis of the text of literary works crowded out almost all considerations of the social milieu among the adepts of the "New Criticism." More recently, the weight of opinion seems to have started swinging back in favor of a study of the environment in which works of art and literature arose. So far, the cultural milieu has been emphasized more than the economic background, but this may be changing as the former topic becomes exhausted and fledgling scholars in search of integrating ideas begin to look to the latter.[h] The problem then, as now, is whether a case can be made for the influence of economic conditions on the subjects chosen by artists and, more difficult still, on their styles. The works of Marxist art historians such as Arnold Hauser, marred as they are by a superficial approach to cultural materialism and a lack of success in establishing clear connections between the material substructure of society and its ideological superstructure, have attracted few followers of note. Little of what I have to say bears directly on the relation of material background to subjects and style. Nevertheless, I hope that my decade-by-decade analysis of the subject matter of nearly ten thousand paintings in Chapter 8 and my discussion of the trends in representation may provide a starting point for an analysis of this relation.

While investigation of economic conditions in Delft has hardly

[g]The only important book written on economic aspects of Netherlandish art was published in the first years of the century, Hanns Floerke's *Die Formen des Kunsthandels, das Atelier und die Sammler in den Niederlanden vom 15-18 Jahrhundert*, Studien zur Niederländischen Kunst- und Kulturgeschichte (Munich, 1905). *Signum temporum*, it has recently been republished (Soest, Holland: Davaco publishers, 1972).

[h]Cf. Svetlana Alpers, "Is Art History?" *Daedalus* 106 (Summer 1977):1-13. For a pioneering attempt to relate economic environment to style in the development of Dutch landscape painting, see Åke Bengtsson, *Studies on the Rise of Realistic Painting in Holland*, 1610-1625 (Stockholm: Institute of Art History of Uppsala, 1952).

begun, some progress has been made on the art-historical front. In the last few years several artists of the Delft school have drawn the careful attention of competent scholars: Arthur Wheelock and Albert Blankert have written on Vermeer, Peter Sutton on Pieter de Hooch and Heyndrick van der Burch, Christopher Brown on Carel Fabritius, and Walter Liedtke on architectural painting in Delft. They have all to some extent delved into the cultural background of their subjects. Their work has been of great help to me in getting a grasp on the art-historical aspects of my socio-economic study. An older book, Max Eisler's *Alt Delft: Kultur und Kunst,* published in Amsterdam in 1923, offers a general synthesis of the arts in Delft, including both painting and the minor arts, based entirely on earlier archival findings. Although I discuss this imaginative work, written in the Romantic tradition, somewhat critically in my concluding chapter, I found some of its ideas useful, particularly on the distinctive character of Delft as a *ville d'art.*

Except for some scattered and unsystematic efforts to generalize about the place of Delft in Holland's economy and culture, my study may be likened to a narrow strip cut from the complex fabric of Dutch society in the first three quarters of the seventeenth century. To tie the loose ends of the strip to its parent fabric a great deal of research will have to be done on other Dutch cities and on the Netherlands as a whole. The source material is there, waiting to be uncovered in the capacious and well-organized archives of the Netherlands. I hope others will join me in taking advantage of it.

ONE

The Arts in Sixteenth-Century Delft

In the Middle Ages, the larger towns of the Netherlands rested their far-reaching political autonomy on charters and privileges granted by their suzerains: first the counts of Holland and Beieren, later, in the fifteenth century, the dukes of Burgundy, and, from the end of the fifteenth century on, the emperors of Germany and kings of Spain. Parallel with the political hierarchy, but by no means coextensive with it, was the hierarchy of ecclesiastic authorities. Delft was subordinate to the bishopric of Utrecht which in turn depended on Rome.[1]

The Church Masters of Delft administered a variety of public institutions, including chapels, hospices, convents, and charitable foundations. But the spiritual life they directed revolved mainly around the two great churches: the Old Church, founded in the third quarter of the thirteenth century, and the New Church, begun at the end of the fourteenth century. These two houses of worship still dominate the townscape today.

What little is known about the arts in early Delft centers on the patronage of the two churches and their satellite institutions. The activities of the guild in which painters, sculptors, glassmakers, and embroiderers were organized—from about the middle of the fifteenth century on—were also bound up with church functions. The evidence is so thin, at least until the fire of 1536 which destroyed a large part of Delft, that we can afford to survey most of the information available on the development of the arts in a few pages.*

*This chapter was written before the publication of a two-volume catalogue of an exhibition on sixteenth-century Delft at the Prinsenhof Museum (Delft: Stedelijk Museum Het Prinsenhof, 1979). The first volume of the catalogue, a collection of articles by several scholars, contains a useful account of social history and art in fifteenth- and sixteenth-century Delft. However, none of the articles in this compendium utilizes the principal sources of this chapter—the accounts of the reconstruction of the New Church and the accounts of the Guild of St. Lucas for the years 1537-1593.

PREHISTORY: DELFT BEFORE THE FIRE OF 1536

The earliest source containing useful material for our survey is the *Chronicle of the New Church*, written in the sixteenth century but drawing on earlier documents, including a number of notarial deeds in which witnesses attested to miracles performed by holy images and relics.[a]

It took a little more than a century to build the New Church. The first stone was laid in 1383. In 1396 work began on the church's single tower. Exactly one hundred years later the building was completed. It was an extraordinary accomplishment for a town with a population of only six to eight thousand inhabitants to finance the construction of one of the tallest and most beautiful spires in the Netherlands.[b] Some of the expense was met from rents on church properties in Delft and the vicinity; but probably the greater part of the receipts stemmed from the donations of pilgrims attracted by the miracle-working images and by the indulgences that were conferred at various times by popes, archbishops, and bishops on all those performing certain rites in the church.

Many pilgrims were drawn to the New Church by a miraculous Pietà. The story is told that this sculpture was made by an out-of-town "artist and master" and brought to Delft a few years before the founding of the Old Men's House on the Voldersgracht in 1411. The master stopped in Delft for the night on the way to the yearly fairs in Antwerp and Bruges where he intended to offer his works for sale. "Some good men who were in charge of the construction of the New Church" asked the master whether he would be willing to sell the Pietà. He said it was indeed for sale, but the price he demanded was too high, and they left. The next morning, when the master was about to set forth on his journey to the south, he went to pick up the sculpture but found, to his great wonderment, that he could not move it. He called the good men back and told them that if they still wanted to buy it, he could come to terms with them. When the deal had been

---

[a]D. P. Oosterbaan, "Kroniek van de Nieuwe Kerk te Delft; inleiding en aantekeningen," *Haarlemse Bijdragen* 65 (1958):5-13. A good portion of the Chronicle of the New Church was already published in 1667 by Dirck van Bleyswijck, *Beschryvinge der Stadt Delft* (Delft, 1667). pp. 196-215.

[b]Oosterbaan, "Kroniek van de Nieuwe Kerk," p. 20. The population estimate, apparently based on the number of houses, seems reasonable.

concluded, the buyers carried off the Pietà very easily because it had suddenly become light.² The donations made by the faithful, out of gratitude for the miraculous effects of the Pietà, helped finance the completion of the church.

The last years of the fourteenth century and the beginning of the fifteenth were marked by prosperity and growth. According to the *Chronicle,* "around the time when the new House of God was consecrated, the whole city of Delft, which had shown little progress formerly, began to increase and to improve. Many cloisters, chapels, and Houses of God such as the sister-house of St. Agatha, the Holy Hospice, the Chapel of St. Cornelis and others were founded, and all sorts of altars in both parochial churches were set up, as of guilds and the like that heretofore never had existed in the town."³ Soon after this reference to the guilds, we find, in the ninth article of the old description chronicling the year 1411, that "in this time there were also consecrated, both in the new [transept] and beneath the wooden church, a Saint Joris altar of the Crossbow Shooters [*Voetboeck scutters*], altars of St. Ann, St. Sebastian, St. Anthony, St. Catherine, St. Obert, St. Joest, St. John the Evangelist, St. Elisabeth, and shortly thereafter others, some out of religious devotion [*wt minne*] and some from the trades [*ambachten*], likewise with the consent of the ecclesiastic as of the lay authorities."⁴ In 1434-1435, the chapels of the New Church, including the "St. Lucas *kapel,*" were finally vaulted. The guilds, whose altars decorated the chapels, contributed to the work, "each according to its [financial] capacities."⁵

Dirck van Bleyswijck in his *Description of Delft*⁶ observes that the Guild of the Holy Cross, which was the first to be founded, "since olden times had authority over all the other guilds" ("van oudts boven alle de gilden schinjnt uytstekende gheweest to hebben . . ."), adding that he perchance came upon "a list wherein the names of the trades and occupations [*ambachten ende neeringhen*] under the authority of the same [Holy Cross Guild] are set forth, as well as many more new guilds later created in this same parish, as St. Joseph's Guild of the carpenters, St. John's Guild of the coopers, St. Stephen's Guild of the brewers, St. Erasmus's Guild of the linen-weavers, St. Adrian's Guild of the cloth-finishers [*droogscheerders*], St. Elizabeth's Guild of the apple-sellers, St. Jacob's Guild of the bargemen, St. Christopher's of the grain-carriers, St. John the Baptist's of the ribbonworkers as well as of the second-hand dealers [*uytdraeghsters*], St. Catherine's of the cobblers, St. Lucas's of the painters, St. Victor's of the millers, St. Obert's of the bakers, St. Michael's of the roofworkers and dyers." This statement is unfortunately too ambiguous to pin down the date of the creation of the painters' guild. My best guess is that the creation of the Guild of St. Lucas coincided with, or followed shortly upon, the vaulting of the chapels in 1434-1435.

From the second half of the fifteenth century on, Delft began to acquire greater importance as an artistic center. At first illuminated manuscripts, later fine illustrated books spread its fame.[7] In 1477 the first Bible in the Dutch language was printed in Delft. The names of the illustrators of manuscripts are lost. Some of the publishers, printers, and lettersetters—Jacob Jacobsz. van der Meer, Christiaen Snellaert, Cornelis Henrikcz., Hendrick Pietersz.—are known, but not the artists who illustrated their books. The anonymous engraver known as the Master of the Virgo inter Virgines is also identified as the author of a number of distinguished paintings (fig. 1). The only other reputed fifteenth-century painter associated with the town is called simply "the Master of Delft."

The names of a few painters and sculptors are known, but their works have not been preserved or can no longer be identified today. In 1428, "Dirck the painter" painted a "beautiful large panel of St. Christopher" for the choir of the New Church.[c] In 1457 the Church Masters gave an order to the figure-carver Cornelis Claessone for thirty-six stalls (*stoelen*) "in the manner of Antwerp," for which he was slated to receive fifty-eight Flemish pounds (108 gulden).[8] In 1484, Master Adriaen of Utrecht, also a wood-carver, was ordered to erect an altar for the New Church "like the one he had made for St. Mary's ([in Utrecht])." He appeared on the scene about two years later and was paid 1,000 rijnsgulden for his work, an enormous sum at the time.[9] It is worth noting that the stone for the towers of the New Church was ordered from a mason in Brabant (1497) and that the copper trellis was acquired from Robrecht van Blaesvelt in Mechelen (1499).[10] As we shall see, the custom of engaging artisans from larger towns with a longer and more distinguished artistic tradition to work in Delft or to send their products there continued into the sixteenth century and lasted well into the seventeenth, especially in the domain of sculpture.

---

[c]Ibid., p. 100. Oosterbaan observes that the traditional identification of "Dirck the painter" with Dirck Bouts, who was born about 1520, is untenable.

FIG. 1 "Master of the Virgo Inter Virgines," Portrait of Hugh de Groot
    (1509), 13⅛ x 8⅝ in. Ackland Gallery, Chapel Hill (Photo: A Dingjan)

THE RECONSTRUCTION OF DELFT AFTER THE GREAT FIRE

From the time of the fire of 3 May 1536, the documentary evidence on the reconstruction of Delft becomes more abundant. The town's artistic life, revolving around the church, begins to emerge with the help of three sources: the St. Lucas Guild's accounts;[d] the account book of the receipts and outlays devoted to the reconstruction of the New Church;[e] and the register of new citizens beginning in 1536, from which may be extracted the names of craftsmen who bought rights of citizenship and of those who stood as guarantors for them in this early period.[f]

The New Church was especially hard hit by the Great Fire. Its books, ornaments, and similar appurtenances were burnt; its tower and much of its woodwork were badly damaged and had to be rebuilt or replaced. Its incomes were reduced because many of the faithful would no longer hear Mass in the half-ruined building and took their donations elsewhere.[11] On 19 June 1537, the Weth (the assembly or "law") held a meeting in the course of which the city fathers resolved to order the Masters of the New Church to reconstruct the tower. They consented for this purpose to allow them to sell various parcels of land, lease rights, and jewels to pay for the repairs to the church. Authorization for these sales also had to be obtained from the bishop of Utrecht. (This, as Van Bleyswijck points out, was further evidence of "the greater power wielded by messrs. the bishops of Utrecht in the land at the time.") The Weth also submitted to His Imperial Majesty, Charles V, ruler of the Netherlands, a letter of supplication requesting that the Church Masters be granted a delay in the payments due on the various obligations—quit- and life-rents—owed to their holders. His Majesty granted the request, appointing commissioners to supervise the schedule of repayments.[12] Of greater concern to our study of

[d]Delft, Municipal Archives, First Division (*1ᵉ afdeeling*), (hereafter cited as Delft MA). "Rekeningboekje (van de deken) van het Sint Lucas gilde te Delft over de jaren 1537-1593" (hereafter cited as "Rekeningboekje"). These accounts were transliterated by Professor J. L. van den Gouw, who kindly gave me permission to use his typewritten text. For a summary and a brief discussion of the contents, see R. W. Scheller, "Nieuwe gegevens over het St. Lukasgilde te Delft in de zestiende eeuw," *Nederlands Kunsthistorisch Jaarboek* 26 (1972):41-48.

[e]Delft, Municipal Archives, Reformed Community (Kerk voogdy), (hereafter cited as Delft RC). "Dit is alsulck uytgheef als die meesters der fabrike van die nieuwe kerck vuijtgegeven hebben" (Hereafter cited as "Uytgheef."), (n.d., ca. 1536-1560).

[f]Delft MA. "Porters der stede van Delft gemaect: Poyrter regyster" (hereafter cited as "Poyrter regyster"), 1536-1649.

artistic life in Delft is the contribution that the Church Masters imposed on the guilds to help finance the work of reconstruction. Before examining this contribution we shall study the role played by various groups of artisans in the town's reconstruction.

For the first twenty years after the fire, work on the New Church and other edifices created a great bustle of craft activity in Delft. Many artisans were attracted to the town, chiefly from other localities in the northern Netherlands, to take part in its reconstruction. Those who wanted to take up permanent residence or to join the guild of their craft, or both, acquired citizenship. In the period 1536 to 1559, twenty to thirty immigrants to Delft acquired citizenship each year. These numbers fell in the 1560s, when religious troubles depressed economic activity in Delft, and were not matched again until the middle of the 1570s at which time the northward trek from the southern provinces began. From 1537 to 1557 we find that seven glassmakers, four sculptors or stonecarvers, and one painter became citizens of Delft.^g These, by the standards of the sixteenth century, were large numbers. We must also consider that many artisans were not specifically identified by their craft in the register of new citizens.

The account book of the New Church contains the only detailed information that has come down to us on the actual work carried out to repair damage done by the fire. The operation was directed by Willem Ariaensz., master of the building site, or church *fabrick*.^h An entry in the accounts for Pentacost 1537, when he was paid three schellings (eighteen stuivers) for a "design of the choirs" (*patroon van de chooren*), suggests that he was a full-fledged architect.[13] Most of the workmen in his *fabrick* were carpenters, woodsawyers, masons, and roofers. Of the artisans of interest to us, that is, of those masters who would normally belong to the St. Lucas Guild, only sculptors or stonecarvers (*steenhowers*) and glassmakers appear in significant numbers in the accounts. Most of the stonecarvers were employed in fairly mechanical stonecutting tasks. One or two at a given time, as we shall see presently, were working as sculptors. There was normally one painter and one wood-sculptor active on the site. Occasionally, artisans who were not regularly employed in the *fabrick* were given special orders that they apparently carried out in their own workshops.

^gThe names of craftsmen were extracted from the "Poyrter regyster."
^hCould he be Willem Adriaenszoon Nagel (also referred to as Willem Adriaensz.), one of the headmen of the St. Lucas Guild in 1542-1543?

During the first decade of reconstruction, from 1536 to 1546, the painter Maertyn,[i] the wood-sculptor Barend, the stonecarver Jeroen, and the glassmaker Jacob Williemsz. were regular employees of the *fabrick,* even though they were paid by the task or by the day. Jacob Williemsz. is the only one of the four who appears to have played a leading role in the Guild of St. Lucas, where he was headman in 1537 and 1546-1547. Some of their tasks were fairly routine, others not. Maertyn *de schilder* had to gild the weathercock (1537)[14] and paint the window frames and doors in the tower green (1539),[15] but he was also entrusted with the task of painting the tabernacle of the Pietà or *nootgods* (12 June 1541).[j] The price he was paid for this last job—three Flemish pounds of six gulden each plus four groot—suggests that it involved more than the mere painting of a sculpted piece.[k] Three other painters are mentioned in the accounts. "Michel de scilder" was paid thirteen schellings eight groot for the paintings of stonework in the transept in July 1537.[16] Jacob (Cornelisz.) Mont received one schelling two groot on 17 February 1538 "for a design of four clocks painted on parchment" ("van een patroon van vier cloquen op franseyn ghevirut") and Jan Lucas received four schellings two groot on St. Martin's Day 1539 "to paint and repair an image of [the Holy] Mary for the towers" ("van dat beelt van Maria voir den thoren te verscylden ende repareren").[17]

Two of these painters, Jan Lucas and Jacob Cornelisz. Mont, are known from other sources. Karel van Mander, in his *Schilderboek,* writes that Maerten van Heemskerk spent some time in his youth in Delft "practicing the art" with Jan Lucas before settling in Haarlem.[18] He was headman of the Guild of St. Lucas in 1540-1541.[19] Mont, again according to Van Mander, was a run-of-the-mill artist (*ghemeen schilder*), the teacher of Augustyn Jorisz. (1525-1552), a talented Delft painter who died young.[20]

Barend, the sculptor in wood, carved all sorts of pieces for the New Church. On 17 February 1538, he was paid nineteen stuivers for "the four evangelists for the choir with the two angels."[21] Less than a

---

[i]He is generally called "Maertyn de scilder" in the manuscript; once he appears as "Maertyn Joost" ("Uytgheef," fol. 148, 16 November 1541).

[j]Delft RC. "Uytgheef," fol. 145. On 17 June 1548, Maertyn also received 15½ stuivers for decorating the tabernacle of Metsekie (?) hanging over St. John ("van't Tabernacel van Metsekie hangende over St. Jan te stofferen").

[k]The sum amounts to 362 stuivers or at least sixty days' work at the typical painter's wage of six stuivers a day. This would be far too long to paint a sculpted tabernacle, although a part of the price he obtained may have covered his expenses for gesso, colors, and gold leaf.

month later he received eleven schellings three groot for "a procession cross" (*een cruijs daermen mede in processie gaet*). Another week went by and he already carved "four statues standing beside the high altar."[22] On 29 December, his wife was paid one schelling (presumably on his behalf) for the varnishing of "heer Hordes kijndekyn (?)"[l] On 28 March 1539, he received two pounds three schellings four groot "to carve our dear Lord [riding] on an ass out of the wood provided by the church" ("van onssen Lijefuen heer op ten eesel te snyden van de kercken hout") and an additional four schellings "to complete the head and to gild [the statue]" ("den heer syn 'thooft metmaecken en te vergulden").[23] On 26 February 1548, he received a small sum for a *patroon* of a statue of a peacock. The only other wood-sculptors that I was able to identify are Adriaen Jeroensz, (possibly the son of the stonecarver Jeroen) who, on 8 October 1553, was given five schellings of six stuivers each to carve a figure of Adam out of willowwood on the high altar;[24] and Hugh Jansz. who got six pounds five schellings to make and deliver the church's pulpit (*preeckstoel*) on 8 September 1543.[m] Neither is mentioned in the guild's accounts. Jeroen carved a great number of pillars, basements, niches, corbels, and other parts of the edifice, but the New Church accounts are silent on the subjects he represented.[n]

The accounts are also sparse on the activities of the glazier Jacob Willemsz., who frequently repaired glass in various parts of the church. I suspect that he did not design or carry out any of the important new stained-glass windows that were made in the 1540s. This task was entrusted to a more accomplished artist. On January 1542, the assistants (*knechts*) of Gerrit Dircksz. de Bye were given one schelling eight groot for "the vidimus [design] of a new glass window

---

[l]Delft RC. "Uytgheef," fol. 117v and 118. Given the low level of literacy of this particular scribe, I should not be surprised if "heer Hordes" was meant to be "Herod" and if the "kijndekyn" were the newborn children that he had ordered massacred. The carving would then represent a "Massacre of the Innocents."

[m]Ibid., fol. 185. Hugh Jansz. was paid "to make and deliver" the pulpit. This and the fairly high single-lump sum paid suggest that he was an out-of-town master. In 1548, a magnificent new pulpit in Italian Renaissance style was installed in the Old Church (still *in situ*). There is at least a chance that it may have been made by the same Hugh Jansz. For a reproduction and description, see Oosterbaan, *De Oude Kerk te Delft gedurende de Middeleeuwen* (The Hague: J. N. Voorhoeve, 1973), pp. 81–82.

[n]Among the numerous other stonecarvers was Claes Heyndricksz., who made "an armature next to the Holy Sacrament" ("van een harniss newins dat heyligh 't sacrament"). This is presumed to have consisted of stone tracery to frame an altar or a window ("Uytgheef," fol. 142v, 21 November 1540). In the 1540s another frequently employed stonecarver was named Pieter Bartholomesz.

on the north side of the transept given by Suete Bom, the widow of Jacob Pietersz. Bom.''[25] This is probably the "Emperor's window," which, according to Van Bleyswijk, had been made in 1544 "on the order of his Imperial Majesty Charles V by the ingenious glass-engraver Gerrit de Bye Dircksz. and set in the Chapel of Our Lady of this church on the north side.''°

When the fathers of the Old Church, to emulate the great works carried out in the New Church, resolved to acquire new stained-glass windows, they opted to order them, at considerable expense, from workshops outside Delft. At least two such orders are known, the first in 1563 from Willem Willemsz. Tybaut of Haarlem and the second in 1565 from Dirck Pietersz. Crabeth of Gouda, both highly reputed glassmakers in their time.[26]

At least as far as painting and sculpture are concerned, home-town work had the advantage of being inexpensive. The highest daily wage on the reconstruction of the New Church, earned by the architect Willem Ariaensz., was fifteen stuivers a day.P

In 1550-1551, Maertyn *de schilder* got only six stuivers a day, as did Jeroen the stonecarver and his presumed son Adriaen Jeroensz. This was barely above the 4½ stuivers a day paid to ordinary workers and to the *knechts* of glassmakers, stonemasons, and so forth. The sum earned by Barend the wood-sculptor to carve "four evangelists with the two angels" (nineteen stuivers) is low enough to infer that he too belonged to the same group of artisans who were paid quite ordinary wages.

These considerations bring us back to the financing of the New Church's reconstruction. In 1538, Van Bleyswijck writes, an order had been issued to all the guilds in the city enjoining them to spend yearly one-half of their guild dues and incomes on the reconstruction of the churches and to deliver the same faithfully into the hands of the Church Masters under whose authority they lay.[27] This was to last until 1547, when they would be freed of this obligation, and the Church Masters would be permitted—in case their finances were not sufficiently restored—to make a collection throughout the city. In

---

°Van Bleyswijck, *Beschryvinge der Stadt Delft*, p. 256. The window made by De Bye, to the extent that it was spared from the ravages of the Iconoclasts, was destroyed by the powder explosion of 1654. Van Bleyswijck had apparently come upon a reference to the *vidimus* delivered to the church fathers, but it was already lost in his time.

P"Uytgheef," fol. 56. This was the highest wage he was paid. On occasion he and his helper together received a total of only thirteen stuivers per day. (Payments made circa 1550-1551.)

1540, the Weth ordered further that "all the guilds of both parishes be obligated to repair and erect their altars and panels including diverse paintings and histories suitable to the occasion."[28]

According to the accountbook of the reconstruction of the New Church, several guilds had already begun to make their financial contributions even before the Weth issued its instructions. As early as 7 September 1536, the Guild of St. Adrian (the cloth-finishers) donated three pounds (eighteen gulden). From then on, the Guilds of St. John (coopers), St. Elisabeth (apple-sellers), St. Joseph (carpenters) St. Jacob (bargemen), St. Erasmus (linen-weavers), St. John the Baptist (ribbonworkers), St. Obert (bakers), St. Catherine (cobblers), St. Michael (roofworkers and dyers), St. Christopher (grain-carriers), St. Stephen (brewers), Our Lady's Annunciation (tailors), and St. Victor (millers), as well as the purely religious guilds—the Guilds of the Holy Sacrament, St. Ann, and the Holy Cross—regularly contributed large sums to reconstruction. In September 1539, the Guild of St. Lucas made a single donation—the death dues of one of its members, amounting to fifteen stuivers.[29] I surmise that the guild was able to satisfy the Church Masters with this token donation because its very small income was barely sufficient to cover the incidental expenses connected with the delivery and the setting up of its altar (as we shall see presently).

The account of these guild receipts ceases in May 1548. At the beginning of August of the same year, we find among the sums expended on the reconstruction an entry concerning the headmen of the St. Joseph's Guild (carpenters) who paid for repairs to the pillar next to their altar. A similar entry is made for the headmen of the cooper's guild. It would have been interesting to know whether some of the receipts from the guilds recorded in preceding years also were spent on projects related to their chapels and altars.

The St. Lucas Guild accounts from 1537 to 1546 unfortunately contain no financial information at all and shed no light on the guild's contribution to the reconstruction of the New Church. Here, for example, is the entry for 1537:

Anno 37 hebben [rekenynghe] ghedaen Jan Mathijsz. ende Claes Claesz. in presency van Jacob Maertsz., Jacob Willemsz. als homansz. ende Dirck Woutersz. ende William Luytsz. als out homans ende Geeryt de Bye Dircksz. ende Jan Cornelisz. Copheer als nieuwe homans. ende is geloeft.	In the year [15]37, Jan Mathijsz. and Claes Claesz. prepared the accounts in the presence of Jacob Maertsz. and Jacob Willemsz. as headmen and Dirck Woutersz. and Willem Luytsz. as old headmen and Geeryt de Bye Dircksz. and Jan Cornelisz. Copheer as new headmen, and is approved.[30]

I surmise that the accounts pertain not to the year in which they were approved but to 1535.[q] Jan Mathijsz. and Claes Claesz., who were *homans* (later called *hoofdmens*, or headmen) in 1535, prepared the accounts, which were approved by the *out homans* (the old or retiring headmen) of 1536, Dirck Woutersz. and Willem Luytsz., and by the *nieuwe homans* (new or incoming headmen) of 1537, Geeryt de Bye Dircksz. and Jan Cornelisz. Copheer. Note that the retiring headmen were still slated to serve through 1537, but the incoming headmen served to the end of 1538. The only two of these six officers whose craft is known to us were both glassmakers: Dirck Wouters, active since 1506,[31] and Gerrit de Bye, already referred to in connection with the glass window he made for the Chapel of Our Lady in 1544. The accounts for the years 1539 to 1546 contain little besides lists of headmen. The only name worthy of note here is that of the painter and designer of stained-glass windows, Jan Lucas, headman in 1540 and 1541, whom we have already encountered in connection with his work for the New Church.

The form of the guild accounts remains the same until the entry for 1547, which reads:

Anno zeven ende veertich hebben re [ke] ninck ghedaen de anno vijff ende veer [tigh] Jan Thonisz. ende Jacob Maertensz. oud hoeftmans in presentie van Jacob Williemsz. ende Cornelis Phillipszoen als oude hoeftmans ende Jan Cornelisz. ende Heynrick Assueruszoen als nieuwe hoeftmans ende is ghepresen van mijn Huych de Groot als deeken van't Ghilden van Sinte Lucas ende bleef in de kist 33 st [uivers].

In the year 1547 Jan Thonisz. and Jacob Maertensz., old headmen, did the accounts for 1540 in the presence of Jacob Williemsz. and Cornelis Phillipszoen as old headmen and Jan Cornelisz. and Heynrick Assueruszoen as new headmen, and [the accounting] is approved in the presence of me Huych de Groot as dean of the Guild of St. Lucas, and there remained in the chest thirty-three st[uivers].[32]

This may be interpreted to mean that the accounts for 1545 were prepared by the old headmen of that year, Jan Thonisz. and Jacob Maertensz., in the presence of the outgoing headmen of 1546, Jacob Willemsz. and Cornelis Phillipsz. and of the incoming headmen of 1547, Jan Cornelisz. and Heynrick Assuerusz. The accounts were certified by the dean of the guild, Hugh de Groot (born in 1511), the grandfather of the famous jurist Hugo Grotius.[r] There remained

[q]The entries for the years 1547 to 1551 make clear that the accounts refer to the years 1545 to 1549 respectively.

[r]As is known to have been the case in the seventeenth century, I presume that the dean of the guild was appointed by the Weth to supervise the activities of the guild members. He was normally not an artist or an artisan himself.

TABLE 1.1

Net Receipts and Assets of the Guild of St. Lucas, 1545-1549

(in stuivers)

	Net Receipts For One Year	Estimated Assets at End of Year
1545	n.a.	33
1546	52	85
1547	70	155
1548	44	198
1549	171	369

SOURCE: "Rekeningboekje (van de deken) van het Sint Lucas gilde te Delft over de jaren 1537-1593."

NOTE: The "estimated assets at the end of the year" are the amounts of money which the chest should have contained if the accounts had been settled immediately upon completion of the year. Note, however, that the assets held in the chest in 1548 correspond to the amount actually stated in the manuscript accounts. The net receipts for 1548 are calculated from the amount given for the assets held at the end of 1547 and of 1548.

thirty-three stuivers in the guild strongbox. Heynrick Assuerusz. was the uncle and teacher of the well-known painter Anthonie van Montfoort, called Blocklandt. According to Karel van Mander, the older man "was a run-of-the-mill master, but rather good at portraits."[5]

In the following year, 1548, there remained fifty-two stuivers left over from the accounts of 1546. "They were placed in the chest along with the above 33 st. herein accounted for."[33] From the accounts for these two years, we may infer that 1546 was the first year that left a surplus to be placed in the guild chest. Prior to that—or at least for the year 1544—outlays must have just matched receipts.

The accounts for the years 1545 to 1551, while incomplete, give us a glimpse into the finances of the guild in these years. The fragmentary data for the years 1545 to 1549 are assembled in Table 1.1.

The question arises as to whether the Guild of St. Lucas was obligated during this period—or at least until 1547—to give half of its gross receipts for the reconstruction of the New Church. Since the net receipts of the 1540s, on average, amount to about as much as the

[5]Karel van Mander, *Het Schilderboeck ... der Edele Vrye Schilderkonst* (Haarlem, 1604), fol. 254. Anthonie Blocklandt is himself recorded on several instances in Delft, but his name does not appear in the accounts. (See below pp. 32-33). It is not known whether he was a member of the guild.

gross receipts of the late 1560s,' when the guild was certainly under no such obligation, I find no reason to doubt that the contributions of the guilds listed in the accounts of the New Church already cited are complete and that the miniscule amount handed over by the headmen of St. Lucas's in 1539 was the only donation that was actually made. As I have already argued, the guild may have been exempted from the obligation to contribute to the reconstruction of the New Church in order to allow it to build up its assets in anticipation of the expenditures that it would eventually have to make on its "altars and panels."

The entry for 1551, referring to the guild's accounts for 1550— there was now a delay of only one year in drawing up the accounts— reveals the purpose of the cumulated savings of the preceding five years.

Anno 51 hebben rekeninck ghedaen de anno 50 Jan Cornelisz. ende Joest Claesz. Schalk afgaende hoeftmans in presentie van Heynrick Willemsz. end Willem Luytsz. hoeftmans ende Jan Claesz. Schalk met Cornelis Jacobsz. nyewe hooftmans ende bleef zuver over 18½ stuver't zelfde in die kist gheleyt.

In the year 1551 Jan Cornelisz. and Joest Claesz. Schalk outgoing headmen did the accounts for the year 1550 in the presence of Heynrick Willemsz. and Willem Luytsz. headmen and Jan Claesz. Schalk with Cornelis Jacobsz. new headmen, and there remained 18½ stuivers which were deposited in the chest.

Willem Luytsz. heeft b[etaelt] 35 s[cellingen] van een maelteyt mr. Maerten gheschonken met wyn ende met costen.

Willem Luytsz. paid thirty-five schellings [at six stuivers the schelling] for a meal for Master Maerten with wine and food.

Noch Mr. Maerten gheschonken 11 s[cellingen] groot tot een gratuyteyt ofte waegen huyr.

In addition, Mr. Maerten was granted eleven schellings as a gratuity or coach-hire.

Noch Mr. Maertens knecht gheschonken 16 st[uivers] doe men't paneel setteden

In addition, the servant of Mr. Maerten was granted sixteen stuivers to set up the panel.

Van't paneel van Haerlem hier te brengen 20½ st[uiver].

For the bringing here of the panel from Haarlem 20½ stuivers.

Noch ghenoemen uuyt die kist een pont vlaems ende ghegheven Frans Dircksz. in't Cromhout op ofcortinghe van die lijst

In addition, one Flemish pound [6 gulden or 120 stuivers] was taken out of the chest and given to Frans Dircksz. in the Cromhout to cut the frame down.

Ergo blijft die kist leech. Ghedaen den 20 Decembris 51.

Hence the chest was empty. Done 20 December 1551.

Mids dat Louris Rijcaertssoen betaelde 15 stuvers bij sijn leeven van sijn doetschulde anno als boven.

Except that Louris Rijcaertssoen paid fifteen stuivers in his own lifetime as death duty in the year as above.[34]

'See below, p. 29-30.

"Mr. Maerten," as Professor van Scheller already recognized,[35] was Maerten van Heemskerck of Haarlem. The total cost of the Van Heemskerck altar, including the setting of the panel, cutting the frame down to size, and gratuities, came to 432½ stuivers (21 gulden 12½ stuivers). If, as I have estimated, there remained 369 stuivers in the chest at the end of 1549 while only 18½ stuivers were left at the end of 1550, the current receipts for the year, including the death duty of Louris Rijcaertssoen, must have been 82 stuivers, an amount which seems plausible.

Since the guild had contributed to the costs of the installation of the new altarpiece, it is probable that the painting was ordered for the Chapel of St. Lucas in the New Church. This would also be in keeping with the city ordinance cited above, that made the guilds responsible for the setting up of the altars dedicated to their patron saints. The Guild of St. Lucas, in any event, was incapable of paying for more than the incidental costs of acquiring its altar. The cost of the painting itself was much in excess of the amounts that had accrued in the chest. The altarpiece painted by Van Heemskerck for the Old Church cost 300 gulden.[36] For the "Three Magi" altar panel, which he painted in 1550 for the St. Aechte (Agatha) Kerk in Delft, he was granted a life-rent of 100 gulden a year.[37]

Cornelis Jacobsz. (Mont), one of the headmen mentioned at the beginning of the above entry in the guild accounts, played a major role in the guild until his death in 1575. He may have been a son of the painter Jacob Mont, cited earlier. He received many commissions from the city, including the recording of an iceberg that drifted into Delfshaven in January 1565. The painting of this extraordinary event—the first known landscape by a Delft painter—survives (fig. 2).[38]

Two contracts of the mid-century cited by Van Bleyswijck illustrate the high cost of the Church-ordered works. In the first, dated 1548, the Masters of the New Church contracted with Cornelis van Scheveling, a Hague painter, to come to Delft to paint the doors of the great organ "with good watercolors [*water-verwen*], both outside and inside, inside on the right-hand door, with the history of David cutting off Goliath's head, and on the other door where David with the head meets the maidens in front of the city, and outside with the histories of Tubal with musical instruments such as organs, harps, and the like."[39] The painter was enjoined to first cover the limewood doors with good glue to make them watertight.

The figures and the rest, both inside and out, should be lifelike in

FIG. 2 Cornelis Jacobsz. (Mont), Ice Scene in Delfshaven (1565), 19¾ x 53½ in. Rotterdam Historical Museum on loan from Koninklijk Oudheidkundig Genootschap (Photo: Fotocommissie Rijksmuseum)

appearance ... and he will be obliged to employ the best and most durable paints that he can find in Antwerp ... and in case the St. Lucas Guild in Delft should legally obtain the right to his guild dues, the Church Masters will be responsible for half and Master Cornelis for the other half. And the said Church Masters will pay him two Flemish pounds cash immediately, and once the doors will have been completed in the manner aforesaid, another five Flemish pounds. And in case the said Cornelis should deliver them as well made as the Church Masters entrusted him to make, they will give him another Flemish pound."[40]

Van Bleyswijck comments that the contracted price (seventy-eight gulden in all), for the organ doors, which were to be seen from afar rather than close up, was not so high as other works, "because there was no one in the city to whom this manner of painting could preferably be entrusted or who would be willing to take on this work at such a low price, even though this city has always been richly endowed with artist-painters."[41] This patriotic statement exaggerates the level of Delft's artistic attainment for the sixteenth century.

The second, better-known contract was made by the New Church Masters with Master Johan van Scorel, canon of St. Mary's Church in Utrecht. The contrast stipulated that the new high altar should exceed in magnificence the one in the cathedral in Utrecht. The dimensions of the chief panel were to be two inches short of eight feet in width and one-and-a-half inches short of nine feet in height, the figures to be six feet high. The New and Old Testament subjects of the double-door altar were to be modeled after the cartoons (*patroonen*) delivered in the hands of the church authorities. For this main altar plus some other side panels, Master van Scorel "requested for his wage fifty Carolus gulden [of twenty stuivers each] yearly during a period of twenty-five years, which demand he left at the discretion of the provost of the Old Church and the pastor of the St. Agatha convent, thereto adding another request for annuities [*lijf-renten*], namely on behalf of his six children, the oldest being twenty and the youngest six years of age, each for two Flemish pounds yearly, which last condition was found to amount to nine gulden per year for each person his life long."[42] These large yearly expenditures for the high altar could only have been financed from general church revenues. The receipts of the guild, which were only of the order of two to four gulden a year, would not even have sufficed to pay the annuity for one of Van Scorel's six children.

The years 1552–1557 are missing altogether from the guild

accounts. The decade 1557–1567 was marked by the accumulation of arrears on the payment of guild dues, delays in closing the accounts, and general confusion. No doubt the nefarious activities of the Iconoclasts—Calvinist extremists who, in the summer and fall of 1566, ran amok in the churches, defacing or destroying all the "graven images" they could reach—contributed greatly to the guild's disarray.[43] According to a letter written by the Delft magistrates to the regent Marguerite of Parma in Brussels just after these events, the officers of the guilds, after hearing about the destruction that had taken place in Antwerp, had tried to remove and safeguard "all the altarpieces, paintings and other ornaments" in the churches.[44] As a result, many small, loose objects had been saved from the onslaught of the image-breakers, but "the large panels and the altarpieces which were nailed fast and other objects of great weight" were, without exception, hacked to pieces and annihilated. Thus, "many incomparable works disappeared which had earned an undying fame for their artful makers."[45] Van Bleyswijck in particular bewailed the loss to the world of the altarpieces by Pieter Aertsen, Anthonie van Blocklandt, Frans Floris, and Maerten van Heemskerck that had graced the New Church. (Some of these, including the Van Heemskerck altarpiece, may have been put away during the time of troubles and were sold or destroyed in the second wave of Iconoclasm after Delft went over to the rebellion in July 1572.)[46]

A severe repression followed. On 23 July 1568, Herman Schinkel, Delft's most important printer, was beheaded on the Market Place for publishing religious pamphlets that the Inquisition considered heretical.

The guilds, as in the years after the Great Fire, were again burdened with contributions to restore the churches; all the "surpluses" (*over-schot*) recorded on the yearly closing of their accounts were to be expended for this purpose. A number of guilds failed to meet this obligation in the following years and were summoned by the Church Masters to acquit themselves of their arrears."

In 1569, the accounts of the Guild of St. Lucas for 1567 were finally drawn up, omitting those for 1565 and 1566. To start afresh all outstanding arrears in members' dues were forgiven. The number of guild brothers was said to be thirty-five, not counting the *hoofdmen,* or thirty-nine in all.[47] The guild officers vowed that

---

"The guild of St. Erasmus (linen-weavers) was obligated to pay six gulden a year and the guild of St. Michiel (roofers and dyers), three gulden a year (Van Bleyswijck, *Beschryvinge der Stadt Delft,* p. 260).

henceforth the collections of dues and other receipts would be regular, that no more years would be skipped, and that the accounts of the guild would be made ready on time. By and large this promise was kept in the following years, until Delft joined the rebellion against Spain in 1572.

The occupational composition of the guild leadership in 1567 gives us some notion of the crafts that were prominent in the organization. The retiring headmen who had presumably been on the board of headmen for the year 1568 were Cornelis Jacobsz. Mont, painter, and Cornelis in den Koninck, who may have been a glassmaker. The *hoefdmen* for 1568 who remained in office in 1569 were Aelbrecht Cornelisz., sculptor[v] and Adriaen Pietersz., glassmaker. The new headmen were Brother Jacob Adriaensz., a monk of the Franciscan (*minnebroers*) order who was also a glassmaker, and Boudewijn Damsz. (or Damasz.), painter.[48] This composition reflects the domination of the St. Lucas Guild by painters and glassmakers, which lasted into the seventeenth century.

The accounts for 1568, which are set forth below, were drawn up as early as January 1569.[49] They provide the first complete breakdown of guild expenditures.

In de eersten die knecht voer een jaer dienen	18 st.	First for the [guild] servant for one year's service	18 st.
Noch van twee nieuwe toertsen	15 st.	For two new torches	15 st.
Noch van die ghilde kaersen ende toertsen te draegen op ommegansdach ende Sacramentsdach	15 st.	For the guild candles and torches to carry on procession day and on Sacrament's day	15 st.
Noch een pont kaersen	1½ st.	For a pound of candles	1½ st.
Noch van twee missen te doen	4 st.	For two Masses	4 st.
Noch van beijeren op't statthuys	6 st.	To ring the bells at the Town Hall	6 st.
Noch van die waskaersen tot den dienst te doen	12 st.	For the wax candles for the service [in the St. Lucas Chapel?]	12 st.
Noch van dat outaer op ende toe te doen	3 gr.	To open and close that altar	3 gr.
Noch die meysens van dat keussuffel te bewaren en den dwael ghedaen tot den dienst	3 st.	Given to the maids to preserve the chasuble and the altarcloth used for service.	3 st.

[v]In the same year 1569, the city gave Aelbrecht Cornelisz. a commission to restore a sculpture of the Holy Mary with two angels for the Town Hall. Cornelisz. Jacobsz. (Mont) was paid for painting the sculpture and for other work related to the commission. Petra Beydals, "Cornelis Jacobsz. uit Delft," *Oud-Holland* 69 (1951):70.

Noch van Jan Cock te daeghen ende weer zijn werck verboen	3 st.	To summon Jan Cock and again to forbid his work.	3 st.
Noch van die toertsen te dragen voer't sacrement van die victory op manendach voer Alre Heylighendach	2 st.	To carry the torches for the consecration of the victory on Monday for All Saints' Day.[w]	2 st.
Noch verteert tot Laurens Rijkensz. doen wij dat rijfelen verboden met consent van mijn heeren die burghemeesters	3½ st.	Expended on account of Laurens Rijkensz. [whom] we have forbidden to hold lotteries, with consent of messrs. Burgomasters.	3½ st.
Noch van luyen ghegeven Jan Willemsz. graefmacker.	6 st.	For ringing the bells, given to Jan Willemsz., gravedigger.	6 st.

The receipts, according to the accounts, exceeded expenditures by 7½ stuivers.

The most interesting entries in the above accounts are those concerning Jan Cock and Laurens Rijkensz. Three stuivers were spent to summon the former "again to forbid his work." In 1582, similarly, complaints were received "from guild brothers about glassmakers and furniture-makers who had been forbidden to work" but apparently had continued to work illegally. Thirty-five stuivers were spent for legal costs.[x] In neither case is it entirely clear whether the men who were forbidden to engage in their trade had failed to pay their master dues in the guild or, perhaps in conjunction with a policy to restrict membership, whether they were barred from entering the guild.

Laurens Rijkensz., the other artisan cited in the 1568 accounts, comes up in connection with a lottery, which was apparently forbidden by the city administration at guild request, as frequently happened both in the sixteenth and the early seventeenth centuries. On 6 November 1578, the guild likewise expended 7½ stuivers on a messenger "to forbid the lottery as our guild brothers were harmed by it" ("om te verbieden het rijveleen also ons ghildebruers daer schade bij hadden").[50]

The accounts for 1569 add only one new entry to those of the previous year. We learn that the headmen spent six stuivers "in den

---

[w]The procession celebrated the victory of the Catholics over the Protestants at Valenciennes (notes of J. L. van der Gouw to his transliteration of the accounts). On these colorful processions, to which the guilds were obligated to contribute, see Oosterbaan, *De Oude Kerk*, pp. 264-65.

[x]The passage of the accounts ("Rekeningboekje," fol. 17v.) reads "In den eersten also wij eenyge duer clachte van gildebroederen 't werck verbooden ende daer tegen te regt gegaen hebben als glaesmaeckers, stoelgroenders Bas Jan Potter an oncosten duer't geheeel jaer daertoe gedan 35 st."

[30]

Bosboem," presumably an inn, on their rounds to collect guild dues. In this same year, the guild receipts were three gulden and one-fourth of a stuiver greater than the outlays. From this surplus headmen were awarded thirty stuivers as "compensation for their work and troubles, according to the old custom, so that they might make merry with others" ("om metten anderen vrolick te sijn").[51] This is the first time that a banquet for the headmen financed from guild revenues is mentioned.

Among the expenditures for the year 1570, there appears an entry of two stuivers "for an extraordinary procession to carry the torches as the pardon was being read" ("als't perd[o]n gelesen werde").[52] This refers to the so-called general pardon of the Duke of Alva given out to repentent rebels. The procession took place in Delft on 25 July 1570, on which occasion it was ordered that for the next few Sundays every one should go to church to pray "for the unity of our Mother the Holy Church."[53] Another two stuivers were spent on torches for a procession to celebrate His Majesty's victory over the Turks. It was doubtless for the guild altar that 1½ stuivers were given out "to open the altar and close it." In this year, the headmen received three stuivers for wine and one gulden ten stuivers for their troubles and to make merry with others. This generous allocation put the guild in the red. The debit balance of fifteen stuivers was to be paid by the new headmen to the old.[54]

From the accounts for 1571 we learn that yearly guild dues were two-and-a-half stuivers, which were received from eighteen guild brothers, and that the death dues of a member came to fifteen stuivers (the same amount as the guild had paid back in 1539 as a token contribution to the reconstruction of the New Church). A relatively large sum was expended in that year—eleven stuivers—"van't outer wech te doen," which may be translated, "to put away the altar" or "to do away with the altar."[55] We have no clue as to what happened on this occasion to the altar, which may or may not have been the one painted by Van Heemskerck in 1550.

In the closing years of Roman Catholic domination in Delft, the Masters of the Old Church ordered a major sculptured altar, in manifest defiance of the Iconoclasts who wanted to rid the temples of all graven images and were apt to do so by force.[y] The 1568 contract went to the famous sculptor Willem Danielsz. van Tetrode (also

[y]It is likely that the new altar was ordered as a replacement for the old, which had been destroyed by the Iconoclasts (cf. Oosterbaan, *De Oude Kerk*, p. 32.)

[31]

known as Guglielmo Fiammingo), almost certainly born in Delft, who had returned to the city not long before this date after spending his formative and early mature years in Italy, working for some time with Giovanni da Bologna.

The contract, which was signed on 5 March 1568 by the Masters of the Old Church and of the Holy Sacrament Guild, called for Master Willem to make a high altar of alabaster, black marble, and other fine stone, "wrought in back as well as in front . . . , all according to the model designed by the aforesaid Master Willem and delivered to the aforesaid Church Fathers and that, very precisely, following the art of sculpture and antiquity" ("Gewrecht soe wel achter als voer . . . , al naervolgende het patroon bij den voersz. Meester Willem daervan geconcipieert ende den voersz. kerkmeesters gelevert ende dat op sijn steck ende voet, naervolgende die cunste van de sculpture ende antiquiteyt"). The work was to be "as good, excellent, and artistic as he had ever made and as good as any master can and is able to make, the like of which will not be found in all the Netherlands."[56] For all this, Willem van Tetrode was slated to receive 1,600 gulden, 300 immediately, a further 900 at regular three-month intervals and the last 400 on completion of the altar. The costs, including the marble and stone which had to be imported from south Flanders, were to be borne equally by the Old Church and the Holy Sacrament Guild. Various payments were made from the church coffers to Van Tetrode until 5 March 1572, when he received some money for the doors of the altar. While the altar may never have been completed, it would appear that the bulk of the work was actually carried out.[57] Willem van Tetrode's altar, whatever its state of completion, was soon set upon and destroyed by the Iconoclasts after Delft went over to the rebellion against Spain.

In 1568, the authorities in Brussels imposed a tax on movable property, called "the hundredth penny," which contributed to Delft's eventual defection from the camp of Roman Catholic orthodoxy. The records of this tax, which have been preserved in the Brussels archive, list all the more substantial citizens whose property was assessed in excess of 100 gulden. Among the 315 citizens so listed, we find one painter, Cornelis Jacobsz. (Mont), assessed at 175 gulden; two printers, Symon Jansz. (287.5 gulden) and Adriaen Heynricsz. (512.5 gulden); one bookseller, Cornelius Puelen (181 gulden); and the land surveyor Jan Jansz. Potter, mentioned on several occasions in the guild accounts (175 gulden). "Mr. Antony," assessed at 1,200 gulden, was probably the painter Anthonie Montfort van Blocklandt.[2] No glass-makers or engravers appear on the list, or at least none that are identified by their craft. The relatively large amount of property owned by the two printers reflects the capital costs of setting up printing establishments. We shall see in Chapter 5 that the master printers, in the first half of the seventeenth century, paid the highest prices for their houses and formed the wealthiest group in the St. Lucas Guild.

THE GUILD AFTER THE ALTERATION, 1572–1593

In July 1572 the great "Alteration" (*alteratie*) took place, whereby Delft became a Protestant city and joined the rebellion against Spain. On 27 December 1572, Prince Willem of Orange issued a placard prohibiting public processions.[58] As a result, the guild was now divested of one of its most important religious functions. Henceforth its accounts would reflect essentially secular activities. For two years—1572 and 1573—the accounts of the guild do not seem to have been kept at all. The accounts for 1574 were brief. After listing three headmen who had died (the painter Cornelis Jacobsz. Mont, the sculptor Aelbrecht Cornelisz., and Jan Claesz. Schallick of unspecified craft), it closed: "And there remained alive Jan Dirricksz. glassmaker [headman in 1571], and it was in the time of trouble, and there were no receipts in that year."[59] The Alteration and the new wave of Iconoclasm had apparently left the guild in disarray.

The last record having to do with the guild's chapel in the New Church, and hence with its religious function, concerns "the altar," probably, but by no means certainly, the one Van Heemskerck painted for the St. Lucas Chapel. In 1575, the receipts included five Flemish pounds for "a panel sold on order of messrs. [the burgomasters] by us the dean and headmen" ("penel vercoft bij mit onthiet van mij heren bij ons deken ende hoemans").[60] On the expenditure side, in the same year, we find two entries that apparently relate to the sale of the [altar] panel: three gulden two stuivers were paid to those who disposed of the altar in the time of trouble ("die't outer ofde[d]en ende wech deen in den trubel") and thirty stuivers were given to Bouven Danes for cleaning and decorating this panel ("van dat peneel schoen te maken ende te versien"). Bouven Danes is presumably

---

[2]He is so identified in the Delft copy of the document (by a later hand). The tax book is preserved in the Algemeen Rijksarchief, Brussels, Audience 618/36.

[33]

identical with Bouwen or Boudewijn Damasz., Dammes, Dammensz., or Damnisz., painter, headman in 1561-1562, 1568-1569, and 1574-1575.

From the time of the *alteratie,* a new item of expenditure makes its appearance in the accounts: moneys spent to succor impoverished guild members. In 1575, Trijn [Catherine] Lucas, "our guild sister," received three gulden "in her extreme need" ("in haer uutteerste noot") by consent of the four headmen. In 1588 Maertgen Louwerijs; Lucas Dircksz., glassmaker; Claes Volckerszoen.; and Willem Gijs-brechsoen., who were also impoverished, each deposited a debt acknowledgment for one Flemish pound (six gulden) in the chest. This was done at the request of the dean in the presence of the four headmen. The headmen were enjoined, in case these people should become sufficiently well-off again to honor their obligations, to collect the money and lay it in the chest.[61] The new guild letter of 1611 contained a similar provision for the repayment, based on a member's formal acknowledgment of any subsidies he might have received from the chest, in case he should "come into means" (article 21 of the guild letter in Appendix B).

The guild, from this time on, also helped out members who had become embroiled in legal difficulties. In January 1572, Jan Cornelisz. Cock, painter, was in prison in Delft. He was released on the pledge and guarantee of Claes Jansz., cloth merchant, and Jan Michielsz.[62] In the accounts for 1575 we find an entry among the outlays for twenty-four stuivers for the legal costs of Jan Cock, painter, and for two overdue debts that had been acknowledged before the sheriffs ("van den cost in recht van Jack Cock scilder ende noch twe verjaerde scepenkennis").

To give readers some notion of the craft-composition of the guild shortly after the *alteratie,* I show below the list of members who paid their annual dues, their initiation fees, or their death dues, and the craft they practiced insofar as it could be ascertained. Where a member's craft is not shown next to his name in the guild accounts but is inferred from other parts of the accounts or from some other source, it appears in brackets. The names are spelled precisely as they are in the accounts.

New Masters in 1575:	Craft	Amount Paid
Jan Louris		25 st.
Maerten Claes	glassmaker	15 st.
Claes Maertensz.		20 st.
Stevenen Jansz.	scabbard-maker	27 st.

New Masters in 1575:	Craft	Amount Paid
Arian Huegenz.		16 st.
Jacob Willems	painter	16 st.
Dues paid in 1575:		
Jan Willems [Puel?]	glassmaker	5 st.
Willem Will[e]ms	painter	5 st.
Lucas Dircxz	[glassmaker]	5 st.
Adriaen Lambrechts		2½ st.
Jacob Bowarts		2½ st.
Broerken Jacob Ariens[aa]	glassmaker	2½ st.
Machtelt Dirkxdr.		2½ st.
Jan Lenderts	[sculptor]	2½ st.
Meester Pieter	schoolmaster	2½ st.
Dignum	scabbard-maker	2½ st.
Cornelis Gerrits	scabbard-maker	2½ st.
Other members mentioned in the 1575 *accounts:*		
Bouven Dames	painter	
Trijn Lucas		
Jan Cock	painter	
Dues paid in 1576 *or* 1577:		
Louweris Rijckaertz.	glassmaker	2½ st.
Meester Willem Danyelsz.[bb]	[sculptor]	0
Meester Willem Willemsz.[cc]	[painter]	2½ st.
Ariaen Lambrechtsz.		2½ st.
Jan Leenaertsz.[dd]	[sculptor]	2½ st.
Jan Willemsz. Puel	[glassmaker]	2½ st.

[aa]Brother Jacob Ariens or Adriaensz., a member of the *minnebroers* or *Fratori Minores* (a Franciscan order) was headman in 1568 and 1569. In the latter year he is identified as *glaesmacker*. It is remarkable that a member of a religious order should have been headman of the guild before the *alteratie* and a member thereafter. (The convent of the order was destroyed a few years after the Alteration).

[bb]The Van der Gouw transcription reads "Willem Danycksz." Professor Scheller apparently read "Willem Danyelsz." and suggested he might be the sculptor Willem Danielsz. van Tetrode, who, as we have already seen, was known to be working in Delft around this time (Scheller, "Nieuwe gegevens over het St. Lukasgilde," p. 43). My reading of the artist's name in the original text confirms Scheller's transcription.

[cc]Perhaps Willem Willemsz. Luyt, the teacher of Michiel Miereveld.

[dd]"Jan Lenaersz. *antycksnyder*" (sculptor *à l'antique*) appears in the preserved inventory of the pre-1618 papers of the Orphan Chamber of Delft. (The papers themselves were burnt in the Town Hall fire of 1618). It may be observed in passing that "Aelbrecht Cornelis *antycksnyder*," who also appears in these papers, is almost certainly identical with "Aelbrecht Cornelisz. *beeldesnyder*" (image sculptor), who was retiring headman in 1570.

[35]

Dues paid in 1576 *or* 1577:	*Craft*	*Amount Paid*
Luycas Dirckz.	[glassmaker]	2½ st.
Bruertgen Jacob Ariaensz.	glassmaker	2½ st.
Gijsbert Ariaensz. Stolck	[glassmaker]	2½ st.
Machtelt Dircksdochter		2½ st.
Dignum	scabbard-maker	2½ st.
Cornelis Gerritsz.	scabbard-maker	2½ st.
Ariaen Pietersz.	glassmaker	2½ st.
Meester Pieter	schoolmaster	2½ st.
Death dues:		
Jan Dircksz.	glassmaker	15 st.

Excluding apparent duplication in the 1575 and 1576-1577 lists, and including "Hadewij" and "Willempgen Ariaens" who paid five groot each in 1578 and are therefore presumed to have been members in 1576-1577, we come to a total of twenty-five members as of 1576. This if of course a lower-bound estimate of guild membership, since some members may neither have paid their dues in the years 1575 to 1578 nor have been mentioned anywhere else in the accounts. Of those twenty-five members, eighteen can, with varying degrees of confidence, be identified with a craft or trade. The members with a known or inferred craft include eight glassmakers or glass-engravers, four painters, three scabbard-makers, two sculptors, and one school-master. The scabbard-makers, who are mentioned in the 1611 guild letter, decorated a variety of leather articles including shoulder belts and knife handles as well as scabbards.[ee] Meester Pieter, the school-master, may have joined the guild in order to be allowed to sell books to his scholars or possibly to sell specimens of fine calligraphy. It is otherwise curious that no printers or booksellers were members of the guild at this time.

In the register of the taxes levied on houses in 1575, only one painter and one painter's widow could be identified: Anthonie van Blocklandt paid three gulden sixteen stuivers nine penningen, and the widow of Cornelis Jacobsz. Mont four gulden seven stuivers four penningen. Cited also were two printers (Aelbrecht Hendricksz., four gulden nine stuivers seven penningen; and Cornelis Jansz. Vennecoel, four gulden seven stuivers four penningen), one bookseller (Simon Pouwelsz., two gulden four stuivers nine penningen), and one scabbard-maker (Cornelis Gerritsz., a headman of the guild in 1575, one

---

[ee]The nature of the craft can be made out to some extent from the death-inventory of Jan Stevens, *scheemacker*, the son of Steven Jansz. mentioned in the above list (Records of Notary Adriaen Rijshouck, no. 1762, 18 July 1610).

gulden twelve stuivers). But the glassmakers dominated this set of better-off artists and craftsmen with six entries (Adriaen Stolck, three gulden four stuivers; Joris Dircksz., two gulden seventeen stuivers; Jan Louris, three gulden four stuivers; Jacob the glassmaker, one gulden twelve stuivers; the widow of Jan Dircksz. two gulden eleven stuivers two penningen; and Jan Willemsz., one gulden twelve stuivers). The important engraver Hans Wierix was renting a house taxed at two gulden eleven stuivers in the year these taxes were collected.[63]

Some of the artists mentioned in the later accounts are still well-known today (Miereveld, Van Tetrode). A few survived until 1611 and were recorded in the first master list of the guild (Appendix A, Table A.1). The most important names found in the accounts are listed in Table 1.2.

Harmen van der Mast, born in den Briel, was a student of Frans Floris, and later of the latter's pupil Frans Francken the Elder. He spent some time in France before settling in Delft, where he died in 1610. His extant portraits are cool, elegant, but somewhat old-fashioned for the 1590s.[64]

Bartelemes Ferrare is presumably identical with "the art-loving Bartholomeus Ferreris" mentioned by Van Mander in his life of Lucas van Leyden, and with the amateur and collector cited by Arnold Buchelius in 1598.[ff] Around 1600, Ferrare left Delft for Leyden where he occupied an important position on the loan board of Leyden and Rotterdam.[gg] Jan Gerbrantsz. de Jong was a rather mediocre portrait painter who seems to have abandoned painting after 1614.[hh]

In addition to this list of artists and artisans, mention should be made of the widow of Lange Pier (the sobriquet of the famed Amsterdam painter Pieter Aertsen). She appears twice in the accounts for 1583, the first time with a payment of four stuivers and then, in the list of members in arrears, with a debit of twenty-one stuivers.[ii]

Table 1.3 shows the craft composition of the headmen of the guild before and after the *alteratie*, insofar as it is indicated in or can be

[ff]Scheller, "Nieuwe gegevens over het St. Lukasgilde," p. 44. A good-quality religious painting by Ferrare hangs in the Lakenhal Museum in Leyden. On the reference to Ferrare in Buchelius, see below, Chapter 2.

[gg]Ferrare had already left Delft in 1605 when he sold a garden by *procuratie* (Camer van Charitate, "Reckeningen van de deuijt op de gulden," 1605).

[hh]A photograph of one of his portraits is conserved in the R.K.D. files, The Hague.

[ii]Pieter Pietersz., the son of Pieter Aertsen, is known to have painted a portrait in Delft in 1583. Did Aertsen's widow pay master dues to be allowed to keep open the atelier where her sons worked? (cf. Scheller, "Nieuwe gegevens over het St. Lukasgilde," p. 43).

TABLE 1.2
Important Names Appearing in Guild Accounts (1578–1593)

Name	First Appearance in Accounts	Last Appearance in Accounts	Craft	Nature of Entry
Jacob Willemsz. Delff* (c. 1550–1601)	1578	1589	Painter	Headman 1578, 1584–1585, 1588–1589
Herman Pietersz.† (c. 1548–1616)	1581	1581	Faiencier	Received as master (from Delft), in 1613 list.
Meynert Fransz.‡ (?- after 1600)	1581	1583	Glass-maker	New master from Groningen
Corstiaen Jansz. van Bieselinge§ (c. 1558–c. 1600)	1582	1592	Painter	New master, headman 1584–1585, 1591–1592
Dirck Reyniersz. van der Douw (c. 1563–c. 1608)	1583	1593	Glass-maker	New master (from out of town), headman 1586, 1593, widow in 1613 list.
Maerten Danielsz. van Tetrode‖	1583	same	Sculptor	Arrears. First name on guild list of sculptors, 1613.
Harmen van der Mast (c. 1550–1610)	1587	1592	Portrait painter	New master (from out of town), headman 1592–1593
Adriaen Gerritsz [Stolck]	1587	same	Glass-maker	New master (from Delft) in 1613 master list
Michiel Jansz. Miereveld (1567–1641)	1589	1591	Portrait painter	Headman 1589–1590, first on 1613 list.

TABLE 1.2 (continued)
Important Names Appearing in Guild Accounts (1578-1593)

Name	First Appearance in Accounts	Last Appearance in Accounts	Craft	Nature of Entry
Bartelemes Ferrare	1589	1592	Painter	New master (from Rotterdam) headman 1591-1592.
Pieter Ariaensz. [van Buyten]	1589	1591	Glassmaker	Headman 1589-1590, first name on the list of glassmakers in 1613 list
Pieter den Boer	1592	1592	Teacher or bookseller	Arrears (6 years), in 1613 list.
Jan Gerbrantsz. de Jong (c. 1573-after 1623)	1593	1593	Portrait painter	New master (from Delft), in 1613 list.

SOURCE: "Rekeningboekje."

NOTE: Last names in brackets have been inferred from other references to the guild member in the accounts or elsewhere.

*All entries are for "Jacob Willemsz." without any designation of craft or profession. However, he is always mentioned first with the other incoming or outgoing headman of the year, once in conjunction with a glassmaker (Jan Willemsz. Poel). I infer therefore that he was a painter. J. W. Delff is the only painter important enough in this period to have been elected headman three times in 11 years.

†The name "Herman de betielbacker" appears in the 1581 accounts (not *"Hennan de becketbacker"* as transcribed by Van der Gouw). He paid only twenty-five stuivers as his entrance fee, although his betrothal act of 1583 stated he was from Haarlem.

‡Mentioned for his work on church windows, *Oud-Holland*, vol. 39, 1921, p. 58.

§Painted "David and Abigail" for the Town Hall as well as portraits and other "histories."

‖Referred to as "Marten den Beldesnyer" in the guild accounts and as "Mr. Maerten" in the guild list of sculptors of 1611.

inferred from the accounts, from the registers of new citizens, or, for the last few years of the entire period, from "notarial protocols" (depositions and other deeds signed before notaries).

The domination of the guild primarily by glassmakers and secondarily by painters is brought out clearly by the numbers in Table 1.3. Scabbard-makers and sculptors played a subsidiary but not insignificant role in the guild. It is characteristic of the guild, both in the

TABLE 1.3

Craft Designation of Headmen of the Guild of St. Lucas

	Painters	Glass-makers	Sculptors	Scabbard-makers	Unknown
Before 1572	6	12	2	2	17
1573-1593	9	10	1	2	1
Total	15	22	3	4	18

SOURCE: "Rekeningboekje."

NOTE: Members of the guild who were headmen before and after the Alteration are listed exclusively in the former period.

sixteenth and seventeenth centuries, that book dealers, embroiderers, painters of furniture, and other minor trades do not seem to have been represented at all among the guild officers. It was not until 1648 that faienciers were regularly selected as headmen.

Among the craftsmen who became citizens of the town in the period of 1537 to 1593, the numerical predominance of the glassmakers over the painters is even more striking than in the officership of the guild (Table 1.4).

For the sake of comparison, I have added the goldsmiths and jewelers to the list of crafts subordinate to the Guild of St. Lucas. The influx of these craftsmen, especially from the southern provinces

TABLE 1.4

Occupation of New Citizens and Their Sureties in Crafts Subordinate to the Guild of St. Lucas

Occupation	Before the Alteration (1537-1571)		After the Alteration (1572-1593)	
	New Citizens	Sureties	New Citizens	Sureties
Glassmakers	8	10	4	3
Painters	1	1	3	0
Sculptors, stonemasons	5	3	0	1
Embroiderers	1	0	0	0
Chair-makers	4	0	4	4
Scabbard-makers	0	1	2	0
Printers, bookbinders	2	0	1	1
Goldsmiths, jewelers*	3	4	8	5
Total	24	19	22	14

SOURCE: Delft MA, "Poyrter regyster," 1536-1649.

*Subordinate to the goldsmiths' guild.

under Spanish rule, was unmatched by any group of artisans belonging to the Guild of St. Lucas in the late 1580s and early 1590s. It is also worth noticing that the preponderance of the glassmakers over the painters was much less marked in the period after the Alteration in both Tables 1.3 and 1.4. (The large number of entries for glassmakers in the tax book for 1575 probably reflects a state of prosperity antedating the Alteration.)

The total list of members by craft that can be reconstructed is unfortunately not much larger than the list of headmen in Table 1.3. I have been able to identify in all—from 1537 to 1593—nineteen painters, thirty-one glassmakers, six scabbard-makers, six sculptors, four chair-makers (*stoelmackers* or *stoelgroenders*) who presumably painted their furniture, one surveyor, one pastry-baker (*pasteybacker*), one engraver, one faiencier, one hookmaker, and two schoolmasters. Out of a total of 106 distinct members mentioned in the accounts, 73 could be associated with a craft with greater or lesser confidence, and 33 could not.

The absence of printers, lettersetters, and other representatives of the book trade—with the exception of the land surveyor Jan de Potter and the teacher or bookseller Pieter den Boer—is surprising. If De Potter and Den Boer joined the guild to be allowed to sell books,[65] at least the masters among the printers and allied trades must have been members of the guild, and we should have expected one or two of them to show up somewhere in the accounts. We saw earlier that Symon Jansz., printer; Adriaen Heynricsz., printer; and Cornelis Puelen, bookseller, were listed among the richer citizens of Delft in 1568, the year in which Herman Schinkel, the famous heterodox printer, was put to death by the Catholic authorities. Shortly after the *alteratie*, Aelbrecht Hendricxsz. started printing again in Schinkel's old establishment, where he employed at least ten men. His shop was then one of the largest in Holland. Cornelis Jansz. Vennecoel was also active, on a smaller scale, as a printer in Delft as early as 1575, when he was listed in the tax book for that year.[66] It may be a coincidence that neither these men nor any their employees appear in the accounts; in any case it is very unlikely that they ever became headmen. If the printers and booksellers were in the guild, their role was apparently as subordinate in the sixteenth as it was in the seventeenth century.

How many members did the guild have after the *alteratie?* The only total given in the accounts is the thirty-nine members cited in 1567, shortly *before* the watershed date. As I indicated above, I was able to identify twenty-five names of artisans in 1575-1576, who may or may

[41]

not have made up the entire membership. In 1583, twenty-three masters paid their yearly dues (five groot each or 2½ stuivers), and seven were listed as being in arrears on their dues. In 1587, three gulden five stuivers were received as yearly dues, a sum corresponding to twenty-six members. From these bits and pieces of information, I deduce, very tentatively, that the membership is unlikely to have recovered, let alone exceeded, its pre-Alteration level by the late 1580s.

In 1613, twenty years after the closing of the last sixteenth-century accounts that have come down to us, the membership reached about one hundred members. In the next two chapter we shall dwell at length on this great expansion.

AN OVERVIEW

Delft in the sixteenth century was a small and undistinguished artistic center. Even though guild life revolved around the Old and the New Church until the *alteratie*, home-town talent received only minor ecclesiastic patronage. For the painting and sculpture of major altars, the Church Masters turned to artists in Utrecht, Haarlem, and The Hague. There were, however, two major exceptions. The sculptor Willem van Tetrode and the painter Anthonie van Blocklandt (who was born in Montfort but lived in Delft) received major church orders before the Alteration. The fame of these artists may have rested more on the work they had done outside Delft (in Italy in the case of Van Tetrode and in Utrecht of Van Blocklandt) than on their local accomplishments. Delft also had a number of painters, such as Jan Lucas, Jacob Mont, and Hendrick Assuerus, who, while undistinguished in their own right, were competent enough to provide training for more talented artists (Van Heemskerck, Augustyn Jorisz., and Van Blocklandt, respectively). In general, the local artists employed in reconstructing the New Church seem to have been paid at low rates for their work, whereas famous out-of-town masters, such as Jan van Scorel and Maerten van Heemskerck, received munificent sums, annuities, or both for their commissions. The difference can perhaps be explained in terms of their respective bargaining positions. The former were more or less exclusively dependent on the patronage of the church authorities in Delft, while the latter profited from competition among various towns, both in the south and in the north, for their services.

The court of Willem of Orange, who resided in Delft from 1583 until his assassination about a year later, seems to have had a little impact on the artistic life of the city. Michiel Jansz. Miereveld, the main recipient of portrait orders from princes and courtiers in the late sixteenth and early seventeenth centuries, must have entered the Delft guild about the time the court moved to The Hague (he was only seventeen years old when the prince was assassinated). Two other portrait painters joined the guild in this period—Harmen van der Mast in 1587, Jan Gerbrantsz. de Jong in 1593—but neither seems to have acquired any great fame either in his time or thereafter.

The relative unimportance of Delft as a birthplace of major painters and sculptors in the sixteenth century may cause us to overlook its importance as a showplace for great works of religious art. The churches and the convents, before the Iconoclastic onslaughts of 1566, were richly adorned with graven images. The altarpieces by Frans Floris, Anthonie van Blocklandt, Jan van Scorel, Pieter Aertsen, and Maerten van Heemskerck were only the most famous among the works that the faithful could adore and art lovers admire. Their destruction in the period of troubles that lasted, with interruptions, from 1566 to 1572 or 1573, must have been felt as a significant loss by the middle and upper strata of Delft burghers, to the extent that they did not themselves join the ranks of the fanatics among the Calvinists (as most of them probably did not). How could they hope to replace these "collective goods," which they had once enjoyed, after the Alteration had stripped the churches of their ornaments and emptied or destroyed the convents? I suggest that private collecting, for many substantial citizens, may have become a substitute for publicly exhibited artworks that had disappeared. The fact that about 45 percent of all paintings with a specified subject in the inventories I sampled for the first twenty years of the century were religious in content is consistent with the notion of a "latent demand" for sacred art that was met privately once its public availability had been curtailed.[67] The hypothesis is very fragile, especially in view of our total lack of information about the contents of burghers' houses before 1600, but the problem is of sufficient importance to put the idea forward, with all due circumspection.

The changeover to a Protestant administration in 1572, on the heels of the havoc wrought by the Iconoclasts, brought about the secularization of the Guild of St. Lucas. Now that it no longer had to spend its dues on the upkeep and repair of chapel altars and on religious processions, the guild had enough money to spare to help out its members in need and to provide a banquet for the headmen and incoming masters. This it could do despite what appears to have been a loss in membership in the late 1560s and early 1570s, which was probably never made up in the ensuing period.

Even though the old guild letter is lost, many of its provisions can be inferred from items in the accounts. Nonmembers practicing their trade in Delft were summoned and fined. Lotteries were prohibited without consent of the guild. Delft-born masters were admitted into the guild at half the price charged out-of-town artists. The dean was a nonmember who kept the accounts and presumably supervised the guild on behalf of the city administration. These and other provisions were maintained in the new guild letter of 1611. Even the trades represented were virtually the same in the two periods, with the possible exception of the *pasteybacker* and the hookmaker, who may have had a secondary craft occupation more in keeping with the rest of the membership. Indeed, I cannot find any point on which the provisions of the new guild letter differed substantially from the old. Guild leadership, moreover, was exercised by the glassmakers and the painters throughout the sixteenth century period covered in the accounts, just as it was to be until 1648 when the faienciers were regularly admitted to the board of headmen. Despite the great changes that took place in the character of artistic life from the sixteenth to the seventeenth century—especially the shift in the bulk of demand from church orders to purchases by individuals in a more or less anonymous private market—there was substantial continuity in the social organization within which artists and artisans operated.

TWO

The Transition Years, 1593–1613

The accounts of the St. Lucas Guild break off in 1593. For the next twenty years, very little is known about the composition of the guild or about its activities. This is a pity, because those transition years—the bridge between medieval and modern Delft—are crucial for the development of artistic and artisanal life in Delft.

Two currents of migration exerted a profound influence on styles, ideas, and techniques in this period. The more important of the two, which will be touched on throughout this chapter, was the migration from Flanders that reached its high point after the fall of Antwerp to the armies of Philip II in 1584. The reverse current took young men—students of both major and minor arts—to France and Italy, where they aimed to perfect their chosen craft.[a] Among the painters of

[a]Two documents of 1616, first summarized in Abraham Bredius, "Twee leerlingen van Jacob Delff die geen voet bij stuk hielden," *Oud-Holland* 47 (1930):189, refer to Italian journeys that occurred at the turn of the century. They reveal that artists and craftsmen active in the minor arts who went to Italy had close links. Some of these links apparently were forged when apprentices who later specialized in different crafts learned the art of drawing together. The documents were drawn up at the request of the trustees of Claes Claesz. Menyt, a *caffawerker* (weaver of fine silk satins) who went to Italy around 1597 and disappeared around 1600 or 1601 without leaving a trace. In the first document, dated 28 June 1616 (Records of Notary Henrick Vockestaert, no. 1580), Pieter Claesz. Bilevelt, goldsmith in Delft, testified that he had learned the art of portraying (*conterfeytsen*) along with Claes Claesz. Menyt from "Mr Jacob, painter on the Brabant peat market" (Jacob Willemsz. Delff?). Some time later, in the year 1597, he had left for Italy "in order to visit these lands and to exercise his handicraft." Toward the end of 1600 or the beginning of 1601 he had met Menyt, who was looking for work, in Florence. Bilevelt told him that there was work to be found in Rome in the jewelry trade. He went with Menyt to the outskirts of Florence "to a place where Netherlanders usually took leave of those that had accompanied them" and never saw him again. In the second document, dated 16 August 1616 (Records of Notary Henrick Vockestaert, no. 1580), the painter Abraham Apersz. van der Hoeve testified that he was living in Milan, Italy, when Claes Claesz. Menyt came to lodge with him in September or October 1600.

Delft, seven[b] are known to have traveled to Italy in the 1590s or early 1600s, most of them spending some time in France on the way thither or back. At least four of these were sons of well-off burghers (Abraham Apersz. van der Hoeve and Johan van Nes, who came from rich brewers' families; Joris van der Lier; and Wouter Jacobsz. Vosmaer). Sending a son to learn the art of painting in Italy was an expensive enterprise with an uncertain pay-off.[c] It was perhaps because wealth rather than talent determined who could travel across the Alps that the impact of this first wave of foreign-trained artists was less than decisive. Another reason may have been that, in contrast for example to Utrecht, which was far more receptive to Italian influence, the Calvinist intellectual climate that prevailed in Delft did not offer fertile ground for the grand religious style of the Counter-Reformation, either in its Mannerist or its Caravaggist manifestations. It was not until Leonaert Bramer, who returned from Italy after a stay of thirteen years, in 1628, that a major artist impregnated with Italian ideas began to have a direct impact on Delft painting. I stress the word "direct" because the influence of the first wave of returnees may have exerted itself through teaching[d] or through the intangible effects that familiarity with Italian achievements might have had on local artists and collectors.

The influence of Flanders was more immediate and profound because both young and mature artists, fully trained in the major centers of the southern Netherlands where the arts were manifestly

[b]Huybert Jacobsz. Grimani (in Venice in the 1590s, returned to Delft around 1598), Abraham Apersz. van der Hoeve (in Milan 1600), Joris Gerritsz. van der Lier (Paris 1610, Rome 1611), Pieter Cornelisz. van Rijck (fifteen years in Italy, returned to Holland circa 1604), Jacob Woutersz. Vosmaer (in Italy early 1600s), Johan van Nes (France and Italy 1600s), and Jacob Pynas (Italy 1605). Pieter van Rijck apparently **never came back to Delft. Jacob Pynas arrived in Delft for the first time in 1632.**

[c]Joris van der Lier (c. 1590-1655) is a case in point. His very mediocre career could hardly justify the money that his parents spent to send him to Italy. His expenses are partly recorded in his estate papers, which inform us that, after learning the art of drawing with Karel van Mander the Younger, he left for Paris in 1611 and about a year later went to Rome. His lack of success as a painter is evident from the very few examples of his paintings contained in contemporary inventories and from the fact that he had felt obliged to ask Wouter Vosmaer to "go over" one of his flower pieces. (Orphan Chamber, *boedel* no. 1847.)

[d]Johan van Nes, for instance, was the teacher of the important Delft artist Corstiaen van Couwenbergh who himself later visited Italy. We do not know whether Huybert Jacobsz. Grimani had any pupils other than Pieter van Rijck, but in view of his long association with the tapestry works of Karel van Mander the Younger, it is likely that he acted as a conduit for the designs and ideas of the great Italian decorators.

[46]

more advanced than in the north, immigrated to the cities of the United Provinces. Their contributions quickened the pace of artistic life and helped to shake Delft out of its provincialism.

Among the specific innovations of the Flemish immigrants were the great tapestry-works founded by Franchoys Spierinx of Antwerp shortly before the turn of the century, which employed weavers and cartoon designers chiefly of southern birth. The faience industry, though founded by a Dutch-born master,[e] received a strong impetus in this transitional period from decorators and potters from Flanders and France. The weaving of fine patterned silks, a southern accomplishment, made its contribution to the renewal of artisanal life in Delft. And, finally it was in the art of painting landscape and still life that the Flemish immigrants were to leave their deepest mark.

The city fathers of Delft encouraged economic development by various measures, including the granting of citizenship for free, instead of for the regular three-gulden fee, to Flemish workers. The production of silk goods was especially favored. For a number of years—from about 1596 to the early 1600s—the city bought up silk goods made by Flemish artisans that could not find another outlet.[f] A great number of textile artisans attracted by these advantages acquired citizenship from 1590 to 1610. As far as I have been able to find out, however, none of the trades grouped under the Guild of St. Lucas enjoyed special privileges of the type designed to attract and hold Flemish textile workers in Delft.

Neither the town authorities nor the two churches seem to have created a major demand for artworks in this period.[g] The convents

[e]Although Herman Pietersz., the first Delft faiencier, who became a master of the guild in 1581, was born in Haarlem (according to his betrothal act of 1583), I suspect that he must have been trained in Flanders, where the only important potteries in the Low Countries were located.

[f]On 8 June 1598, the town authorities resolved to continue for one more year "to take delivery [*afnemen*] of the silk goods made by those of the Flemish trades so that they may not be obliged, by reason of the failure to sell their silks, to depart from here" (Delft MA, Resolutie boucken van veertigen ende vroedschappen der stadt 1592-1625," fol. 58v). There was also a plan afoot in 1595 to negotiate directly with master weavers in Leyden to attract textile workers to Delft by paying the cost of their transfer to Delft, but the idea seems to have been finally rejected as "impractical" (ibid., fol. 24v., fol. 124). On the interest of Haarlem in following Delft's example in the pursuit of similar mercantilist policies, see Briels, J.G.C. *De Zuidnederlandse immigratie 1572-1630* (Haarlem: Fibula van Dishoeck, 1978), p. 128.

[g]In 1601, Willem Willemsz. Luyt is the only painter paid by the treasurer of the city. He received three small payments, totalling twenty-nine gulden ten stuivers, all for

that had been so active in the Middle Ages as patrons of the arts were liquidated in the 1570s and 1580s. Some, like the Franciscan convent to the south east of the New Church, were destroyed; others were sold or leased to private buyers and were converted into workplaces. This was the fate, for example, of the St. Agatha and the St. Ann convents that became the sites of the tapestry-weaving works of Franchoys Spierinx and Karel van Mander II respectively. The only really important order by an ecclesiastic institution for work by Delft artisans was destined for the adornment of an out-of-town edifice, the Church of St. Jan in Gouda. This was the glass window commemorating the lifting of the siege of Leyden, started by Dirck Jansz. Verheyden and completed after his death in October 1603 by Dirck Reyniersz. van der Douw. But even here it is remarkable that the design of the window was not entrusted to a Delft artist but to Isaac van Swanenburgh of Leyden, in contrast to the window donated by the town of Dordrecht which was both designed and executed by the Dordrecht glassmaker Gerrit Cuyp, the grandfather of the painter Albert Cuyp.

Fortunately the growth of the market for individual consumption more than picked up the slack left by the decline of public patronage. The shift of demand from glass products and sculpture toward painting and decorated earthenware, which we can infer from the change in the numbers of individuals active in these various trades, was a consequence of this individualization of demand.

The immigrants from Flanders not only supplied new skills; they also contributed to demand. The population of Delft, which may have been of the order of seventeen thousand in 1590, increased at a fairly rapid pace during the transition years, reaching an estimated twenty-three thousand inhabitants in 1622[h] Many businessmen and a number of artisans prospered in these ebullient times. The new fashion for decorating homes with paintings and colored tiles and the rise in

---

broad-brush work (Delft MA, "Reckening; Meester Jan Hogenhouck Tesoryer der Stadt Delff van den jaere 1601," fol 196v., 204, and 208). Town orders for glass are also of small importance (ibid., fol. 204, 208). Payments to book dealers and printers are larger. Niclaes de Clerck, for instance, is paid thirty gulden for a print of the victory of Prince Maurice (ibid., fols. 179v., 180) and Floris Balthasar the same amount for a print of the Battle of Nieuwport (ibid., fol. 180).

[h]The population of Delft in 1622, according to the States General head count made in that year, was 22,769. Johannes G. van Dillen, "Summiere staat van de in 1622 in Provincie van Holland gehouden volkstelling," *Economisch-historisch Jaarboek* 21 (1940):174. If the population increased at the same rate as the average number of betrothals (which averaged 240 in the period 1587-1590 and 340 in the

burgher wealth all made for a stronger local demand for artworks than in the generation earlier.

While we lack guild documents during the transition period, we are far better endowed with other evidence pertinent to artistic life. The betrothal and marriage books, starting in 1582 and the burial books, starting in 1593, provide precious vital statistics on the practitioners of the arts and trades embraced by the guild.[i] The accounts of the city of Delft and the day-to-day records of the decisions of the sheriff and aldermen of Delft (*Camer boeken*) supply more relevant material, starting in the 1590s, than in the earlier periods. The records of the Camer van Charitate, which received 0.625 percent of the value of all real-estate transactions, are preserved from 1597 on.

The principal new source, at least by the 1600s, consists of notarial records. The first preserved notarial books date back to 1574, but there are large gaps in the 1580s and 1590s.[j] The harvest of names of artists and artisans for the first decade or so is disappointingly small. It is only in the last two or three years of the sixteenth and in the first decade of the seventeenth century that names of artisans begin to crop up with any degree of frequency and that interesting documents containing references to their lives or to their works make their first appearance. Because of the Town Hall fire of 1618, which burnt more or less beyond retrieval[k] the papers of the Orphan Chamber that had been preserved there, very few settlements of estates (*boedels*) have survived for the transition period. Those that are to be found among the "notarial protocols" mention only an occasional panel or painted

---

years 1622-1626), then the population was roughly 16,000 in 1590. A similar calculation using the number of deaths in 1593-1594 (the first years for which records are available) and 1622-1623 yields a population of 18,000 in 1593-1594 (based on an average of 323 deaths per year in the first period and 410 in the second).

[i]The first baptismal books preserved are dated 1616, after the end of the period under consideration.

[j]Altogether thirteen wrapped or bound sets of record ("protocols") produced by six notaries are preserved for the sixteenth century. Of these, eleven contain only testaments or marriage contracts, which yield little information on our subject except for occasional signatures of artists and artisans as witnesses. Even the testaments of such persons, when they are available, rarely contain material of any significance. The most informative documents, both for the sixteenth and seventeenth centuries, are depositions or affidavits (*attestatien*) and, much more rarely, "insinuations" (*insinuatien*), notifying the addressee of the addresser's intent (usually of bringing suit against him).

[k]The calcinated papers are held in boxes at the Delft archive. A technique may yet be found that would make them legible at a reasonable cost.

board, with no artist's name cited. In spite of all these gaps and deficiencies in the data, a much clearer picture now emerges of the relative importance of the different crafts and of the general nature of their production than in the pre-1590 period covered in the preceding chapter.

OLD AND NEW CRAFTS

The books recording the acquisition of Delft citizenship give an approximate idea of fluctuations in the number of new immigrants from Flanders. In the early 1580s, new citizenships average thirty-one a year; they rise to thirty-eight in the period 1586 to 1589, and reach a peak in the period 1590 to 1594 with an average of forty new citizens per year, the overwhelming majority of them from Flanders. After this crest the numbers recede to an average of twenty-six per year from 1595 to 1607. Around the time of the truce with Spain, the number of new citizens rises again to an average of thirty-seven per year from 1609 to 1614. Among all the factors affecting the relation between the actual number of immigrants and the number of new citizenships granted, the policy of the guilds may have been the most crucial. Where a guild was well in control of the activities of the individuals engaged in the trades under its jurisdiction, new migrants wanting to establish themselves as independent craftsmen in Delft were forced to buy their right of citizenship prior to entering the guild. Where the guild was weak, craftsmen practiced without becoming members and dispensed with citizenship rights too. The goldsmiths apparently belonged to a relatively strong guild: five of them obtained citizenship from 1590 to 1599 and two from 1601 to 1611. The St. Lucas Guild during the 1590s and early 1600s must have been quite weak, considering that very few of the newly migrated artisans normally falling under its jurisdiction became citizens during the period (Table 2.1).

In addition to directly acquired citizenships, a number of painters who later became members of the guild of St. Lucas were the sons of Flemish immigrants. Gillis de Berch from Ghent, sailmaker, the father of Gillis and Matheus de Berg(h), became a citizen on 13 February 1590; Michiel Stael, baker, from Maestricht, father of Peter Stael on 19 April 1594; Gillis Gillisz. van Couwenburch from Mechelen, silversmith (later also engraver), the father of Corstiaen Gillisz. van Couwenbergh, on 4 July 1606; Evert Harmensz. from Steenwyck, spectacle-maker, father of Harmen and Pieter Steenwyck, on 10

TABLE 2.1
New Citizens and Their Sureties, 1590-1611

Occupation	1590-1599		1600-May 1611	
	New Citizens	Sureties	New Citizens	Sureties
Painters	1	0	0	0
Glassmakers	0	2	1	1
Printers, bookbinders, and allied trades	1	3	1	2
Chair-makers	2	3	1	0
Sculptors, stonecarvers	1	1	0	0
Scabbard-makers	1	0	0	0
Faienciers	0	0	1	2
Tapestry-makers	0	0	1	0
Jewelers, goldsmiths	5	2	2	1

SOURCE: All years except 1596-1600, Delft MA, "Poyrter regyster, 1536-1649." For the years 1596-1600, Delft O.R.A. 168, "Camerbouck."

NOTE: Sureties (*borgen*) were Delft citizens who acted as sponsors for the new citizens.

1611; Michiel Nouts, faiencier and tile-painter from Antwerp, father of Servaes Nouts, on 5 October 1611. Some immigrants from the south, however, seem to have become citizens de facto without ever formally acquiring citizenship. Examples are the painter Hans Jordaens, who stood as surety (*borg*) for his son Simon when the latter became a citizen on 3 August 1612; and Palamedes Stevensz., agate-polisher from Flanders, both of whose sons, Anthony and Palamedes, became members of the guild in the 1620s as native citizens (paying only six gulden). Neither Hans Jordaens nor Palamedes Stevensz. is registered in the "Poyrter regyster."

To show that the new citizenships in Table 2.1 represent only a fraction of the new arrivals from Flanders, we need only consider that, by a conservative estimate that excludes individuals who de facto or de jure derived their citizenship from their parents or who are known to have married in Delft but worked elsewhere,[l] thirty painters of Flemish origin practiced their trade in the city in the late 1590s and early 1600s who were not citizens.[m] Of the sixteen painters in the

[l] Including Gilles de Hondecoeter, Conradius du Laeij, and Peter Stalpaert.
[m] Abram Bonaert; Guillamme Gillis and Willem Willemsz. van den Bundel; Hans van der Burch; Jacques Francois (Musscher?); Michiel Hack; Adriaen, Claes, and Hans de Hondecoeter; Hans, Abraham, and Simon Jordaens; Hendrick de Koninck;

[51]

above group who were still working in Delft at the time the new guild regulations came out in May 1611, seven acquired citizenship the following year and one in 1617.[n] It is likely that some of those who did not formally become citizens were allowed to join, or perhaps to remain in the guild, because their father or another family member was already inscribed in the citizenship rolls. It is evident in any case that the sudden rush to obtain citizenship in 1612 was linked to the tightening of guild regulations in the preceding year.

I have not found any direct evidence about the weakness of the Guild of St. Lucas around the turn of the century nor about the city authorities' concern over this problem. It is worthy of note, however, that the sheriffs and burgomasters thought it well to remind the people of Delft in 1602 that only master masons, carpenters, smiths, stonecarvers, glassmakers, and roofers who were guild members and citizens should be employed in the construction of new houses.[1] Since we can be fairly certain that the regulations of the Guild of St. Lucas already made this citizen and guild status mandatory for the stone-carvers and glassmakers, we may conclude that evasion of this rule had become frequent and flagrant.

The ascendancy of the painters and faienciers in the first decade of the century and the decline of the glassmakers, who had been numerically and organizationally so important in the guild in the sixteenth century, are the most striking features of Table 2.2, where the first mention of artists and artisans in a variety of contemporary sources are enumerated.

Besides the painters and faienciers, the sculptors and the stonecarv-ers,[o] the tapestry-makers and the embroiderers were clearly in the

---

Mathys, Augustyn Mathysz., Cornelis Mathysz., and Pieter Mathysz. Pastenax; Jan Pietersz., van der Schoot (alias Schotelman); Jan Jansz. van der Schoot (alias Schotelman); Servaes (Boerman?); Jan van Thielt; Heyndrick Thysz.; Esdras Thysz.; Elias Lucasz. and Francois Eliasz. Verhulst; Hans Verlinden; Pieter Pietersz. Vromans de Oude; Pieter Pietersz. Vromans de Jonge; Pieter Jansz. Vromans; Jacques van der Wyer.

[n]The following painters (from the list in note m) were working in Delft in 1611. The date in parentheses shows when those that became citizens acquired their citizenship. Bonaert (1617), Willem van den Bundel, Jacques Francois, Adriaen Hondecoeter, Hans Hondecoeter (1612), Hans Jordaens, Simon Jordaens (1612), Pieter Pastenax (1612), Cornelis Pastenax, Jan Jansz. van der Schoot (1612), Jan Pietersz. van der Schoot, Francois Verhulst (1612), Hans Verlinden, Pieter Pietersz. Vromans the Elder (1612), Pieter Pietersz. Vromans the Younger, Pieter Jansz. Vromans (1612).

[o]The increased number of stonecarvers was probably due more to intensified building activity—and hence the demand for stone-cutting—than to the need for

TABLE 2.2
First Mention of Artists and Artisans in Delft Sources

Occupation	January 1590–December 1599	December 1600–May 1611
Painters	23	54
Glassmakers	30	20
Printers, book trades	17	17
Chair-makers	23	21
Sculptors, stonecarvers	10	15
Scabbard-makers	5	6
Faienciers	3	24
Tapestry-makers	11	24
Embroiderers	2	5
Total	124	186

SOURCES: Delft MA, Notarial archives; ibid., "Poyrter regyster," 1536-1649; Delft O.R.A. 168 and 169, "Camerbouck"; Delft MA, "Regyster boek(en) van de getroude personen," 1590-1611; ibid., "Begrafboeken van de Oude en Nieuwe Kerck," 1593-1611; Delft, Camer van Charitate, "Register van Ambachtsjongens," 1597 (no. 174), 1609 (no. 175); ibid., "Reckeningen van de deuijt op de gulden," 1597-1611; Delft RC, "Thienste reckening," 1597; and "Twede generale reckening," 1608-1609.

NOTE: When an artist or artisan is first mentioned in the 1590s and then is mentioned again in the 1600s, he is entered only in the first period in this table.

ascendant. Even if we take into account that many of the individuals counted in the first period continued to work in the second, the more or less unchanged number of newly recorded printers and other bookworkers, chair-makers, and scabbard-makers suggests that these trades did not share the extraordinary expansion of the other four occupations. The only trade where employment regressed absolutely appears to have been glassmaking, which, as I have already pointed out, must have been adversely affected by the prolonged decline in church patronage after the Alteration.[P]

The register of hearths of 1600, which was the basis for taxing both owners and renters of houses, gives a first approximation of the number of individuals in each craft who were working in Delft at that

---

sculpture. It is my impression that the number of full-fledged sculptors in Delft was very small both in the 1590s and in the early 1600s. In the original Master List of 1611, there are only seven sculptors (*beeltsnyders*).

[P]Dirck Jorisz. is the only glassmaker paid by the church authorities in 1595 (150 gulden) and in 1608 (101 gulden), apparently for repairs to glass windows in the Old or the New Church.

TABLE 2.3
Artists and Artisans Identified by Their Craft in the "Haardsteden Register" of 1600

Occupation	No.
Painters	24
Glassmakers	12
Printers, book trades	11
Chair-makers	13
Sculptors, stonecarvers	9
Scabbard-makers	5
Faienciers	3
Tapestry-makers	11
Embroiderers	0
Total	88

SOURCE: Delft MA, "Haardsteden register," 1600.

time (Table 2.3). The data in the table seriously underestimate the absolute number of individuals in each craft for two principal reasons: 1) by no means all individuals are identified by their craft in the survey; and 2) poorer artisans renting a room or two in a private house were probably not recorded by the tax collectors. The painters and printers are likely to be better represented in this sample than the glassmakers or chair-makers, many of whom were poor and escaped registration. When all this is said, however, one should keep in mind that many of the individuals mentioned in notarial archives or in the marriage and other registers of vital statistics lived only in Delft a year or two before moving on to another town. A number of painters, some of whom were of Flemish origin, belonged to this transient category.[9]

According to my very rough calculations, the 1600 register of hearths comprised about three thousand persons, including many individuals without designation of trade or craft. The eighty-eight artists and artisans listed in Table 2.3 represented a little less than 3 percent of this number. This percentage, which is already fairly significant, should only be considered as a lower bound in the light of the above arguments.

[9]Among these cases may be cited Jan van Ravesteyn (moved to The Hague), Bartholemeus Ferrare (to Leyden), Hans Rem and Abram Jordaens (Amsterdam) and Pieter Dircksz. Cluyt (unknown destination). We have already noted that painters who married in Delft but who are thought not to have resided there are not included in the name counts in this chapter.

THE VISIT TO DELFT OF ARNOLD VAN BUCHELL

In May 1598, Arnold van Buchell, itinerant scholar and canon of St. Peter's in Utrecht, visited Delft and wrote down in his diary a number of observations that give a first *vue d'ensemble* of the state of the arts in the city.

Van Buchell first mentions the stained-glass window by Willem Thibaut in the Old Church, which he judges to be of moderate quality (*"artis non extrema"*). On painting, he makes two entries. First:

> The painters here are Michael Jansz. [Miereveld] and Hubert [Jacobsz. Grimani];[r] the art-lovers are Melchior Wyntgis and Aper Fransz. [van der Hoeve][s]
>
> (Pictores hic sunt Michael Johannius et Hubertus, amatores Melchior Vineus et Aper Franciscus.)[2]

Van Buchell probably did not mean to write that the portrait painters Miereveld (fig. 3) and Hubert (or Huybert) Jacobsz. were the only painters worthy of note in Delft. After describing the collection of Aper Fransz. van der Hoeve, which included small statues by Willem van Tetrode and a life-sizing painting of Hercules by Jan Gossaert (Mabuse), and the gems, medals, and other precious objects belonging to the goldsmith Abraham Gorlaeus, he goes on to write:

> I saw in the Market Place at the shop of a goldsmith[t] various types of shells and a rather large petrified sea-mushroom [*sic*]. From there we went to the house of Elias, whose wife showed us pictures painted by him from life of almost all types of flowers. He also is

[r]Huybert (or Hubert) Jacobsz., already mentioned in connection with his trip to Italy, was born in Delft in 1562 or 1563; he spent ten years in Venice, where he attached himself to the future doge Marinus Grimani, whose surname he adopted. He returned to Delft in 1598 and died there in April 1631. He is mentioned as a portrait painter by both Van Mander and Van Bleyswijck. None of his portraits have been identified.

[s]Both Melchior Wyntgis and Aper Fransz. van der Hoeve were rich brewers. Wyntgis sold his brewery for 12,500 gulden and left Delft in 1601 for Campen where he became master of the Mint. The inventory of his important collection of paintings was published in *Dietsche Warande*, n.s. (1889):267-76. According to Karel van Mander, *Het Schilderboeck ... der Edele Vrye Schilderkonst* (Haarlem: Paschier van Wesbursch boek vercooper, 1604), fol. 24v., Aper Fransz. studied painting with Frans Floris in Antwerp. The name of his son Abraham Apersz. van der Hoef (or Hoeve) appears on the guild's master list of painters of 1611.

[t]The goldsmith on the market square was perhaps Jan Michielsz. Miereveld, the father of the painter.

given to expressing the forms of shells and animals by the same technique, in very vivid color.

(Vidi in Foro apud quondam aurifabrum varia concharum genera, fungum item marinum, satis amplum, petrificatum. Inde ad Eliam pictorem ivimus, cujus uxor nobis monstrabat omnium fere florum vivas ab eo depictas imagines. Hic idem concharum animaliumque eodem artificio solet exprimere formas, colore ad-modum vivido.)[3]

The painter Elias is almost surely Elias Lucasz. Verhulst, an artist of Flemish origin. The only known work by his hand is a flower piece engraved by Hondius.[u] He was buried in Delft on 21 January 1601.

Van Buchell concludes the account of his stay in Delft with a description of a visit to the atelier of Franchoys Spierinx, which was installed in the former convent of St. Agatha. Spierinx showed him tapestries "made with the greatest art, worthy of a prince, unequaled in mastery."[4] The colors of the animals and figures represented, he observed, exceeded in verisimilitude anything that could be made with the painter's brush. He noted that Spierinx used many cartoons drawn by Karel van Mander (the Elder). It was probably those first contacts of Karel van Mander with the great *tapissier* that led to the introduction of the painter's son, Karel van Mander the Younger, into the business, at about the time of his father's death in 1604.

Was there much else to see in Delft in 1598? In the field of painting Van Buchell might have mentioned the work of Hans Jordaens (fig. 4), who became master in Antwerp in 1581 and was active in Delft in 1590s, and of Rochus Jacobsz. Delff, who produced a few religious paintings of good quality, dated from 1581 on, as well as competent group portraits. Christian Jansz. van Bieselingen, who is remembered chiefly for a *David and Abigail* in the Town Hall of Delft, had already left town to return to Middelburg, his native city. The group portraits of *Schutters* by Rochus Jacobsz. Delff and by Miereveld preserved in the Town Hall are competent but hardly innovative.

Neither these nor the workaday portrait painters of the time, such as Harmen van der Mast and Jan Gerbrants de Jong, were worthy of any special consideration on the part of a man who was familiar with the fine work going on in Utrecht (Bloemart, Uytewael) and Haarlem (Cornelis Cornelisz. van Haarlem, Van Mander, and Goltzius), let alone with the exciting achievements of Renaissance Italy. It is perhaps more surprising that he did not mention the fledgling faience

---

[u]The only known copy of the print was destroyed in Berlin during World War II.

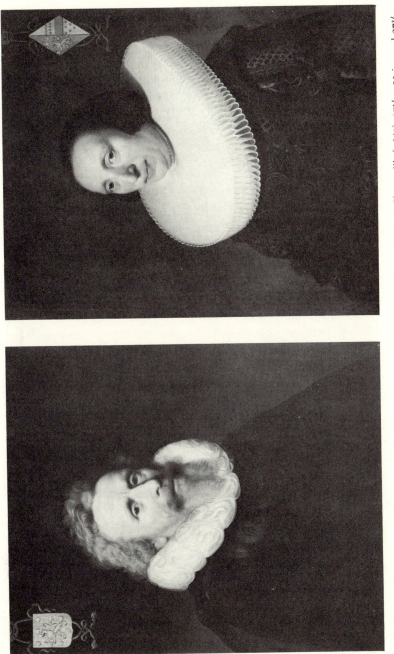

FIG. 3 Michiel van Miereveld, Portraits of Jacob van Dalen and his wife, Margaretha van Clootwijk (1640), 27½ x 23 in. and 27¾ x 22⅛ in. The Metropolitan Museum of Art, Bequest of Collis P. Huntington, 1925 (Photo: Museum)

industry of Delft, founded by Herman Pietersz., which already produced fine decorative majolica in this early period.

Van Buchell, as an observant tourist, was more interested in artistic accomplishments than in the seeds of future growth. He had nothing to say about the critical contribution of Flemish immigrants or about the innovations that were being brought back from France and Italy by the young artists who had spent their formative years in these more "modern" countries.

THE MAJOR ARTS

Few inventories and still fewer notarial documents dealing with painting or sculpture in the years preceding the issuance of the new guild letter have survived. There were no attributed paintings or sculptures in the inventories that I studied. By far the largest collection of works of art that I have recorded for the period belonged to the tax-collector Cornelis van Coolwijck. Shortly after the death of his wife Geertgen van den Aa in December 1605, his vast possessions were appraised.[5] The paintings were estimated by the painters Hans Jordaens and Huybert Jacobsz. Grimani.ᵛ Not a single painter's or sculptor's name is cited in connection with the 120 paintings recorded in the house and the manor belonging to the couple. The failure to attribute any of the works is all the more striking in view of the detail lavished on the descriptions (e.g., "large square panel with white pine frame and support representing a certain noble manor in the countryside with a hunt and a promenade of noble men and ladies, twenty-four gulden").

As in the period 1610-1619, for which we have more abundant data (see Table 8.3, Chapter 8), "histories"—religious, mythological, and allegorical—dominated the subject categories. Combined, they made up nearly half of the total. Within this group, mythological scenes, called "poëteries," were well represented. They came to 8 percent of the total, twice the share in the sample for 1610-1619. Subjects drawn from Ovid and Homer were more commonly collected by nobles and rich burghers with some knowledge of the humanities than by more plebeian types who favored simple religious scenes. The share of landscapes in Coolwijck's collection was 17.5 percent, compared to about 25 percent for the 1610-1619 sample. Landscapes, while by no means rare at the time, did not enjoy wide popularity until later decades. There were of course many portraits

ᵛGrimani's first name was written "Jacob," presumably by error of the clerk.

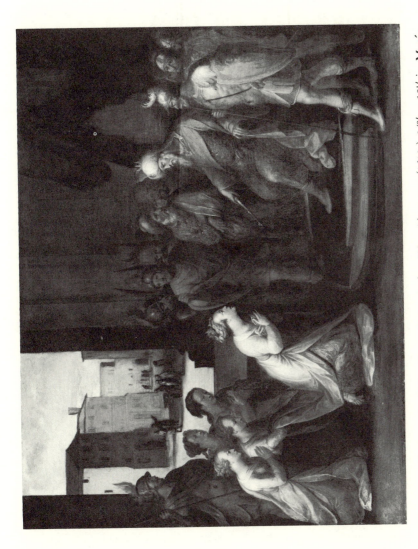

FIG. 4 Hans Jordaens the Elder, Queen Esther before King Ahasuerus (1610s), 34⁹/₁₆ x 12½ in. Musée des Beaux-Arts de Montréal, Horsley and Annie Townsend Bequest (Photo: Museum).

among the possessions recorded (22 percent of the total), including, besides family mementos, heads of princes and of famous theologians (Luther, Melanchton). Two still-lifes—both of them flower pieces— and five genre pieces (market men and women, the "five senses" in one picture) completed the collection. These last two thinly represented categories only became significant in the second quarter of the century. There was also a great abundance of wood, lead, stone, and alabaster sculptures, elaborate embroidery pieces, and brass trellis-work. While the proportion of sculpture and other artworks to paintings may have been unusually high in rich houses of this sort, the evidence from later periods indicates that pictures only gradually acquired the dominant position they finally commanded from the 1630s or 1640s on.

Other inventories of this period were much smaller and laconically described. Old and New Testament scenes and portraits were by far the most common subjects.[w]

Our first reference to paintings in a notarial document is of interest chiefly because it mentioned painted panels in conjunction with silver and other objects of luxury, a juxtaposition we shall often encounter. The petitioner or *requirant* in this notarial deposition, a man named Rogier Laurensz., is also of incidental interest because he was closely involved in the affairs of the grandparents on both sides of Johannes Vermeer's family a quarter of a century later. On 24 May 1596, a young man by the name of Maximiliaen brought a basket of goods belonging to Rogier Laurensz., operator of a market stand,[x] to the house of the deponent Jantgen Jacobs, wife of a shipper, and left them in her care. Later he came back and removed some of the goods "on the pretext that he had been sent to do so." The goods that he

[w]Here are a few typical small collections: On 25 November 1607, a panel, of Abraham's Sacrifice worth eight stuivers is recorded (Records of Notary Adriaen Rijshouck, no. 1759). On 4 December 1607, a Delfshaven collection is said to contain two portraits, a landscape in gilded frame, two small prints, a picture of the Prodigal Son, and a man's face (ibid.). On 17 February 1608, the paintings in an estate are listed as "four old landscape panels, two panels written in French, portraits of the four Evangelists, a Tamar, and the King of France" (ibid., no. 1760). The widow of a butcher owned "a large panel with naked persons" (probably a mythological scene), a Rebecca, a Dead Prince, Daniel in the Lions' Den, two portraits, and nine other paintings of various shapes of unspecified subjects. The painter Sybrant Andries Balkenende signed the inventory (ibid., no. 1758, 20 November 1606).

[x]The original Dutch word is *kramer* which is usually, but inaccurately, translated as peddlar or itinerant merchant. Rogier Laurensz. apparently sold his wares from a stand (*kram*) on market or fair days, but he did not necessarily carry his goods from place to place as peddlars did.

removed from the basket were declared to be: a beer stein, a silver spoon, a silver belt (*onderriem*),[y] two large gilded square mirrors, along with two or three small panel paintings (*bordekens*).[6] We shall see later that, in the lottery of luxurious objects organized by Roger Laurensz. in 1620, silver and gilded vessels, mirrors, and paintings made up a large proportion of the total value of the items that were raffled off.[z]

The second reference to paintings is more substantial. I cite it here even though the painter concerned, Hendrick Splinter, was normally active in The Hague,[aa] because the suit in which he was involved came up before the sheriffs in Delft.[7]

On 29 November 1596 Splinter sued his mother-in-law Magdalena de Lant, demanding from her: 1) 340 gulden for various paintings according to his register; and 2) 54 gulden 6 stuivers that he had paid on her behalf to a certain Jan Yemantsz. Bosman in Utrecht. Magdalena asserted to the contrary that he owed her 822 gulden 18 stuivers. She claimed that to keep him from going around idly claiming that he had no work, she had agreed to buy every painting that he would make for one Flemish pound (6 gulden) each, herself paying for the panels, oil, colors, and other costs. She had taken delivery of various paintings that she had paid for at this price, with the exception of two pictures that were markedly larger and for which she had herself volunteered to pay more money and had done so to his satisfaction. The painter denied that the defendant had undertaken to buy the paintings for one Flemish pound each. He conceded that she had once brought colors from Amsterdam worth thirty-five or thirty-six stuivers, which he was willing to substract from his demands. He acknowledged that Magdalena had taken delivery of all pictures (except the Venus piece) but claimed that he had received no payment for them. She persisted in her defense, mentioning some panels she had bought for his use. Besides the Venus picture, a painting of the Virgin Mary (*een Maria Beelt*) is also mentioned in the suit.

The division of labor within the Splinter-Lant family was remarkably complete. The painter supplied his labor. The mother-in-law was the capitalist. Not only had she contributed a dowry (*huwelyck goed*)

[y]A belt or girdle, frequently made of silver, that women wore under their outer garments and from which hung keys, a purse, or other apparel.

[z]For details, see the discussion of lotteries in Chapter 7.

[aa]Splinter is listed twice in the books of The Hague Guild of St. Lucas (F.D.O. Obreen, *Archief voor Nederlandsche Kunstgeschiedenis*, 7 vols. [Rotterdam, 1877-1890], 3:283, 286).

[61]

which, according to her statement, "he had enjoyed and from which he had profited," but she had agreed to bear all the painter's costs of production. She was apparently responsible for marketing the goods produced by this system. Yet the paintings in question, judging by the price she had paid, were not cheap wares that were sold at the fair for ten to twelve stuivers. If she sold them, as I suppose she did, for about ten gulden each, they could already be said to belong to the category of luxury goods that competed with silver objects, mirrors, and similar items.

We have three short documents for this period on the sale of paintings, prints, and maps, all of which characteristically refer to fairs, free-market days, or both. On 22 March 1605, the burgomasters and aldermen of Delft granted Hans Jacobs of Amsterdam permission to hire for eight gulden a space in the side hall of the Town Hall to exhibit "maps and such" as he had done in the past on the market days of St. Odolphus (6 to 7 June) and St. Gillis (28 to 29 August). The surety for this arrangement was the painter Claes de Hondecouter, which leads me to suppose that paintings may have been part of the "and such."[8]

The art goods that were sold at the Delft fair that took place each June were not all cheap daubed panels. We learn that King Christian IV of Denmark, through his *homme de confiance* in the Netherlands, Jonas Charisius, bought an important painting of David and Abigail by the sixteenth-century Leyden master Jacob Cornelisz. van Ootsanen at the Delft kermess for six Flemish pounds, or about twenty-four gulden.[9]

To supplement his earnings in Delft, an art dealer who was a member of the Delft guild could also sell his wares in the Inner Court (Binnenhof) of the princes of Orange in The Hague.[bb] Niclaes Jansz. de Clerck, a prominent book and print dealer in Delft, was "given preference over others to be permitted to exhibit in the Binnenhof in the Gallery, between the two doors of the Chamber of State, all sorts of books, maps, and paintings during the fair and on other high days." In the years 1614 to 1617, the same De Clerck rented the front hall of the Town Hall in Delft in order to exhibit during free-market days.[10]

The impression I formed from the very limited material at my disposal is that dealers specializing exclusively in paintings, as distinguished from dealers in luxury goods (such as Rogier Laurensz.), and book and print dealers who sold paintings as a sideline (such as

[bb]For a later example of this practice, see Chapter 7, p. 196.

Niclaes de Clerck), make their appearance in Delft only in the 1620s. But as we shall see in greater detail later, specialized intermediaries were by no means necessary to transfer ownership of artworks. Painters could and no doubt did sell their works directly to consumers.[cc] Paintings were also exchanged or bartered against other luxury goods, in the absence of any intermediary, as the following example testifies.

On 23 March 1611, about a month before the issuance of the new guild regulations, a Delft goldsmith named Anthony Govertsz. bore witness at the request of Pieter van Battelerat, jeweler in Amsterdam, that a certain Octaby, merchant living in Delft, had agreed, without any reservation, to buy a large oriental ruby from Van Battelerat (the petitioner) and to pay for it as follows: first, in cash fifteen Flemish pounds; second, a piece of cambric of twenty-two ells worth three gulden per ell; third, a painting, representing a landscape, made by Droncken Fr[a]ns [Frans the Drunk], who may perhaps be identified as Frans Floris.[dd]

The last set of documents in this section are dated shortly *after* the issuance of the new guild letter but refer to events that took place *before* it was issued. On 9 February 1612, Andries Pietersz. Prins, waiter in the tavern In de Vergulden Bosboom, testified at the request of the Delft merchant Heyndrick Jansz. van der Hooch. In 1610, when he, Prins, was still practicing the occupation of tapster, Cornelis Eliasz. van Walscappelle, merchant in Dordrecht, lodged in his house a number of times. He and the petitioner Heyndrick de Hooch frequently ate and drank together. On such occasions, "Cornelis Eliasz. had brought from the aforenamed Heyndrick de Hooch various paintings at different times and that on condition of the ringing of the bells at the Town Hall of the aforesaid city of Delft" ("Cornelis Eliasz. van den voorsz. Heyndrick Jansz. gekocht heeft gehadt diversche stucken schilderyien op verscheyden tyden ende dat op conditie van't luyen van de groote clocke van't stadhuys binnen der voorsz. stede Delff.") Andries Pietersz. testified further that "the aforenamed Cornelis Eliasz. did not buy these paintings at a single

---

[cc]It is symptomatic of the poverty of the material available before 1611 that I could not find a single document referring to the direct sale of a painting by any artist in this period.

[dd]Records of Notary Jan de Molijn, no. 1559. Karel van Mander wrote that Frans Floris was "as great a drunkard as a painter" (*als groot dronkaert als Schilder*) (cited by B.P.J. Broos in his review of *Frans Hals* by Seymour Slive, *Simiolus* 10 [1978-79]:119).

time but at many and various times, several days in a row, as some times eight days, some times ten days, more or less, and that in all honesty without my getting to see or noticing any unseemliness and that the aforenamed Cornelis Eliasz. also, in the course of purchasing this merchandise, asked me 'how many times the great clock was rung in the year [?], and that I answered I did not know and that this was uncertain." He testified further that "he understood and in part had knowledge of the fact that, in the end, the acknowledgements of debt (*obligatien*) arising from the merchandise that had been transacted between them had been rendered null and void and that these obligations had all been consolidated into a single obligation." Finally, he attests that "the bill for food and drinks consumed by the two merchants had been reduced by two-thirds by Cornelis Eliasz. in favor of Heyndrick Jansz." ("dattet gelach twelck by de voorsz. Cornelis Eliasz. ende Heyndrick Jansz. werde verteert by den voorsz. Cornelis Eliasz. den voorsz. Heyndrick Jansz. tweederdepaerten van dyen werden gecort.")[11]

A year and four months later Cornelis Eliasz. van Walscappelle (now called Van Walschipper and living in Oud Beyerland) went to another notary and requested that two more depositions be drawn up on the same subject. On 24 June 1613, the painter Simon Jordaens (c. 1585–after 1644), aged twenty-eight years, and Jan Ariensz., cloth merchant, aged twenty-three, stated that they had often heard it said that Heyndrick Jansz. (the merchant named in the previous year) frequently concluded transactions upon the ringing of the great clock at the Town Hall. Simon Jordaens recalled that Heyndrick Jansz. had sold him some goods on that condition four or five years ago. Both deponents said that they knew Heyndrick Jansz. still made his living honestly in this manner to this day. Jan Ariensz. testified that he had been present when Heyndrick Jansz. had bought goods for sale on the condition of the ringing of the clock, whereupon the petitioner (Walscappelle) had asked him how many times a year the clock was rung. The deponent answered that he did not know for sure but that he guessed twenty-six or twenty-seven times a year. Whereupon the petitioner had concluded the transaction, and the deponent had received some money for drinks (*voor't gelach*). On 28 June 1613, a bowmaker testified at Walscappelle's request that for many years he had earned his living in the selling of goods on the condition of the ringing of the Town Hall bell in Delft, and that, according to the notes he had taken, the clock had been rung thirty-eight or forty times in 1608 and 1609, forty-two times in 1610, and fifty times in 1611.[12]

The reader who has had the patience to follow the translation of these documents may well find them obscure. I have quoted them *in extenso* as a good example of notarial depositions written legibly, but virtually impenetrable given our lack of knowledge of the context in which they were drawn up. I can only offer the following highly tentative interpretation. The accounts of the Guild of St. Lucas in the sixteenth century inform us that the guild spent small sums "for the ringing of the bells at the Town Hall." This is likely to be the same ringing of bells referred to in these documents. It is my guess that the guild had the bells rung on free-market days and on other occasions when paintings and other works of art could legally be sold. The transactions between the two merchants had somehow violated this legal procedure—i.e., had not always taken place on days when the bells had been rung. As a result the acknowledgments of debts incurred by the Dordrecht merchant for paintings purchased were no longer valid. Perhaps those that were valid had then been consolidated into a single debt. There is a suggestion that Cornelis Eliasz. may have been the one who was at fault, since he had agreed to reduce the part owed by Heyndrick Jansz. for their bill at the inn.

The new guild regulations stated, as we shall see in the next chapter, that paintings could only be sold by persons who were not members of the guild—as Heyndrick Jansz. and Cornelis Eliasz. were not—on well-defined weekly market or Delft-kermess days. The question remains whether these occasions were announced by the ringing of the Town Hall clock.

EARLY DEVELOPMENT OF DELFTWARE POTTERIES

Herman Pietersz., as we saw in the first chapter, joined the Guild of St. Lucas in 1581, the first faiencier to do so. In the summer of 1593, he was forty-one years old, according to a deposition he made before a notary.[13] He was thus twenty-nine years old when he joined the guild and presumably began to operate his pottery. For nearly twenty years, he seems to have remained without competition. Among the taxpayers listed in the 1600 "Haardsteden register," there were only two other faienciers (*plateelbackers*), Heyndrick Gerritsz. and Egbert Huygensz. The first, as far as we know, was never established on his own.[14] Egbert Huygensz., born about 1568, bought a house in Delft

[65]

in 1598 for 3,100 gulden, a very high price for the time;[15] it was presumably in this house that he set up his pottery. The next faiencier to establish himself in Delft was Pouwels Boursett (or Bourseth), probably from Rouen in France, who bought his house for 1,150 gulden in the first half of 1606 but arrived in Delft at least three years earlier.[ee] In the second half of 1606, Cornelis Rochusz. (later "van der Hoeck" or "van der Hoeven"), acquired a house-cum-tileworks (*pannenbackerye*) for 3,400 gulden.[ff] He also was already in Delft in 1603.[16] Only two other masters started producing delftware before the new guild letter of 1611 was issued. Thomas Jansz. van Boonen, a young man of twenty-five was already operating on his own a delftware pottery in January 1611.[gg] The second was Abraham Davidsz., who bought a house in Delft in the first half of 1609[17] and took on Jan Bartelemesz. as an apprentice in March 1611.[18] Thus in a little more than a decade—from 1598 to 1611—the number of delftware potters went up from one to six. At least three of the six potteries—those of Herman Pietersz., Pouwels Bourseth, and Abraham Davidsz.—were located in the east end of Delft, a populous section of the city. I suspect that my count of twenty-five faienciers for 1611 falls short of the real number of individuals engaged in this craft, since this averages only four employees per works, whereas there were likely to be approximately ten workers in each establishment. (In an attestation of 5 December 1613, nine employees of the master faiencier Hans de Wint, all *plateelbackers*, from eighteen to forty-four years of age, testified against Lenart Jansz., the foreman of De Wint's works.)[19] The total number of employees in the industry would then amount to about fifty in 1611, not including young apprentices. How many children labored in these establishments in addition to the full-fledged workers is anybody's guess.[hh]

[ee]Bourseth already appears in a deposition with Egbert Huygensz. and his wife in 1603 (Records of Notary Jan de Molijn, no. 1557, 22 March 1603).

[ff]Camer van Charitate, "Reckeningen," vol. 28, p. 10, fol. 22. Cornelis Rochusz. van der Hoeck, faiencier, is noted in Delft on 5 July 1603 (Records of Notary Jan de Molijn, no. 1557.) A *pannenbackerye* made floor or roof tiles but not the tin-glazed delftware tiles.

[gg]Records of Notary Adriaen Rijshouck, no. 1768, 28 January 1611. His age emerges from a document of 23 November 1610 cited by A.H.H. van der Burgh ("Aanteekeningen betreffende de oudste Delfsche plateelbakkers," *Oud-Holland* 21 [1903]:40.

[hh]We know the names of a few orphan boys who were sent by the Camer van Charitate to work in faience works before 1611. One such apprentice was Corstiaen Louys, nine years old, who was assigned to Thomas Jansz. soon after 1609 (Camer van Charitate, no. 175, "Register van Ambachtsjongens," 1597–1611, fol. 84).

Five out of six notarial documents summarized below concern the employment of journeymen or apprentices. In the first, dated 9 October 1606, Herman Pietersz., the earliest established of the Delft faienciers, hires an apprentice named Abram Gillisz., who will learn the craft of faience-making for four years.[20] In the first three years he will learn to make dishes or plates, large and small. If Abram Gillisz. proves apt at his work, his employer at his discretion will teach him potting. During the four years, the apprentice will be paid nine stuivers per day, board and lodging not provided. He must not quit his master's employment for any reason, including marriage. In case his employer Herman Pietersz. should die, he will remain in the service of his widow if she undertakes to continue the business.

On 28 January 1611, Thomas Jansz. signed a contract for one year with Peter Herx (or Herp), journeyman faiencier (*plateelbackersgesel*),[21] who, though he never became a master of the guild, was clearly an experienced hand. Herx was supposed to pot 1,600 pieces for each oven-load that Thomas Jansz. would wish to bake during the year. For each such load he was to turn out 400 large dishes, 600 middle-sized, and 600 small ones. He was slated to receive eight stuivers per hundred for the large, six stuivers per hundred for the middle-sized, and five stuivers per hundred for small dishes. He must never cause any delay in setting the dishes ready for baking. At the same time Thomas Jansz. must make ready in time for Herx the balls of clay, from which the dishes are made; but Herx must in turn give his employer warning a half day in advance whenever he needs to have the balls on hand. Any failure or delay in loading the ovens would be at Herx's cost. Lenert Pietersz., also a journeyman-faiencier, presumably working for Thomas Jansz., witnessed the contract.

On 11 March of the same year, Abraham Davidsz. took on the nineteen-year-old Jan Bartholomesz. as a boy-learner for four years.[22] The young man was expected to do whatever his master ordered him to, but in particular he was to learn how to pot, load the ovens, prepare lead and tin glazes, and also help to put on color (*verru*) and cover (*couvaert*)[ii] and tread the clay. He was to receive eight stuivers a day the first two years and ten stuivers a day the last two. He also must not take on any employment by any other master "by day or night," except if Abraham Davidsz. could not provide him with work, in which case Jan Bartholomesz. would earn his regular "outside wage." After the expiration of four years the apprentice was to remain in the

---

[ii]The "cover" is the translucent white lead or tin glaze that is applied over the entire dish or tile.

employ of his master and to be paid the same wages "as other masters give."

On 1 May 1611 Egbert Huygensz. hired Jan Jansz. Vullens, *plateelbackersknecht*, as a faience-painter for three years, according to the contract signed on 7 June 1611.[23] He, like Pieter Herx, was set chiefly on piecework. According to the rates set in the contract he was to earn thirteen stuivers per hundred *"blompotten in de ruyt,"* which I interpret to mean tiles painted with vases of flowers, framed in a lozenge. For vases framed in a medallion (*"ronde blompotten"*), he was slated to earn twenty-six stuivers per hundred and for gold flowers (*"enkelijk goutsblomkens"*), meaning probably gold-colored flowers without a medallion or lozenge frame, sixteen stuivers per hundred. Whenever his employer wished to hire him by the day, his wage was to be eighteen stuivers per day. If he was employed in loading the ovens, he would get ninety-five stuivers per oven-load, where each oven-load contained at least 200 "gold flowers," meaning presumably 200 polychrome tiles with flowers.

We have just summarized four apprenticeship or employment contracts in the delftware industry between 1606 and 1611.[ii] Not a single contract of this type drawn up by a painter has been found for the entire transition period, even though there were perhaps six or seven times more master painters in Delft at the time than master

[ii]Only two other apprenticeship contracts were found in the Delft notarial archives for the period 1593 to 1611. The first, characteristically dated before the turn of the century, refers to the apprenticeship of a glassmaker, the second, dated 1608, to that of an embroiderer. The first contract involves a three-way barter of services, along with a side payment, between two glassmakers and a surgeon. Willem de Vries, glassmaker, living in France in Chatelrault near Poitiers, sent his son Moyses to live for two years with, and at the expense of, Jacob Poelenburg, surgeon in Delft. During this time Moyses was to learn glass-engraving with the well-known master Dirck Reyniersz. (van der Douw). Poelenburg contracted to pay Dirck Reyniersz. four pounds (twenty-four gulden) for the apprenticeship from his own pocket. In counterpart, Willem de Vries agreed to take Jacob, the son of Poelenburg, to live with him in Chatelrault and let him learn the practice of surgery with a surgeon for a year-and-a-half entirely at his, De Vries's, expense (Notary records of Vranck van Uytenbrouck, no. 1528, 20October 1596). The second contract bound the fourteen-year-old Maerten Fouquier, son of an Amsterdam merchant, to the embroiderer Pieter van der Heyden for three years. The boy was to live in Van der Heyden's house and to learn "all that concerns the craft of embroidery, including drawing." For these services Maerten's father agreed to pay 150 gulden (Notary records of Adriaen Rijshouck, no. 1760, 18 October 1608). This contract, as well as later documents, suggest that embroidery was a highly skilled occupation, the training for which was approximately as expensive as learning how to paint (and indeed involved, in common with painting, the art of drawing).

faienciers established on their own account. The difference in the
frequency of occurrence of contracts in the two trades is unlikely to
be a coincidence. My guess is that it was crucial for faienciers to bind
their apprentices for a minimum period of years in a time of rapid
expansion of the industry. Once an apprentice was trained, other
potters had an incentive to bid him away by proferring higher wages
than his initial master wished to pay. Painters' apprentices, on the
other hand, once they were fully trained, could make only a marginal
contribution to the master's own works.[kk] If they produced marketa-
ble paintings on their own, they could join the guild for a relatively
small fee and set themselves up as independent masters.

A contemporary document gives some support to this conjecture.
On 6 January 1612, Abraham Davidsz., master faiencier, asked two of
his *knechts* to testify that a certain Hans Arentsz., *plateelbackersknecht*,
had been seen turning dishes at the house of Egbert Huygensz.,
despite the fact that it was known to all masters here that he was
bound to him.[24] (There presumably was no legal document to prove
it.) In a second deposition made on the spot Jan Bartholomesz., the
same young man who had been apprenticed by contract to Davidsz. in
March 1611, together with another *knecht*, testified that some masters
had offered five Flemish pounds (thirty gulden) to Hans Arentsz. if he
was willing to leave his master to work out of town. This is surely one
case when a master must have regretted he had not drawn up an
employment contract in good and due form.

We finally come to the only document that was not directly
concerned with apprenticeship and employment. On 21 January
1612, "Hans Cools, faience-painter (*schilder*), potter (*draier*), and
brick baker (*steen maecker*), and a full-fledged master of the craft of
faience-making,"[ll] testified at the request of Lucas Arentsz., tilebaker,
in Leyden, that twelve to fourteen months ago Thomas Jansz., master
faiencier, who was at the time Cools's master, had come to the house
of Herman Pietersz., also master faiencier, where he had been offered
by the latter's wife a large number of unbaked tiles made by the
petitioner (Lucas Arentsz.), to be sold by the thousand. Herman's wife
had given Thomas Jansz. a few tiles as a sample. Hans Cools further

---

[kk]I am arguing essentially that the *knecht* of a faiencier furnished work that was a
complementary input to his master's, whereas the work of a fully trained painter's
apprentice was a substitute for his master's.

[ll]Hans Cools does not appear in the list of master-faienciers in the 1613 masterlist
of the St. Lucas Guild. He may have been a master in his craft, but he was not a
master in the legal sense (I assume that he did not die or leave town before January
1613).

attested that the tiles "once they were baked and colored (*verruwet*) were as good as the best, even though these unbaked tiles had not been colored as one usually colors tiles." Yet he could detect no shortcoming in them.

We have here I think one more revealing sign of an expanding industry. Given a very strong and growing demand for Delft tiles, faienciers must have looked around for cost-cutting measures that would enable them to step up their output. One of them was to buy the raw unbaked tiles from producers in another industry and to limit the in-house work to baking and decorating. As we shall see in the next chapter, the practice of ordering semifinished goods from outside the faience industry, which offered the advantage of getting around guild regulations on the hiring of apprentices, was unsuccessfully combated by the town authorities in later years.[mm]

THE TRUCE OF 1609 AND THE GUILD OF ST. LUCAS

By April 1609 when the States General and Spain signed the truce that was to last twelve years, Delft had been on the side of the rebellion for nearly forty years. Its contributions to the confederate cause, like those of every other city on the side of the Prince of Orange, had been heavy and had eaten into the funds that would otherwise have been available for the improvement and beautification of the city.[nn] The help and succor given to the refugees from the south was a further drain on the budget. From the artist's viewpoint, though, the war with Spain had not been without advantages. Competition from Flanders had been, if not completely eliminated, at least severely reduced.[25] The truce created new conditions to which the community of artists was impelled to respond. Three documents, including one from members of the Delft Guild of St. Lucas, have been preserved that chronicle the attempt of the artists of Leyden to form a guild in 1609 and 1610. These documents tell us more about the effects of the truce on the arts at that time than any other contemporary evidence.

[mm]There may also have been a shortage of suitable clay in Delft which could thus be obviated (Cf. below, Chapter 9).

[nn]On the financial contributions of Delft to the "war for freedom," see J. H. van Dijck, "Rekeningen betreffende het financieel aandeel van Delft aan den vrijheids-oorlog," *Bijdragen en mededeelingen van het Historisch Genootschap* 54 (1933): 43-124.

The first document, dated 11 March 1610, contains a petition presented by the painters of Leyden to the burgomasters and tribunals of the city of Leyden.[26] They begin by reporting that in October 1609—thus less than six months after the truce was signed—"some individuals had come here from Brabant and other neighboring places with various paintings which they had sold with the help of the public caller."[∞] They would also have sold the paintings left over from this public sale if the petitioners had not secured an injunction against such further sales from the town authorities. In February 1610, a number of these same individuals had come from Amsterdam to sell paintings "publicly (*door uytroupen*) and the rest in open shops (*'t overige met opene winckel te vercopen*), as if they were living here, which is permitted in no other cities, nor is the practice allowed here, with great damage to the petitioners." The Leyden painters asked the town authorities to prohibit the sale of paintings except on free-market days "so that the supplicants may earn money and care for their families in those hard times." Almost as an afterthought they requested permission to set up a guild.

In the margin of the document the town clerk had written that the petitioners should show what the practice was in neighboring towns, especially with regard to the question of whether or not out-of-town paintings were allowed to be sold.

The decision of the town authorities was written on the back of the same document. They had resolved to forbid anyone not living in Leyden to sell any paintings on any but free-market days, whether through public sale or otherwise, except with the consent of the burgomasters. They also rejected "for the time being" the petition to set up a painters' guild.

The petition of the dean and headmen of the St. Lucas Guild in Amsterdam, which was appended to the petition of the Leyden painters, was dated 10 November 1608, thus some months *before* the truce was signed. The Amsterdam painters reported how, "a short time ago, some foreigners, who were neither citizens nor members of the guild, had on various occasions sold by public auction and otherwise various kinds of paintings coming from Antwerp and other enemy quarters." These paintings "as a result of the cunning and ungodly pressure of certain individuals had been sold far above their worth (being mainly poor copies)." Now the same sellers, "drawn by

[∞] The text reads "door den uytrouper," thus perhaps by auction. This is also suggested by the word "overblijfsels" (leftovers) in the next sentence.

[71]

the profit they are expecting and seeking to continue this trade, are attempting with all diligence to pick up all the paintings they can get in Antwerp and elsewhere; such that they now have a great many paintings on hand to be sold here in the same manner as before." They will do so even though "according to the ordinance of the petitioners' guild, no foreign persons may sell any paintings except on free-market days," with the consequence that "through the introduction or the admittance of such malicious public auctions on the part of foreigners, which will be increasing from day to day, in a short time, this city, yea the whole country, will be flooded with rubbish and the work of poor boy-apprentices, such that all the painters living here will be adversely affected in the necessary earning of their bread, and also held back in their diligent studies in the art of painting (which is promoted by all princes and well-constituted republics); and yea also the good burghers who on the whole have little knowledge of painting will be cheated." All this was meant to justify the plea for protection of the petitioners "in the honest and necessary earning of their bread especially in these costly times" and for allowing the dean and headmen of the guild to prevent "these newly practiced and illegal auctions." The Amsterdam authorities acceded to the request.

We come finally to the attestation of the members of the Guild of St. Lucas in Delft, which will be cited in full.

Today the 27th of March 1610 there appeared before me Otto van Setten, public notary admitted by the court of Holland and the witnesses mentioned below: Pieter Ariens, glass-engraver, 47 years old; Mr. Cornelis Jacobsz. Delft, 39 years old; and Jan Garbrants de Jongh, 37 years old, painters, all living in Delft, and declared by their conscience and salvation in place of oath, at the request of Mr. Cornelis Boissens, painter in the town of Leyden, also on behalf of the other master painters in the aforenamed town, to be aware that, in the memory of man, it has been the practice in the town of Delft, among those of the craft of painting or otherwise named St. Lucas Guild, that no one in the trade or craft may exercise any craft or mastery unless he be first and beforehand a citizen of the same town and in the guild of St. Lucas, and that also such persons being from places where the citizens of this town are not free likewise may bring or sell no paintings within this town, except on the yearly and weekly markets, unless they pay a certain fine which has been set from olden times.

Declaring by reason of knowledge to have been headmen of the aforesaid guild at various times and the aforenamed Mr. Jan

Garbrants to be presently headman, and is used in conformance with their guild letter.[pp]

The aforesaid witnesses declared besides that, to their knowledge or to the knowledge of any of the past headmen, no persons not being in the aforementioned guild may hold any *boelhuis* sales[qq] of their paintings, and if they wish to effect these public sales on market days, it should be understood that they may not do so.

Presenting the foregoing and ready at all times on request to reinforce the same by oath.

Thus done and executed in the town of Delft, at the house of the notary, on the day and year aforesaid, in the presence of Niclaes van Nes my clerk.

OTTO VAN SETTEN
Notary Public

The language of these attestations is somewhat obscure and confusing, but their general meaning is clear. The resumption of trade with the enemy, starting a year or so before the truce, threatened to pierce the curtain of protection behind which the artists of Holland had prospered these many years. Flemish artists, I conjecture, were not only numerous and skilled at painting inexpensive pictures that could easily be marketed in Holland; they were also more impoverished by war and devastation than their Dutch cousins, and much of their traditional clientele among Flemish burghers could no longer afford the luxury of buying art goods. Demand was thus displaced to the north, and the tradition of supplying cheap artworks in exchange for the grain, dairy products, and other goods that the Dutch possessed in abundance was reinforced.

The community of artists in Delft, swelled by the immigration of their colleagues from Flanders, must also have suffered from the competition of the impoverished south. It was no doubt at the initiative of these local artists that the town authorities set about tightening guild regulations in 1611. The new regulations and the amendments of subsequent years form the subject of the next chapter.

[pp]The original reads: "ende conform heinl. gildenbrief is gebruyct." It is not clear whether the attestants were acting in their legal capacity as duly constituted headmen or whether the contents of their declaration were in conformance with guild practice.
[qq]Public sales of estates by the *boelhuismeester* are discussed in Chapter 7.

THREE

Rules and Regulations of the St. Lucas Guild

About the time of the truce, the authorities of several Dutch cities, moved by the considerations discussed in the preceding chapter, issued new "letters" for their respective St. Lucas Guilds. This happened in Rotterdam in the very beginning of 1609 and in Gouda in May 1609; in Utrecht the painters and sculptors, who were formerly thrown in with the saddlers, were allowed to form a separate guild in September 1611.[1] In Haarlem the regulations were already tight enough, apparently, to deal with the undesirable competition from the south. Of all the major cities, it was only in Leyden that the authorities refused to be swayed by the petition of the painters to found a guild, either together with or separate from other crafts.[a]

THE NEW GUILD LETTER OF 1611

On 29 May 1611 the sheriff, burgomasters, aldermen, and counsellors of the city of Delft handed down to the Guild of St. Lucas a complete set of regulations or "New Guild Letter." These regulations were generally patterned on Rotterdam's, except for the jurisdiction and ambit of the guild, which were defined in line with the Utrecht guild letter.[2] The Guild Letter of 1611 and its amendments promulgated by "the law" (Weth) of Delft from 1611 to 1675 are translated in Appendix B. The translation is fairly literal, to give the reader a flavor of the original, but a careful reading will reveal the sense of the ordinances and the intent of the lawmakers.

The guild rules covered five broad areas. They 1) defined the craft

---

[a] In 1615, the glassmakers of Leyden were allowed to form a guild. G.J. Hoogewerff, *De geschiedenis van de St. Lucasgilden in Nederland* (Amsterdam: P.N. van Kampen en Zoon, 1947), p. 176. The painters were finally granted permission to have a guild of their own in 1648.

occupations and the activities which required status of master in the guild for their exercise; 2) specified the qualifications for becoming a master; 3) regulated the internal administration of the guild; 4) governed in certain respects the relation between masters and their apprentices and the registration of apprentices in the guild; and 5) set the level of guild dues—entrance fees, annual dues, and fines—and stipulated the kinds of expenditures on which these receipts could legitimately be spent. It is important to observe that the town authorities issued no price or quality controls for goods sold by masters, or limits on the persons to whom they might be sold. I doubt whether the headmen could have enforced such rules without the general authority of the guild letter to support them. In any case, there is no evidence whatever for the existence of any such regulations.

The next section discusses the rules on membership—the first two areas covered by the guild letter and its amendments—in the light of the fairly abundant information at our disposal on the extent of compliance to these provisions of the letter.

Membership

The introductory paragraph of the guild letter defined the crafts and occupations encompassed by the guild. The guild was to include "all those earning their living here by the art of painting, be it with fine brushes or otherwise, in oil or watercolors; glassmakers; glass-sellers; faienciers; tapestry-makers; embroiderers; engravers; sculptors working in wood, stone, or other substance; scabbard-makers; art-printers; booksellers; sellers of prints and paintings, of whatever kind they may be." This definition was amended three times in the seventeenth century: On 19 October 1620, the tapestry-makers were excluded from the guild, even though they were still obligated to pay the regular death dues contributed by members of the guild; on 1 July 1630 the book printers were added to the list of trades under the guild's jurisdiction; finally, on 21 March 1661, sellers of faience wares were also obliged to join.

There is no separate mention in the list of crafts that the guild encompassed of the "chair-painters" (*stoel-verwers*), who held a sort of associate status in the guild. These artisans, who were regular members of their own guild, paid twenty-five stuivers to join the Guild of St. Lucas if they were born in Delft and fifty stuivers if they were born elsewhere.[3] These entrance fees were identical with those charged according to the Old Guild Letter of the sixteenth and early seventeenth centuries.[b] Their names were listed in the Master Books of 1613-1649 and 1650-1714. They were not inscribed in the "Register of All the New Masters that Have Come into the Guild Since 1613," but a few of them appeared in the "Register of New Masters and Shopkeepers" for the years 1650 to 1714. The "chair-painters" were actually furniture-makers who in effect had to pay a fee to the Guild of St. Lucas to be allowed to paint their wares.

There were a few other anomalous registrations in the guild. Claes Matteus was inscribed in 1625 as a gilder (*vergulder*), Aelbrecht Aelbrechtsz. in 1632 as a printer on linen (*lindedrucker*), Pieter Gerritsz in 1644 as a block-and-tackle-maker (*blockmacker*), Aelbrecht Teunisz. Vermeulen in 1650 as a compass-maker. Conrad Harmansz. Broukman, whose name frequently crops up in notarial papers as a clockmaker, joined the guild in 1651 so that he would be allowed to paint the faces of his clocks.[4] The most curious entry is for Jacob Pietersz. van den Ende, who registered in 1651 as a *"mutssetrekker,"* perhaps a deformation of *mutsescreerer,* a man who prepared skins for fur hats.[5]

The preamble to the Guild Letter of 1611 states that "all those earning their living here" in the crafts listed were to be members of the guild. A few articles or clauses of the letter were more specific about this requirement. Article 8 required membership of any one who "shall make with his own hand a painting or any other work comprised under the aforesaid guild." The same requirement applied, according to article 9, to any individual setting glass panes in the apertures of windows and, according to article 10, to sellers of paintings imported from outside Delft and its jurisdiction (except at certain specified times). By an amendment of 4 February 1615, no glass-engraver or painter could "set someone to work in his house to engage in a trade or activity in the Guild of St. Lucas unless he be of the same art-craft or trade and that he himself have been received master." In my view, this implies that no one was to take on an apprentice to learn the trade unless he was a master in the guild.

How closely were these membership clauses observed? To answer this question we must examine the membership lists and compare them with the names of individuals known to have practiced any of

[b]It seems inconsistent with this principle that Jan Thielmanse Hallingh had to pay a full six gulden in May 1654 for permission to paint "white goods" (*witwerck*, perhaps pine furniture). He also undertook to paint only the goods made in his shop (F.D.O. Obreen, *Archief voor Nederlandsche Kunstgeschiedenis*, 7 vols. (Rotterdam, 1877-1890), 1:57.

the crafts under the guild's jurisdiction. For this procedure to be valid, our guild lists must be complete—the name of every guild member must appear in a master book, a register of new members, or both.

To verify whether or not the guild lists, which comprise a total of 640 members for 1613 to 1714, are complete, we can make use of the following information: 1) The register of newly admitted members records the lower dues paid by sons of members (three gulden, instead of six gulden for new members born in Delft whose fathers were not members). For the lists to be complete they must include the names of the fathers of the new members admitted for three gulden. 2) There are frequent references in the register of new members to headmen of the guild (listed in Appendix C). The names of all such headmen should be recorded at an earlier date, when the artist or artisan first joined the guild, in the master book, in the register of new members, or both. 3) The registers of new members sometimes refer to guild brothers who registered a second time (usually because they changed their craft) or who came back to Delft after a long absence and paid their accumulated yearly dues. All the names of these individuals should be found inscribed in the guild records at some earlier point. 4) Occasional references to individuals qua guild members in notarial records or in the estate-settlements of the Orphan Chamber, most of which are preserved in the Delft archives, provide a small supplementary list.[c]

Analysis of these four sources reveals no demonstrable gap or cluster of omissions, although a few problem cases arise among the masters' sons and daughters that could not be settled beyond a doubt. The fathers of all but ten of the ninety-three new guild members who registered as masters' sons or daughters between 1613 and 1724 can

[c]Our guild sources, reprinted in Obreen, 1:4-120, are these: 1) The first Master Book which begins in 1613 and ends in 1649; 2) the second Master Book, which begins in 1650 and ends (in fact) in 1686; 3) the first Register of New Masters which begins in 1613 and ends in 1649; and the second Register of New Masters and Shopkeepers which begins in 1650 and ends in 1714. The master books and the registers of new members carry some information that is not common to both. Thus the painter Adriaen Lynschoote (usually spelled Linschoten) is listed in the Master Book of 1613 to 1649 but not in the Register of New Masters. On the other hand the painter "Harman Evertsz., son of the spectacle-maker" (Harman Evertsz. Steenwijck), was inscribed in the register in 1637 but in neither of the master books. A few names are repeated in the master books without apparent reason. Examples are the painters Hans Verlinde and Heyndrick van den Burch. (The painters' lists are analyzed in greater detail in Chapter 6.) The names of faienciers and book-printers and -sellers are carried over from the Register of New Masters to the Master Book of 1613-1649 up to the mid-1630s, but to no other list subsequently.

be identified with some confidence. Of the remaining ten, three are believed to have been sons of guild masters who died before 1613,[d] and six are uncertain but can all be linked with a putative father-member.[e] One appears to be the result of confusion or error.[f] With a single exception, which I attribute to a clerical error,[g] all ninety-four headmen mentioned in the guild records and in the estate settlements were originally registered in one of the two master books or in the register of new masters. (For the years 1613 to 1680, see Appendix C.) The members who, according to the membership register, returned after a long absence (including the painters Engel Rooswyck and Heyndrick van der Burch who were both away from Delft for nearly ten years), were all recorded previously. So were the members who registered a second time, with one exception. The housepainter Ary Jacobsz. Kortendonck, who paid twelve gulden in 1646 "to register himself anew,"[6] does not appear to have been inscribed previously. It is possible that he had appeared before the clerk earlier but, because he had not paid his entrance fee, his name was not entered in the book.

The only doubtful cases that were found in estate-settlements papers concern the painter Jan Serange, the book- and paper-seller

---

[d]Pieter Jorisz. Cabbesyn, glazier, presumed son of Joris Jorissen Cabbasin, headman of the guild in 1593; Cornelis Dircx van der Dou, glazier, presumed son of Dirck Reyniers van der Dou, headman in 1586 and 1593; and Jan Jansz. de Jonghe, perhaps the son of Jan Jansz., glassmaker, who became master in 1580. All three presumed fathers are mentioned in the Delft MA, "Rekeningboekje (van de deken) van het sint Lucas gilde te Delft over de jaren 1537-1593." In this and in all subsequent notes referring to guild members I follow the spelling of the name as it occurs on the first mention in the guild books.

[e]In all six cases (two glassmakers, three faienciers, and one bookbinder), a possible father whose first name corresponds to the patronymic of the new member and whose date of registration precedes his presumed son's by a reasonable number of years has been identified. The search for father-son links, incidentally, must be made within the same trade, since the son or daughter of a guild member choosing to follow a different trade from his or her father often had to pay the full six gulden.

[f]Arent Jansz. Cosyn, faiencier, was called a master's son when he registered as foreman or master-apprentice (*meesterknecht*) in 1648. However, when he became a master decorator (*plateelschilder*) in 1675, he paid the full six gulden as an ordinary citizen of Delft. Cosyn could not be linked with any father in the guild, and I suspect a clerical error in the 1648 entry.

[g]The 1714 list of headmen shows "Reijer Heij in plaets van C. Fictor." The "C. Fictor" who was replaced by Reijer Heij, faiencier, was presumably Louwijs Victor, faiencier, who served as headman during a number of previous years and is registered as a new master in 1689.

Heyndrick Jansz. Verpoort, the art dealer Heyndrick Jansz. Vockestaert, and the painter of ceramic plaques Frederick van Frijtom.
Abraham Bredius had already drawn attention in his *Künstler-
inventare*[7] to the fact that neither Serange nor Verpoort were listed in
the Obreen transcription of the guild records, even though an item in
the estate papers of Jan Serange referred to a small sum (twenty-four
stuivers) expended for calling the members of the Guild of St. Lucas
to his funeral. This sum had been paid to Heyndrick Verpoort, who is
likely therefore to have been a fellow member of the guild. Serange's
name, as it happens, does appear in the first master book of the guild,
not among the painters but among the printers, illuminators, and art-
and booksellers. His name is entered in the manuscript as "Hans
Cerange," which in the published transcription by Obreen was
misread as "Hans Cernage."[h] As to Heyndrick Verpoort, he seems to
have registered in the guild as a bookseller under the name of
Heyndrick Jansz. in 1616.[i]

The nonappearance in the guild records of the art dealer Heyndrick
Jansz. Vockestaert is also puzzling. The estate papers prepared after his
death on 20 September 1624[j] show that he sold paintings on alabaster
and on panel, among other objects of luxury. Such sales, of course,
called for his membership in the guild. An item at the end of his *boedel*
reads: "The headmen of the St. Lucas Guild maintain that they are
owed as the remainder of the entrance [fee] into the aforesaid guild
three gulden, for death dues thirty stuivers, and for costs pertaining
thereto twelve stuivers, altogether five gulden two stuivers." This may
be interpreted to mean that Vockestaert had been
summoned to register in the guild (which summons or other legal
costs amounted to twelve stuivers), and that he had subsequently paid
a part of his entrance fee (three out of six gulden, since he was a Delft

[h]Obreen, *Archief,* 1:8. The correct reading is due to Mrs. Petra Beidals, the former
director of the Delft archive. Hans Lichtlam (or Lichtalem), who is referred to in
contemporary documents as a painter, also appears among the printers and illuminators.

[i]Heyndrick Jansz. Verpoort appears in the estate papers of Dirck Jansz. de Vogel,
who died on 22 February 1622 (Orphan Chamber, *boedel* no. 1821 I), in connection
with a debt of five gulden sixteen stuivers for delivered paper and books. Jan
Heyndericxs, painter-in-the-rough, who registered as a master's son in 1636, was
probably his son, and Heindrick Jansz. Verpoort, who registered in the guild as a
master's son in 1661, his grandson.

[j]Records of Notary Johan van Beest, no. 1661. This merchant should not be
confused with the well-known Delft notary Hendrick Adriaensz. Vockestaert, who
died in 1634.

citizen). He was thus technically responsible for his death dues. Although many cases are known, including that of Johannes Vermeer,[k] where newly registered members paid initially only a part of their entrance fee, in this instance no formal registration seems to have taken place, perhaps because the dealer had not made a personal appearance before the headmen. Our last doubtful case is that of the well-known painter on faience Frederick van Frijtom. Although his name appears nowhere in the guild registers, his second wife called him a "guildsman" in her testament.[8] Since the names of all employees of delftware potteries were supposed to be inscribed in a separate register for *knechts*, he may technically have been a guildsman without being a master. With these possible exceptions, all the guild members referred to in estate papers were found to be registered in the guild.[l]

I conclude from this survey that the membership books of the St. Lucas Guild in Delft are reasonably complete. The possible exceptions in any case do not fit into a pattern that would suggest that there are substantial gaps in the record. My next task was to verify the guild's ability to compel all individuals making a living in any of the trades under its jurisdiction to acquire membership.

We already observed in the last chapter that a number of painters acquired Delft citizenship in 1612-1613 as a necessary condition for guild membership. This suggests that membership rules were strictly enforced. Contemporary inventories and notarial evidence also provide a good deal of information that can help us determine whether or not painters who were working and selling their works in Delft were registered in the guild. All twenty-three of the Delft-based painters I found in contemporary documents selling their services or their paintings directly to customers were registered in the guild.[m] Virtually all the exceptions to the membership rule that I have been able to find belong to the following categories: 1) painters who lived in Delft but are not known to have sold their works there; and 2) outsiders who sold their works in Delft.

Hans van Asch (c. 1570-1571-September 1644) who is said to have

---

[k]In December 1653, Vermeer paid one gulden five stuivers out of six gulden for his entrance fee. He only settled the rest in 1656 (Obreen, *Archief,* 1:567).

[l]One of the more interesting cases is that of the rich silk merchant Willem Jorisz. Roscam (who died in February 1643) whose estate papers show an entry for a death duty (*dootschuld*) to the St. Lucas Guild (*boedel* 1452 I of the Orphan Chamber). His name appears among the embroiderers in the Master Book of 1613.

[m]A partial exception, discussed below, is that of Jacob Ariensz. Korstendonck, who contracted for a housepainting job in 1661, even though he was registered at the time as a glassmaker rather than as a painter.

painted portraits, lived all his life in Delft but never registered.[n] Since no portraits by him seem to be recorded in Delft inventories,[o] it is possible that he did not work as an independent master. The second exception is the still-life and landscape painter Johannes de Haes (c. 1631-1666), noted in Delft from 1661 to 1666. No paintings by him were found in contemporary inventories, except in his own death inventory. The fact that he worked as a *knecht* for a merchant suggests that he may not have earned his living by his art.[p] The requirement that anyone making a painting with his own hand should be a master in the guild was apparently not taken literally. There were a number of amateurs whose paintings are cited in their own death inventories who never joined the guild.[q]

The painter Jan Steen, in my opinion, does not represent a genuine exception to the membership rule. We do known that on 22 July 1654 he rented a brewery in Delft for a term of six years[9] and that he painted a portrait in 1655 with a Delft background.[r] But there is no evidence that Steen was actually living in Delft in this period.[s] The case of the landscape painter Adam Pynacker comes closer to a true exception. He is recorded in Delft on a number of occasions from August 1649 to May 1651, and he must have sold some of his work locally since once of his paintings (a Nativity!) is to be found in a Delft inventory as early as 12 November 1652.[t] In most of these

---

[n] The fact that his son, the landscape painter Pieter Jansz. van Asch, paid six gulden to enter the guild in 1623 rather than three gulden as a master's son proves that the father was never a member.

[o] It must be acknowledged, however, that the great majority of portraits in inventories are anonymous.

[p] On De Haes, see Abraham Bredius, *Künstler-inventare: Urkunden zur Geschichte der Holländischen Kunst des XVI^{ten}, XVII^{ten}, XVIII^{ten} Jahrhunderts*, 7 vols. (The Hague: Martinus Nijhoff, 1915-1921), 3:825-28. On 30 April 1663 Johannes de Haes was working as *knecht* for Harmen Jansz. Honwer, merchant in Delft (Records of Notary Nicholaes Vrienbergh, no. 2060).

[q] On paintings by amateurs, see below, Chapter 8.

[r] For a brief discussion of the subject of this painting, traditionally said to represent a Delft burgomaster, see National Gallery, *Art in Seventeenth Century Holland* (London, 1976), pp. 82-83.

[s] Another Hague painter, named Adam Andriesz. Staender, whose works, if he *was* an artist-painter, are totally unknown to us, owned an inexpensive house in Delft in the 1620s. (He was first taxed twenty-six stuivers and later thirty-nine stuivers in the "Legger van der verpondingen op den huysen ende gronden" 1620 (hereafter 1620 *Verponding boek.*) According to the Bredius notes in The Hague's Rijksbureau voor Kunsthistorische Documentatie, he was living in The Hague both in 1608 and in 1625.

[t] Pynacker signed as a witness on 11 August 1649 (Records of Notary Johan van Ruiven, no. 1960); 27 October 1649 (Records of Notary Frans Boogert, no. 1996); 3

[81]

documents, however, he is associated with Adam Pick, painter and innkeeper; it is my guess that he came to Delft only from time to time, staying at Pick's inn rather than establishing himself in town.

There were a number of other painters who are known to have spent a short time in Delft and who did not become members of the guild, whether or not they actually painted and sold pictures there. The most instructive example is that of the Haarlem-based marine painter Hendrick Cornelisz. Vroom (1566-1640) who painted two panoramas of Delft at the request of the burgomasters. Vroom was apparently not compelled to pay any guild dues out of his earnings.[u]

In 1638 Pieter de Grebber came from Haarlem to Delft to paint the portrait of the Roman Catholic pastor Frederick Uyttenhage van Ruyven.[v] He also avoided making any payment to the guild. I should also mention that the Hague painter Everhardt van der Maes painted a coat of arms for the Hoogheemraadschap, which he may or may not have executed in Delft. (The Hoogheemraadschap was the administration of waterways in Delftland which had its luxurious headquarters in Delft.)

Out of twelve sculptors or stonecarvers who are known to have sold their products against payment and hence were independent artists or artisans, all but three were registered and of the latter three only one lived in Delft. Hendrick de Keyser of Amsterdam was paid 200 gulden in 1620 for a statue of Justice for the newly reconstructed Town Hall.[w] On 18 September 1655, De Keyser's son Willem and Rombout Verhulst, who also lived in Amsterdam, were engaged by the widow

---

December 1649 and 16 May 1650 (ibid., no. 1997); and 8 May 1651 (ibid., no. 1998). The inventory of 12 November 1652 is listed in the Records of Notary Simon Mesch, no. 2049.

[u]On this commission, see below, Chapter 7. We saw in Chapter 1 that when Cornelis van Schevelling of The Hague painted organ doors for the New Church in 1548, the Church Masters promised to pay half of his guild obligation "in case the St. Lucas Guild should legally obtain the right to his guild dues." While guild regulations may have been stricter in the mid-sixteenth century, we should also consider that the time spent in Delft to paint a set of organ doors must have been greater than that needed for a city panorama, which could have been carried out in Vroom's Haarlem studio on the basis of sketches.

[v]That he came to Delft to paint the portrait, which is dated 1638, is indicated by his signature on a notarial document, together with that of the still-life painter Gillis Gillisz. de Berg(h), dated 13 March of that year (Records of Notary Cornelis Coeckebakker, no. 1616). The portrait is still *in situ* in a Beguinage called *Het klaeuwshofje* in Delft.

[w]On Delft's commissions to adorn the city, see Chapter 7, Table 7.1.

and heirs of Admiral Tromp to build a monument to the naval hero's memory in the Old Church at a contracted cost of 10,000 gulden.[10] Neither sculptor joined the guild on this occasion. Our third failure to register appears to be in flagrant violation of guild rules. The sculptor Gerrit Heyndricksz. van Ratinge (*antyckdrayer*), noted in Delft from 1655 on, appeared before a notary on 5 April 1666 to appoint a correspondent in Amsterdam to collect a debt of forty-nine gulden twelve stuivers owed to him for "sculpted work" ("ter sacke van gedrayt werck").[11] It is conceivable of course (but highly unlikely) that Van Ratinge was working for a registered master and collecting the debt on his behalf, or that he had sculpted the piece or pieces for which he was trying to collect payment before he arrived in Delft.

Sellers of prints and paintings, as we already know, were supposed to belong to the guild. We have also seen that one of these—the dealer Hendrick Vockestaert—owed the guild his entrance and death dues. The important dealer Abraham de Cooge was a member, but his son Meynard, who also was engaged in buying and selling pictures, was not in the guild. Some but by no means all of the merchants and craftsmen who occasionally sold paintings joined the guild. Among those who did may be listed the frame-makers Nicholas Breda and Anthony van der Wiel (the brother-in-law of Johannes Vermeer) and Johannes de Renialme from Amsterdam; among those who didn't, Cornelis Walscapelle and an English merchant named Hendrick Stiers, who sold five pictures representing the Five Senses to a barber in 1627 in part exchange for barbering services.[x]

We now move on to the more difficult cases of the glassmakers, faienciers, book-printers and booksellers. For these we must base our research chiefly on known cases of products delivered, the evidence for which lies mainly in estate settlements. In a sample of cases of glass products delivered by glassmakers or of window panes repaired by thirty-five distinct glassmakers or glass-sellers, I found the following exceptions to the registration rules: seven glass merchants, one out-of-town glassmaker, and two doubtful cases who may have been dealers or makers of glass. The glass merchants were chiefly out-of-town operators of market stands and may not have been compelled to register if they were not regular dealers established in Delft.[y] All

[x]Records of notary Adriaan van Twelle, no. 1654, 12 April 1627. Stiers may have been exempted from the necessity of becoming a member of the guild because he belonged to the English community. (See below, p. 86).

[y]In one month—from 31 January to 28 February 1667—four glass-sellers, two men and two women, joined the guild, paying twenty-five stuivers each (as did furniture-

twenty-three glassmakers who repaired broken window panes were registered.

With regard to Delft faience, I found sixty-five cases of delivery by forty-four individuals. Twelve suppliers among them were not registered in the guild as master faienciers. Three were widows of registered *plateelbackers* who were allowed by guild rules to continue the business.[z] One supplier of faience, named Jan Harmensz. van Dijsel, was the second husband of the widow of Claes Jansz. Verstraten, who had been a member of the guild; he too was allowed to operate the faience works of his wife while she was still alive. Four were merchants who dealt in faience and apparently did not have to register:[aa] Daniel Jacobsz. van der Walle, dish-seller (*plateelvercoper*), in 1632; Lambrecht Kruck (or Kruyck), who sold crocks and delftware from a market stand in the thirties;[bb] Pieter Jacobsz. Lust, a buyer of delftware in 1664; and Louris Andriesz. Blommendael, merchant of "all sorts of earthenware" in 1656. Two were guild-registered stone-cutters who delivered tiles that they probably set in the walls themselves (Heyndrick Swaeff and Adriaen Samuels). There are only two suppliers left whose absence from guild records I cannot satisfactorily explain. One, named Willem Jansz. de Rieu, seems to have operated a Delft pottery for a brief period in the early 1620s, then left for Haarlem where, having translated his name into the Dutch Willem Verstraten, he became the city's most important faiencier in the mid-1620s to the 1630s. The second, named Jacob Scholier, is virtually unknown to me.[cc] I originally thought he might

---

painters). (Obreen, *Archief*, 1:72). This rash of registrations may have resulted from a new guild policy or town ordinance which has not come down to us.

[z]These were the widows of Heyndrick Marcellisz. van Gogh, Cornelis Harmensz. Valckenhoff, and Dirck Jeronimusz. Kessel.

[aa]Whereas glass-sellers were specifically mentioned in the introductory paragraph of the 1611 guild ordinance, sellers of faience were not. They were not obligated to register until the "faienciers' ordinance" of 21 March 1661 (Appendix B). The exceptions listed are all before this date, except for Pieter Jacobsz. Lust (1664) who seems to have *bought* delftware for resale out of town.

[bb]Kruyck joined the guild in April 1640 when he began to operate his own faience works.

[cc]I found his name among suppliers of earthenware who were owed money by the estate of Pieter Jacobsz. Lust, buyer of delftware (exact date illegible, August 1664, records of Notary Cornelis Cornelisz. Brouwer, no. 1660). There were seven other suppliers listed among the creditors who were either members of the guild or, in one case, the widow of a member.

have been a *knecht* who delivered faiencewares for a registered master, but he is actually called *meester plattielbacker* in a document of 1653 and therefore should have been a member of the guild himself.[12] On the other hand, he almost certainly did not own a pottery. I conclude that he was either in the guild and his name was omitted from the master and membership books by error, or he was not and escaped detection by the guild authorities.

Among the faienciers who were at least at one time in violation of guild statutes should be mentioned Benedictus van Houten (1631–1675) who is known to have operated his own faience works for a few months in 1657 before he was received as master in the guild. On 9 July 1657 he was fined seven gulden ten stuivers "for violating the first article of the guild letter." On 6 August 1657, the date he finally became master, he was fined another two gulden ten stuivers for exercising the faiencier's trade "during the forbidden period."[dd] Another indication that membership was a virtual necessity for faienciers who actually operated their own works is that those who bought or associated themselves with owners of faience shops in the period 1613–1660 became members within a few months of their purchase, if they were not members already.[ee]

To summarize the situation for the glassmakers and faienciers, we may say that the guild rules on membership were rarely, if ever, infringed for established makers of glass or faience products, but that dealers in both types of goods, many of whom were not residents of Delft, were frequently permitted to operate without becoming members. Perhaps the distinction was made between those who had regular shops in Delft from which they sold their wares and those who operated only on weekly market days that were not subject to guild

[dd]Van Houten drew up a contract to set up a *plateelbackerye* with Jacob Wemmersz. Hoppesteyn on 15 January 1657 (Records of Notary Cornelis Pietersz. Bleiswijck, no. 1909). The fine is cited in Obreen, *Archief*, 1:61). It is not entirely clear what was meant by the "forbidden period" ("verbooden tijt"). If this was just the time when van Houten was not yet a registered master, why should this particular violation differ from the violation of the first article of the guild letter?

[ee]The following faienciers bought a delftware pottery within a year of their (previous or subsequent) registration in the guild: Hendrick Beuckelsz. van den Burgh (1616), Jacob Jacobsz. Ducarton (1653), Pieter Gerritsz. Durven (1654), Dirck Jeronimusz. van Kessel (1628), Pieter Jeronimusz. van Kessel (1634), Lambrecht Ghysbrechtsz. Kruyck (1640), Joost Lievensz. Cuys (1655–1656), Frans Paulusz. van Oosten (1640), Harmanus Outhuesden (1635), and Hans de Wint (or Windt) (1613). The evidence on the purchase of a pottery is either from the Camer van Charitate, "Reckeningen van de deuijt op de gulden," or from a notarial act.

[85]

rules. This is a distinction that usually cannot be made out from the notarial documents in which these dealers are mentioned.

The book-printers and booksellers working in Delft may be divided along national lines: Netherlanders of either northern or southern origin and English. Most of the Netherlanders who worked as printers or who supplied books or paper products were in the guild (though a few were not).[ff] None of the English booksellers, book-printers, lettersetters, or bookbinders were registered in the guild. Of the nineteen nonregistered individuals, including employees of printing establishments, that I found cited in sources in the 1630s, ten were English or in association with English businessmen. I was not able to find any Delft town ordinance to cover this group of exceptions. It may be conjectured that the town authorities did not enforce guild rules on these foreigners because most of the books they printed and sold were meant to be exported rather than sold locally.

So far we have investigated the enforcement of membership rules for suppliers of the types of goods cited in the preamble of the Guild Letter of 1611. I have already referred to the amendment of 4 February 1615 that stipulated that any painter or glass-engraver employing anyone to do any work encompassed by the Guild of St. Lucas in his house or shop must be a master of that same craft or trade and hence a member of the guild. A similar ordinance was later applied to the faienciers. It is presumed the rule applied to all the trades subsumed under the guild. To study the extent to which this rule was enforced I collected a sample of contracts and of notarial references to master-apprentice relations and checked whether or not the masters with whom the apprentices studied actually belonged to the guild.[gg] My sample consisted of thirteen painters (twenty-three pupils), two glassmakers, nine faienciers, two sculptors, six book-printers, and four embroiderers who are known to have had pupils or apprentices. All these individuals were masters in the guild with the exception of two English printers (Thomas Cowper and H. Hincliff).

[ff]I found five exceptions. Ludolf Cloeting was not in the guild when he delivered paper to the Hoogheemraadschap in 1644, but he was probably working for one of his relatives Andries Jansz. or Simon Jorisz. Cloeting. Pouwels Calmbach, a master printer who worked for various English owners, also failed to register. The exceptions that were most clearly in violation of guild statutes were those of Carel Warnaertsz. Turenhout (1641), Abram Pietersz. Heukelom (1652), and Michiel Stael (1649). For details, see Chapter 9.

[gg]A very large number of references to apprentices and journeymen working for faienciers were also found. These individuals were invariably working for masters in the guild.

The evidence marshaled up to this point only helps to establish whether or not the artists and artisans who should have been masters in the guild actually acquired membership in it at some point in their career. A more difficult point requiring very detailed investigation, is to ascertain how promptly they met this requirement. From bits and pieces of evidence about seven artist-painters, I conjecture that most foreigners who were already masters in some other guild before they arrived in Delft joined the local guild anywhere from six months to two years after their arrival. The time elapsed between the first mention of an artist's presence in Delft and the date of his registration was less than a year in the case of Simon de Vlieger, Emanuel de Witte, and Louis Elsevier, about fifteen months into the case of Pieter de Hooch and two years and two months in that of Carel Fabritius (assuming that he was already a master in Amsterdam or elsewhere). Van Beyeren was cited in The Hague on 30 June 1655 and became a member of the guild in Delft on 15 October 1657. But even for these few cases, the estimates are highly tentative.[hh]

My general conclusion on the observance of guild rules on membership is that the guild authorities were able to enforce these fairly effectively, frequently allowing a grace period, for almost all those artists and artisans who were living and practicing their craft in Delft and who sold their products or services there or had pupils and apprentices. The only important group of exceptions consisted of the printers. The English printers did not join the guild at all and as many as five Dutch-born printers also escaped registration. Since, in the other trades, the few artists or artisans who did not appear in the guild

[hh]For dates of registration in the guild, see Appendix, Tables A.2 and A.3. Simon de Vlieger rents a house for three years on 26 February 1634, presumably for the first time (Records of Notary Willem van Assendelft, no. 1858). He joins the guild in Delft on 18 October 1634 Emanuel de Witte rents, also apparently for the first time, on 15 September 1641 (Records of Notary Johan van Ruiven, no. 1858); he joins the guild 23 January 1642. Louis Elsevier was a member of the guild in Leyden in 1645 and joined the guild in Delft in September 1646. Pieter de Hooch was in Lier, not far from Delft, on 29 April 1654 (Records of Notary Frans Boogert, no. 2000) and joined the guild in Delft on 20 September 1655. Carel Frabritius was married in Delft on 20 August 1650 and became a master of the guild in Delft on 29 October 1652. However, Fabritius had borrowed money in Delft on 1 October 1647, possibly on an earlier visit (Records of Notary Nicholaes Vrienbergh, no. 2052, 7 February 1653). Abram van Beyeren was last noted in The Hague on 30 June 1655 (Bredius, *Künstler-inventare* 4:1,168) and joined the guild in Delft on 15 October 1657. Similarly, Abram van Beyeren may have left The Hague some months after he last appeared before a notary there. The delay in Carel Fabritius's registration appears to be the longest of those we have on record and the best established.

records and who seem to have been established on their own account—one painter, one art dealer, one sculptor, and one faiencier—were all noted in the sources in the 1650s and 1660s, there is a possibility that the guild rules were not enforced quite as effectively in this period as in previous years.

Once a member of the guild left town, he was supposed to pay "separation dues" in lieu of "death dues" amounting to thirty stuivers (twice the amount stipulated in the Old Guild Letter). If he came back to Delft after an absence of several years he could be readmitted provided he was willing to pay yearly dues, at the normal rate of six stuivers per year, for the entire period of his absence. The painter Heyndrick van der Burch, for instance, left town in late 1654 or early 1655, joined the guild in Leyden that same year, and returned to Delft in 1664. He paid two gulden fourteen stuivers on 8 December of this latter year, a sum corresponding exactly to an absence of nine years.[ii] This shows that in this respect also the guild exercised fairly close surveillance on the artists and artisans working in Delft who were nominally subject to its jurisdiction.

QUALIFICATIONS AND ENTRANCE DUES OF
MASTERS JOINING THE GUILD

To function as masters in the guild, according to amendments of the guild letter dated 1615 and 1654, painters, glass-engravers and faienciers (*plateelbackers*) had to have studied for six years with a master in the same craft. Printers, bookbinders and booksellers, by an amendment of 1658, had to be apprenticed for only two years. No ordinances concerning the apprenticeship requirements of embroiderers and sculptors have come to light. However, surviving contracts indicate that a period of at least two years was required (and more probably four or six).[ii] One piece of evidence demonstrates that the rules of the guild on apprenticeship were not always formalized in the

---

[ii]Van der Burch was still in Delft on 20 April 1654 (Records of Notary Frans Boogert, no. 2000). In 1658 he claimed that he had remitted his entrance dues to the Leyden guild in the hands of Cornelis Stoter who actually died in 1655 (Leyden, Municipal Archives, no. 849, "Deeken ende hooftmans boek vant gilde van St. Lucas Ordre," fol. 129). His absence from Delft therefore is unlikely to have lasted more than nine years. On the payment of the yearly dues that he owed during his absence, see Obreen, *Archief*, 1:70.

[ii]See below p. 89 and Chapter 5, pp. 117-18.

guild letter or its amendments. On 1 July 1613, forty-one years before the amendment was issued prescribing a learning period of six years for faienciers, Hans de Wint, a former lance-maker, was admitted into the guild as a faiencier even though his admission violated article 1 of the letter "as he had not spent the required amount of time in the trade" ("als niet den behoorlicken tyt aen't ambacht geweest hebbende"). The burgomasters had given De Wint a document validating the exception.[13] The next year, the lords of the Weth also interceded in the case of Franchoys du Boys Joli, another faiencier who had not fulfilled the apprenticeship requirement.[14] Forty years later, the owners of faience shops who had not themselves learned the trade were able to "release" their establishment from the necessity of being run by a master in the craft by naming a manager (*meester-knecht*) who ran the business for them. These *meesterknechts* had themselves to be masters in the guild. Even though this practice started in the early 1650s,[15] it was only formalized by an amendment to the guild letter in March 1661.[16]

An entry in the register of new masters for 10 January 1661 states that a former glassmaker named Gedeon Jacobse had been admitted as master painter "upon having shown an appropriate record of his years of apprenticeship in painting" ("leer jaren wegens sijn Schilder-en"). Four months later another glassmaker became a painter under the same condition ("hebbende vertont acte van voldoening van't schilderen").[17]

The only notarial evidence we have on the fulfillment of training requirements refers to years antedating the issuance of the Guild Letter of 1611, but it is nevertheless relevant to the later period since the document in question, which is dated 1618, was almost certainly drawn up to satisfy a contemporary, at present unascertainable, requirement. On 17 March of that year, the sculptor Maerten Danielsz. (van Tetrode), sixty years of age, testified at the request of Mathys de Been that Jacob Mathys de Been, the petitioner's son, was apprenticed to the deponent with whom he learned the "handicraft of antique or image-carving" (*antycq ofte beeldsnyden*), that in 1596, 1597, and 1598 he had spent a full two years learning the craft and that he had completely satisfied his master. He declared further that Jacob de Been had also met the requirements of the guild in Delft as far as his apprenticeship years were concerned." Finally, Van Tetrode declared Jacob Mathysz. de Been to be a "free master as having well and completely fulfilled his apprenticeship years."[18] As is frequently the case with depositions of this type, there is no hint in the document itself of the reason for the testimony. Since Jacob Mathysz. de Been appears among the sculptors on the original Master List of 1613, it is hard to see why, at this late date, there should be any question as to whether he had satisfied his apprenticeship requirement. However that may be, the document provides one more example of the continuity in guild practices between the sixteenth and seventeenth centuries.

The original Guild Letter of 1611 did not specify any "proof" or masterpiece requirement that a master had to satisfy before being admitted into the guild. On 14 July 1614, the sheriff and aldermen, with the advice of the burgomasters, issued an ordinance requiring glassmakers to furnish a "proof" of their mastery before the headmen in the form of a "lantern with prunts or a glass with a stem."[19] Six years later, the headmen ordered a glass with a stem "such as young masters make" and had it approved by the Weth as a model for candidate masters doing their proof. In February 1615, the Weth stipulated that painters could fulfill their learning or apprenticeship requirement in less than six years if they gave "evidence of their work" demonstrating their capacity to become masters. A marginal note specifically referred to the masterpiece (literally "proof-piece") that a painter or a glassmaker could make if he wished to become a master before his six years' apprenticeship was up.[20] There is no mention in any other ordinance of a masterpiece requirement for painters.[kk] In 1654, an "amplification" of the guild letter was promulgated requiring faienciers to produce a proof or masterpiece (described in some detail in Appendix B) if they had not been apprenticed in Delft for six years. Widows of masters wishing to continue the business, and even their husbands in case they should remarry, were exempt from the requirement, except that, if the second husband of a master's widow wished to keep open the shop after his wife's death, he had to submit to the test within six weeks after that event.

[kk]J. Soutendam, "Eenige aateekeningen betreffende Delfsche Kunstenaars," *Neder-landsche Spectator* (1870):11, found among some papers of the guild that cannot presently be located in the Delft archives "a model (in small scale) that must be painted for the painter's proof before one can become a master," together with "the proof of the broadbrush or *kladschilders*." These undated papers may refer to pieces that had to be executed by apprentices wishing to become masters before their six years' apprenticeship was up or to proofs that became compulsory in the late seventeenth or early eighteenth century beyond the period of the present study. Two paintings of identical size representing a bull's head and painter's equipment preserved in Delft's Prinsenhof Museum are thought to be proof-pieces for *kladschilders*. They were almost certainly painted in the eighteenth century.

The register of new masters for the period 1650–1714 contains many entries of receipts from new masters in the glassmaking and faience crafts who rented the facilities of the guild to do their proof. On 28 March 1667, for instance, Johannes Antonisz. van der Poel paid three gulden by way of entrance dues (at the lower rate granted to master's sons) and another three gulden for twelve days use of the chamber for his proof ("12 dagen camerrecht van de proef").[21] On 17 May 1677, Mijgijel Torenburgh registered as master-*knecht* in the faience works called De klaeuw for six gulden and paid one gulden ten stuivers for the use of the chamber for his proof "which lasted five days" (at six stuivers per day).[22]

Notarial mentions of *plateelbackers* who took the masterpiece test to enter the guild crop up occasionally. On 4 April 1656, Jacobus van Veen, who at the time was not yet registered as a shopkeeping faiencier, signed a contract with Lucas Jansz. Netteswey, *plateelback-ersknecht*, in which they agreed that Lucas Jansz. would submit to the masterpiece test of the faienciers' guild in Delft eight days after the contract was signed. Provided the headmen of the said guild approved the test he would be permitted to work as master-*knecht*. He would then begin to manage Van Veen's delftware pottery for a period of three years.[23] Lucas Jansz. in fact registered as a full master in the guild on 29 May 1656, paying six gulden. Van Veen did not register as shopkeeper (*winckelhouder*) until May 1662, presumably after he had passed the test. (The reference in the above-mentioned document to a faienciers' guild is not untypical. In estate inventories, the death dues of a painter or glassmaker are often referred to as being due to the painters' or to the glassmakers' guild, instead of to the Guild of St. Lucas.)

In a document of 1663,[24] the faiencier Benedictus van Houten declared that, sometime after May 1656 when he began his association with Jacob Hoppesteyn, he had done his proof for both himself and Hoppesteyn; in the same document, Jan Otten Schaek testified that, when he was working for Jan Aelbrechtsz. Groenlant who owned a "Delft-porcelain bakery," he had also "done the requisite proof" for both. This deposition was probably made in response to a complaint by the officers of the guild about the practice of having only one of several owners of a faience shop register as master.

Entrance dues for new masters in the guild remained at the same level throughout the seventeenth century. Masters born in Delft and its dependencies, including Delfshaven and Overschie, paid six gulden and "foreigners" twelve gulden. Masters' sons, as we have already seen, paid the privileged rate of only three gulden. From the cases where the place of birth of a new member is known, we may infer that these rules were rigorously observed.[11]

I have assumed, therefore, that it was legitimate to deduce whether a member of the guild whose place of birth could not be ascertained from other sources was born in Delft and its dependencies or not from the amount he paid on entering the guild. (Such inferences are starred in the last column of entries in Appendix Tables A.1 to A.3.)

In the case of "foreign" candidates, the headmen interpreted the rule that candidates must be citizens of Delft in order to be admitted by demanding that they show evidence of citizenship within a specified period. Thus the glassmaker Claes van Rooeij was inscribed in the register of new masters on 19 April 1632 after he pledged that he would show proof of his citizenship within half a year. If he failed to do so his twelve gulden entrance would be confiscated (and he would be required to pay it again).[25] It was presumably to avoid such problems that the Weth amended the guild letter in 1649 to require that a "foreigner" must already have become a citizen *before* he could pay his guild dues.[26] "Individuals of small means" could also be admitted at lower rates at the discretion of the burgomasters, but I have only found one instance where this actually occurred when the painter Jacob de Vries—a "poor fellow" (*arm gesell*)—was taken in, apparently for no fee at all, on 10 May 1683.

The headmen of the guild at their weekly sessions must have debated and resolved many cases where the rules on the payment of dues left room for ambiguity: Should the son of a master engaged in a different craft under the guild pay the privileged rate? How much

---

[11]The painter Heyndrick van der Burch, born in Naaldwijk, paid six gulden as his entrance fee (Obreen, *Archief,* 1:42). It is not certain whether he was exempted from paying the higher dues levied on foreigners because Naaldwijk was considered a Delft dependency or because his father Rochus van der Burch was a longstanding citizen of Delft. The father of Abraham van Beyeren, named Hendrick Gillisz. van Beijeren, registered as a painter on 10 October 1639, under the name "Hendrick Gillesen" (Obreen, *Archief,* 1:34). Six months later he brought in the rest of his entrance dues under the name Heinderijck van Beijeren. When Abraham joined the guild on 15 October 1657, he paid six gulden "as he said he was a citizen." Actually, he was born in The Hague where his father was a glassmaker (Bredius, *Künstler-inventare,* 4:1,164). The six-gulden fee was perhaps a compromise between the three-gulden fee paid by masters' sons and the twelve-gulden fee paid by foreigners. This compromise was made explicit in the case of the stonecarver Heyndryck Bellaert who, in July 1682, paid the entrance fee of six gulden "being a master's son but not born here" (Obreen, *Archief,* 1:87).

should masters pay who were admitted as masters in one craft and now wished to take up another? Their policy on the first question was not always consistent. Take, for example, the painters Corstiaen Couwenbergh and Johannes Vermeer, who were both sons of members in the guild belonging in principle to the group defined in the master book of 1613 as "illuminators, art dealers, and booksellers." Yet Corstiaen, the son of an engraver, paid only three gulden as a master in 1627 while Johannes Vermeer, the son of an art dealer, paid the full six-gulden fee in 1653. (Perhaps the difference was that the former's father was still alive when he joined the guild, while the latter's was not.) Jacob Corsendonck, the son of the broad-brush painter (*kladschilder*) who wrote his name "Ary Kortendoeck," registered as a glassmaker in 1655 for only three gulden, despite the fact that his trade was basically different from his father's. Six years later he was readmitted, this time as a painter (probably also broad-brush), again paying three gulden.[27] The practice of requiring a guild member in one trade to complete several years of apprenticeship and a second payment of entrance dues for a new trade was by no means exceptional. Altogether three glassmakers converted their skills to become painters in the 1660s, probably because they could expect greater earnings in that trade. Interestingly enough Jasper Saroth became a headman in the position on the board reserved for the glassmakers in 1670 after he had reregistered as a painter in 1661. He apparently practiced both crafts at the same time.

Craft divisions were quite fine: Michiel van Eemst, six years after being admitted to the guild as a master decorator on faience (*plateelschilder*) for twelve gulden plus one gulden ten stuivers for the use of the guild chamber to do his proof, was compelled to pay another twelve gulden to become a master painter. Such decisions may have been left to the discretion of the headmen.

THE ADMINISTRATION OF THE GUILD

According to article 22 of the Guild Letter of 1611, the guild was to be governed by four headmen. While the letter is not explicit on this point, it implies that each headman served two years. The first year he was said to be "ongoing" (*anblijvende*) and the second "retiring" (*affgaende*). Each year the two ongoing headmen chose four men from the guild rolls and delivered their names to the burgomasters. From among these four, the burgomasters selected two headmen to take the place of the retiring headmen of the year. The election and the changeover were slated for the feast of St. Lucas, the guild's patron saint, 18 October. Initially, there were no explicit rules on the craft composition of the board of headmen. However, the usual sixteenth-century practice of appointing painters and glassmakers to the board persisted. This at least is the picture that emerges from the incomplete lists of headmen's names that we have been able to reconstruct. In 1633, for example, the headmen were Jacob Vosmaer and Willem van Vliet, artist-painters, and Dirck Joersen Blaenoker and Jan Dijercksen (van der Laen), glassmakers.[28] The same pattern may be observed in 1619, 1622, 1625, 1633, 1638 and 1640 (see the list of headmen in Appendix C). The only exception occurred in 1616 when Pouwels Bourseth, faience-maker, served on the board.[29]

On 19 October 1620, the day after St. Lucas's, the lords of the Weth governing Delft, upon observing that a dispute had arisen concerning the faience trade about which the headmen of the guild had no competent knowledge, decided that henceforth a faience-maker ("claybaker") would be appointed by the burgomasters to help settle and compose all such disputes.[30] This individual was not, however, a full-fledged headman. Precisely twenty-eight years later, on 19 October 1648, the faienciers finally won access to the board. From then on, the board was to be composed of "two painters, two glassmakers, and two claybakers." It looks, though, as if passive resistance on the part of the other headmen continued, since it was not until three years later that the headmen-faienciers were formally entitled to receive a key to the strongbox that held the guild's moneys.[31] From 1648 on, the lists of headmen were more or less regularly written down in the register of new masters. From these lists we may infer that the composition of the guild conformed to the new rules, at least until 1714 when the register of new masters and shopkeepers breaks off.

The dean of the guild also played an important role in guild affairs, even though his functions are only incidentally referred to in the guild letter and its amendments. Dirck van Bleyswijck in his description of Delft gives a brief account of the dean's responsibilities in the various guilds of Delft. He was appointed by the burgomasters "to supervise the guilds on their behalf" and "to see to it that the ordinances of the magistracy are observed in their full vigor." One of his duties was to audit the accounts of retiring headmen.[32] The deans were not themselves artists or artisans but distinguished members of the "burgher-noblesse." Three names of deans of the St. Lucas Guild in the seventeenth century have come down to us: S. Groenewegen van der Made (1627), Sacharias Hofdijck van Beresteijn (1654), and Dirck Meerman (1661).[33] The last of these was dean when the new guild hall in the Old Men's Home on the Voldersgracht was opened for the gatherings of the members in 1661. The former burgomaster, counsellor of Delft, and knight (*ridder*) had his name and titles inscribed in a painting representing a Triumphal Arch hung over the mantle of the newly refurbished hall.[34]

Since the records of the guild meetings have long been lost—they were discarded along with many other books of the guild around 1850—and notarial records contain no documents dealing with intraguild disputes, we have no way to know precisely how guild problems were settled. The only clue we have to the extent of participation of the various groups in guild decision-making lies in the preamble and justification of the ordinances amending the guild letter. At first the Weth acknowledged only the requests of the headmen, as in October 1620, when the headmen submitted for approval an example of a stemmed glass for the glassmaker's proof. In May 1641 "my lord the sheriff and aldermen with advice from the lord burgomasters all having been heard previously in the matter, as well as the dean and the headmen of the aforesaid St. Lucas Guild who were also heard, together with the ordinary masters and servants (*knechts*) of the faienciers" reaffirmed an ordinance of 1614 limiting the number of boy apprentices hired to two a year and ordered the faience shops to desist from engaging any new boys for two years for each boy who had been hired previously in violation of the earlier ordinance. The ordinance also enjoined masters setting to work any servants coming from out of town to demand proof from these newly hired employees that they had "honestly and loyally satisfied their master," by which was meant that they had completed the term of their apprenticeship contract or agreement. In 1658, Aelbrecht Keyser, a well-known master faiencier, owner of "De twee scheepjes," who was at that time a headman of the guild representing his craft, addressed a request to the Weth, together with "some faienciers' servants," asking that the words "honestly and loyally satified their master" be altered to "satisfied their master for the period of six years."[35] In 1673, the *knechts* of the faienciers asked to be brought "under the supervision and governance of the guild in all respects." The Weth granted the request after consideration of "the written report and advice of the headmen." The *knechts* had also implored the Weth to reaffirm an old regulation according to which no faiencier could "put out any work belonging to the dish-turner's craft." This

[95]

request was granted on the 3 July 1673. On the 21st of August the Weth rescinded the order "upon request of virtually all the master faienciers," who alleged that the consent of the headmen had been obtained "without the knowledge of the ordinary master faienciers."[36] From the noble dean to the humble *knechts* employed by the master faienciers, everyone apparently had his say—or her say in the case of a widow who continued her husband's business—in matters that were important to them. The town's governance, at least in cases where its interests were not at stake, was responsive to pressures from the membership. It is worthy of note that in the unique case we have just considered of a disagreement between masters and *knechts*, the masters won the support of the Weth, even though the headmen had sided with the *knechts*. In 1673, when this incident occurred, business was poor, due to the war with France. The gentlemen of the Weth were perhaps swayed by the ordinary master faienciers' arguments about the necessity for fewer restraints if the industry was to be restored to health (in opposition to the *knechts* who feared that their jobs would be jeopardized if some of the dish-turning work was given to individuals outside the guild.) It is clear from all this that the initiative for the various ordinances restricting the expansion of employment in the industry came from these *knechts*.

The paramount role of the headmen in running guild affairs emerges in connection with the new hall already mentioned. On 3 September 1661, the burgomasters, at the request of the dean, consented to allow the guild, until further notice, the use of "the great upstairs hall with a little room beside it in the chapel of the old men's and women's house on the Voldersgracht."[37] This chapel had been used since 1596 as a drapers' or silk merchants' hall but had become too small for the members of the cloth and silk industry, who moved to new premises about this time. The resolution of the burgomasters further stipulated that all the costs of converting the drapers' hall should be borne by the Guild of St. Lucas "and in no manner shall any of it be charged to the city." The total expense, according to a summary accounting preserved on the reverse side of a memorandum[38] recording the contributions "in kind" of Leonaert Bramer and of other members, came to 1,342 gulden 12 stuivers.[mm] On 19

[mm]Bramer painted the ceiling; Cornelis de Man painted the space around the mantelpiece; Aelbrecht Keyser and Quiring Kleynove, faienciers, paid for ten "Spanish chairs," covered with Russian leather; Adriaen Engelbrechtsz. van de Velde and Arent van Saenen, glassmakers, donated to the guild hall new glass windows.

October 1661, Dirck Meerman, old burgomaster and dean of St. Lucas's Guild, together with the headmen of the guild in that year—the painters Leonaert Bramer and Cornelis de Man, the glass-makers Adriaen Engelbrechtsz. and Arent van Saenen, and the faienciers Quiring Kleynove and Aelbrecht Keyser—acknowledged before Notary Williem van Assendelft a debt of 800 gulden, for money received from Sybrant Jansz. van der Laen in the form of silver ducats of sixty-three stuivers each and rijcksdaelers of fifty stuivers each, which sum was "to be employed for the making or preparation of the guild hall in this town."[39] The money was to be returned *by the guild* in the same currency and at 3½ percent interest per year at a time to be set either at the request of the holder of the obligation or of the headmen of the guild serving at the time with three month's notice. The debtors promised not to oppose any condemnation for failure of payment and to bear responsibility for any and all payments arising from such a condemnation. All the guild's possessions and future incomes were pledged as a guarantee of repayment.

In February 1662, the headmen of the guild submitted a petition to the lords of the Weth "to be relieved of the obligation" (the debt they had incurred) and to lighten "the burden of the common guild brothers" who, if new measures were not found to raise revenues, would have to help meet this obligation. The main change the Weth introduced, in response to the petition, was to triple the entrance fees of out-of-town *knechts*, which rose from ten stuivers to two gulden ten stuivers. This measure had a beneficial effect on the guild's finances, to which we shall return in the next chapter.

The registration of *knechts*, incidentally, was rigidly enforced by the guild authorities. Already in the late sixteenth century, when the sculptor Jacob Mathysz. de Been had been apprenticed to Maerten Danielsz. van Tetrode, "the apprentices were duly registered by those in the guild practicing the same craft" ("de leer-knechts so pertina-mentlijck by dye van't gilde van't voorsz. handt werck werden

---

These donators were all headmen of the guild in 1661. The total expense included fifty-four gulden paid to Johannes Druyf, broad-brush painter, for painting inside and outside portions of the hall, forty-two gulden nineteen stuivers for upholstering, six gulden for keys to the hall, and thirty gulden eight stuivers for a green tablecloth and for sewing fringes on the same. These and other small sums account for only 142 gulden out of 1,343 gulden. Most of the remaining expenses probably went for masonry and carpentry work connected with the alteration of the old drapers' hall to accomodate the guild.

[97]

gheregisteert").[40] In 1656, a faiencier was fined twelve gulden for failing to register a boy apprentice on time; for what would seem to be the same infraction, a glassmaker paid two gulden in 1657.[41]

While we have had numerous occasions in this chapter to cite schedules of guild dues, the only guild expenditure we have commented on so far was for the new guild hall. Unfortunately, with this exception, the only information that can be pulled together concerns the rules for spending guild moneys, not the items on which they were actually spent. Article 27 of the Guild Letter of 1611 ruled that one-third of all guild receipts should go for "the necessary expenditures and sittings of the guild and the yearly gatherings of the headmen" and the rest for the upkeep of impoverished guild brothers. The one-third share was spent in part on the heating of the guild hall in winter, and on paper, pen, and ink for the records of the guild. Some of it must have gone to defray the costs of the yearly banquets at which the headmen enjoyed themselves in a local tavern as they had done in the sixteenth century. In the early 1660s, the refurbishing of the new guild hall was surely the main item of expense, which, as we have seen, had to be underwritten by loans. As for the impoverished guild brothers, there is not a trace in surviving documents about the payments they may have received or even about who they may have been. It is remarkable that when the painter Leonaert Bramer was old and penurious in 1669, it was the burgomasters and not the guild that succored him with 100 gulden at his written request.[42] While we know nothing about the guild's support of impoverished members, a couple of documents mention a "poor-box" (*arm-bos*) for the *knechts* employed by the faienciers. On 27 May 1669, for example, Jan Fransz., an ordinary *knecht*, and Ary Jansz. Ham, a dish-turner with a long career in the industry, declared that they had each borrowed fifty gulden from the box and acknowledged their debt to the "headmen of the same box"—presumably the two headmen representing the faienciers' craft.[43] The box was probably financed by contributions from both masters and servants, in the same manner as a similar fund set up for his employees by the tapestry manufacturer Karel van Mander the Younger (described in Chapter 9).

How Restrictive Was the Guild?

The straws of evidence gathered in Chapter 2 led us to suppose that the old guild rules were only laxly enforced prior to the issuance of the new letter. Many artists were active in Delft who had not acquired citizenship and almost certainly had not gained admission to the guild. Paintings from other towns, perhaps chiefly from Flanders, were probably as easily imported into Delft, as they were into other Dutch cities (if we are to believe the letter addressed by the painters in Amsterdam to the burgomasters of Leyden).[44] What difference did the issuance of the new guild letter make? There can be little doubt that membership rules were much more strictly enforced from this time on. Just about everyone living and earning his livelihood in Delft in any of the trades and crafts subsumed under the guild became a member either when he had completed his apprenticeship or within a year or so after he settled in town. Restraints on foreign competition aside, this "closed-shop" aspect of artisanal life meant that the guild administration had authority over virtually all the individuals practicing the trades under its jurisdiction—whether they were masters or servants. The guild had control, via the proof or masterpiece requirement, over the qualifications of all master glassmakers and faienciers. There is some likelihood, the evidence for which is briefly considered in Chapter 9, that it restricted the number of master faienciers in the 1630s and 1640s, perhaps by imposing excessively high standards on those wishing to undergo the test. There was no masterpiece requirement for painters or sculptors in the period covered in this study,[nn] but the six-year apprenticeship rule could be enforced to maintain the quality of new entrants. Guild revenues were also considerably larger than they would have been if membership had been strictly voluntary. A half-century after the new letter was issued, the elegant premises into which the guild moved in 1661 finally consecrated its more powerful situation (notwithstanding the fact that a loan had to be negotiated and various dues raised to finance the improvement).

How successful was the guild in limiting employment? To what extent did the *knechts* use the guild as a union to restrict competition and keep wages up? We have already seen that it was at their initiative that an ordinance was passed forbidding master faienciers from setting individuals to work at potting dishes who were not regularly registered as *knechts* in the Guild of St. Lucas. It was probably also these same *knechts* who had pressed for the amplification of 1614 which forbad any faience-shop from "keeping and hiring" more than two boy-apprentices at the same time. Even though the faienciers

[nn]Painters in other towns of Holland were also exempt from the proof requirement (*proef-vrij*). However, in certain places, including Amsterdam, sculptors and stone carvers had to produce a masterpiece (Hoogewerff, *De geschiedenis van de St. Lucasgilden*, p. 144).

succeeded in interpreting this ordinance—contrary to its literal text—
as meaning that no more should be *hired* than one boy every two
years, this injunction was also violated, and the old ordinance had to
be strengthened in 1641. All boys hired in excess of the permissible
number were to be discharged within a period of ten days, subject to a
"double fine" (presumably twice the twelve-gulden fine imposed on
those who had hired such supernumerary boys in the first place).[45] It is
hard to believe that the faïenciers, who were enjoying a boom in
demand at this time, complied zealously with this regulation. On the
other hand, it may have been one of the factors that kept down the
number of workers employed per faïence-making shop and that
fostered the remarkable increase in the *number of shops* which took
place in the next twenty years.[oo]

The degree to which the guild was empowered, or when empowered was effective, in restricting trade is less clear. There were a
number of free-market kermess days when anyone could sell paintings
or other works comprised under the guild in Delft.[pp] By article 10 of
the guild letter, if a foreign seller was willing to pay a fee of one
gulden ten stuivers he was also allowed to market his wares at any
time during two periods of twenty-four hours. Out-of-towners were
not permitted to sell pictures or books at public auction without
securing the prior consent of the burgomasters (article 11 and
amplification of 4 November 1658). It was not until February 1662
that an ordinance was issued prohibiting the sale of paintings brought
in from out of town at estate sales.[46] (*Boelhuys* sales, scheduled every
week, were organized to liquidate the estates of deceased persons yet
frequently contained items consigned by dealers.) These were, as far as
I am aware, the only restrictions to which the importation of
out-of-town products subsumed under the guild was subject. Any
guild-registered dealer was apparently allowed to sell imported paintings or other works of art. The fact that about half the attributed
paintings in Delft inventories between 1610 and 1680 were made by
out-of-town masters who at no time in their life belonged to the guild
in Delft[47] indicates that there was no lack of such imports. It would
have ill behooved my lords of the Weth to clamp down on private
purchases of works of art by artists from other towns when they had
no qualms about ordering paintings and sculptures from well-known
"foreign" masters for Delft's adornment.[48]

[oo]See Chapter 4, Table 4.2 and Chapter 9, Table 9.2.
[pp]After the kermess of 1657, some art dealers continued to sell their merchandise.
They were fined eleven gulden nineteen stuivers and nine penningen (Obreen, *Archief*,
1:61).

[100]

FOUR

Guild Masters and Their Apprentices

In this chapter I estimate the total number of masters in the guild at various benchmark dates and analyze the composition of the membership of the guild by crafts. Since the registers of the servants or apprentices of guild masters have disappeared, we can only get an idea of their numbers by counting the references to these *knechts* in a variety of sources. The great majority of these individuals, it turns out, worked for faienciers or makers of delftware. The leitmotiv of the chapter is the vigorous expansion of employment in the faience industry, which continued throughout most of the seventeenth century, coupled with the gradual decline of the other crafts, including painting, after the mid-century point. The chapter concludes with some observations on the consequences of the changing composition of the guild for its finances.

THE COMPOSITION OF THE GUILD OF ST. LUCAS

The first Master Book of the guild begins in 1613 and ends in 1649. With the help of the Register of New Masters, which also begins in January 1613, we can segregate the members who were already in the guild at this initial date from those who were inscribed afterwards. This at least is possible for all the trades except for the painters of furniture (*stoelverwers*) who appear on the master list but not in the register of new masters. These artisans, who paid only 2½ gulden to become members, compared with the regular fee of six gulden, did so only to obtain the right to paint the furniture they made. Because of their marginal status in the guild and the absence of reliable data on their numbers, I have chosen to leave them out of the analysis of the guild membership that follows.

On 1 January 1613, the names of ninety-four members were inscribed in the first Master Book, classified in seven groups, marked A to G. In group A there were forty oil-painters, in group B seven watercolor painters (*waterverw-schilders*), in group C seventeen glass-engravers, glassmakers, and glass-sellers, in group D ten illuminators (*verlichters*), art dealers, and booksellers, in group E five embroiderers, in group F seven sculptors, and in group G eight painters on faience (*plateelschilders*). There was one last group for which a separate page was provided in the Master Book as early as 1613 (i.e., before the tapestry makers were listed). This space was reserved for the scabbard-makers (*scheemackers*) who, as we saw in the first chapter, had played a significant role in the sixteenth century. The numbers 1 to 5 were written on the page but the names were left blank. There were apparently no such artisans left to inscribe or none who wished to be inscribed by this date.[a] The tapestry-makers inscribed after January 1613 and the furniture-painters completed the roster.

The formal names of the groups within the guild, which I have literally translated, give an imperfect idea of the structure of membership. Thus group D also included engravers, printers, and bookbinders, all three of which were a good deal more important by 1613 than the "illuminators." The sculptors in group F were thrown in with the stonecarvers. Group G was not restricted to the painters on faience but comprised all the master *plateelbackers* (dishbakers or faienciers). The total of ninety-four members in groups A to G was between two and three times as great as the membership in the second half of the sixteenth century.

The number of guild members in 1650 is more difficult to estimate because we lack a firm date of departure from Delft for a few painters. The first fifty-three painters[b] in the Master Book of 1650-1714 had all become members before 1650. All but three—Willem van Aelst, Paulus Potter, and Corstiaen Caescooper—are believed to have been in Delft in January 1650. The next six names on the list are inscriptions of the 1650s, with the exception of Cornelis de Man who joined the guild in 1642 but then left for nine years of travels in France and Italy. The names that follow, numbers 59 to 69 inclusive, were written down by the same hand. The word *vertrocken* (departed) appears after each of them. All eleven are listed in the order of the date they joined the guild (from 1627 to 1647). I conjecture that the headman or guild servant who kept these lists, some time in the early 1650s, combed through the register of new members of the pre-1650

[a] The blank page with the title and numbers is not mentioned in the transcription of the Master Book in F.D.O. Obreen, *Archief voor Nederlandsche Kunstgeschiedenis*, 7 vols. (Rotterdam, 1877-1890), 1: 4-11.

[b] Oil and watercolor painters are no longer distinguished in the 1650 membership rolls. For a complete list, see Appendix, Table A.2.

period in an attempt to account for all the members who were still nominally in the guild but had not been listed in the Master List of 1650, perhaps because they had not been in Delft when the headmen went on their yearly rounds (*ommegang*) to collect dues. He then concluded that every one had already departed, presumably without paying his death or separation dues, as the guild statutes stipulated. Five of these masters are known to have moved out of Delft before 1650—Corstiaen Couwenbergh, Geraerd Houckgeest, Simon de Vlieger, Pieter Steenwijck, and Isaac Junius— and I have not been able to find any record in Delft of any of the others in or around 1650. The next two painters on the list, inscribed in the manuscript in another hand, are Heyndrick van der Burch (registered in 1649) and Pieter van den Vin (registered in 1645). After the first we find the word *vertrocken* and after the second *vertrocken en doot* (departed and dead). It is not clear whether either of them was in Delft in 1650; but, if they did leave, they were back shortly afterwards.[c] They could not have been absent very long during these years, so no serious mistake will be made by assuming both to be in Delft in January 1650. This leaves us altogether with fifty-two painters in 1650, as compared with forty-seven oil and watercolor painters in 1613. The Master List of 1650 also contained eighteen glassmakers, two stonecarvers, three sculptors, and three embroiderers who became members before that date. Neither the faienciers nor the printers, bookbinders, and art dealers are shown separately in the 1650 membership list. From the evidence at my disposal about the deaths or absences in these two groups of individuals who registered before 1650, I estimate that there were thirteen master faienciers active in Delft in 1650, plus one widow who carried on the business of her late husband,[d] and seventeen art dealers and representatives of the printing trades. In all

[c]Heyndrick van der Burch witnessed the baptism of Johannes Rudsz. van Aert along with Jannetgen van der Burch, the future wife of Pieter de Hooch, on 10 August 1649. He signed a document in Delft with the painter Pieter de Hooch on 5 August 1652 (kind communication of Peter Sutton) and again on 29 April 1654 (Records of Notary Frans. Boogert no. 2000). He was also present in Delft at the baptism of Pieter de Hooch's child, Heyndrick, on 2 February 1655. Pieter van der Vin was a witness to notarial documents on 8 and 18 August 1654 (Records of Notary Frans van Hurck, no. 2090).

[d]Not included in this list is the master faiencier named Cornelis Cornelisz. Schipper who was still alive in 1650 but was no longer active in the profession (see the records of Notary Adriaen van der Block, no. 1748, 30 November 1648). The two *plateelbackers* in Delfshaven (Esaias de Lindt and Jan Loquefier) are included, but the decorator on faience, Cornelis van der Plaat, who appears in the list of painters in the 1650s, is counted among the latter.

there were an estimated 109 members, excluding the furniture-painters. Compared to the similarly defined membership of the guild in 1613, which consisted of ninety-four individuals, there was a moderate increase of 16 percent in thirty-seven years.

From 1650 on, we have no master books for any group within the guild to control our estimates. We must now rely on such information as we may come by on the death or departure dates of newly inscribed members. Wherever these vital statistics were missing, I have arbitrarily assumed that an artisan would remain active for twenty years after his registration in the guild or until he reached the age of sixty-five (provided his birth year was known), whichever came first. This method is likely, if anything, to overestimate the number of individuals active in Delft at any one time, since it makes no allowance for departures. The data for painters, faienciers, and printers, which are better than those at my disposal for the other crafts, are show in Table 4.1.

The drop in the number of active painters and the increase in the number of faienciers are so pronounced that the overall tendencies must be correct even if the numbers are not quite precise. The number of printers, booksellers, and allied trades was fairly stable until 1670, then seems to have declined precipitously. Whereas the decrease in the number of painters corresponds, in my opinion, to a real decline in the artists' colony, the rise in the number of faienciers is not *only* a reflection of a corresponding expansion in the total labor force of the entire industry. For it appears that membership policy underwent an important change with respect to the faienciers starting in the 1650s. In the 1630s and 1640s, very few faienciers became masters; almost all those who did were owners of potteries. Thus, out of the estimated fourteen master faienciers active in 1650, thirteen are believed to have owned a pottery by themselves or in association. After the guild letter

TABLE 4.1
Registered Painters, Faienciers, and Printers Active in Delft from 1650-1680

Occupation	1 Jan. 1650	1 Jan. 1660	1 Jan. 1670	1 Jan. 1680
Painters	52	51	41	31
Faienciers	14	29	48	57
Printers and allied trades	17	21	20	12

SOURCES: Obreen *Archief*, 1:49-82; Delft MA, "Begrafboeken van de Oude en Nieuwe Kerck" (burial files), 1650-1680; Records of notaries in Delft.

[104]

was amended in February 1662, we find an increasing number of *plateelbackers* and *plateelschilders* joining the guild to become foremen or managers of potteries owned by "companies" or by individuals possessing capital who were not themselves skilled in the trade. According to my estimate, there were only twenty-eight owners or part-owners of faience works in 1670 out of forty-eight registered faienciers in the guild.[1] Nearly half the guild members in this trade were working for other masters, as compared with only one in 1650. We recall from Chapter 3 that the owner of a delftware pottery, if he was not himself a master in the craft, was expected to register his *meester knecht* (foreman managing the shop) in the guild provided this foreman had passed his masterpiece or "proof" requirement.

With respect to other crafts, the data available show a general downward trend starting in the 1660s. The number of glassmakers and sculptors, after registering an increase in the 1650s, fell off in the 1660s and 1670s, at least as far as we can make out from the number of new registrations.[c] The embroiderer's craft was in complete decadence: no new master-embroiderer was registered from 1650 to 1680.

During a period of thirty years, which bracketed the short active life of Vermeer as a painter—he registered in the guild in 1653 and died in 1675—the composition of the membership was completely transformed. Painters in the early 1650s made up about half of the total membership (as they had done in 1613) and faienciers less than one-seventh; by 1680, the painters were down to about one quarter, while the faienciers reached nearly half of the total. The total number of members in the guild was probably not substantially greater by the end of this period than it had been in 1650, that is, 115 to 125 in 1680, again excluding painters of furniture.

Delfts's distinction as an artistic center in the 1640s and early 1650s was of course a reflection of the quality of the painters who resided there at the time; but this burst of creativity could scarcely have occurred if there had not been a critical mass to sustain it. Because there were many painters in town, young people had a choice of masters from whom to learn; a wide variety of ideas sprouted to fructify even the barest soil; and there were good statistical chances that an extraordinary talent such as Vermeer's would one day or

[c]There were eight new registrations of glassmakers in the 1640s, thirteen in the 1650s, eight in the 1660s, and three in the 1670s. The corresponding number of sculptors' registrations were four in the 1640s, seven in the 1650s two in the 1660s, and one in the 1670s.

another reveal itself. It is paradoxical that by the time Vermeer's talent had ripened the critical mass that had nurtured it had vanished.

MASTERS AND SERVANTS

To write about guild membership exclusively in terms of masters would be misleading. For as we saw in the last chapter *knechts* and even boy-apprentices also had to be registered in the special books kept for this purpose (which have all disappeared). If they were not full-fledged members, they were at least subject to guild rules so far as these rules pertained to them. We have no way to know whether all apprentices were in fact registered as they were supposed to be; the fact, mentioned in the last chapter, that a master was fined for failing to register some of his boy-learners suggests that the rule may at times have been ignored. This is all the more likely in the case of the faienciers who, in a period of expansion of the industry, must have found it profitable to hire more young people than the one additional learner that they were entitled to each year.

Our next task is to estimate the number of masters and the number of *knechts* (apprentices, journeymen) in each craft subsumed under the guild. I focus my comparison on the years 1620 to 1650 for which we have more complete information than in other decades. There are *Verponding boeken* (real-estate tax assessment books) and records of real-estate transactions in the Camer van Charitate that are not available in other decades. The records of notaries are better because the names of witnesses and other individuals are usually accompanied by a mention of their occupation and age (which helps distinguish individuals with similar names); in the second half of the seventeenth century both types of information, more often than not, are absent.[f]

The data in Table 4.2 refer to the number of artists and artisans who first registered in the guild in a given decade or were cited in a document in that decade as an approximation to the number of individuals who may have been active at any one time in a given craft. When an individual has been recorded in several decades from 1620 to 1650, he is only counted in the first decade of his appearance.

The number of nonregistered individuals in the 1620s is somewhat inflated, as compared with the following two decades, because it includes not only artisans who first became active in that period but

[f]The only positive aspect of later notarial protocols is that they more often mention the last name of individuals. In earlier times most people were satisfied to call themselves by their first name and their patronymic.

TABLE 4.2
Date of Registration (Guild Members) or of First Mention in Sources (Nonmembers)
of Delft Artists and Artisans

Occupation	1620-1629	1630-1639	1640-1649
Painters			
Newly registered guild members	33*	23	33
Nonmembers mentioned	28	13	13
Total	61	36	46
Faienciers			
Newly registered guild members	4	4	10
Nonmembers mentioned	120	99	96
Total	124	103	106
Printers and allied trades†			
Newly registered guild members	11	8	9
Nonmembers mentioned	5	17	7
Total	16	25	16
Glassmakers			
Newly registered guild members	10	7	8
Nonmembers mentioned	11	4	0
Total	21	11	8
Sculptors			
Newly registered members	3	5	4
Nonmembers mentioned	6	5	5
Total	9	10	9
Embroiderers			
Newly registered guild members	4	1	1
Nonmembers mentioned	2	1	0
Total	6	2	1

SOURCES: For all trades: Delft MA, "Legger van der verpondingen, 1620 and 1632; Delft MA, "Haardsteden register," 1638; Delft MA, Notarial archives; Delft, Camer van Charitate, "Opperste Kleed Boeken," 1615-1650; Delft, Camer van Charitate, "Reckeningen van de deuijt op de gulden," 1620-1644; Obreen, *Archief*, 1: "Het St. Lukas-gild te Delft," pp. 1-11, and 4: "Necrologium van Delftsche kunstenaars opgemaakt uit de begrafenisboeken in het archief van Delft," pp. 4-26. For painters: manuscript notes of A. Bredius (based on notarial archives and on the registers of births, deaths, and marriages in Delft), preserved in the Rijksbureau voor Kunsthistorische Documentatie in The Hague. For printers, bookbinders, and allied trades: J.G.C. Briels, *Zuidnederlandse boekdrukkers en boekverkopers in de Republiek der Verenigden Nederlanden omstreeks* 1570-1630 (The Hague: Nieuwkoop and B. de Graaf, 1974); A.M. Ledeboer, *De boekdrukkers, boekverkoopers en uitgevers in Noord Nederland sedert de uitvinding van de boekdrukkunst tot de aanvang der negentiende eeuw* (Deventer, 1872). For faienciers: Henry Havard, *Histoire des faïences de Delft . . .*, 2 vols. (Amsterdam: "Vivat," 1909) vol. 2. Handwritten notes of A.A.H. van der Burgh in the Delft municipal archives.

NOTE: All numbers include individuals working outside Delft but within its jurisdiction, particularly in Delfshaven. The numbers of nonmembers in the table do not comprise apprentices who later became masters.

*Including one gilder.

†Including art dealers.

also those who began their activity in earlier years and continued to
work in the 1620s. This may account for the relatively high numbers
of recorded "first mentions" in this decade.

There are two sources of understatement in the data for all three
decades in Table 4.2: 1) A few masters were *knechts* before they
registered in the guild. 2) A number of apprentices and journeymen
probably escaped detection in our sources: they never showed up in
the tax books and left town before they could be picked up in the
register of burials; or, if their names did appear in any of the sources
used, they were not identified by their trade. Neither of these
deficiencies in the data will be critical to our analysis provided they
affect all trades to more or less the same extent, since we shall use the
numbers in Table 4.2 as a reflection of differences among the trades
rather than as an indication of their absolute values.

The data in Table 4.2 show that in all three decades there was less
than one new mention of a nonregistered painter, glassmaker, and
embroiderer per newly registered member in these trades. Among the
printers there were about two nonmembers mentioned for each newly
registered member in the 1630s, but less than one in the 1620s and
1640s. For my small sample of sculptors and stonecarvers the ratio
was two mentions of unregistered individuals per registered member
in the 1620s and about equal numbers of registered and unregistered
individuals in the 1630s and 1640s. Among the faienciers by contrast,
there were thirty mentions of nonmembers per newly inscribed
member in the 1620s, while the ratios were twenty-four to one in the
1630s and a little over nine to one in the 1640s.

The ratio we should really like to have, of course, is that of
nonregistered to registered artisans in a given trade at a particular date.
This is very difficult to estimate since, for many *knechts*, we have only
one or two dates of mentions from which to reconstruct their entire
period of activity in Delft. To make a stab at the problem, I estimated,
on the basis of rough expectations of working-life expectancy, that in
the beginning of the year 1640, there were about 150 unregistered
faienciers active in Delft, compared to 8 registered masters (7 of them
owners of delftware potteries) plus 3 widows continuing to run their
late husband's business.[8] The ratio of unregistered to registered

[8]My initial method of estimating the number of unregistered faience workers was as
follows. Where I had only a date of marriage, I assumed that the individual was
already working for one year and that he was active for another five in the faience
trade in Delft after his marriage. Where only the date of death was available I assumed
activity for five years previously. For a date of baptism or an occasional mention in a

members was then about fourteen to one in 1640, whereas for the painters it was at most two to one in the same year. Since there were, by my count, ten active faience works in the beginning of 1640, the number of employees per establishment works out to fifteen. As virtually all the *knechts* in our lists were adults, we may readily imagine that with a full complement of five or six boy-learners, the complete crew of the average pottery amounted to twenty or so individuals of all ages. All these figures, if one takes account of possible omissions, might have to be raised by 10 to 20 percent but, in my judgment, not by any more. If it is assumed, as appears probable, that most of the *knechts* employed in the faience industry were former boy-apprentices[h] one may wonder how such a high level of employment could have been achieved without substantial violations of the rules on their employment. (We recall that no more than one boy-apprentice could be added to a pottery's work force each year.) The guild leadership's efforts to tighten up the relevant regulations—because of misuse and abuse—suggest how serious these violations must have been. Until the late 1650s, as we have seen, almost all master faienciers owned a delftware pottery or at least a share in such an enterprise. Indeed many examples can be invoked to show that artisans only joined the guild just before or shortly after they had purchased a pottery.[i] Before that, if they were not "capitalists" who entered the business as just another

---

notarial source, I assumed three years of activity before this date and three thereafter. For the great majority of individuals for which I disposed of more than one date, I assumed that activity began three years before the first date of mention and continued three years after the last mention (except in case of death). On the basis of these assumptions, the number of active faience workers at the beginning of 1640 was 136. When I lengthened the assumed initial and terminal periods from three to four years, I obtained a count of 155. When I increased these periods to five years, the number rose to 160. Given the few new names that cropped in notarial books in the last few months of this study, I doubt very much that the number of faienciers who did not show up at all in the archival sources I used was in excess of 20 percent of the number I listed. In a few cases of very common first names and patronymics (e.g., Jan Jansz.), I had to guess from the dates at my disposal whether two or more mentions corresponded to the same or different individuals. But the error in the final estimates due to these identification problems is probably less than 3 percent.

[h]The only information we have on this point comes from the accounts of the guild that are extant from the year 1723 on. In 1723, only two individuals coming out of town were registered as *knechts* in the guild, as compared to a total of thirty-five former boy-learners who became *knechts*. (See Delft MA, "Rekkenningen ... St. Lucas gilde 1723," fols. 1–3)

[i]On the faienciers who bought a delftware pottery within a year of their (previous or subsequent) registration in the guild, see Chapter 3, note ee.

line of trade, they generally worked for their father or their widowed mother. It is not surprising therefore that faienciers on average should have been considerably older when they joined the guild than painters, most of whom became members as soon as they had completed their apprenticeship or had come back from their *Wanderjahre* abroad. The average age of thirty-four faienciers with a known year of birth who became masters from 1613 to 1674 was 33.4 years. By contrast, the average age in a sample of forty-seven painters was 24.5 years. Most Delft-born painters who did not leave town to travel to Italy or elsewhere after their training was over joined the guild when they were twenty-one years of age.

Among the unregistered painters, not all were ordinary *knechts*. We also find a fair number working for their fathers who were members of the guild, including Willem Willemsz., the son of Willem Bundel; Garbrant Jansz., the son of Jan Garbrant de Jong; Jan Michielsz. and Pieter Michielsz., the sons of Michiel Miereveld; and Johannes Willemsz., the son of Willem Jansz. Ploij. Every one of these artists died before his father did; none had a chance to set himself up on his own account. Virtually no names of journeymen painters, not family members, who worked all their lives for master-painters can be cited.

Our analysis of the ratio of members to nonmembers in the various trades is complicated by the fact that not all guild members were necessarily working as independent masters. Among the glassworkers, book-printers, and booksellers, it was not unusual for a *knecht* to register as a guild member and to continue to work for a master. Jacobus Dircksz. de Geus, for example, registered in the guild as a master bookbinder in January 1654. Two-and-a-half years later he was still called a bookbinder's *knecht*, working for an independent master.[2] The ratio of unregistered to registered faienciers is especially high in the period 1630–1650 because *knechts* never registered as masters in the guild in this period. From the mid-1650s on, as we have already seen, the foremen-managers of faience works were also admitted into the guild.

The relation between the number of masters and the number of *knechts* is not only important to understand differences in how trades grouped under the guild were organized; it had significance for the finances of the guild and probably also for the distribution of power within it. Approximate calculations indicate that by 1672 the master faienciers, *knechts*, and boy-apprentices contributed about two-thirds of all guild receipts from new entrants and yearly dues.[j] It was no

[j]The guild's yearly receipts for entrance fees averaged twenty-nine gulden for

doubt the "flourishing state of the faience industry" (as Van Bleys-wijck put it in 1667)[3] and its great number of employees that made it possible to finance the new guild hall on the Voldersgracht in 1661. The soundness of the guild's finances becomes apparent when we consider that by 1723, the year in which surviving accounts of the guild resume after breaking off in 1593, the guild possessed obligations totaling 1,325 gulden and had no outstanding debt of any kind.[4]

The delftware industry, which dominated the community of artists and artisans belonging to the guild from the 1670s on, more than made up for the losses of entrance fees and yearly dues stemming from the decline in other crafts. The period during which Delft's painters' colony flourished and its art-crafts prospered was brief. It lasted perhaps one generation, from the early 1630s to the late 1650s or early 1660s. After that, with a very few exceptions among the painters and the printers, only the potteries were left to proclaim its fame.

---

faienciers and their *meesterknechts* in the period 1667–1672 and twenty-eight gulden for all other trades. If there were 160 *plateelbackersknechts*, their yearly guild dues alone (at six stuivers per individual) must have been about forty-eight gulden. If one assumes that boy-learners replaced one-fourth of the total number of *knechts* each year, they brought in another twelve gulden as entrance fees. The yearly dues of masters in the faience trade and of masters in all the other trades came to about fifteen gulden each. If we add to the latter the masters' entrance fees plus a minimum of ten gulden for the entrance fees and yearly dues of boy-apprentices in the trades other than faience-making, we obtain a total of fifty-three gulden, as against a total of 120 gulden for the faienciers. (The entrance fees and yearly dues used in these calculations are extracted from the guild regulations in Appendix B.)

FIVE

The Economic Status of Artists and Artisans

In 1622, when the only more or less reliable population count was made in Holland in the first half of the seventeenth century, Delft numbered 22,769 inhabitants.[1] It was the fourth most populous town of Holland, after Amsterdam (104,932), Leyden (44,745), and Haarlem (39,455). Delft was well known in the seventeenth century for the quality of its wares. It was outstanding for its beer, its embroidery, and for the weaving of fine cloth, brocaded satin, and velvet textiles; starting from very humble beginnings in the 1580s, its faience industry burgeoned forth and eventually brought wide fame and riches to the makers of "delftware." Its fine craft traditions, supported by a discriminating upper-class clientele, helped create the conditions in which Delft's community of artists and artisans flourished.[2]

About the middle of the century, an adult apprentice or journeyman in the faience industry earned from eighteen to twenty-five stuivers per day.[3] A skilled carpenter took a job in Switzerland for forty gulden a month.[4] A kitchenmaid hired for a banquet earned eight stuivers a day. The hired manager of a prosperous delftware workshop received about eight hundred gulden a year. A pound of veal cost 4 stuivers, a chicken 11 stuivers, a pound of butter $5\frac{1}{2}$ stuivers, a three-pound loaf of brown bread $4\frac{1}{2}$ stuivers, and a glass of beer at an inn $\frac{1}{2}$ stuiver.[5] A house cost anywhere from 150 gulden for a tiny cottage to 6,000 gulden or more for a patrician residence. The inventories of 461 estates of Delft residents who died in the period 1600 to 1679 (analyzed in Chapter 8) reveal that the mean and median values of the movable possessions in this fairly large sample were 531 gulden and 938 gulden respectively. The distributions were similar in the subperiods 1600 to 1639 and 1640 to 1679. Increases in the cost of living, which had been rapid in the last quarter of the sixteenth century, were apparently quite moderate from about 1620 to 1680.[a]

[a]N. W. Posthumus's wholesale index rose from 126 in the 1620-1624 period to a high of 141 in the 1650-1654 period, then subsided to 115 in the 1676-1680

HUMAN CAPITAL

The traditional measures of individual material well-being in modern times—income and net worth—are almost never ascertainable in the seventeenth century. Lacking these summary measures, we must find indirect ways of assessing the economic status of the artists and artisans of interest to us, relative to each other and to other occupations. Some of the indicators I shall use will be very indirect indeed: for example, I take the ability of a person to sign his name in a literate manner as an indication of formal education (and that he built up a minimum amount of human capital with which to start his career). Some will be more direct: the amounts paid for real estate and property taxes must surely be highly correlated with income and wealth. I shall also use as indicators of wealth the death donations made by relatives of recently deceased individuals to the Camer van Charitate, Delft's charitable institution, and the estimated inventories or auction sales of estates.

When we speak of the economic status of an individual or of a group, we may lose sight of the fact that income and wealth vary over the life cycle of individuals. In the case of seventeenth-century artists, in particular, I am struck by the rise in apparent wealth until mid-career and the decline thereafter.[b] Unlike rentiers and other individuals with settled incomes, even successful artists may become quite poor toward the end of their lives. Death donations and estate inventories will then be biased downward in their case, at least if our conception of status is stretched to cover the entire life history of individuals, instead of being reduced to a single reading at a point in time.

While a young man growing up in Delft in the seventeenth century could sometimes achieve a fairly high economic status even though he never went to school or received specialized training at the cost of his parents, starting under these adverse conditions was a great handicap. Maximiliaen van der Gucht, a prominent tapestry-maker, is an

---

period. Retail prices in Leyden and Utrecht may have gone up by about 25 percent from 1610-1620 to 1630-1640 then held steady to 1655, after which date they eased slightly; by 1675-1679 they were about 10 to 15 percent higher than 1610-1614. Price quotations for Delft alone are not available. The index numbers cited in this note are taken from Posthumus, *Inquiry into the History of Prices in Holland*, 2 vols. (Leyden: E. J. Brill, 1946), 1:ci and 2:xciii.

[b]Examples include Rembrandt in Amsterdam, and Evert van Aelst and Leonaert Bramer in Delft.

exceptional case: despite his illiteracy he ran a successful tapestry business for over thirty years. For most families, however, sending a child to school was the first essential step in eventually ensuring at least a tolerable living. The second step was for him to receive solid training by an established master in one of the better-paid trades. This was also, as we shall see, a significant expense for his parents.

Sending a child to school involved both out-of-pocket and (much greater) indirect costs. Parents had to pay only two to six gulden a year for school tuition,[c] but they had to feed and clothe their child at a time when he could have been earning his keep as an apprentice. The expenses of keeping a child of twelve or thirteen at home depended of course on the status of the parents; but even for the ordinary craftsmen, it could not have been much less than fifty to sixty gulden a year.[d] If the child went to school full time for three years, the accumulated expense might be 150 to 200 gulden. There can hardly be any doubt that outlays of this magnitude were beyond the means of most working men's families, especially when they were burdened with many children.

Masters in the Guild of St. Lucas, with the partial exception of the furniture-painters, were almost all literate. As for apprentices and journeymen, the incidence of literacy depended very much on the trade. Generally speaking, painters, printers, and bookbinders were literate. Most faienciers were not. The picture was mixed among the *knechts* of glassmakers, embroiderers, and stonecarvers.

As regards the painters belonging to the guild, I found only a few instances of illiteracy, and these almost exclusively among the painters-in-the-rough (*kladschilders*). The only artist-painter I discovered who could not sign his name even though he was a master in the guild was Jonas Jansz. van der Burch, who painted tapestry cartoons for Franchoys and Aert Spierinx.[e] The *kladschilders* named Rytsaert

---

[c]See Orphan Chamber, *boedel* no. 405, 6 October 1617, estate of Barent Claesz., where Mr. Jonas, schoolmaster, is paid three gulden for a half year's school money. The amount owed by another individual for one year's schooling was four gulden. (Orphan Chamber, *boedel* no. 187, 21 May 1631).

[d]In the 1620s it cost about twenty-five to thirty stuivers a week to keep a child with foster parents or wards (Inventory of Willem Jansz. Decker, Records of Notary Adriaen Rijshouck, no. 1816, 18–19 November 1624). The Camer van Charitate provided the children it placed in apprenticeship with a subsidy sufficient to bring up their earnings to twenty to twenty-three stuivers a week.

[e]Jonas Verburch was inscribed as an oil painter in the Master List of 1613. See F.D.O. Obreen, *Archief voor Nederlandsche Kunstgeschiedenis*, 7 vols. (Rotterdam, 1877–1890), 1:4). For an example of his mark, see Records of Notary Adriaan van Twelle, no. 1654, 26 June 1627.

Jansz., Aryen Jacobsz. Corsendonck I, Pieter Mathysz. Pastenackel (or Pastenox), Jacob Pouwels van Schooten, Jan Jansz. and Jan Pietersz. Schotelmans (Schoot), and Heinderick Jansz. Verpoort II were all illiterate.[f] However, the most important painting contractors in Delft, named Jacob Jansz. and Jan Jacobsz. Molyn and Willem van Odekercken (who also painted an occasional picture) were quite literate. In a sample of thirty unregistered painters, all apparently working for Delft masters, who appeared before notaries as attestants or witnesses in the period 1613 to 1672, twenty-nine signed in a clearly literate manner and one (Jan Pietersz. Vromans in 1629) in a barely literate way.

I will not dwell on the printers, booksellers, and the bookbinders for whom reading and writing were skills necessary to their trade.

Almost all the master glassmakers, sculptors, and embroiderers were literate.[g] I have only a very small sample of unregistered apprentices in these crafts, from which I can only conclude that a fairly high percentage (perhaps a third) of the unregistered sculptors or stonecarvers were illiterate.

Illiteracy was common among the furniture-painters even when they were masters in the guild. In a sample of twelve masters, I found six who set down their mark in lieu of signature and one who signed so clumsily that he must have been illiterate.

The numbers of both registered and unregistered faienciers are so large and the evidence so readily available in notarial archives that a more systematic study of literacy for this craft is possible. With regard to the master faienciers, I need only report that out of a sample of thirty-nine individuals who joined the guild between 1613 and 1675, all but two signed their name in a more or less literate way. Both of these exceptions—Egbert Jansz. van Swenne, who registered in 1613, and Claes Jansz. van Straten, who registered in 1650—owned faience works. The literacy of apprentices and journeymen in the faienciers' trade is summarized in Table 5.1.

If, as I believe, we can safely assume that the extremely clumsy signatures that I have classified as "illiterate" in the table belong to individuals who really could not read or write, we may conclude from these data that about twice as many faience workers were illiterate as

[f]The *kladschilder* Johannes Druif could sign his name but he wrote so clumsily I suspect that he could neither read nor write.

[g]The only exceptions I found were the glassmaker Jan Jacobsz. (van der Burgh) who was listed in the original Master List of 1613, and the embroiderer Salomon Pietersz. Booms (or Boots) who registered in 1618.

TABLE 5.1
Literacy Among Faience Workers, 1613-1675

	Clear Signature	"Illiterate" Signature	Mark	Total
1613-1619	0	3	11	14
1620-1639	10	2	25	37
1640-1659	19	9	21	49
1660-1675	32	8	44	84
Total	61	22	101	184

SOURCES: Delft MA, Notarial Records, 1613-1675.

were literate. The ratio of literate to illiterate workers seems to have risen up to 1660 and then to have stabilized or declined. It is not clear whether the increase in literacy up to 1660 refects a general tendency for more people in Delft to send their children to school or whether it is indicative of an improvement specific to the industry.

The register of boys in the trades ("Register van Ambachtsjong-ens") of the Camer van Charitate provides information on the apprenticeship of children of poor families that gives us some idea of the relative status of the various crafts. Two registers have been preserved—one for the period 1597 to 1611 and one from 1612 to approximately 1630—in which are recorded the details of each child's apprenticeship and earnings and of the subsidies he or his family received from the Camer. The children assisted by the Camer were sometimes orphans but more often lived with their widowed or deserted mothers. Many of them, particularly in the period 1597 to 1611, were children of immigrants from Flanders.

Out of a total of 275 children "served by the Camer" in the second volume, fifteen were apprenticed to trades belonging to the Guild of St. Lucas. Five boys were sent to learn faience-making, four stonecarving, five furniture-making, and one glassmaking. None were apprenticed (in either register) to painters,[h] printers, or embroiderers (or to silversmiths who are comparable in status to these three occupations). Three cases will be described to give the reader an idea of how this welfare institution operated.

[h]Felix Jansz. was called painter (*schilder*) in the index of names of the second register (no. 54), although he was actually apprenticed to a faiencier (Thomas Jansz.) The clerk's error is probably due to the fact that he was the son of the painter Hans van der Burch (or Verburch) who died young in 1608, leaving several small children.

In 1612, Corstiaen Louys, nine years old, was apprenticed to Thomas Jansz., master faiencier. He was to receive six stuivers a week from the Camer as subsidy and he was given the opportunity of going to school during the period of his apprenticeship. Two years later, in 1614, he went to work for Hans de Wint, also master faiencier. De Wint said that he would put the boy on piecework and that he could earn three-and-a-half to four gulden a week. He no longer needed a subsidy from the Camer.[6]

On 3 February 1617, the Camer resolved to send Willem Pietersz., fifteen years old, to learn glassmaking with the master Jan Jacobsz. van der Burgh, for three years. He was to receive a subsidy of ten stuivers from the Camer in the first year, nothing thereafter. His master committed himself to provide him with food and clothing and to teach him the trade for the entire three years.[7] Jan Korssen, sixteen years old, went to work in June 1613 for the well-known sculptor and architect Adriaen Willebortsz. van Weena. In the first year he was slated to earn six stuivers per week and to receive a subsidy of sixteen stuivers per week from the Camer.[8] In general, the Camer saw to it that the family (usually the mother) of boys of fourteen to eighteen received a total of twenty to twenty-three stuivers per week between their earnings and the subsidy. While young children—starting at age six—were sometimes subsidized for a number of years, adolescent boys could expect to earn enough to dispense with the Camer's help after one or two years of apprenticeship.

The reason why children assisted by the Camer were not apprenticed to painters, printers, or embroiderers is obvious: these were higher-status trades, whose masters demanded more money to train a boy than the Camer could afford. The period required before a boy could earn his keep was also much longer than in the common trades.

Four apprenticeship contracts of embroidery-workers from this early period have survived, which give an idea of the training costs that parents had to bear. In the first, dated 18 October 1608, Pieter van der Heyden, a registered master embroiderer, hired Maerten Fouquier, fourteen years old, for three years. The boy's father committed himself to pay a total sum of 150 gulden to cover learning costs, including drawing lessons, and his son's room and board.[9] In 1621 Jacob van Halmael (registered in the master book of the guild as Jacob van Halma) undertook to teach a boy the embroidery trade for two years at a cost of 100 gulden per year.[10] In 1629 an eleven-year-old boy named Jan Bruynsz. was apprenticed to Anthony van Biesen, master of the guild, for a period of seven years, to learn embroidery at a cost to his guardians of fifty gulden per year.[11] It was perhaps a sign of the decline of the embroidery trade that the last apprenticeship contract that I found, dated 25 June 1634, only called for the payment by the guardians of the apprentice's clothing and laundry for the eight-year term, plus, in case the apprentice died, any food costs that might have been incurred by his master up to the boy's death.[12]

Apprenticeship contracts for artist-painters are described in detail in the next chapter. From these contracts and from other mentions of debts for art lessons in estate papers, I conclude that a pupil living at home might expect to pay anywhere from 20 to 50 gulden a year and one living with his master anywhere from 50 to 110 gulden. Even at the lower range, for an apprentice living with his master the amount paid by the parent or guardian was about twice as large as the subsidy given by the Camer van Charitate to the family of the boy who had been apprenticed to a glassmaker. We should also keep in mind that being apprenticed to a glassmaker was a good deal more promising than going to work as a spinner or chair-maker, which was a much more common assignment by the Camer.

We can estimate from these contracts that the total cost, including schooling, of training a boy for six years until he became master embroiderer or painter in the guild or could travel as a journeyman on his own and practice one of these occupations was of the order of 300 to 350 gulden. In addition to these direct costs, we have to figure in the earnings of the apprentice in a lower-status occupation which he had to forego in learning the higher-status trade. If we assume that, from the age of fifteen on, he could earn as an apprentice faiencier two gulden more a week than his parents had to expend on feeding and clothing him, the foregone cost would amount to about 100 gulden a year, or 300 gulden from age fifteen to age eighteen.[i] The total direct and indirect costs of training the boy were then in the neighborhood of 600 to 700 gulden. This expense was roughly equal

---

[i]On weekly boarding costs, see above, note d. An adult apprentice earned about eighteen stuivers a day. A boy of fifteen was able to earn at least twelve stuivers a day, or seventy-two stuivers a week. (This is somewhat less, as we have just seen, than the amount Hans de Wint claimed that a thirteen-year-old boy should be able to earn on piecework). His earnings, after the deduction of upkeep, were then about forty to fifty stuivers a week or over 100 gulden a year.

to the average price of houses bought or sold by apprentices and journeymen in the faience industry (see Table 5.2).

The sacrifices that an ordinary journeyman or even a master furniture-maker had to make to bring his boy up so that he could accede to one of the higher-status trades in the guild were heavy enough. But in addition he had to take into account that these sacrifices would be in vain if the boy died before maturity, as very many did in those times. It is no wonder then that few children of artisans who worked in lower-status occupations ever gained access to the more prestigious trades in the guild.

HOUSES

While people with similar incomes may elect to live in houses of widely disparate market values—I need only mention the size of the family as a critical variable— the prices of houses bought and sold and the rents paid for housing probably reflect differences in income and wealth at least as well as any alternative at our disposal. There is also more evidence with which to work in the area of housing with respect to prices, rents, and taxes, than in the case of any other indicator. For the years 1597 to 1644, all real-estate transactions in Delft were recorded in the books of the Camer van Charitate, which collected a tax of one *duijt* (doit) per gulden or 0.625 percent of the value of property sold.[13] I shall make use of the books covering the years 1620 to 1644, which may be considered a homogeneous sample despite the slight upward trend in prices of houses during this twenty-four-year period. I shall also draw on the "Verponding boeken" of the city of Delft, dated 1620 and 1632, which record municipal property taxes. Finally, I will refer to a small, unsystematically collected sample of house rentals.

Table 5.2 below provides information on the mean (arithmetical average) and the standard deviation of the prices of houses bought and sold within each craft group belonging to the Guild of St. Lucas. My total sample amounts to ninety-seven houses.

The most striking differences in the table are those between the average prices of houses bought or sold by masters (registered members of the guild) and apprentices or journeymen (unregistered).[j]

[j]In the case of the furniture-makers, there is a statistically insignificant difference in favor of the unregistered members, some of whom may have been members of the guild of chair-makers (the registers of which are lost.)

TABLE 5.2

Prices of Houses or Business Establishments Paid by Artists and Artisans of Trades Represented in the St. Lucas Guild (1620-1644)

Occupation	Size of Sample (N)	Mean Price of House or Establishment (gulden)	Estimated Standard Deviation* (gulden)
Painters			
registered	17	1,785	1,383
unregistered	2	275	35
Glassmakers			
registered	9	1,249	600
Printers†			
registered	7	2,300	770
Furniture-painters‡			
registered	6	817	571
unregistered	3	851	996
Faienciers			
registered	20	1,647	1,274
unregistered	33	672	545

SOURCE: Delft, Camer van Charitate, "Reckeningen van de deuijt op de gulden," 1620-1644.

*Computed as the square root of the sum of squared deviations divided by $N - 1$.

†Including bookbinders, book-sellers, and art dealers.

‡Furniture-makers (*stoelgroenders*). In the "Verponding boeken" and in other sources, the individuals registered in the guild as furniture-painters (*stoelverwers*) are generally identified as *stoelgroenders*, never as *stoelverwers*.

The four highest group averages are those of master printers, painters, faienciers, and glassmakers. Our estimated standard deviations in all groups, but particularly for the master painters and faienciers, are quite large so that differences between and among means may easily be due to chance.

To check on the statistical significance of differences between group averages, I made use of standard small-sample formulae.[k] The

[k]First I calculated, for every pair of means i and j, the average standard deviation s_{ij} as follows:

$$s_{ij} = \frac{d_i^2 + d_j^2}{N_i + N_j - 2}$$

where d_i^2 and d_j^2 are respectively the squared deviations from the means of craft

statistically significant differences in the mean prices of housing and business establishments paid by or to the members of various trades in the Guild of St. Lucas are 1) those between printers and allied trades, on the one hand, and glassmakers and furniture-painters on the other; and 2) between registered and unregistered faienciers. The variance among the prices paid by or to painters is so high that even the large difference in the mean prices between painters and furniture-painters is only significant at the 90 percent probability level ($t = 1.6$).

The large dispersions about each of the means that greatly reduce the significance of differences between group means are due not only to group disparities in wealth and family-size but also to a technical factor. Many of the richer residents of Delft who already possessed a house bought second and third houses as an investment. In many cases, these houses were less expensive than their own house, which may not have been on the market during the period under consideration. Thus, when I record the price of a secondary house, which has actually been leased by another individual, as if it were the principal residence of a painter, printer, or other master, I impart a downward bias to the average for that group. This bias could only be eliminated by research into each particular transaction, which I have not been able to carry out.

The prices of houses bought or sold by registered painters ranged from 500 gulden (sold by Cornelis de Man, twenty-one years old, registered in the guild in the same year 1642) to 6,000 gulden (bought by the art dealer Abraham de Cooge in 1644). Among the high prices may be cited the houses bought or sold by Anthony Palamedes (3,400 gulden in 1638), Willem Jacobsz. Delff (chiefly an engraver, but registered with the painters in the guild's master list, 3,200 gulden in 1631), and Michiel Jansz. Miereveld (2,010 gulden in 1639). The median price was 1,383 gulden, somewhat lower than the mean of the sample (1,785 gulden). The two prices that turned up in the source for

---

groups i and j, and N_i and N_j are their sample sizes. I then computed t-values as follows:

$$t = \frac{\overline{X_i} - \overline{X_j}}{s_{ij}} \sqrt{\frac{N_i N_j}{N_i + N_j}}$$

where $\overline{X_i}$ and $\overline{X_j}$ are the means of the taxes paid by representatives of groups i and j. Standard tables were then used to ascertain whether differences between group means were statistically significant at the 90 and 95 percent levels of probability.

houses purchased or sold by an unregistered painter (250 gulden in 1638 and 300 gulden in 1642) are lower than the lowest price for any registered painter.

The prices paid by or to delftware potters or faienciers are also heterogeneous. In this category, a group of six high-priced observations may be singled out that represent the purchase or sale of delftware potteries, ranging from 2,590 to 3,614 gulden and averaging 3,267 gulden. When this group is excluded, the fourteen remaining observations average 1,068 gulden, still 398 gulden over the average for unregistered faienciers. When the prices of potteries are excluded, the average for the remaining faienciers is significantly smaller than the average for the printers.

Even though the property tax statistics for 1620 and 1632 are based on a larger sample than those of housing prices in Table 5.2, these data are still marred by their high variances, which limit the number of statistically significant differences between group means.

For my first comparison, I drew on real-estate taxes from the "Verponding boek" of 1620, covering the years 1620 to 1631, levied on individuals active in eight trades or professions, only three of which are represented in the Guild of St. Lucas (painters, glassmakers, and faienciers). In the case of these three trades I have recorded exclusively the taxes paid by individuals registered in the guild.

The standard deviation of the difference between the mean taxes paid by painters and the mean for each of the other trades or professions separately was calculated and was then used to test the significance of the difference between each pair of means. The mean taxes paid by the pinmakers, the carpenters, and the glassmakers turned out to be significantly lower than the mean taxes paid by painters (at the 95 percent probability or better).[1] The mean for the apothecaries was significantly higher than the mean for painters. In our sample, the painters paid somewhat higher taxes, on the average, than the faienciers, but the difference was not statistically significant ($t = 1.15$). There was no significant difference between the mean taxes paid by painters, silversmiths, and notaries.

The coefficient of variation (the standard deviation divided by the mean, expressed in percentage terms) is fairly high throughout—in excess of 50 percent for several of the trades represented in Table 5.3.

[1]The *t*-values of differences with respect to painters were 2.82 for the pinmakers, 4.5 for the carpenters, 2.0 for the glassmakers, and 3.65 for the apothecaries.

TABLE 5.3

Real-Estate Taxes Paid by Representatives of Eight Trades or Professions
(1620 to 1631)

Occupation	Size of Sample (N)	Mean Taxes Paid (stuivers)	Estimated Standard Deviation* (stuivers)
Painters	39	177.8	102.5
Glassmakers	10	110.8	42.9
Faienciers	14	142.8	80.9
Pinmakers	5	44.0	20.8
Carpenters	39	103.2	62.6
Notaries	12	196.0	103.7
Apothecaries	7	340.6	133.9
Silversmiths	10	179.6	77.4

SOURCE: Delft, MA, "Legger van der verpondingen op den huysen ende gronden,"
1620.

NOTE: When an individual appears more than once in the source, the highest tax
paid on any of the houses he owned or rented was used in the calculations. All
painters, glassmakers, and faienciers in the samples listed were registered members of
the Guild of St. Lucas.

*Computed as the square root of the sum of the squared deviations from the mean
divided by $(N - 1)$.

This is a reflection of the heterogeneity of the individuals grouped in
these categories. Among the carpenters, for instance, there were
well-off masters paying as much as nine or ten gulden (180 or 200
stuivers) taxes on their houses; the bulk of the carpenters, however,
paid two to four gulden (40 to 80 stuivers). Most of the individuals
designated in the source as apprentices (*knechts*) or as workers
(*opermen*) were taxed less than forty stuivers. At the other end of the
scale, we may mention a burgomaster taxed twenty-two gulden ten
stuivers; surgeons—a sample of seven individuals—who averaged
twelve gulden eight stuivers; and an attorney (*advocat*) who paid
thirteen gulden eight stuivers.

The data collected from the 1632 "Verponding boek" allow us to
analyze in greater detail the taxes paid by artists and artisans in trades
subsumed under the St. Lucas Guild. The results are summarized in
Table 5.4.

Because of the high variance within each group and of the small size
of the samples collected in most groups, few differences between the

mean taxes paid by the various trades in Table 5.4 can be shown to be statistically significant. Even the large observed difference between the means for printers (215 stuivers) and for glassmakers (151 stuivers) is barely significant at the 90 percent level of probability ($t = 1.82$). The difference in the mean taxes paid by painters and glassmakers could also be due to chance ($t = 1.34$), but it too may reflect a real gap. The taxes paid by the registered furniture-painters do appear to be significantly lower on average than those paid by printers ($t = 2.93$). The most revealing and significant difference, however, is between the taxes paid by faienciers in the guild and apprentices, journeymen, and other practitioners of this craft who were not registered in the guild. The difference of over five gulden between the two means is significant at the 99 percent probability level. It supports the conjecture stated earlier that the great majority of the *plateelbackers* who were not registered in the guild were relatively poor apprentices and journeymen. The taxes they paid on

TABLE 5.4

Real-Estate Taxes Paid by Artists and Artisans in Trades Represented in the St. Lucas Guild (1632–early 1650s)

Occupation	Size of Sample (N)	Mean Taxes Paid (stuivers)	Estimated Standard Deviation* (stuivers)
Painters			
registered	34	193.6	97.6
Glassmakers			
registered	11	151.0	78.8
Printers and allied trades			
registered	7	215.0	68.4
Furniture-painters			
registered	4	103.2	41.3
unregistered	5	85.6	57.6
Faienciers			
registered	22	163.5	154.9
unregistered	64	62.0	46.0

SOURCE: Delft, MA, "Legger van der verpondingen op den huysen ende gronden," 1632.

*Computed as the square root of the sum of the squared deviations from the mean divided by $(N - 1)$.

TABLE 5.5
House Rent Paid by Painters (1628-1674)
(In Gulden per Year)

Name	Amount	Year
Artist-painters		
Willem Jansz. Decker	98	1628
Jan Willemsz. Decker	130	1632
Pieter Groenewegen	1,380	1633
Simon de Vlieger	{ 108	1634
	130	1638
Herman van Bolgersteyn	180	1639
Corstiaen Couwenbergh	100*	1647
Emanuel de Witte	{ 192	1647
	140	1650
Adam Pick	300	1654
Pieter van Asch	108	1655
Daniel Vosmaer	80	1665
Mean (excluding Groenewegen)	142	
Painters-in-the-rough		
Willem van Odekercken	84	1648
Jacob Pauwels van Schoten	100	1657
Abraham Corsendonck	44	1668
Uytterant B. Post	38	1670
Aryen Bodan (or Boude)	40	1673
Johannes Molyn	100	1674
Mean	69	

SOURCE: Delft, MA, Notarial records.

NOTE: In cases where more than one figure was available for a given painter, his average rent was used to represent him in the calculation of the average for the entire group.

*Rent charged by Couwenbergh (Records of Notary Jacob Spoors, no. 1674, 16 October 1647).

their houses were typically of the order of twenty-four to thirty-six stuivers, on a par with ordinary carpenters and masons.

The highest tax recorded for any painter was twenty-one gulden, or 420 stuivers, paid by Abraham de Cooge, who is known to have painted grisailles and decorated faience but who seems to have earned most of his income as a dealer in paintings and other luxury objects, including organs and tulip bulbs (in the late 1630s). Leonaert Bramer, who was probably the best-known painter in Delft in the 1630s with the possible exception of the aged Michiel Miereveld,[m] was runner-up with sixteen gulden.

The only available evidence on rentals or leases comes from notarial records. I have collected a sample of sixteen contracts involving painters and a dozen cases for all the other crafts combined. The complete list of painters' leases and their dates is shown in Table 5.5.

The average rent for artist-painters in this sample was 266 gulden. But this figure was so influenced by the extremely high rent paid by Pieter Groenewegen[n] that an average excluding this outlying observation may be more meaningful. Excluding Groenewegen's rent, the average rent falls to 142 gulden per year, which comes much closer to the median of the entire sample of artist-painters (130 gulden). The average for the painters-in-the-rough (*kladschilders*) was sixty-nine gulden. The difference between the two groups was statistically significant at a high level of probability (even when the high rent paid by Groenewegen was left out). The separation of the two groups of painters helps to reduce the variance in the sample but by no means eliminates it. In addition to talent and commercial success, inherited wealth (e.g., Groenewegen) and lucrative side occupations (e.g., Adam Pick, innkeeper) also influenced the amount of rent painters could afford to pay.

I have very little information on the rents paid by masters in other trades subsumed under the guild. As to apprentices and journeymen employed by master faienciers and stonecarvers, the rents they paid were low, as we should expect. In a sample of six such individuals the range of rents paid was from thirty to fifty gulden per year.

---

[m]Miereveld paid twenty gulden three stuivers in the 1620 "Verponding boek," the highest tax paid by any painter in the 1620s. Many of the lesser-known painters, however, such as Peter Anthonisz. Bronckhorst (religious scenes) and Joris Gerritsz. van Lier (still-lifes) seem to have lived in low-taxed, inexpensive houses. Furthermore, some of the painting contractors (*kladschilders*) such as Jacob Molyn and his son Jan Jacobsz. paid relatively high taxes (twelve gulden and fourteen gulden five stuivers respectively). The young Molyn succeeded his father as "town painter." Both received lucrative contracts from the city.

[n]The lease contract states that Christoffel Huygensz. van der Schie leases to Pieter Anthonisz. van Groenewegen "Het Gouden Hooft" near the Fish Market for three years at 230 pounds *Vlaems* a year (1,380 gulden), payable each quarter (Records of Notary Willem van Assendelft, no. 1857, 28 December 1633). The rent is so high that it seems possible the house was intended to lodge the extended Groenewegen family, including his father, Anthony van Groenewegen, who was a successful attorney in Delft and The Hague.

DEATH DONATIONS AND THE VALUE OF ESTATES

When an individual died in seventeenth-century Delft, the Camer van Charitate sent a chest to the house of the deceased in which his or her relatives were supposed to place the best upper (or outer) garment (*beste opperste kleed*) that he or she had possessed. After the chest had gone back to the Camer, the relatives could "redeem" the garment by paying its value to the Camer.[°] These donations provide a measure of the wealth of the deceased, although the fact that the amount of the donation was more or less optional and was presumably influenced by the religious faith and civic commitment of the donors introduces a significant source of variance that may affect our comparison of the averages of the various groups in the guild.

Perhaps the most significant statistic in Table 5.6 is the percentage of nondonors—deceased persons whose names are mentioned but who contributed nothing to the Camer—in the sample of observations for each trade. The median donation is also a more representative average measure than the arithmetic mean because it eliminates the upward bias due to isolated, unusually large donations, particularly evident in the case of registered faienciers. The rank orders of the percentage of nondonors in each sample, starting from the lowest, and of the median donation, starting from the highest, are in perfect agreement for all groups with a sample size of nine or more individuals. (The statistics for the furniture-painters, embroiderers, and sculptors may be discounted, being based on very small samples with a high variance.) The rank order begins, as usual, with the printers (no nondonors, median 440 stuivers), followed by the painters (eight nondonors out of thirty-one, median 120 stuivers), the registered faienciers (five nondonors out of eleven, median 100 stuivers), the glassmakers (six nondonors out of nine, median zero), and the unregistered faienciers (nine nondonors out of eleven, median zero). This is of course the same rank order we have already found in the case of our other indicators of economic status. The large differences between the statistics for registered and unregistered artisans in the case of faienciers and furniture-painters are also noteworthy.

While much can be inferred from the estate papers (*boedels*) of a

---

[°]The system did not always operate in this manner. Wealthy people made donations in their will which were then paid by the heirs or trustees of the estate directly to the Camer. As the century wore on, moreover, it would seem as if money donations were more often collected directly, irrespective of the wealth of the deceased.

TABLE 5.6

Value of the Death Donations to the Camer van Charitate by Artists and Artisans in Trades Represented in the St. Lucas Guild (1620–1649)
(In Stuivers)

Occupation	Sample Size	Mean Donation, All Observations	Median Donation, All Observations	Number of Nondonors	Mean Donation, Exclusive of Nondonors
Painters					
registered	31	339	120	8	457
Glassmakers					
registered	9	23	0	6	68
Printers					
registered	10	518	440	0	518
Furniture-painters					
registered	4	50	40	2	100
unregistered	4	6	13	3	25
Faienciers					
registered	11	447*	100	5	821*
unregistered	11	59	0	9	325†
Embroiderers					
registered	3	413‡	240	1	620‡
Sculptors					
registered	5	426	65	2	710

SOURCE: Delft, Camer van Charitate, "Opperste Kleed Boeken," 1620–1649.

NOTE: In the case of the even-numbered samples, the median was computed as the average of the middle two observations.

*The very large bequest (200 Gulden or 4,000 stuivers) by the faiencier Hans de Wint (a former lance-maker) imparts a strong upward bias to the average.

†Based on an average of two donations, one of 600 stuivers and the other of 50 stuivers.

‡Based on an average of three observations amounting to 240, 0, and 1,000 stuivers respectively. This last donation was contributed by Willem Jorisz. Roscam, a rich cloth merchant, who may have registered in the guild as an amateur rather than as a full-time embroiderer.

particular individual, the information does not lend itself to aggregation and to statistical analysis. The papers are far from homogeneous in content. Some include only inventories of movable possessions, some only of real estate holdings and of financial papers. If the inventory is present, the goods listed in it may not be priced. The net worth of the estate, including the value of debts due to and by it, is rarely supplied. For these reasons, I have chosen to describe in some detail a few representative *boedels* rather than present averages based on very small samples and incomplete information.

We may begin with Willem Jacobsz. Delff and his father-in-law Michiel Miereveld, respectively the most successful engraver and painter in Delft in the first three decades of the seventeenth century. Willem Jacobsz. died on 14 April 1638. When his movable goods were sold at auction by the *boelhuysmeester* in January 1640, they brought a total of 2,516 gulden 6 stuivers.[14] Of the 461 valued inventories that I have collected, only 28 were of this size or greater.[P] The value of the paintings and prints sold amounted to nearly 300 gulden or a little over 10 percent of the total.

The goods left behind by Michiel Miereveld, who died on 30 June 1641, were probably not sold at auction, and we have no *contracedulle* (list of auction prices) for his possessions. However, we have detailed information about his other assets. He owned two houses, one of which, as we have already seen, was worth 2,010 gulden. Another was leased for 180 gulden a year. He owned ten parcels of land, from three to ten hectares in size, that were rented out to farmers and brought him a combined income of 1,237 gulden a year. He held debentures or bonds (*obligatien*) issued by the States General, the Province of Holland and other bodies amounting to 14,500 gulden, which yielded about 900 gulden in interest a year. Various other interest-bearing debts incurred by private individuals brought him another 250 gulden a year. Thus, he enjoyed a yearly revenue, from his capital assets alone, of over 2,500 gulden. At his death 5,829 gulden in cash were found in his house. We do not know how much he earned from his paintings each year, but the finished portraits—delivered and undelivered—for which he was owed money at the time of his death were valued at nearly 1,200 gulden.[15] Miereveld clearly belonged to the wealthiest stratum of the bourgeoisie in Delft.

We have information also on three artist-painters who earned a fairly good living but were not as rich as Miereveld or Willem Jacobsz.

[P]If anything, the inventories in my sample overrepresent the large estates, since I did not systematically collect the *boedels* of poor people who owned few or no paintings.

TABLE 5.7
Value of Movable Goods of Three Artist-Painters

Name	Date	Total Value of Goods (gulden)	Value of Paintings and Artists' Materials (gulden)
Willem Jansz. Decker	1624	857*	343*
Hans Jordaens	1630	1,265	1,067
Cornelis Daemen Rietwijck	1660	1,172	180

SOURCES: Decker: Orphan Chamber, *boedel* no. 446; Jordaens: Records of Notary Willem de Langue, no. 1686, 3 July 1630; Rietwijck: Orphan Chamber, *boedel* no. 1428 I.

*Including various items sold privately (outside auction).

Delff. These were Willem Jansz. Decker (d. 1624), Hans Jordaens (d. 1630), and Cornelis Damen Rietwyck (d. 1660). Since we have a *contracedulle* of the movable goods for all three and since these goods represent the bulk of their assets, a summary comparison of their levels of wealth is possible.

That paintings comprised such a very high share of the value of Hans Jordaens's possessions is puzzling. Perhaps the sale of his possessions, which had been ordered by his widow, failed to include some of his goods. It is hard to believe that a man who held such a valuable stock of paintings[q] owned no silver or pewter and that his clothes were limited to "one gray and one black cloth mantle." These items of clothing were perhaps just those that his widow had no use for and therefore disposed of by auction.

The next inventory is that of a painter who died poor. The still-life painter Evert van Aelst, the uncle of the better-known Willem van Aelst, had enjoyed considerable success in Delft, at least if we may judge from the large number of his works listed in contemporary inventories, including those of rich collectors. Nevertheless, when he died in February 1657, he was renting rooms from a tailor and he owned little else besides his panels, easel, and other artists' materials. "A bed, some clothes, two portraits, and various odds and ends (*rommeling*)" was little to show for a life of work. His nephew Willem, who was living in Amsterdam, thought that these few goods were not worth collecting and "repudiated" the estate in April of the same

[q]Very few of the paintings were attributed in the inventory. I presume that most of the unattributed ones were painted by Jordaens.

year.[16] Pieter van der Vin, a little-known artist-painter who studied with Emanuel de Witte, seems to have been bankrupt when he died in 1655. His *desolaet boedel*, which was sold at auction for 192 gulden 4 stuivers, comprised paintings that brought 93 gulden 7 stuivers.[17] Judging from the clothing and the low value of bedding in the sale, I should think that he was fairly poor even before his creditors seized his assets.

Printers, as we have had several occasions to show, formed the wealthiest group of masters in the guild. Jan Pietersz. Walpoth, whose establishment was located on the Market Place between the Town Hall and the New Church, was among the more successful representatives of his profession. When he died in October 1667, he owned, in addition to his large house and printing shop, some 21,000 gulden worth of debentures, a staggering amount by Delft standards.[18] He was also owed fairly large amounts for books delivered in Delft and elsewhere and he had a large inventory of books in stock. We unfortunately do not have the *contracedulle* of his rich inventory of movable goods.

Simon Cloeting (d. 29 July 1676), bookbinder and bookseller, was less wealthy. His possessions were more typical of the book trade as a whole. He owned obligations valued at 1,630 gulden and about 350 gulden in cash. Some of his furniture, paintings, and clothes were sold at auction for 585 gulden, which represented about half of the total value of his movable goods.[19] I should judge that he was about as well-off as the middle group of artist-painters listed in Table 5.5. His brother Ludolf Cloeting, also a bookseller, who died in 1669, was apparently somewhat richer than he was, even though he himself was not registered in the guild, perhaps because he worked with Andries Jansz. Cloeting who *was* a member of the guild. He owned debentures totaling nearly 5,000 gulden, which put him in the class of rich notaries and silversmiths, just below the richest brewers and merchants of Delft.[20] I did not find any estate papers of really poor printers or booksellers. The apparent absence or rarity of such individuals may explain why the averages for the group in Tables 5.2 to 5.5 were so high.

Most owners of faience works—the closest thing to capitalists in the guild—had both large assets and liabilities arising from their heavy needs for capital. Their assets also were differently distributed from those of well-off painters in that they invested in their own establishments rather than in fixed-yield obligations and spent relatively little on the embellishment of their households. A typical instance is that of

Lambrecht Ghysbrechtsz. Kruijck whose assets, when his wife died in 1641, amounted to 22,626 gulden and his liabilities to 11,245 gulden. The estate's net worth was then just over 11,000 gulden. Among the assets were a house estimated at 4,000 gulden, faience works at 6,000 gulden, merchandise at 1,521 gulden, and 220 gulden in cash. The household goods of the couple were evaluated at only 900 gulden.[21]

When Jannetge Hendricxdr., the widow of the master faiencier Jeronimus Pietersz. van Kessell and the wife of Ary Jansz. van Hamme, died in 1667, a complete accounting was made of her estate, including the faience works called "De Vergulde Astonnens." The assets totaling 9,367 gulden were made up of a house and *plateelback-erie*, together worth 6,000 gulden; household goods and merchandise, 1967 gulden; unbaked faiencewares, 200 gulden; and debts due to the estate, 1,200 gulden. The liabilities, consisting chiefly of obligations for capital borrowed for the business, amounted to 16,072 gulden, leaving a negative worth of 6,705 gulden.[22]

Whether or not the master faienciers owned assets that exceeded their liabilities, they had command over substantial resources and lived on a scale that was far higher than that of their employees. We have already seen that a *knecht* earned eighteen to twenty-five stuivers a day in the 1640s. If he had two or three children, he could barely feed his family, and his opportunities to accumulate any significant assets were slight. When these decorators on faience or dish-turners died, they generally left very modest estates (even though most of them were still larger than those of many miserably poor people who died in Delft whose assets consisted of some sacks, a table, and a few pieces of earthenware). A few instances are listed in Table 5.8.

The larger estates listed in Table 5.8 were those of owners of houses (the value of which was included in their assets) and of workers who had long been established in the industry. Dirck van der Cram and Maerten Pietersz., for instance, were houseowners who had been active over twenty years in the industry by the time they died. Maerten Pietersz.'s house was valued at 250 gulden or almost half of his widow's assets. Grietgen Pietersdr., the widow of Joost Cornelisz., at the time of her death owned movable goods worth only 19 gulden 9 stuivers, but her house, valued at 518 gulden, brought her estate up to 537 gulden. Similarly, the value of Tobias Esch's house, estimated at 488 gulden, represented the bulk of his estate of 600 gulden. The poorer *knechts* did not own a house but rented a room or two: their estates, accordingly, were extremely meager.

TABLE 5.8

Estates Left by Faienciers' *Knechts* or Their Widows (1638-1670)

Name	Date	Assets (gulden)	Liabilities (gulden)	Net Worth (gulden)
Widow of Maerten Pietersz.	1638	517	221	296
Diert Jacobsz.	1644	326	144	182
Pieter Jansz. van Rijn	1651	80	84	−4
Dirck van der Cram	1652	489	280	209
Tobias Phillips Esch	1660	600	531	69
Willem Dassonvylle	1662	162	n.a.	n.a.
Corstiaen Pietersz. van den Burch	1663	104	n.a.	n.a.
Hendrick Dasonville	1666	88	n.a.	n.a.
Widow of Joost Cornelisz.	1667	537	n.a.	n.a.
Michiel Jansz. Soete*	1669	523	592	−69
Widow of Josua Peltier	1670	24	n.a.	n.a.
Frans Jacobsz. Rotshouck	1670	17	n.a.	n.a.

SOURCES: Notarial records in Delft MA for all estates except those of the widow of Joost Cornelisz. (Orphan Chamber, *boedel* no. 281) and Tobias Esch (Orphan Chamber, *boedel* no. 565).

NOTE: All assets and liabilities are rounded off to the nearest gulden.

*The estate was "repudiated" by Soete's heirs.

OVERVIEW

In Delft, as elsewhere, a young boy's chances in life depended on his parents' ability to finance his training. If he was poor, as were the wards of the Camer van Charitate, the best he could hope for, within the range of trades encompassed in the Guild of St. Lucas, was to become apprenticed to a glassmaker or a furniture-maker. If he survived adolescence, as many of these poor boys did not, and he was eventually admitted to the guild as a master glassmaker or furniture-maker, he would then accede to the status of the fourth or fifth rank of masters listed in descending order of economic status. It was much more likely for him to be apprenticed to a faiencier or a stonecarver and to remain a *knecht* all his life. To become an artist-painter was not normally within his reach. Painters either were from families who could afford the relatively high cost of the six-year training or were themselves the sons of painters.

Artists and artisans in Delft can be divided into four broad economic and social groups, the first two consisting of registered members of the guild and the last two of nonmembers.

The first group includes: 1) successful artists (e.g., the painters

[133]

Anthony Palamedes, Leonaert Bramer, and Michiel Miereveld, the engraver Willem Jacobsz. Delff, the stonecarver and architect Adriaen Willeboortsz.); 2) wealthy amateurs (e.g., the painters Arent van Renoy and Adriaen Arentsz. Gouda, the embroiderer Willem Jorisz. Roscam); 3) art dealers (e.g., Abram de Cooge and Reynier Jansz. Vermeer, the father of Johannes Vermeer); 4) owners of print and book shops (e.g., Jan Andriesz. Cloeting, Felix van Sambich de Jonge, Jan Pietersz. Walpoth); and 5) owners of delftware potteries (e.g., Heyndrick Marcellis van Gogh, Lambert Ghisbrechtsz. Kruck, Aelbrecht Keyser). This was the aristocracy of the guild, living in houses that cost 2,000 or more gulden, paying ten to twenty-five gulden in property taxes, and, if they retained their status until the end of their life, bequeathing fifty gulden or more to the Camer van Charitate upon their death. The value of the assets in their estates could easily exceed 15 to 20,000 gulden; however, their liabilities, especially in the case of the faienciers, were often also large, due to their heavy capital requirements. Most of the headmen of the guild were picked from this group. Their status was comparable to that of notaries, surgeons, silversmiths, and successful merchants.

The second group is made up of less successful artists in the guild—housepainters, glassmakers, most sculptors and embroiderers, printers and faienciers not established on their own, and at the lower end of the scale for this group, the furniture-makers. They typically lived in houses costing 800 to 1,500 gulden, paid three to seven gulden in taxes on their houses, and left small amounts to the Camer van Charitate upon their death. The value of the movable goods in their estates was generally also in the 800 to 1,500 gulden range. A number of the guild members in this group became headmen, especially from among the glassmakers, who were guaranteed two places on the list of headmen each year, even though their industry had substantially declined in importance since the sixteenth century.

The third group consists of artists and artisans who were not registered in the guild, but by virtue of their education and training could aspire to master status. These included the sons of painters working for their fathers, and more generally, apprentices and journeymen who had not yet succeeded in establishing themselves but who could expect eventually to do so (e.g., the painters Mathys Mathisz. Spoors, who was apprenticed to Carel Fabritius and died in the explosion of the Delft powderworks in 1654, Johan Willemsz. Ploij, and Gerbrand Jansz. de Jong). These, like almost all the members of the first two groups, were literate. Little is known about

[134]

their economic circumstances, because most of them lived with their master or with their family and paid no taxes on their own account.

The fourth group, the overwhelming majority of whom were apprentices and journeymen in the delftware industry, may be said to belong to the proletariat of Delft. A majority were either totally illiterate or could only sign their names. They typically lived in "little houses" (*huysgens*) selling for 150 to 300 gulden, paid eighteen to thirty-six stuivers in taxes if they owned a house, or rented for thirty to fifty gulden a year if they did not, and left little or nothing to the Camer when they died. The gross value of their estates rarely exceeded 500 gulden. Within this fourth group, we should perhaps distinguish the long-established workers of the faience industry, some of whom are presumed to have been *meesterknechts* (foremen), whose material conditions were at the upper end of the range for the group as a whole. But even in this subgroup, few if any individuals ever had a chance to set themselves up as independent masters.

When the first two groups are aggregated and all guild members are considered together, significant differences among the various trades show up in our indicators of economic status. The printers, booksellers, and art dealers, on average, seem to have lived in more expensive houses, paid higher taxes, and left larger estates than the representatives of any other trade. The painters were next, then—in descending order—the faienciers, the glassmakers, and the furniture-painters. The relatively low status of the glassmakers may reflect the declining fortune of their industry, which never recovered from the loss of the Church's patronage after the break with Rome.

SIX

Painters in Delft, 1613–1680

This chapter focuses on the painters who were masters in the guild, from 1613, when the first list of members appeared after the promulgation of the new Guild Letter of 1611, to the end of 1679. We shall study the composition of the "painters' guild" in 1613 and 1650, the geographic and social origin of painters, their specialization by subject matter, their training, and their relative success or failure.

Altogether, 206 painters held membership in the guild in this period. According to my estimates, the master painters in the guild numbered forty-seven in 1613, fifty-eight in 1640, fifty-two in 1650, fifty-one in 1660, and thirty-one in 1680.[a] There were an estimated twenty-five artist-painters in the 1613 list and thirty-five in 1650; but only twelve artist-painters can be more or less securely identified as being active in Delft in 1680.[b] At various points in this chapter, I shall comment on the expansion (up to 1640), the stagnation, and the subsequent contraction in the size of the painters' community.

[a]For the method and assumptions used in arriving at these figures, see Chapter 4. The apparent decline in the number of artist-painters from 1650 to 1680 may in part be attributed to the fact that information about guild-registered painters is more limited at the end of this period than at the beginning.
[b]The artist-painters in 1613 have been tallied from Table A.1. The following artist-painters were known or presumed to be active in Delft on 1 January 1650: Willem van den Bundel, Pieter Bronckhorst, Cornelis Rietwijck, Joris Gerzitsz. van Lier, Jonas Verburgh, Willem Jansz. Ploij, Abraham Vromans, Claes Engelen, Johannes van Nes, Gillis de Bergh, Anthony Palamedes, Evert van Aelst, Leonaert Bramer, Dirck van der Mast, Pieter van Asch, Balthasar van der Ast, Heyndrick van Vliet, Adriaen Jaspersz. Pelleman, Andries van der Linde, Pieter Vromans II, Abraham de Cooge (dealer), Mattheus de Bergh, Jacob Delff, Emanuel de Witte, Adam Pick, Abraham Vosmaer, Jacob van Velsen, Herman Steenwijck, Heereman Witmont, Claes Vosmaer, Jochum de Vries, Cornelis van der Plaat, Johannes Songe, Heyndrick van der Burch, and Pieter van der Vin. The artist-painters known or presumed to be active on 1 January 1680 were: Mattheus de Bergh, Cornelis de Man, Gijsbrecht Verbruggen, Abraham Corssendonck, Antony Issendoorn, Pieter Born, Pieter Jansz. van Ruijven, Johannes Verkolje, Michiel van Eemst, Johannes Elsevier, Jan Willemsz. van Spriet, and Johannes Hoendermans.

Forty painters in oil and seven painters in watercolors were listed in the Master Book of 1611-1612. These guild members were by no means all professional artists. Some were housepainters or painters-in-the-rough; some were wealthy amateurs. A number of them left such a faint trace in Delft records—if they left any trace at all—that we cannot even tell whether or not they were artist-painters. The primary specialty of all these painters, their year of birth or death, and their place or origin, to the extent the information could be found, are set down in Table A.1 of Appendix A.

Only the first, third, and fourth names in Table A.1 (Miereveld, Willem Luyt, and Jan Gerbrantsz. de Jong) are recorded in the sixteenth-century accounts of the guild. The fact that three of the first four painters on the list were registered before 1598 and that none of the subsequently listed painters are known to have belonged to the guild before that date suggests that the names appear in order of the date of their accession to the guild.[c] This would explain why the immigrants Hans Jordaen[s] (the Elder) and Pieter Stael appear after some of their younger and less well known colleagues.

Several painters on the list, including Olivier Willemsz., Claes Hals, Jan Pietersz., and Bruijn Jansz. are virtually unknown. Since the few references to them in the notarial archives occur around 1611-1613, I presume they left town, retired, or died only a few years after their inscription.[d] It is unlikely that any of them were artists. They were perhaps itinerant painters of houses, signboards, or other coarse work. They may have been induced to join the guild in the years 1611-1612 because they had to pay only the low entrance fee of the Old Guild Letter (twenty-five stuivers for Delft-born citizens, fifty stuivers for out-of-towners), in what I suppose must have been a period of grace.

A small group of amateurs—Pieter Molshoeck, Reyer Crabmoes, and Arent van Reynoy—may be singled out. Molshoeck and Crabmoes were merchants;[e] the profession, if he had any, of Arent van Reynoy (who is always called "Jonckherr" and must therefore have

[c]The name placed at the head of the faienciers' list, Harman Pietersz., is also the earliest representative of this trade known to have registered in the guild. (above, Chapter 1, Table 1.2). Maerten (Danielsz.), the first sculptor listed in the master book, was already a master in 1596 (above, Chapter 3, p. 89).

[d]A note in the master book indicates that Oliver Williemsz. and Bruijn Jansz. both left town. At some point, Jan Pietersz. went to reside "in St. Jeronimus," an old men's home.

[e]Molshoeck sold cloth (Records of Notary Adriaen Rijshouck, no. 1767, 15 December 1615); Crabmoes went to Spain in 1599 as a merchant (according to his testimony of 11 February 1623 in the Records of Notary Gerard Camerling, no. 1650

been of noble origin) is unknown. Another member of the guild, Pieter den Dorst, may also have been an amateur. In his estate papers, delivered to the Orphan Chamber after his death in 1620, a number of his paintings are described, including a Judith, an Entombment, a Last Supper, a Venus, an Annunciation, and an unfinished portrait of Prince Maurice. The sale of these paintings brought altogether the respectable sum of 134 gulden. None of Den Dorst's works, however, appear under his name in any Delft inventories. Molshoeck, Den Dorst and Arent van Reynoy, who were roughly of the same age, must have been closely acquainted with each other, since the first two signed as witnesses to the third's testament, and Arent van Reynoy acted in the capacity of trustee to Den Dorst's estate, of which he was also one of the heirs via his wife.[f] Jan Pietersz. van Ghilt (or more usually Van Ghils or Gils) may also not have been a full-time professional. When his wife died in early 1621, an inventory was made of his possessions, which, among other valuables, included a long list of paintings with distinguished names (e.g., a Crucifixion by Karel van Mander estimated at 200 gulden and a church interior by Hendrick Steenwijck the Elder for 150 gulden), besides his own paintings, some of which were copied after Dirck Barendsz., Cornelis van Haarlem, and Michiel Miereveld. By this time he had bought the office of process server of the Court of Holland (*deurwaerder van den Hoeve van Hollant*), which was apparently a fairly lucrative position.[1] Finally, as the notes to Table A.1 indicate, Willem Luyt, Jan Gerbrantsz. de Jong, Jan Cornelis Schoonhoven, and Adriaen Rypevelt all appear to have given up painting some time after they were inscribed in the guild.

The distinction between watercolor and oil painters made in the 1613 Master List was short-lived. After 1619, newly registered master

---

II). The former is mentioned once in the notarial protocols as a painter (9 April 1612, Records of Notary Adriaen Rijshouck, no. 1764), at all other times as a merchant or without profession; the latter, who frequently comes up in documents, never appears as a painter. Both were quite well-off (Crabmoes bought a house for 3,500 gulden in 1616; Molshoeck's widow sold her house for 2,900 gulden).

[f]Arent van Reynoy's testament is dated 19 April 1611 (Records of Notary Adriaen Rijshouck, no. 1763). The papers of Pieter den Dorst's estate are conserved in the Orphan Chamber estate papers, *boedel* no. 500. The approximate ages of Van Reynoy and Crabmoes are known from notarial depositions (respectively, 14 November 1620, Records of Notary Gerard Camerling, no. 1650 II; and 30 April 1620, Records of Notary Herman Jansz. van der Ceel, no. 1637). That Molshoeck must have been born in the late 1580s appears probable, given that he married for the first time in March 1608.

painters are no longer called one or the other, with the sole exception of Claes Engelen, who registered as a watercolor painter in 1625. It is remarkable that all the watercolor painters in the master list, including some who registered after 1613, came from Flanders. One likely reason, since tapestry cartoons were usually painted in watercolor on paper, is that a number of them were employed as designers in the tapestry works of Franchoys Spierinx and Karel van Mander the Younger, themselves of Flemish origin who mainly hired artists and artisans from the southern provinces.[8] The fact that tapestry-makers were excluded from the guild by an amendment to the guild letter of 19 October 1620 may explain why watercolor painters, with the single exception noted above, no longer appeared in the register of new masters after 1619.

PLACE OF ORIGIN AND PRIMARY SPECIALTY

In the 1613 list, twelve out of the twenty-five oil painters whose place of origin is known (or at least can be inferred with a certain confidence) came from Delft; five from Gouda, The Hague, Leyden, and Rotterdam; and six from the southern provinces including Maestricht. If we throw in the watercolor painters, thirteen out of thirty-two painters of known origin were born in Flanders.

The consolidated data on the origin of painters in 1613 may be compared with the periods 1613 to 1649 and 1650 to 1679 in Table 6.1.

In comparison with subsequent periods, the low proportion (38 percent) of Delft-born members and the high proportion of members born in Flanders (40 percent) in 1613, both reckoned on the basis of totals excluding painters of totally unknown origin, are quite striking. The high number of members of totally unknown origin in 1613 (15 out of 47) throws some doubt on these comparisons since the proportion of Delft-born members in 1613 would be almost as high as in the two subsequent periods if all the members in the unknown group were merged with the Delft-born group. However, it is unlikely that all these "unknowns" were born in Delft. Moreover, the proportion of members born in Flanders would remain abnormally high in 1613, irrespective of how the unknown group was apportioned. Among the new masters joining the guild in the 1613–1649 period,

[8]Thus I infer from very indirect evidence that Francois Verhulst and Cornelis Pastinocx (or Pastenax) were both tapestry designers.

TABLE 6.1

Geographic Origin of Guild Members Registered as Painters, 1613-1679

Place of Birth	Master List (1613)	New Inscriptions (May 1613 to Dec. 1649)	New Inscriptions (May 1650 to Dec. 1679)	Total (1613-1679)
Delft and its dependencies	12	64	30	106
Outside Delft				
Flanders*	13	5	0	18
Rotterdam	2	3	2	7
Haarlem	0	3	1	4
Dordrecht	0	2	0	2
Gouda	3	0	0	3
The Hague	1	2	1	4
Leyden	1	2	2	5
Amsterdam	0	1	1	2
Other, Holland	0	5	3	8
United Provinces (other than Holland)	0	3†	0	3
Unknown	0	10	11	21
Total "Outside Delft"	20	36	21	77
Unknown	15	5	3	23
Total	47	105	54	206

SOURCE: Obreen, Archief, 1:1–119; Appendix Tables A.1, A.2, and A.3.

NOTE: Delft origin is inferred in most cases from the payment of six-gulden entrance dues into the Guild of St. Lucas (new members originating outside Delft and its dependencies paid twelve gulden). "Dependencies" include Delfshaven, Naaldwijk, and Waelwijk (one new member each originating in these towns paid six gulden as the entrance fee).

*Including Maastricht.   †Two from Middelburg and one from Friesland.

four Flemish immigrants became members in 1613-1641, only one in the period 1615-1649, and none in the period 1650-1679. Delft-born master painters represented 64 percent of the new guild members from 1613 to 1649 and 58 percent from 1650 to 1679 (excluding members of unknown origin). The high proportion of Flemish masters about the year 1613 was evidently an exceptional phenomenon brought on by the great current of migration in the years 1580-1610.

Rotterdam, Leyden, and Haarlem, in that order, supplied the greatest sources of immigrant members from other parts of Holland, but the absolute numbers in all periods were quite small (at most two to three new members from each of these cities in each period). It is remarkable in view of the influence of the Utrecht school on painters such as Corstiaen Couwenbergh and Johannes Vermeer that not a single artist belonging to the Delft guild is known to have originated in Utrecht or its dependencies in the entire period 1613 to 1680. (The flower-painter Balthasar van der Ast did spend some time in Utrecht before registering in Delft, but he was born and began to work as a master in Middelburg.)

Some information is available about the professional specialization of thirty-four members on the 1613 list. One was primarily an engraver (Willem Jacobsz. Delff); five were *kladschilders* who painted houses, signboards, and did other "broad-brush" work; one was probably a decorator on faience (Claes Jacobsz. Spierinckhoeck) and four, including Karel van Mander the Younger, the son of the famous author of the *Schilderboeck*, were designers of tapestries. This leaves twenty independent artist-painters, of whom five are known to have painted chiefly portraits, eight "histories" (Bible, mythology, etc.), two flowers (Jacob Woutersz. Vosmaer and Herman Bolgersteyn) and one fruit still-lifes and "kitchens" (Cornelis Jacobsz. Delff). The specialties of painters who were members of the guild in this and in subsequent periods are summarized in Table 6.2.

The painters who registered in the guild from 1613 to 1649 and from 1650 to 1680 are listed in Tables A.2 and A.3 of Appendix A, together with their primary specialty and their probable place of origin.

Of the 105 painters listed in Table A.2 who became guild masters between 1613 and 1649, five are known to have worked in Delfshaven, the sea outlet of Delft located near Rotterdam. Most of these were broad-brush painters of naval vessels or ship's equipment. This leaves 100 guild members working in Delft or its vicinity. We have some information about the professional specialty of eighty-five of these

TABLE 6.2

Primary Specialty of Guild Members Registered as Painters, 1613–1679

	Master List (1613)	New Inscriptions (May 1613 to Dec. 1649)	New Inscriptions (May 1650 to Dec. 1679)	Total (1613–1679)
Artist-Painters				
Portraits	5	9	4	18
"Histories" (Bible, mythology, history)	8	7	3	18
Landscapes	4	9	3	16
Seascapes	0	4	1	5
Still-lifes (including flowers)	3	14	3	20
Battles	0	3	0	3
"Perspectives" (churches, palaces)	0	4	0	4
Genre	0	6*	3	9
Tapestry designs	4	5	0	9
Amateur	3	0	0	3

Specialty unknown	0	7	5	12
Total	27	68	22	117
Others				
Kladschilders	5	11†	6	22
Art dealers	0	2	1	3
Painters in Delfshaven‡	2§	5‖	2	7
Miscellaneous	0	4‖	3#	9
Total	7	22	12	41
Unknown	13	15	20	48
Grand Total	47	105	54	206

SOURCE: See Table 6.1.

*Including Jacob Fransz. van der Merck, born in Sgravendael, believed to have registered in the guild in 1628 as "Jacob Fransz. van Sgravendael." He was also a portrait painter.

†Including Willem van Odekercken who was chiefly a painting contractor but also painted still-lifes and other subjects.

‡Most painters in Delfshaven painted ships, ship's equipment, and houses.

§One engraver and one decorator on faience.

‖Three faienciers or decorators on faience and one engraver.

#One painter of clock faces, one compass painter, and one decorator on faience.

painters, none about the remaining fifteen. Eleven in the first group were *kladschilders*. I suspect that a large proportion of the unknown group was also in this category.

Fifty-four new members were registered as painters from January 1650 to December 1679. Nothing is known about the specialty of 37 percent of these painters (a higher proportion than in the other two periods). Very few of the painters of unknown specialty are likely to have been artists. Thus the proportion of *kladschilders* in the total number of painters may be substantially higher than the 18 percent ratio of *kladschilders* to painters with a known specialty, which was already higher than in the two previous periods. This high proportion of artisan-painters may be related to the fall in the number of newly registered masters in the 1660s and 1670s. Both may perhaps be explained by the decline of Delft as an artistic center, which must have had a more profound effect on the number of artists than on the number of painters of houses, fences, and armories, the demand for which probably depended on the overall level of the city's economic activity, and was less affected, if it was affected at all, by the causes of the fall in artistic activity.

Important changes also occurred from period to period in the distribution of artist-painters among the primary specialties of Table 6.2. There was a pronounced decline in the relative number of painters specializing chiefly in biblical, mythological, and other "history" paintings (from 30 percent in 1613 to 10 percent of the sixty-one artist-painters with a known specialty in the period 1613 to 1649). The tapestry designers, who were heavily represented in the guild in the first quarter of the century, virtually disappeared, perhaps because the demand for large tapestries with historical subjects declined, perhaps because tapestry-makers in general were no longer expected (or allowed) to become members of the guild after 1620.

The specialties that made relative gains from 1613 to 1649 were landscape and still-life painting. Those that first developed after 1613 included the painting of seascapes, battle scenes, "perspectives" (churches and palaces), and "genre" scenes.[h] If we are willing to treat painters of seascapes and battle scenes as landscape-painters, the difference between the pre- and post-1613 period becomes especially salient. Sixteen landscape painters of all sorts became members of the guild from 1613 to 1649, or 26 percent of the total number of newly

[h]Seascape painting was already a well-established genre in Haarlem by 1613 (Hendrick Vroom, Adam Willaerts). Hans Vredeman de Vries (born in Leeuwarden), Hendrick Steenwijck the Elder (Antwerp), and Pieter Neefs the Elder (Antwerp) practiced "perspective" painting in Flanders before this date.

Fig. 5 Anthony Palamedes, Corps-de-Garde Scene (1653), 18¾ x 25 in. Art Trade (1978), The Hague (Photo: A. Dingjan)

registered artists with a known specialty, as against only four landscape painters who were members of the guild in 1613, representing not quite 15 percent of the number of masters with known specialties. The landscape specialty seems to have receded slightly in the period 1650 to 1679, but the numbers in this last period are so small that no firm inference can be drawn from relatively small differences.

The apparent fall in the relative importance of artists specialized in "perspective" painting from the period 1613 to 1649 to the period 1650 to 1679 is misleading. In fact three out of four of the painters in this category who registered before 1650 (Hendrick van Vliet, Geeraert Houckgeest, and Emanuel de Witte) developed the art of painting church interiors chiefly after 1650. This said, it is remarkable that they had no pupils or followers in the genre who joined the guild after the mid-century point.

The newly registered members who specialized in genre painting—starting with Anthony Palamedes in 1621 (fig. 5)—represented 11 percent of the artist-painters with a known specialty from 1613 to 1649; their proportion rose to 18 percent in the period 1650 to 1679 when the painting of "society pieces" reached its high point in Holland. These changes in the relative importance of artistic specialties mirrored changes in taste and fashion. On the other hand, there must have been a fairly steady demand for portraits, which were less subject to the vagaries of taste. Not surprisingly the relative importance of portraits, as measured by the number of new inscriptions who specialized in this branch, fell when Delft's importance as an artistic center grew from 1613 to 1649 and many painters practicing new specialties were attracted to the city, and then rose again (from 15 percent of the number of artists with known specialty in 1613 to 1649 to 24 percent from 1650 to 1679) once the burst of activity was over.

The misleading impression may have been given so far that painters had an exclusive specialty. Many of them did; but a number were many-sided. Painters with widely differing primary specialties such as Anthony Palamedes (genre), Hendrick van Vliet ("perspectives"), Bramer and Linschoten ("histories") also painted portraits, probably because they were a fairly reliable source of income. Some were quite eclectic. Carel Fabritius painted "histories," portraits, "perspectives," and still-lifes.[1] Bramer did landscapes and still-lifes in addition to

---

[1] A still-life by Fabritius (almost surely Carel) was in the inventory of Pieter C. Mole, wine merchant, who died on 7 October 1658 (Records of Notary Govert Rota, no. 1989, 4 December 1658).

Fig. 6 Leonaert Bramer, Judgment of Solomon (1630s), 31⅛ × 40½ in. The Metropolitan Museum of Art, Gift of National Surety Co., 1911 (Photo: Museum)

portraits and religious and mythological pictures (fig. 6).[j] Vermeer's small *oeuvre* includes townscapes as well as religious scenes, genre pictures, and portraits. On the basis of rather casual observation, I conjecture that early training in painting "histories" allowed painters to switch fairly easily from one type of painting to another, whereas painters who began their career by specializing in more mundane subjects were tethered to their specialty. Such was the case at least for the still-life painters Pieter and Harmen Steenwijck, Cornelis Jacobsz. Delff, and Willem van Aelst; and the landscape painters Willem van den Bundel, Daniel Vosmaer, and Pieter van Asch who, as far as I know, always stuck to their genre.[k]

While the distinction between painters-in-the-rough and artist-painters became increasingly marked in the first half of the seventeenth century, some overlap between the two persisted. Both types, for instance, on occasion painted armories. Willem van Odekercken painted still-lifes, genre scenes, and an occasional church interior in addition to his regular contracts decorating the inside and outside of houses. Jacob Molijn, who carried out all sorts of orders for the city in the period 1608 to his death in 1649, was quite versatile. He usually painted walls, statues, and armories but he could also paint a man's or a woman's face, as he did in 1608 when he was asked "to distinguish the privies where the men and the women go" ("om te stellen tot onderscheyt voor die secreten waer die mens ende die vrouwen gaen"). His son Jan Molijn, who was also a contractor for the city, is known to have signed a copy of a picture by Adriaen van Ostade.[2]

SOCIAL ORIGIN

It is commonly believed that Dutch painters in the seventeenth century stemmed mainly from and worked for the "lower strata" of

---

[j]A still-life by Bramer was in Adriaen Gouda's collection (Abraham Bredius, *Künstler-inventare: Urkunden zur Geschichte der Holländischen Kunst des XVI^{ten}, XVII^{ten}, und XVIII^{ten} Jahrhunderts*, 7 vols. [The Hague: Martinus Nijhoff, 1877–1890], 2:685) and a waterfall in the estate papers of Dr. Johan Hogenhoeck (Orphan Chamber, *boedel* no. 810).

[k]Both Pieter Steenwijck and Pieter van Asch, however, are known to have painted their own portraits (the first was in the museum at Ypres before World War I; the second is in the Rijksmuseum). The flower specialist Jacob Woutersz. Vosmaer began his career as a landscape painter. A picture by "Jacob Wouters" (almost surely Vosmaer) representing ships and rocks, the staffage by (Hans) Jordaens, was in the collection of Jacob Jansz. Helm, who died in 1626 (Orphan Chamber, *boedel* no. 761).

society. There is some truth in this notion, to the extent that the majority of artists were the sons of craftsmen and shopkeepers, but it is misleading in that it overemphasizes class and occupational status to the detriment of wealth and purchasing power.[l]

I know of only one attempt to look at the social origin of Dutch artists empirically. Åke Bengtsson, in his book *Studies on the Rise of Realistic Painting in Holland, 1610–1625,* concluded from a small-sample study that 1) the wages of common people—textile workers, small craftsmen, road makers, and so forth—were too low to afford any but the most wretched pictures, such as "copies, workshop pictures, engravings, and second-rate paintings," and 2) that painters in Haarlem and Amsterdam of known social origin came mainly from the middle and upper classes (artists' families, master craftsmen, merchants, and up).[3] His results, based on a sample of twenty-six artists (thirteen in Haarlem, thirteen in Amsterdam) born in the period 1575 to 1600, divided into five wealth classes, are roughly comparable with those of my study of Delft painters, which are summarized in Table 6.3.[m]

Out of twenty-five artist-painters born before 1600 whose father's (or guardian's) occupation is known with more or less confidence, twelve were the sons of painters, two of silversmiths or goldsmiths, three of practitioners of assorted handicrafts, four of members of

[l]Cf. the citation by K. W. Swart in Chapter 8, note 36.

[m]The lowest of Bengtsson's five classes consisted of workers of the textile industry, sailors, and other very low-paid workers (he gives as an example the spoolers, who received sixteen stuivers per week in 1620). Class 4 was made up of general laborers, small unorganized craftsmen, masons, carpenters, et al., earning perhaps fifteen to twenty-four stuivers per day around 1620. Included in class 3 were the small merchants, barber-surgeons, goldsmiths, ironmongers, and master craftsmen, such as the city carpenters, engineers, professors, humanists, notaries, ministers, and other representatives of the "intellectual bourgeoisie." In class 2 he placed the large-scale merchants, tradesmen, and producers, including the owners of breweries and textile establishments. The top class was made up of regents, mayors, and other wealthy bourgeoisie living off their assets in land, ships, and government bonds (*Rise of Realistic Painting* [Stockholm: Institute of Art History of Uppsala, 1952], pp. 35–36). In his sample of thirteen Haarlem painters, nine came from group 3 (including six from artist families), three from group 4, and one from the higher groups. Bengtsson concludes that both the "modernists" and the "academists" among painters came chiefly from the upper layers of "government officials, intellectuals, well-to-do tradesmen, producers, and merchants" (ibid., p. 51). My only objection to his classification is that he did not distinguish independent craftsmen who were masters in their respective guilds (e.g., master carpenters or masons) from their "servants" (*knechts*) who were far more numerous in most occupations than their masters. The distinction requires very detailed research, but it is crucial for any such investigation.

TABLE 6.3

Craft, Trade, or Profession of Fathers or Guardians of Artist-Painters in Delft

Occupation of Father or Guardian	Artist-Painters Born				Total
	Before 1600	1600 to 1619	1620 to 1639	1640 to 1659	
Guild of St. Lucas					
Painter	12	6	1	2	21
Engraver	0	2	0	0	2
Art dealer	0	0	1	0	1
Glassmaker	0	1	1	0	2
Other handicrafts or services					
Goldsmith or silversmith, jeweler	2	3	4	0	9
Spectacle-maker	0	2	0	0	2
Candlemaker	0	0	1	0	1
Mason	1	0	1	0	2
Baker	1	0	1	0	2
Nailmaker	0	0	1	0	1
Carpenter	1	0	0	0	1
Sailmaker	0	2*	0	0	2
Innkeeper	0	0	1†	0	1

					Total
Liberal professions					
Attorney	0	1	0	0	1
Notary	1	2	1	0	4
Notary's clerk	1	0	0	0	1
Schoolmaster	0	1	1	0	2
Official	2	0	0	0	2
Minister	0	1	0	0	1
High bourgeoisie					
Brewer	2	0	2	0	4
Merchant	1	1	0	1	3
Unknown	1	0	1	0	2
Unknown	25	16	5	4	50
Grand Total	50	38	22	7	117

SOURCE: See Table 6.1.

NOTE: A number of artists are included in the table whose birth year is not precisely known. However, in all cases, an approximate year of birth, thought to be accurate within three to five years, has been estimated from the artist's year of marriage or from some other evidence.

*Gillis and Mattheus de Berg, the sons of the sailmaker Gillis de Berg, became the wards of their uncle, the silversmith Daniel de Berg (cf. the latter's testament, records of notary Guillaume de Graeff, no. 1721, 30 March 1644).

†Pieter van der Vin was the ward of the innkeeper Rocus Rocusz. van der Vin (cf. the exchange of painting lessons for rent in a contract between Emanuel de Witte and the innkeeper, dated 17 September 1641).

liberal professions or officials, two of rich brewers, and one of a wholesale merchant (the father of Jacob Pynas); one (Arent van Reynoy) evidently stemmed from a well-off (noble) family but the occupation of his father could not be ascertained. In terms of Bengtsson's five classes of economic status, I am inclined to place all the practitioners of handicrafts in the third class from the top. The three members of the liberal professions were either in the upper layer of class 3 or the lower layer of class 2. The brewers, merchants, and other well-off burghers were all in class 2. In sum, three-fourths to four-fifths of the artists represented originated in class 3 and one-fourth to one-fifth in class 2. If anything the proportion of artists in the Delft sample originating in the middle and upper classes was higher than in Bengtsson's Haarlem and Amsterdam samples.

My entire sample for the seventeenth century consists of sixty-seven artists of known origin who either were members of the guild in 1613 or registered between 1613 and 1679. Of these, twenty-six were the sons or wards of painters, art dealers, engravers, and glassmakers who belonged to the St. Lucas Guild (in Delft or elsewhere); nine of goldsmiths, silversmiths, and jewelers (including Anthony and Palamedes Palamedes, the sons of an agate-polisher); eleven of practitioners of other handicrafts; one of an innkeeper; eleven of representatives of the liberal professions; and nine of the rich bourgeoisie, including brewers and merchants. These last two groups (comprising members of liberal professions, brewers, and merchants) made up 30 percent of all the artists' fathers of known occupation or status. As far as I know, not a single son or ward of a farmer, a textile worker,[n] a sailor, or a manual laborer (e.g., the numerous corn- or peat-carriers) became an artist-painter. More surprisingly, the faienciers' industry, with all its masters and *knechts*, produced no artist-painter in this period.

Let us now examine more closely the artists' fathers or guardians who practiced a handicraft. Of those who belonged to the Guild of St. Lucas and to the guild of the goldsmiths and silversmiths either in Delft or elsewhere, all but one were guild masters (the painter Hans van Asch, father of Pieter van Asch). Among the artists born before 1600, we found one whose father was a baker (Peter Stael, the landscape painter), one a carpenter (Sybrand Balkenende, also a

---

[n] The father of Johannes Vermeer was first trained as a *caffawercker,* a highly skilled craft involving the weaving of patterned silk velvets and satins. But by the time Vermeer was born in 1632, in any case, his father had become an art dealer and innkeeper, which two occupations seem to have gradually edged out his *caffa*-weaving.

landscape painter), and one a mason (Joris van Lier, still-lifes). The first of these fathers was a well-known master baker, the second was city carpenter of Rotterdam, the third was city mason of Delft. (A city carpenter or city mason was a master who regularly obtained contracts to do work for the city; these contractors were usually among the best-paid in the trade.) Among those born from 1600 to 1639, the spectacle- and lens-maker (father of the still-life painters Harmen and Pieter Steenwijck), the candlemaker (father of the genre painter Heyndrick van der Burch), the sailmaker (father of Gillis and Matheus de Berg), and the nailmaker (father of the landscape painter Jan Gabrielsz. Songe) were all independent masters or tradesmen. Similarly, Pieter de Hooch's father was the son of a master mason in Rotterdam.° It is curious that the proportion of painter-fathers declined sharply, starting with the generation of artist-painters born after 1600. A plausible explanation may be that talent, which was perhaps more or less randomly distributed in the population, gradually became more important in painting than craft traditions which could be learned by anyone from his family.

No doubt my sample of fathers or guardians of artist-painters of known occupation is biased in the direction of the more substantial citizens who left a trace in the archival material—if they were master craftsmen or tradesmen because they were owed money by their customers—but even making the broadest allowance for the lower social origin of the artists about whom we have no information, I think I can uphold the view that most artist-painters came from a solidly middle-class background. Artists with rich parents (such as Johan van Nes, Abraham van den Hoef, Pieter Groenewegen, Geraerd Houckgeest, Adam Pick, and Willem van Kerckhoven) in fact made up a significant proportion of the entire artists' community.

RELIGION

There is of course a good deal more to the social background of an artist than his father's or guardian's occupation. In seventeenth-

---

°Various debts owed for candles and salt delivered by Rochus Hendricksz. van der Burch are cited in Delft inventories, including the inventory of Ariaentge Wemmers, who died 17 December 1633 (Orphan Chamber, *boedel* no. 1899). On the nailmaking business of Johannes Songe's parents, see the Records of Notary Johan van Beest, no. 1671 (24 July 1652). I am indebted to Peter Sutton for information on Pieter de Hooch's father.

century Delft, his position in society was also critically influenced by his religious affiliation. For one thing, if he was not a member of the Reformed Church community, he could not obtain any municipal office. About all he could aspire to was to become a headman in a guild. Even though the data that I could assemble on the religious denomination of artist-painters are only fragmentary, their detailed presentation may be warranted by the importance of the subject.

Most of the immigrants from Flanders at the end of the sixteenth and the beginning of the seventeenth centuries were probably Protestants. Many painters registered in the Reformed Church community soon after they arrived in Delft, among them numerous members of the Pastenox or Pastenackel family, Abram Bonaert, Hans van der Burch (father of the tapestry designer Jonas Jansz. Verburch), Adriaen Ivenssen, Heyndrick Thyssen, and Jacques van Weyer.[4] Some of those who joined the established church in these transitional years were from prominent Delft families, such as Willem Willemsz. Luyt and Pieter Dircksz. Cluyt, son of a well-known local apothecary and botanist. Pieter Cluyt, at the time he became a member of the church, was said to be living "at the house of Jan Michielsz." The latter was probably the father of his teacher Michiel Miereveld. This young member of the established church seems to have had no qualms about learning the art of painting from the Anabaptist Miereveld, at a time when the two communities were at loggerheads.

That Miereveld took his religious obligations seriously, yet was fairly broad-minded, can be read from the donations he made in his will: 400 gulden to the Lutheran poor, 400 gulden to the Flemish Anabaptists, 600 gulden to the Waterlanders Anabaptists, and 500 gulden to the Remonstrants (Arminians).[p] The only other artist belonging to the Anabaptist sect that I have been able to identify was the genre painter Johannes Verkolje, who joined the guild, coming from Amsterdam, in June 1673.[q]

Among the families that immigrated to Delft in the 1590s was that of the baker Michiel Stael, born near Maastricht. His elder son Pieter, called "de hyger" (the panter or stutterer), born about 1576, became a fairly successful landscape painter with a predilection for representing

---

[p]Miereveld also left 2,486 gulden to charitable institutions, such as the orphanage in Delft, which were under the dominion of the Reformed Church community. Henry Havard, *L'Art et les artistes Hollandais*, 4 vols. (Paris, 1879-1881) 1: 13, 54.

[q]The highly successful faiencier Hendrick Marcellisz. van Gogh was also an Anabaptist.

[154]

Old Testament scenes set in landscapes (Lot and his daughters, Sodom and Gomorrah).[1] In 1617, he took part, as a witness and minor participant, in an incident that arose from the great religious controversy that was raging in Delft at that time as the strict (Gomarist) Calvinists struggled for ascendancy with the more liberal (Arminian) Remonstrants. (A year and a half later, in April 1619, the Synod of Dordrecht, convened by Maurice, Prince of Orange, who, largely for political reasons, favored the strict faction, ruled against the Arminians who were deprived of all secular and ecclesiastic offices: Oldenbarnevelt, the leading Arminian statesman, was beheaded.) The attestation regarding the incident in question had been made at the request of Henricus Arnoldus, a well-known Reformed minister in Delft.[5] The dispute started when Bouwen Dircxsz., shoemaker, fell into conversation on the marketplace in Delft with a minister named Slatius, pastor in Bleyswijck, regarding a broadside (*libel*) that Slatius had written against (fundamentalist) "barn preachers" (*scheurpredikanten*). Bouwen Dircxsz. had suggested that Slatius meet with "weavers and furriers" (apparently to debate his views). Slatius had answered that "those people invoke the Scriptures but do not understand them," and suggested that Henricus Arnoldus should come to debate with him. Bouwen then objected that Arnoldus respected himself too highly to do so. Slatius said he also had too much self-respect to debate with weavers and furriers. Boùwen retorted that the weavers and furriers "would give you Arminians and the like enough to do." Slatius: "At least they don't say about the Arminians what they say about your Henricus [Arnoldus] being a usurer." The shoemaker asked Slatius whether he would openly say that Henricus was a usurer, which Slatius confirmed he would. All these "insulting words" concerning Henricus Arnoldus were overheard by Pieter Stael and two other witnesses (a basketmaker and an individual of unspecified occupation).

Three days later, Pieter Stael and two other attestants again came before the notary and related how, immediately after the above conversation, Slatius and the previous witnesses met the brother-

---

[1] Abraham Bredius claimed to have seen a religious landscape by Pieter Stael, perhaps with staffage by Pieter Bronckhorst, signed and dated 1616, but this painting, said to be in the style of Joost de Momper, cannot now be identified. No painting can be securely attributed to him today. See the discussion on this point in Laurens. J. Bol, *Holländische Maler des 17. Jahrhunderts nahe den grossen Meistern: Landschaften und Stilleben* (Braunschweig: Klinkhard and Bierman, 1969), p. 151.

in-law of Henricus Arnoldus, who, hearing what had transpired, asked
Slatius whether it was true he had alleged Arnoldus was a usurer.
Slatius answered that Arnoldus was not only a usurer but a liar. They
then walked toward Arnoldus's house. When Slatius was invited to go
into the house (to confront Arnoldus), he refused, despite repeated
urgings, saying he did not wish to repeat his insults in the house.
Whereupon Arnoldus himself appeared on the doorstep, and Pieter
Stael said to Slatius: "Here stands the man, go to him." When Slatius
still refused and he was asked why, he said that he had sworn falsely.
Stael laid his hand on the hand of Slatius and perceived that he was
trembling. He said to him: "See here, had our Lord come upon you,
you might well have gotten a seizure" ("Soe mocht onse lieve heer uw
comen, hier mocht ghy wel een popelsie op u hals krigen"). A seizure
or apoplexy was presumably the punishment of God for a false oath.

The significance of the testimony, from our viewpoint, is that Pieter
Stael apparently sided with the strict Calvinist Arnoldus against the
Remonstrant Slatius.[s] His allusion to the punishment that God might
visit on a false-swearing Arminian suggests he may have shared the
fundamentalist beliefs of the conservative party, along with the barn
preachers, the weavers, and the furriers. This would square well with
his own relatively low-class background.

The Lutherans, officially called at that time "members of the
community of the Augsburg confession," if they did not enjoy
anything like the status and privileges of the officially recognized
Calvinists, were tolerated and were treated a good deal more liberally
than the Roman Catholics. Hans Jordaens the Elder, who was born in
Antwerp around 1560 and had emigrated to Delft about 1585, was a
dean of the Lutheran community toward the end of his life.[t] The
landscape painter Andries Pietersz. van der Linde was no less than the
pastor of the Augsburg community. He had arrived in Delft in 1625
(or perhaps even earlier) and signed a document with his fellow-
Lutheran Hans Jordaens in 1626; but he did not take out citizenship
in the town until 20 August 1631, three weeks before joining the
guild as a painter.[u]

[s]Bredius, *Künstler-inventare*, 5:1,758, points out that in 1623 the Remonstrant
minister Slatius was condemned to death for his part in a plot against Prince
Maurice.

[t]He is thus referred to in the Records of Notary Adriaan van Twelle, no. 1653, 24
February 1625.

[u]Andries van der Linde appears in Delft on 22 June 1625 (Records of Notary
Willem de Langue, no. 1684). He signs with Hans Jordaens on 16 July 1626 (Records

Our knowledge of the Roman Catholic community, probably quite numerous in Delft, is limited in part because its activities—especially baptisms and marriages—had to be more or less secretly conducted in "hidden churches." The Roman Catholic sculptor Adriaen Samuels and Hendrick van den Velden, who was very active in Catholic affairs, testified before a notary on 20 October 1659 that many marriages had been performed in Delft in the Roman Catholic manner "despite the oppression with regard to the free exercise of the Roman Catholic faith, which may not be done here" ("mits de benautheyd int reguardt men de vrye exercitie die alhier te landen niet en mach gedaen werden").[6]

P.T.A. Swillens, himself a Dutch Catholic, has collected what little evidence was available on Roman Catholic artists, his information coming largely from parochial records in Rome where Dutch artists took Holy Communion.[7] (He does not consider the question whether the act of taking communion in a Roman Catholic church when an artist was abroad necessarily meant that he was a Roman Catholic back home in the Netherlands.) According to Swillens, the following artists of the Guild of St. Lucas in Delft were Roman Catholics: Leonaert Bramer, Simon de Vlieger, Willem van Aelst, and Johannes Jordaens the Younger. It is surprising, but by no means impossible, that Johannes Jordaens the Younger, who was the grandson of the Lutheran Hans Jordaens the Elder, should have been Catholic. In addition, we have almost direct evidence that the wealthy genre painter Jacob Jansz. van Velsen was Catholic. In 1654, two years before his death, Van Velsen testified before a notary that a certain Lambrecht Jansz. Stam was "of good and pious religious character and of the Roman Catholic religion."[8] This type of attestation, as far as I can make out, was always made by fellow members of the same religious community.

Another convert to Roman Catholicism, I believe, was Johannes Vermeer. The artist was born in a Protestant family: his paternal grandmother claimed in 1622 that she "was a sister and member of the Reformed Church";[9] his uncle Reynier Balthensz. (his mother's

---

of Notary Adriaen Rijshouck, no. 1818). When he joined the guild he was called "predicant van de Ausburgsche Confessije" (F.D.O. Obreen, *Archief voor Nederlandsche Kunstgeschiedenis*, 7 vols. [Rotterdam, 1877-1890], 1:27); in 1654 he is referred to as "bedienaar des godel. worts der Aug. Confessije" (Records of Notary Nicholaes Vrienbergh, cited in the handwritten notes of Abraham Bredius in the R.K.D.).

brother) had joined the Reformed Church community in Rotterdam and Gorinchem. It is highly unlikely that Vermeer's father and mother had already converted to Catholicism in view of their decision to baptize their daughter Geertruyd in 1620 and their son Johannes (the artist) in 1632 in the New Church in Delft. The following facts strongly suggest, without proving beyond a doubt, that Vermeer became a Roman Catholic after his marriage. To begin with, he married the daughter of a distinguished Catholic family from Gouda. The couple chose to perform the marriage in Schipluy, a village near Delft with an overwhelmingly Catholic administration. None of their children—they had at least fourteen—were baptized in either of the Reformed Churches of Delft. Vermeer and his wife lived during most of the artist's working life (from 1660 to 1675) in a Catholic neighborhood known as the Popish Corner. They called one of their sons Ignatius, a name with Jesuit connotations, that would hardly have been imaginable in a Protestant family. Finally, the iconography of one of his paintings, *Allegory of Faith* (in the Metropolitan Museum of Art), has some specifically Jesuit features; it has been speculated recently[10] that the picture may have been ordered by the Jesuits who held secret services in a hidden church in close proximity to the house of Vermeer's mother-in-law, where he lived at the time.

From these scattered bits of evidence we can only form a very general idea of the religious composition of the artists' colony in Delft. Nevertheless, one impression emerges vividly: the large number and the relative importance of the artists who did *not* belong to the orthodox Calvinist community. The most important portrait painter in the first half of the seventeenth century was an Anabaptist (Miereveld); the two most reputed "history" painters were, respectively, a Lutheran (Hans Jordaens I), and a Roman Catholic (Bramer); in the second half of the century, the Catholic Willem van Aelst was the best still-life artist in town (before he left for Amsterdam); Johannes Vermeer, who was probably also Catholic, was Delft's greatest painter of genre and landscape. I have named altogether ten non-Calvinists out of a possible total of 117 artists active in the period 1613 to 1679. Many, if not most, of the remaining 107 artists were Calvinists. Among the more prominent artist families who were most probably Calvinist—judging by the fact that members of these families acceded to various municipal and military functions—were the Delffs, the Vosmaers, and the Steenwijcks.[v] These important exceptions notwith-

---

[v]Jacob Delff II was master of the port of Delft (Havenmeester); Jacob Woutersz.

FIG. 7 Johannes Vermeer, The Little Street ("Het Straatje") (c.1660), 21⅓ × 17⅓ in. Rijksmuseum, Amsterdam (Photo: Museum).

standing, I suspect that the established church was most heavily represented among the less well known painters, many of whom were of lower-middle-class origin (such as Pieter Stael), while the minority Protestant sects and Roman Catholicism predominated among the more successful artists of middle- or upper-class background. If I am right, the reason would not be far to seek. Individuals from well-to-do families belonging to minority faiths were generally barred from the more prestigious careers and offices in city government. Most handicrafts were below their status. If they had no inclination for business, a career in the arts, the status of which was rising in the seventeenth century, may have been one of the few attractive opportunities open to them.

APPRENTICESHIP OF ARTIST-PAINTERS

In Chapter 5, I conjectured that only fairly well-to-do parents could afford to pay the direct and indirect costs of training an artist-painter. The painters' relatively high indicators of wealth, to the extent that they correlated with income, were likely to reflect the increments in income they could expect as a return for these training costs. Clearly, the sons of painters and engravers, who made up about one-third of the number of artist-painters of known social origin, had an initial advantage over other young people: they could get their basic training at no direct cost from their father (if he was still alive); the only money outlays their family might have to sustain were the "finishing costs" of sending the boy to another master for his last two years of apprenticeship. Attention in this section will be focused on young men who could not get training from their father or guardian and who had to be contracted out as apprentices to masters in the guild.

The archival evidence is in the form of apprenticeship contracts and debts due to painters for "learning costs." Because few documents have survived bearing on this matter, my survey will cover this material more or less exhaustively.

In all, three regular apprenticeship contracts have survived; at least no more have turned up in my systematic search of the notarial archives and of the estate papers of the Orphan Chamber. One was

---

Vosmaer was "Captain Major" of a Delft regiment of militiamen; Herman Steenwijck was a militiaman (*schutter*) of the third regiment in the free quarter of Delft, according to an attestation of 13 July 1637, Records of Notary Arent Bogaard, no. 1876).

discovered many years ago by Abraham Bredius (Van Lier-Linschot-en) and two are new (Bolgersteyn-Reymbrant Verboom and Cornelis Jacobsz. Delff-Jan Joppens). In addition, I discovered a contract whereby Emanuel de Witte agreed to teach painting to the young Pieter van der Vin in exchange for free rent of an apartment.

By the terms of our first contract, dated 7 December 1618, the three legal guardians of Reymbrant Cornelisz. Verboom, son of the late Cornelis Reymbrantsz. Verboom, confectioner, with the agreement of the masters of the Orphan Chamber, apprenticed Reymbrandt Cornelisz. to the painter Herman Arentsz. van Bolgersteyn.[11] (Bolgersteyn, a member of the guild in 1613, painted still-lifes, portraits, and an occasional "history.") The apprenticeship was to last one year. Bolgersteyn promised to teach Reymbrant what his disciple "could learn of the art of painting, and in particular the making of portraits." All the colors that the young man would require were to be supplied by Bolgersteyn, "with the exception of a few costly ashes which the aforesaid guardians, together with the panels, would charge to the expense of the aforesaid Reymbrant.'"[w] The apprentice was allowed to "have in property and to keep ... all the paintings that he would make, in order to make his profit thereof." In return for teaching Reymbrant the art of painting and portrait-making "as a good master should do," the guardians promised to pay Bolgersteyn fifty gulden. Since there is no mention of board and lodging in the contract, as there usually is when the master takes on the obligation to provide his apprentice with these services, I presume that Reymbrant was slated to live at home during the period.[x]

On 8 February 1620, Bolgersteyn wrote in his own hand a twelve-line receipt for the fifty gulden that he had received. On 2 April 1621, the accounting of the estate of Cornelis Reymbrantsz. included an item of sixty-nine gulden due to Bolgersteyn for one year's teaching of Reymbrant Cornelisz. for the year 1620, plus three gulden for money expended on his behalf (Orphan Chamber, *boedel* no. 1760 I). These two years were surely not the first that Reymbrant

[w]The guardians appointed by the Orphan Chamber were accountable for all the receipts and outlays of the estate of their ward. The contract called for them to pay for the rare ashes and panels and to charge the estate accordingly.

[x]Frans Cornelisz., the brother of Reymbrant, was apprenticed, by a contract on 28 August 1618, to Corstiaen van Borselen, silversmith. The guardians were to pay the silversmith eighty-four gulden per year. However, the apprentice was slated to sleep and eat at his master's house and at the latter's cost (Orphan Chamber, *boedel* no. 1760 II).

had spent learning the art of painting: as early as 17 January 1617, a document was drawn up by a notary "in the presence of Reymbrant Cornelisz. Verboom *schilder.*"[12] The two years during which he was the pupil of Bolgersteyn were probably the last two years in the normal six-year apprenticeship required of master painters.

Despite all this preparation for a professional career as a painter, Reymbrant Cornelisz. Verboom never joined the guild, and I did not find a single one of his paintings mentioned in a Delft inventory. Yet he did not disappear without a trace. On 26 November 1629, he was said to be a servant or clerk (*dienaer*) in the company of Count van Cuylenburgh holding garrison in 's Hertogenbosch.[13] Less than a year later, on 13 May 1630, he reappears as a painter.[14] Robbrecht Jansz., shoemaker, twenty-eight, testified at the request of Gillis and Frans Verboom (brothers of Reymbrant) that Reymbrant Verboom owed him eight gulden eleven stuivers for shoes delivered in 1628, for which Verboom had promised to deliver a painting. The shoemaker had asked him many times for the money due, but he never received anything, despite many appointments made to go to Reymbrant's house, which he, the debtor, always broke. Finally Reymbrant told him that he was unwilling to pay the debt unless three gulden were rebated from it.

Heyndrik Jansz. Verpoort,[y] bookbinder, fifty-eight, then testified that two years before, during Lent, he and Reymbrant Verboom had bartered two paintings, one a St. Peter and the other a St. Paul, against books, "on condition that he, Verboom, should paint a key in the hand of St. Peter." Shortly thereafter Verboom had fetched the two paintings from the witness's house, promising to paint a key in the hand of St. Peter and to touch up (literally, improve somewhat) the St. Paul. He undertook to deliver both paintings again soon afterwards. The witness, despite repeated entreaties, never succeeded in getting the paintings back. Finally, he told Verboom that he would be forced to send the bailiff, to which Verboom retorted that he would receive him with a dagger, adding "many other unseemly words." This ended the testimony, which was witnessed by Verboom's old teacher Harmen van Bolgersteyn. Gillis and Frans Verboom probably paid Reymbrant's debts and then had the attestation drawn up to help them collect from their errant brother (or from their late father's estate). This is the last we hear of the namesake of Holland's most famous painter.

[y]On Verpoort, see above, Chapter 3.

In the second of our apprenticeship contracts the still-life painter Cornelis Jacobsz. Delff took on the youngest son of Jan Joppens van Waterwijck, named Jan Jansz., for one year, starting 1 April 1620.[15] Delff promised to provide his pupil with food, drink, and lodging and "to instruct him in all that concerns the art and science of painting." All that Jan Jansz. makes will belong to his master. The guardians of Jan Jansz. will give Cornelis Jacobsz. eighteen pounds Flemish (108 gulden) for the year, payable in two installments. Cornelis Jacobsz. will do everything for Jan Jansz. that a good master should for his apprentice-learner (*leerknecht*). (The usually stipulated obligations of the *knecht* toward his master are omitted.) Absolutely nothing is known of the subsequent career of Jan Jansz., who is presumed to have died young or to have left town. Jan Joppens van Waterwijck was a wine merchant. He was well-off, considering that his movable goods, after his death in late 1619, were sold for 1,956 gulden. Among the debts to his estate, probably for wine delivered, were ninety-eight gulden ten stuivers owed by the same Cornelis Jacobsz. *schilder* who later taught his son, and forty-eight gulden ten stuivers by "Mr. Michiel *schilder*," who could be no other than Miereveld. Among his possessions was a large panel with a frame in which his portrait was to have been painted (perhaps by Miereveld). In counterpart to the debt owed by Cornelis Jacobsz. was a debt owed to him of 132 gulden for "teaching money" for Jan Joppens's son, which may have included besides the 108 gulden stipulated in the contract some colors or other extra costs. The painter also claimed unspecified damages for a broken painting.

The third contract, dated 28 May 1623, bound Adriaen Cornelisz. van Linschoten, who was fifteen or sixteen years old at the time, to the flower painter Joris Gerritsz. van Lier.[16] It is of interest that Van Lier registered in the guild the very next day after this apprenticeship contract was signed, presumably to comply with the regulation requiring that all instruction in the trades under the guild's jurisdiction be given by guild masters. Adriaen's father, the master glassmaker Cornelis Ariensz. Linschoten, agreed with Van Lier that the latter would provide his apprentice with food, drink, and lodging and would instruct him in the art of painting for the next two years, starting 1 June 1620. All the work done by Linschoten was to accrue as profit to his master. Linschoten Senior committed himself to pay Van Lier eighteen pounds Flemish (108 gulden) for board and instruction costs for the two years. On a yearly basis, this was precisely one-half as much as Jan Joppens van Waterwijck had paid for his son, under identical conditions. The lower rate of payment may perhaps be explained by the fact that Van Lier had only recently come back from a stay in France and Italy and was not yet established in Delft,[2] whereas Cornelis Jacobsz. Delff, who was already in the guild in 1613, enjoyed a considerable reputation as a painter of fruit and vegetable still-lifes and kitchen scenes by the time he had been engaged to teach Jan Jansz.

After Adriaen Cornelisz. Linschoten completed his apprenticeship, he went to Italy, where according to Houbraken, he became a pupil of Giuseppe Ribera. Upon his return, he became a member of the guild in Delft (around 1635), and spent at least ten years in his native town; he then moved to The Hague, probably in the late 1650s. If we may judge by the number and the high prices of his paintings in Delft inventories, he was a successful painter, chiefly of religious subjects, but also of portraits and still-lifes. He seems to have been prone to violence, which frequently brought him in conflict with the law. In 1645 he assaulted Jan Arentsz. van Bolgersteyn, baker, the brother of the painter Herman Bolgersteyn, with a curved dagger.[17] It was apparently for this misdeed, carried out in front of witnesses, that he was banned for fifty years from the states of Holland and West Friesland. In 1662 he was banned for another ten years for violating the first ban. Nevertheless, he came back to The Hague, where complaints continued to reach the judges about his restless life. He was banished again for ten years in 1669.[18] He died in The Hague in 1677.

According to the terms of our last contract, dated 17 September 1641,[19] Rocus Rocusz. van der Vin, brewery foreman (*opperbrouwer*), agreed to lease to

> Emanuel de Wit *schilder* the following parts of his, Rocus Rocusz.'s, house standing in the Choorstraet: namely the upstairs room, the attic above the upstairs room and the back-attic, with the understanding that the lessor and the lessee will both be able to use the back-attic to dry linen [canvas] and clothes, and this for the duration of one year, starting All Souls' Day 1641 and expiring All

[2]Van Lier was said to owe thirty-four stuivers to the estate of the flower-painter Jacob Woutersz. Vosmaer because the latter had "helped him with and gone over a painting of a flowerpot" ("verhelpen ende overgaen van een blompottgen") (Orphan Chamber, *boedel* no. 1847). From this and the fact that he became collector of taxes by 1640 and apparently abandoned painting, we may perhaps conclude that he was not very talented. (On his post as tax-collector, Records of Notary Johan van Ruiven, no. 1958, 30 April 1640.)

Souls' Day 1642. Instead of paying rent money, the lessee will instruct Pieter Leendertsz. van der Vin, the lessor's nephew, in the art of painting without concealing any knowledge and science understood or known to him in this art but to reveal and to inform him about everything as if the forenamed Pieter Leendersz. were his own child. . . . Besides which, all that Pieter Leendersz. will paint will belong to Rocus Rocusz.

At the time this contract was signed, Pieter Leendertsz. was fifteen years old.[aa] Emanuel de Witte, who was only about twenty-four himself, had just arrived in Delft from Rotterdam where he had spent the last two years. As he did not join the guild until nine months later, on 23 June 1642, he must have technically violated in the interim the guild regulation forbidding nonmembers to give instruction to their craft. It probably took some time for the headmen to detect and repress (by fine or otherwise) a violation of this type, which may not have been considered too serious anyway since no money changed hands. Pieter van der Vin joined the guild four years later, on 7 November 1645, when he was only nineteen. Shortly after his death in May 1655 his bankrupt estate was sold at public auction.[20] An original work of unspecified subject by the painter sold for twenty-one gulden, while a portrait of Van der Vin and his wife by Fabritius went for forty-five gulden (an unusually high price for a portrait). All his possessions, as we saw in Chapter 5, brought 192 gulden 4 stuivers, of which 93 gulden 7 stuivers was for paintings and painter's equipment.

Occasional references to debts for painting lessons and for other costs of achieving mastery in art can be found in estate papers. One of the earliest and most revealing concerns a series of debts paid on behalf of Joris Gerritsz. van Lier (the future teacher of Linschoten) by his guardians from the estate of his father Gerrit Jorisz., about 1619.[21]

First, the painter Karel van Mander (the Younger) was paid twenty gulden by the estate for teaching Joris up to January 1610 "when he departed from here." The young man was about twenty-one at the time.[bb] There follow various small amounts of money, totaling twelve gulden twelve stuivers, given to him in connection with his craft ("om costen van zijn hantwerck"), then two gulden fourteen stuivers for an

[aa]He was christened on 9 August 1626 ("Delft MA, Doopboek").

[bb]He was said to be about fifty years old on 18 July 1639 (Records of Notary Adriaen van der Block, no. 1739).

outer garment paid when Joris was going to France, thirty-two gulden eight stuivers for his expenses in France, and three gulden ten stuivers for sending Joris a package and letter in Paris. In July 1611, thirteen gulden four stuivers were transferred to Joris in Paris via Michiel Block, envoy in Paris. Later his guardians sent him fifty-five gulden in Rome, Italy, at his urgent request. Another twelve gulden that was also dispatched to him through Michiel Block may have reached him on his return from Italy. Payments by the estate of three gulden to a captain's wife and fifty-one gulden ten stuivers to a skipper were also presumably made to defray the young man's travel costs. All these payments when Joris was wandering about France and Italy came to less than 160 gulden, a sum that seems eminently reasonable if it covered his entire financial support for the journey.

Some forty years later when a rich bourgeois of Delft, named Arent Adriaensz. Goud'A (or Gouda) sent his son Adriaen Arentsz. to Italy "because he had let him learn the practice of painting," he spent over 3,000 gulden for the young man's tour of Italy and "other places."[22] While there was probably some rise in prices (especially in the years 1610 to 1625) between the time Joris Gerritsz. van Lier went to Italy and young Goud'A's journey, I suspect that the latter's expedition was on a much grander scale than the former. Incidentally, Adriaen Arentsz. married in Italy, then came back to Delft, where he died in 1667. He never joined the guild. His death inventory was ample enough to suggest that he did not need to sell his paintings for a living.

The expense of traveling to Italy was so high, in any event, that only a small number of families could afford to send their boy to complete his training beyond the Alps (or even in France). In the period 1590–1610, Abraham Apersz. van der Hoef, Pieter Bronckhorst, Huybert Jacobsz. Grimani, Joris van Lier, Jacob Vosmaer, and Johannes van Nes had gone from Delft to Italy. Linschoten made the trip some time in the late 1620s or early 1630s. Leonaert Bramer was in France from 1614 to 1616 and in Italy from 1615 to about 1625. Pieter Groenewegen was noted in Rome in the early 1620s. Corstiaen Couwenberg spent some time in Italy between 1624, when he was recorded in Delft, and 1635, when be bought a house in his native city.[23] Cornelis de Man wandered for nine years in France (Paris) and Italy (Rome, Venice) between 1642 and 1653. Johannes (Simonsz.) Jordaens is known to have painted in Rome in the early 1650s. Willem van Aelst spent four years in France and seven years in Italy, then came back to Delft in 1656. Finally, Jacob Pynas, who was born in Haarlem around 1590, went to Italy as a very young man (around 1605) long before he joined the guild in Delft in 1632. Altogether out of 116 artist-painters who were masters in the guild between 1613 and the end of the 1670s, only fourteen are known to have made the ultramontane journey.

Resuming our survey of documents citing art instruction, we find that the painter Cornelis Daemen (Rietwijck), who, as we shall see presently, had a drawing school in Delft in the 1650s, received twenty gulden ten stuivers in 1621 to teach "portraying" for one year to Nicolaes Pietersz. van Roon, the orphaned child of the goldsmith Pieter Dircksz. van Roon.[24] It is likely, in view of the small amount involved, that the instruction was given while the pupil lived at home. Nothing is known about the subsequent fate of the goldsmith's son.

According to Arnold Houbraken and Jacob Campo-Weyermann, the famous eighteenth-century chroniclers of Dutch painting, the still-life painter Evert van Aelst taught painting to his nephew Willem van Aelst, Emanuel de Witte, and Jacob Denys.[cc] An entry in the 1638 estate papers of the rich brewer Thomas Jansz. Pick states that Evert van Aelst claimed seventy-two gulden, including twelve gulden for colors, for having instructed Adam Jansz. Pick in the art of painting.[25] Adam Pick, the grandson of Thomas Jansz., joined the guild in 1642. His one extant painting, a barn interior in the Rotterdam style in the Prinsenhof Museum in Delft (fig. 8), betrays a mediocre talent. By the later 1640s, Pick had become an innkeeper. It is not clear whether or not he continued to paint.[dd]

The last reference to art lessons that I could find was to a nephew of Reymbrant Cornelisz., named Aryen Gillisz. Verboom.[ee] He was the orphan son of well-to-do parents. In 1642 the custodian of the estate paid to the painter Anthony Palamedes twenty-two gulden "for one

---

[cc]Arnold Houbraken, *De Groote Schouburgh der Nederlandsche Konstschilders en Schilderessen*, ed. P. T. Swillens, 3 vols. (Maastricht: Leiter-Nypals, 1943), 1:179–80; and Jakob Campo-Weyermann, *De levensbeschryvingen der Nederlandsche konstschilders ende konstschilderessen* 3 vols., (The Hague, 1729), 3:62. According to Campo-Weyermann, De Witte "learned the art of painting in Delft" (and Evert van Aelst was his teacher). If this is true, De Witte, who apparently began to teach Pieter van der Vin as soon as he arrived in Delft, was both taking and giving lessons at the same time.

[dd]The inventory made on 11 March 1653, a year after his wife's death, of the common property of the couple contains many paintings, including at least one by Pick himself, but no painter's equipment (Records of Notary Frans Boogert, no. 1999).

[ee]This individual should not be confused with the landscape painter Adriaen Hendricksz. Verboom (1628–1670), who lived in Rotterdam.

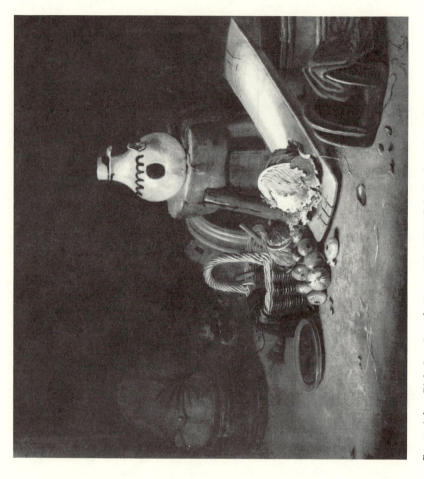

FIG. 8 Adam Pick, Interior of a Barn with Still-Life (1640s), 10⅛ x 11¾ in. Museum Het Prinsenhof, Delft (Photo: A Dingjan)

year's instruction in drawing and painting."[26] (I surmise from the wording of the debt that no board or lodging was involved.) In addition three gulden were spent from the estate to buy Aryen Verboom paints and brushes. The amount paid was so small that it leads me to wonder whether the instruction was not in a group. Perhaps Anthony Palamedes was operating a drawing school similar to the one described below that Cornelis Daemen Rietwijck taught in the 1650s. By 1646, in any event, Aryen Verboom was clerking for the notaries Govert Rota and Adriaen van der Wiel.[27] Nothing is known of his later career.

From all this disparate evidence on the costs of training, we may infer that 1) the parents or guardians of the young men who were taught painting by established masters were burghers who were all at least moderately well-to-do; 2) all the teachers were, or soon after became, masters in the guild; 3) costs of instruction varied appreciably according to the reputation of the master, whether the pupil or apprentice lived with his master or at home, who paid for the paints, and who was allowed to keep the work produced by the fledgling artist. A fact that doubtless influenced learning fees was also the age and previous training of the young artist before he joined a new master or renewed a contract. Unfortunately neither the contracts that have survived nor the additional information I was able to pick up allow us to gauge the relative importance of this point. Leaving aside these and other obscure determinants of training costs, we may estimate, *grosso modo,* that a pupil living at home might expect to pay 20 to 50 gulden a year, one living with his master 50 to 110 gulden.

How do these fees compare to those paid to painters in other towns? The evidence collected from secondary sources by Hanns Floerke unfortunately does not always distinguish the students and apprentices who lived with the master from those that lived at home. The "learning moneys" he cites range from a yearly barrel of herring due to the master in the case of an apprentice living with the painter Isaac Isaacsz. in Amsterdam to 100 gulden per year paid by the pupils of Honthorst, Dou, and Rembrandt to their masters.[28]

These last fees would be on the high side but normal for Delft, judging from my sample, for pupils living with their master, but excessively high if they were solely paid for instruction. My guess is that they did *not* include board and lodging: it is hardly possible for Honthorst who taught "twenty-four or twenty-five students" at the same time or for Rembrandt who had at least as many students[29] to have housed them all. The fees these famous masters were paid were

TABLE 6.4

The Specializations of Artists and Their Disciples

Artist	Artist's Specialty	Disciple	Disciple's Specialty
Michiel Miereveld	portraits, "histories"	Jan van Ravesteyn	portraits
Michiel Miereveld		Pieter Dircksz. Cluyt	flowers, "historical" staffage in landscapes
Michiel Miereveld		Pieter Gerritsz. van Montfort	unknown
Michiel Miereveld		Paul Moreelse (Utrecht)	portraits, "histories"
Michiel Miereveld		Jan van Nes	figures, portraits
Michiel Miereveld		Willem van Vliet	portraits, "histories"
Willem van Vliet	portraits, "histories"	Hendrick van Vliet	"perspectives," genre
Cornelis van Haarlem	"histories"	Jacob Delff II	portraits
Cornelis van Haarlem		Cornelis Jacobsz. Delff	still-lifes
Karel van Mander II	"histories," tapestry designs	Joris van Lier	flowers
Herman van Bolgersteyn	still-lifes, portraits, "histories"	Reymbrant Verboom	"histories"
Cornelis Jacobsz. Delff	still-lifes	Jan Jansz. van Waterwijck	unknown
Joris van Lier	flowers	Adriaen Linschoten	"histories," still-lifes

Emanuel de Witte	"histories" (1640s), church interiors	Pieter van der Vin	unknown
Anthony Palamedes	genre, portraits	Adriaen Gillisz. Verboom	genre, landscapes
Anthony Palamedes		Ludolf de Jongh	unknown
Hendrick van Vliet	church interiors	Floris de la Fée	unknown
Cornelis Damen Rietwijck	portraits	Nicolaes van Roon	unknown
Carel Fabritius	"histories," portraits	Mathys Spoors	unknown
Evert van Aelst	still-lifes	Emanuel de Witte	"histories," church interiors
Evert van Aelst		Willem van Aelst	still-lifes
Evert van Aelst		Jan (or Jacob) Denys	still-lifes
Evert van Aelst		Adam Pick	landscapes, genre, still-lifes
Johannes Verkolje	genre	Thomas van der Wilt	portraits, genre

SOURCES: Standard references (Fabritius, Moreelse, Hendrick and Willem van Vliet, Jacob Delff) are omitted as well as teacher-pupil relations documented in the text. In the inventory of Jacob Jansz. Helm (died 7 July 1636, Orphan Chamber, *boedel* no. 761), there were three landscapes by Pieter Stael with "historical" staffage by Pieter Dircksz. Cluyt and one staffed by the same painter with a shepherd and sheep; the reference to flower-painting is from the photographic files of the Rijsbureau von Kunsthistorische Documentatie in The Hague. Ludolf de Jongh, according to Houbraken, left the atelier of Cornelis Saftleven in Rotterdam to study with Anthony Palamedes (*De Groote Schouburgh*, 2:33). Jacob Denys's study with Evert van Aelst is mentioned by Campo-Weyermann, *De levensbeschryvingen der Nederlandsche Konstschilders*, 3:62. (A painter named Jan Denysz., or Danijse, working in Delfshaven, registered in the Guild of St. Lucas in Delft on 12 June 1649, who may be identical with "Jacob Denys.")

considered unusually high at the time precisely because the learners lived at home and continued to be a burden on their families.

What little is known about Delft teachers of painting and their pupils and about their respective specialties is set forth in Table 6.4. About the only thing that can be concluded from this small sample is that most students painted subjects, at least as a secondary specialty, that coincided with the primary specialty of their teachers. The three most obvious exceptions are the pairs Cornelis van Haarlem-Cornelis Delff, Karel van Mander II-Joris van Lier, and Evert van Aelst-Emanuel de Witte, whose specialties did not overlap in any way.

Only two documents turned up in the Delft archives supplying any sort of information on the relation between master-painters and their apprentices or "disciples." The first refers to Hendrick van Vliet, the well-known painter of church interiors (fig. 9). On 7 February 1646 a carpenter named Jeronimus Leendertsz. testified at Van Vliet's request as follows: He was working in the attic of Van Vliet's house where Floris de la Fée, "then disciple of the petitioner," sat drawing when De la Fée said to him that he could easily cut his face up with his little knife in the position in which he (Jeronimus) was lying on the floor. Jeronimus answered, "Boy, you must not think so, or I should trounce you." Whereupon De la Fée reached into his bag and brought out another knife, saying that this knife had already served, adding: "I shall stick the knife once more into my master's ribs." When the carpenter punished him, De la Fée persisted (in his threats?) but asked him to keep quiet about it. "The master's wife," he said, "is a goddamned hog (*een sacraments varcken*)." Next Van Vliet's maid, who was seventeen years old, declared that three weeks before the kermess, when De la Fée had come down after being called to eat in the evening, his master had asked him whether he had snuffed out the candle that he had had upstairs. De la Fée claimed he had extinguished it against the wall.[ff] When the maid went upstairs to see, it turned out it had been left on the windowsill and that the wick of the candle was still hot. On hearing this Van Vliet gave De la Fée a couple of slaps. When De la Fée, upon running upstairs, was asked by the master's wife where he was going, he answered "to The Hague." He was then told it was too late for passage (on the canal). Thereupon the apprentice said, "I shall hire a barge out of my own purse." The

[ff] A small part of the document is missing here. From what I can reconstruct of it, the master was worried about the fire that might be started if the candle was left to burn out next to a wooden wall.

FIG. 9 Hendrick van Vliet, Interior of the Oude Kerk, Delft (1660), 32½ x
26 in. The Metropolitan Museum of Art, Gift of Clarence Dillon,
1976 (Photo: Museum)

master's wife warned him that if he went away that evening, she would not let him in again. She held the trapdoor to prevent him from going out but the maid said, "Woman, let him out, or something worse still could happen." The master's wife opened the door, and De la Fée ran from the house. Some time after nine o'clock that same evening, De la Fée knocked on the door after the master and his wife had both gone to bed. The maid would not let him in. He came back the next day, put on his best clothes and went away again, this time apparently for good. Finally some other witnesses testified that De la Fée had not been thrown out of the house but had run away.[30]

If we ignore the incidentals of the dispute between Van Vliet and his pupil, we come away with the impression that the relationship was a close one. The boy lived in the master's house, probably took his meals with the family, and was treated much as a child of the house would be (including the slaps). Finally, we may infer from the document that De la Fée must have had well-to-do parents if he could afford to hire himself a barge out of his own purse. It is very unlikely that an apprentice could earn that kind of money.

The next deposition illustrates a totally different master-pupil relationship. Here the setting appears to be that of some sort of drawing academy where a number of boys, who were not necessarily all future painters, learned how to draw. The deposition refers to a young man named Adriaen Duvese (also spelled Duvers or Duyvemen) who, as early as 1651, had signed a document with Cornelis Daemen Rietwijck, who was presumably already then his master. It is interesting, in view of his inability to learn the craft, alleged in the later document, that he already was called *schilder* at that time.[31] On 15 January 1659, Cornelis Daemen Rietwijck, who was then nearly seventy years old, and his wife Adriana Joosten testified at the request of Mr. Johan Soutman, attorney before the Court of Utrecht, about a certain Adriaen Duvese, "then over nineteen years of age," who had been brought to Rietwijck's house some time previously—the attestants could not remember precisely how long ago[88]—by his mother and his late godmother so that he might learn drawing. These ladies had said that "they feared he would not be able to learn, because he was short on intelligence, but their principal aim was to keep him off

[88]In any case not later than December 1651 when Duvese was already working with Cornelis Daemen. The reference in the later part of the document to the beginning of the Anglo-Dutch Wars in 1652 is consistent with this date. The document is from the Records of Notary Engelbert van der Vloet, no. 2069.

the street and away from bad company." Adriaen, as it turned out, was not only lacking in memory and understanding, but totally retarded (*innocent*).

During the four years that he lived with the deposant, he was considered crazy by the other students. Even though he, Rietwijck, did his utmost to teach and instruct him, young Duvese could make no progress. He was "always seeking delays (*soeckende gestadich het futselboek*), now he must do this, now that," and got nothing done. He would promise his fellow students some candy that he had received from his godmother (of the kind that is given to small children) because they had drawn something for him. This the master closed his eyes to because he did not want to lose heart. Sometimes he would take the young man to his own room to let him draw beside him, but Duvese could not make headway ("wiste daer geen mouwen aen te passen"), and he would start howling like a child. He would then, with many promises, say he was doing his best. Nevertheless his work at the end of four years was not much different from what it had been at first. The attestants then related how the other pupils had made fun of Duvese's inability to make the simplest arithmetic calculations.

Toward the beginning of the war with England (i.e., in 1652), it happened that Duvese, who had been out of the house, came home all amazed because some people, who had had an eye on him for some time, had informed him that all the smiths had been urged to go from Delft and The Hague with axes to cut off the tails of the English who, they said, had landed in Scheveningen. Whereupon he had asked for his best clothes and for permission to go to Scheveningen, with the promise that he would be careful. When this was refused and he was told he was crazy to let himself be told such a thing, he began to cry heartily, saying he was sure he had heard it from people worthy of belief.

The imbecility of the young Duvese was confirmed by Huybrecht Bonefaesz. van der Gaech, carpenter, and Jan Hendricksz. van Es, baker, who had both lived at and frequented the house of Cornelis Rietwijck. Among other contacts with Duvese they mentioned that they had "drawn for him," presumably to help him out. If, as would appear, the carpenter and the baker were really fellow-pupils of Duvese, then it may safely be conjectured that Rietwijck did not just give instructions to boys who later became professional artists but in effect ran a school where boys going into any craft occupation could get basic training in the art of drawing. The young men who attended

Rietwijck's school may also have received the rudiments of a technical education including the simple mathematics that poor Duvese could not cope with.

These two depositions still leave us completely in the dark about technical aspects of the instruction for future artists. We might ask for instance whether painters and their apprentices drew from life in Delft as some of them are known to have done in Amsterdam. My evidence on this point is amusingly ambiguous. A notarial deposition of 1652 has come down to us in which witnesses testified that the petitioner had been accused of letting herself be painted naked and that she had earned quite a bit of money thereby ("sy haer naect hadde laten uijtschilderen ende dat sy gelts genoeg daermede wist te winnen").[hh] Even if the accusation was unwarranted, I doubt that the woman who had made this scurrilous claim would have thought up her story if the practice had not existed.

SUCCESS OR FAILURE

What constituted success or failure for an artist in Delft in the seventeenth century? At the extremes the answer is fairly straightforward. Miereveld died a rich and famous man; Evert van Aelst died so poor his estate was repudiated by his nephew.[ii] The in-between cases are harder to classify. One empirically useful notion is to treat as a relative failure any painter who quit painting and took up another trade. There is also a category of individuals who may not have been a failure as artists per se but who left Delft because they could not make a living there or because there were better prospects elsewhere. We also have to consider other aspects besides material prosperity or adversity, which may have come about through factors unrelated to

[hh]Records of Notary Frans Boogert, no. 1999, 16 February 1652. On 22 March 1670, the wife of an apprentice-faiencier complained at the request of Burghia Dirxdr. that a certain Cryntge Boudewyn had said on various occasions that the petitioner was a whore and that she had let her mother be painted naked outside The Hague (Records of Notary Jacob Spoors, no. 1679).

[ii]Even in Van Aelst's case, doubt arises as to whether it was his lack of success as an artist which caused his financial penury or his intemperance. Abraham Bredius already noted how Van Aelst was forced to deliver paintings for a large debt incurred to an innkeeper in Nootdorp for food and drinks. He mentions also some other debts for beers and "quantities of Rhine and Mossel wine" (Bredius, "Drie delftsche schilders," *Oud-Holland* 6 [1888]: 291). Hendrick van Vliet also did fairly well during his lifetime but died poor, perhaps as a consequence of the depressed conditions of the early 1670s (*Vide* Bredius in Obreen, *Archief,* 5: 56-61).

an artist's talent. Jacob Jansz. van Velsen, for instance, died wealthy, but chiefly because he married a rich wife. I consider him to have been only "moderately successful." Hans Jordaens the Elder did not leave an especially rich inventory, but he was still a highly successful painter, judging by the very large number of his pictures in Delft collections and their high prices. Vermeer died in financial trouble (his widow had to declare bankruptcy); yet he cannot be said to have been a real failure, in the light of the high prices he obtained for his works and of his respected position in the guild (headman in 1662-1663 and 1670-1671). Depending on the weight that is placed on spiritual and material factors, he may be classified either among the moderate successes or the moderate failures (I have arbitrarily classified him among the former). On the other hand, I have opted to consign to the "unknown" category a number of artists whose financial circumstances did not seem to depend at all on their success as artists (e.g., Karel van Mander II, who was a partner in a tapestry business, and the Protestant minister Andries van der Linde).

No matter how approximate and conjectural the distribution of artists may be among the various categories of success or failure listed in Table 6.5, one conclusion emerges strongly: the proportion of painters who either failed, left town, or changed occupation was substantially greater in the period 1640 to 1679 than it had been from 1613 to 1639. Moreover, it can be shown that the outward migration from Delft started in the 1640s, at a time when the yearly number of new registrations was still high, then continued after the supply of new masters began to dry up. The artists' colony in Delft began its numerical decline even before the school of original painting for which the town is best known—the church interiors of Houckgeest and Emanuel de Witte, the townscapes of Fabritius, Daniel Vosmaer, and Egbert van der Poel, the genre scenes of Pieter de Hooch and Johannes Vermeer—reached its maturity.

The attraction of Amsterdam as a buoyant commercial city with many rich potential clients and as a center where artists could congregate and exchange ideas cannot be overestimated. In the period 1640 to 1670, the balance of exchanges between Amsterdam and Delft was almost all one way: only one Amsterdam-based painter came to Delft—Carel Fabritius (who was born in Middenbremster)—whereas a number of prominent painters in Delft moved to Amsterdam, either directly or via The Hague, including Jacob Pynas (moved to Amsterdam in 1642), Simon de Vlieger (1648), Willem van den Landen (about 1650), Emanuel de Witte (early 1650s), Willem van

[177]

TABLE 6.5
Relative Success or Failure of Registered Artist-Painters (1613-1679)

	Pre-1613-1639	1640-1679	Total
Very successful	3	0	3
Moderately successful	15	5	20
Moderate failure	1	2	3
Engaged in other occupations	6	3	9
Left town	15	12	27
Died poor in Delft	2	2	4
Total known or estimated	42	24	66
Unknown	29	22	51
Grand Total	71	46	117

SOURCE: See Table 6.1.

NOTES: The year of inscription in the guild has been placed after the name of the master. Very successful: M. Miereveld (1613 master list), Hans Jordaens I (1613 master list), Jacob Vosmaer (1613 master list). Moderately successful: Pieter van Asch (1623), Balthasar van der Ast (1632), Gillis de Berg (1624), Leonaert Bramer (1629), Pieter Bronckhorst (1613 master list), Willem van den Bundel (1623), Jan Willemsz. Decker (1613 master list), Carel Fabritius (1652), Jacob Willemsz. Delff II (1641), Pieter Groenewegen (1626), Hubert Jacobsz. Grimani (1613 master list), Hans Jordaens II (1657), Cornelis de Man (1642), Anthony Palamedes (1621), Cornelis Rietwijck (1613 master list), Pieter Stael (1613 master list), Jacob van Velsen (1625), Jochum de Vries (1628), Johannes Vermeer (1653), Willem van Vliet (1613 master list). Moderate failures: Matheus de Berg(h) (1624), Claes Bronckhorst (1641), Claes Vosmaer (1645). Engaged in other occupations (and more or less gave up painting): Abram de Cooge (1632), Louis Elsevier (1646), Jan Gerbrantsz. de Jong (1613 master list), Jan van Ghils (1613 master list), Isaac Junius (1640), Joris van Lier (1623), Dirck van der Mast (1627), Johannes van Nes (1618), Adam Pick (1642). Left town: Willem van Aelst (1643), Bartholomeus van Bassen (1613), Abram van Beyeren (1657), Abram Bonaert (1613), Hendrick van der Burch (1649), Corstiaen Caescooper (1643), Pieter Hoevenaer (1622), Jan Damen Cool (1614), Corstiaen Couwenbergh (1627), Jacob van Geel (1628), Pieter de Hooch (1655), Gerard Houckgeest (1639), Willem van den Landen (1635), Adriaen van Linschoten (1635), Egbert van der Poel (1650), Paulus Potter (1646), Jacob Pynas (1632), Jan Songe (1646), Jan Spangaert (1632), Jan van der Spriet (1675), Pieter Steenwijck (1642), Abram Stulling (1626), Maerten Hendricksz. Tol (1625), Simon de Vlieger (1634), Abram Vosmaer (1639), Daniel Vosmaer (1650), Emanuel de Witte (1642). Died poor in Delft: Evert van Aelst (1632), Sijmon Fangaert (1647), Pieter van der Vin (1645), Hendrick van Vliet (1632).

Aelst (about 1657), Paulus Potter (moved first to The Hague then to Amsterdam around 1652), Pieter de Hooch (1660-1661), Isaac Junius (early 1660s), and Abram van Beyeren (moved to The Hague around 1663 then to Amsterdam in the late 1660s).

A final note on success-or-failure: all the artists considered became masters in the guild. This was in and of itself a mark of sufficient talent to finish a six-year apprenticeship or otherwise satisfy the headmen of one's capability to operate as an independent painter. Many apprentices never reached this stage. Given the low costs of setting oneself up as an independent painter, I doubt whether many artists long remained apprentices for lack of means after their learning period was completed.[ii] Reference was already made to Reymbrant Cornelisz. Verboom who did not join the guild after his apprenticeship was over. A clearer case in point is that of Jacob Jansz. Dinsich, the nephew of the landscape painter Williem Williemsz. van den Bundel. Dinsich was mentioned a number of times as a painter in Delft in the period 1622 to 1624, when he was almost surely an apprentice.[32] However, on 3 November 1625, Van den Bundel's sister apprenticed her son, Jacob Jansz., to a baker to learn the trade of bread-baking (records of Notary Willem de Langue, no. 1684). The young man had apparently not been able to earn a living as a painter.

DELFT AS AN ARTISTIC CENTER

The period during which Delft distinguished itself, at least by present-day standards, as a center of artistic activity was very brief. It can hardly be said to have begun before the mid-1640s or to have extended much beyond 1660, with the conspicuous exception of Johannes Vermeer.

In the first decade of the century, Delft's only real strength had lain in portrait painting (Michiel Miereveld and the now-forgotten Hubert Jacobsz. Grimani). The Flemish immigration brought a fair number of painters and tapestry designers to Delft, but none with a dominating artistic personality like Frans Hals or Esaias van de Velde in Haarlem. It may also be argued[33] that Delft's conservative political and religious climate, its well-marked and long-established class cleavages, and the preference of its high bourgeoisie for solid craftsmanship over dash and imagination, did not create a favorable climate for the type of forceful, baroque art that Rubens, Hals, and Rembrandt were popularizing elsewhere at the time.

The first forty years of the century witnessed the slow but steady growth of the artists' community. New specialties developed in seascape painting, church interiors, and battles scenes. Yet Delft in 1640 could still not be said to host an original "school" of painting: its artists went their separate ways, exempt for the most part from any

---

[ii]I conjectured in Chapter 4 that very few artist-painters lived out their lives as apprentices.

FIG. 10 Pieter de Hooch, *Two Women in a Courtyard* (1657-1660), 27¼ x 21¼ in. Royal Collection, Buckingham Palace. Copyright reserved to H. M. the Queen (Photo: National Gallery)

leadership or even from strong currents of influence, beyond the imitation by the weaker among them of their more talented colleagues (as in the case of Pieter Vromans the Younger's imitation of Bramer's style). No more disparate group of painters can be conceived than Michiel Miereveld, Balthasar van der Ast, Jacob Pynas, Anthony Palamedes, Simon de Vlieger, and Leonaert Bramer who were all active—and more or less successful—in Delft in the 1630s. It is only toward the end of the 1640s and the beginning of the 1650s that common interests began to take shape and new trends to emerge among some of the Delft's painters, conspicuous among whom were talented out-of-towners who immigrated about this time, such as Paulus Potter and Emanuel de Witte who arrived in 1647, Carel Fabritius in 1650 (or perhaps earlier), and Pieter de Hooch in 1652 (fig. 10). These innovative "foreigners," together with their Delft-based colleagues, including Gerard Houckgeest and, some time later, Johannes Vermeer, shared a sensibility to the effects of light and air and an interest in space construction and perspective.[kk] The upper-classes of Delft with their fondness for fine craftsmanship and their sense of good taste could not fail to give a hospitable reception to the simplifying-clarifying ("classicizing") tendencies that were spreading over Holland at the time.

By the mid-1650s, weaker personalities such as Heyndrick van der Burch (genre), Daniel Vosmaer (city views), and Hendrick van Vliet (church interiors) had fallen under the sway of the innovators of Delft art. A genuine school—in the sense of a community with intersecting interests in subject matter and techniques, with some similarity in aesthetic approaches, and with significant cross-influences—had at last come into existence. But a critical mass, in the sense of a number of individuals large enough to preserve the intensity of interaction necessary to keep a community of artists from drifting apart, is sooner lost than won. When the community is small to begin with, it only takes a few deaths or departures for it to disintegrate. By 1660, Carel Fabritius was dead, and Amsterdam had attracted some of the school's best elements (Emanuel de Witte, Paulus Potter, Pieter de Hooch). When Vermeer became headman of the guild in 1662, he had little left to preside over. What artistic vitality the town still possessed was concentrated in its booming blue-and-white faience industry, while easel painting was shrinking in importance. The talented artists who continued to exercise their art in Delft—Cornelis

---

[kk]I have profited here from the suggestions of Peter Sutton.

de Man, Johannes Verkolje—contributed little that was new or important beyond the achievements of their predecessors. It is a wonder that Vermeer, the greatest talent that Delft brought forth, did not forsake his native town after most of the gifted painters of his generation had left it to seek better prospects elsewhere.

SEVEN

The Art Market

There is a wide range of possible relationships between patrons and artists: from the close links that bind an artist to the prince or the Maecenas who feeds and lodges him all the way to the casual and intermittent contact between a painter or sculptor and the client who buys an occasional piece from him. Throughout this chapter, I shall limit the meaning of the word patronage to a personal relationship between the artist and the client who commissions a work of art from him and normally influences the carrying out of the commission in some way. Buying ready-made works, whether from the artist himself or through an intermediary, will not be considered patronage.

INSTITUTIONAL PATRONAGE

In Renaissance Italy, most artists belonged to the households of the rich and the noble or worked on commissions for churches, city edifices, princely courts, and wealthy burghers. The market for ready-made works was still narrow and underdeveloped.[1] In early sixteenth-century Delft it is also likely that artists worked chiefly for ecclesiastic and civic authorities. But by the 1600s the situation had changed. Since the Protestant Alteration, monasteries were closed. Churches were no longer buying works of art on any scale.[a] Only civic

[a]No paintings seem to have been bought or commissioned by either the Old or the New Church. The sculpted monuments that were erected in these churches were for the most part commissioned from out-of-town artists and paid for by the States General or private parties. Thus the famous monument to Willem the Silent in the New Church begun by Hendrick de Keyser and finished by his son Pieter was commissioned by the States General in 1614. Another pupil of Hendrick de Keyser is probably responsible for the 1611 funerary monument for Elisabeth van Marnix. Pieter de Keyser executed the monument for Admiral Piet Heyn, while the monument for Tromp was the work of Willem de Keyser (Hendrick's second son) and the Mechelen-born, Amsterdam-based Rombout Verhulst. Most Delft sculptors, according to Max Eisler's short chapter on sculpture in his book on Delft, hardly rose above the level of tradition-bound artisans (*Alt-Delft: Kultur und Kunst* [Amsterdam:

organizations—the town, the guilds, the militia organizations known as the *schutters*—maintained some level of public patronage. Sculptors by the very nature of their art still depended largely on commissions. Painters had no alternative but to work "for the market."

Delft, in any event, was no place for high-class patronage. The Court of the princes of Orange, whose support of the arts was never on a royal European scale to begin with, had moved from Delft to The Hague in the last decades of the sixteenth century. The court now had little to offer Delft artists. Exceptional orders emanated from The Hague for the decoration of Prince Frederick Henry's castles at Rijswijck and Honselaersdyck, which Leonaert Bramer and Corstiaen Couwenbergh executed in the late 1630s, and for the Huis ten Bosch near The Hague for which Couwenbergh supplied some paintings in the 1640s, along with colleagues from The Hague, Haarlem, and Antwerp.[b] It should be observed that Couwenbergh, aside from the little-known Mattheus de Berg(h), was the only artist in Delft in the 1630s and 1640s who specialized in painting classical nudes in the Italian manner, of the type that princely patrons favored for the decoration of their great houses.

Only Michiel Miereveld enjoyed anything like steady patronage from the court: he not only painted portraits of the princes of Orange and their families on commission but obtained monopoly privileges from the States General to make copies of these portraits and sell them to the burgomasters in Delft and elsewhere.[2]

Elsevier, 1923], pp. 72-82). Pieter Rycx, cited below, may have been an exception. Because the Roman Catholic churches were barely tolerated, there is hardly any record of their patronage. A number of anonymous early seventeenth-century pictures, so far unattributed, are preserved in the vestry of the "hidden" Catholic church in Delft that were perhaps acquired shortly after they were painted. Vermeer's *Allegory of Faith* in the Metropolitan Museum of Art, New York, may have been painted on a commission from the Jesuits, who were in charge of the Catholic church in Delft in the 1660s (Albert Blankert, *Vermeer of Delft: Complete Edition of the Paintings* [Oxford: Phaidon, 1978], p. 59).

[b]Couwenbergh received 800 gulden for the paintings he made for Honselaersdyck in 1638. On Frederick Henry's patronage, see J. G. van Gelder, "De schilders van der Oranje-zaal," *Nederlandsch Kunsthistorisch Jaarboek* 2 (1948-49):118 ff.; and Jacob Rosenberg, S. Slive, and E. H. ter Kuile, *Dutch Art and Architecture 1600-1800*, Pelican History of Art Series, rev. ed. (Baltimore: Penguin Books, 1972), pp. 298-300. In all the inventories of Frederick Henry and Amelia Soms, except for the paintings by Couwenbergh in the Huis ten Bosch, I found only two small paintings by Balthasar van der Ast representing the Delft artists' community. *Inventarissen van de inboedels in de verblijven van de Oranjes* (The Hague: M. Nijhoff, 1974), p. 191.

The patronage of the burgomasters of Delft and the authorities constituting the Weth was neither steady nor particularly generous. Of the artists that the Weth patronized, only Leonaert Bramer received commissions that were important enough to support him for any length of time. The city of Delft paid Miereveld about half as much money over the years as it did to Bramer for the portraits of the court of Orange that he painted for the Town Hall, but his other sources of income were so large that these local orders, which amounted to less than 1,200 gulden from 1620 to 1632, can hardly have been decisive for him.

Table 7.1 summarizes the receipts by painters and sculptors of city commissions from 1619 to 1675. Some of the individual commissions listed in Table 7.1 merit more detailed consideration. Hendrick de Keyser, master sculptor of the city of Amsterdam, received 200 gulden in 1620 for the statue of Justice he made for the Town Hall, newly rebuilt after the fire of 1618. In 1622 Pieter Bronckhorst was commissioned to paint a "perspective" (i.e., an architectural piece) with "the judgement of Salomon between the two whores" to hang in the Court of Justice (Verschaar). This rather mediocre picture in the style of Hans Vredeman de Vries can still be seen in Delft's Town Hall. Bronckhorst was awarded twenty Flemish pounds (120 gulden) for the picture according to his original specifications plus thirty gulden as a present "because he complained, and the lords of the Weth judged, that he had (initially) received too little."

Joris Gerritsz. van Lier obtained a commission in 1629 for "22 little upright panels for the ordinaris (?) in prayers for the burial of the dead" ("voor de ordinaris biddens van de dooden ter begrafenis"). These were perhaps little signs with writing on them, or, less likely, holy images for the marchers to carry in funerary processions.[c]

The commission of two paintings from the marine painter Hendrick Cornelisz. Vroom in 1634 is of sufficient interest to quote the full entry for payment in the "Lopende Memorialen":

> Master Vroom from Haarlem presented this city with a portrait of the city of Delft made with his own hand. In consideration of the fact that his mother was buried in the Old Church in Delft, that Mr. Vroom in his youth learned his art here, and that he has always borne great affection for this city, Messrs. the burgomasters have

[c] I do not feel sufficiently confident of the correctness of Wichmann's transcription of the original text or of my own translation to affirm this interpretation.

TABLE 7.1

Sums Paid by the City of Delft to Various Artists for Commissions
(1619–1675)

Artist	Date	Commission	Sums Received (Gulden)
Michiel Miereveld	1619–1632	Various portraits	1,161
Hendrick de Keyser	1620	Statue for Town Hall	200
Pieter Anthonisz. van Bronckhorst	1622	A "history" painting	150
Cornelis Jacobsz. Delff	1629	Painting of pennants and other small commissions	44
Hendrick Vroom	1634	Two panoramas of Delft	150
Simon de Vlieger	1640–1641	Various paintings*	700
Joris Gerritsz van Lier	1641	Twenty-two small panels	17
Corstiaen Couwenbergh	1643–1645	Two tapestry cartoons and a picture for the Drapiers' Hall	174
Adriaen Diest†	1646	Painting of new pennants for the Shooting Gallery	400

Carel Fabritius	1654	Painting of coats-of-arms	12
Jacob Delff	1659	Repair of paintings hanging in the Doelen	200
Leonaert Bramer	1660-1668	Various paintings*	2,330
Pieter Rijcx	1660	Statues for the new Doelen	1,672
Pieter van Asch	1669	A painting	100
(?) Van der Hoor	1669	Restoration of a painting by Van Heems-kerck in the Town Hall	63
Willem van Odekercken	1672	Painting of armories and pennants	126
Cornelis de Man	1675	Portraits and copies	63
Total (1619-1675)			7,562

SOURCES: Soutendam, "Eenige aanteekeningen," pp. 1-10; Wichmann, "Mitteilungen über Delfter Künstler," pp. 65-70.

*Described in the text below.

†Possibly an error in transcription for Adriaen Delff, *kladschilder*. In any event this "Adriaen Diest" should not be confused with The Hague painter Adriaen van Diest (1655-c. 1704)

accepted the portrait with thanks and presented Mr. Vroom, as an expression of their gratitude, 150 gulden.

This was surely as elegant and courteous a formula for a sales transaction as anyone could devise.

On 2 December 1640, when Simon de Vlieger received 300 gulden for paintings that were apparently designed as projects or sketches for tapestries, he was called a "painter in Amsterdam." Four months later another 400 gulden were paid to him on this same account. Neither the sketches nor the tapestries, as far as I am aware, have been preserved. The unusually high payments and the fact that he was commissioned when he had already left Delft, at a time when at least one fairly successful marine painter was still active in the city (Jochum de Vries), are evidence of Vlieger's contemporary reputation.

In 1643 Couwenbergh painted a cartoon for a tapestry of fifteen ells at six gulden the ell and "for making an additional two ells at the same price." Two years later he made a picture for the Drapiers' Hall for seventy-two gulden. In July 1654, Fabritius, three months before his death in the explosion of the powder magazine of Delft, received twelve gulden for painting "one large and a few small armories of the city." For 200 gulden, Jacob Delff in 1659 repaired the damage done by the explosion to four paintings hanging in the Doelen (the "targets"). This was probably the hall next to the alley where the *schutters* had their target practice.[d]

On 2 April 1669, a year after the repairs to the paintings in the Doelen had been paid for, Bramer obtained 300 gulden for three paintings in the New Doelen plus 100 gulden for the upkeep of those paintings his whole life long, together with a picture on canvas for the mantelpiece, apparently also for the New Doelen. The paintings for whose upkeep Bramer was responsible were presumably frescoes. Shortly thereafter a payment to Bramer of 150 gulden was authorized in two installments for "painting in the shooting-piece in the shooting gallery of the Doelen" ("over het schilderen int schietstuck van de scutterye inden doele"). In mid-July 1661, he received twenty-two gulden for painting an outdoor signboard hanging in the horse market. In 1663, various payments totaling seventy-five gulden were made to him for repairs to and upkeep of the "painted room and the

---

[d]These were perhaps group portraits of the *schutters* such as Jacob Delff himself had painted in 1641 (reproduced in Eisler, *Alt-Delft*, p. 143). Their large size would explain the expense of the repairs.

shooting-piece." In May 1667, sixty-three gulden were given to Bramer for "repairing the painted room in the Doelen and for two sketches for the mantelpieces in the great hall in the court." These sketches were made for the Prinsenhof, whose decoration occupied Bramer for the next year. During the remaining months of 1667 and up to October 1668, by which time the commission seems to have been completed, various payments were made to the painter for work on the Prinsenhof totaling 1,620 gulden. Despite these large payments—a part of which may have defrayed the remunerations of assistants—Bramer was apparently still in financial straits. A month after the last payment of 800 gulden in October 1669, Bramer, at his request and in consideration of his pecuniary difficulties, was awarded 100 gulden as a present "for his upkeep."[e]

In 1660 the sculptor Pieter Rijcx received the munificent sum of 1,672 gulden "for the making of various sculptures for the New Doelen." These sculptures have unfortunately disappeared. Finally the landscape painter Pieter van Asch was paid 100 gulden for a mantelpiece painting destined to hang in the hall of the Prinsenhof.[f] The other entries in Table 7.1 refer to minor commissions for the painting of pennants and armories and for restoration.

The variety of subjects commissioned—portraits, "histories," landscapes, seascapes, armories, and signboards—is striking. Prices, while higher than those one would expect to encounter in contemporary inventories for typical pictures by the painters listed, are not unreasonable. It is remarkable that the town authorities had no qualms about commissioning artists who were not residents of Delft (De Keyser, Vroom, De Vlieger) to carry out commissions. In this respect they remained true to the sixteenth-century practice that the churches had followed of ordering works from the most competent artists, irrespective of whether or not they were presently members of the guild in Delft.

Besides orders from the burgomasters, to what other institutional sources might artists look for support? The Hoogheemraadschap,

---

[e]This last sum, not being a payment for a commission, was omitted from Table 7.1. The city treasurer's payment of 25 gulden 9 stuivers to Anthony Palamedes "as an extraordinary subsidy" is the only other known example of Delft municipal support for an artist that did not call for delivery of a work of art (Heinrich Wichmann, "Mitteilungen über Delfter Künstler des XVII Jahrhunderts," *Oud-Holland* 42 [1925]:69).

[f]Perhaps the landscape which he painted with Hendrick Verschuring of Dordrecht, presently in the Municipal Museum Het Prinsenhof in Delft.

which financed and supervised all waterworks in Delftland, had fairly sumptuous quarters in Delft, yet the accounts of its expenditures in its archives show only routine orders for tiles, the painting of mantelpieces, and the decoration of coaches. Some of the numerous guilds of artisans commissioned works for their quarters, but the records of these orders have for the most part been lost. The Anatomy Lesson of Dr. W. van der Meer designed by Michiel Miereveld and executed by his son Pieter in 1617 was a commission of the Guild of Surgeons. This same guild later had Anthony Palamedes paint portraits of its headmen on the doors of an instrument case.[3] The painted decoration of the new quarters of the Guild of St. Lucas strictly speaking was not a commission at all: it was carried out by Bramer and Cornelis de Man as a voluntary contribution, "out of love and in honor of the guild."[4] If we may judge from the written records that have come down to us including notarial and estate papers that should show some trace, if only through contracts, of such patronage, there was little here that artists could draw on besides an occasional commission for a group portrait, which was at the limit between private and institutional patronage.[g]

PRIVATE PATRONAGE

Turning now to private patronage we find hardly any evidence of protracted employment of artists by wealthy clients. The only case that I can document is the employment by Justus de la Grange of the painter Pieter de Hooch as a *knecht*, a term that may refer to the supplier of domestic as well as of artistic services. However, the fact that De la Grange turned over paintings by De Hooch as collateral on a loan in 1655 suggests the genre painter painted for his master.[5] No evidence has turned up of painters regularly employed as copyists or otherwise by dealers.

In December 1637, Simon de Vlieger, then living in Delft, did sign a long-term contract with the Rotterdam dealer Crijn Hendricksz. Volmarijn that obligated him to deliver paintings regularly to the merchant, although this was not for wages but as the equivalent of installment payments on the purchase of a house. De Vlieger, who had bought the house from Volmarijn for 900 gulden, committed

[g]On group portraits in Delft, see Eisler, *Alt-Delft*, pp. 140-45.

himself to deliver pictures worth thirty-one gulden a month, starting 1 January 1638, until the entire sum was paid (with the provision that any delays in delivery would entitle Volmarijn to collect a fine of six gulden).[6] De Vlieger could supply each month a large picture worth thirty-one gulden or a "seven-stuiver panel"[h] worth eighteen gulden and a marine worth thirteen gulden. In addition De Vlieger would vouchsafe a gift (presumably of a picture) by May 1638. This was all to be "good work, of the kind the painter produced for other people." All costs (of panels and paints) would be shared by the painter and the dealer.

We can document a few instances of artists working directly for clients on the decoration of their houses. In 1653 Leonaert Bramer signed a contract[7] with his next-door neighbor Anthony Bronckhorst whereby he undertook to paint in fresco the walls and ceiling of a corridor or passage, apparently situated between the houses of the contracting parties "according to such prescription (*ordonnantie*) as may please Bronckhorst," together with two doors opening into the corridor, all "according to the requirements of the work, which the contracting parties shall refer to the judgment of the notary." If I interpret this last passage correctly, the Notary Willem de Langue, a well-known collector of paintings and friend of many artists in Delft,[i] was expected to judge the manner of execution and quality of the work performed. Bronckhorst promised to pay Bramer 300 gulden upon completion of the commission plus a silver flagon worth 50 gulden.

Samuel Hoogstraten in his *Inleyding tot de Hooge Schoole der Schilder-konst* tells of a similar commission for a fresco painting of a ceiling given by a Delft physician, Dr. Valentius, to Carel Fabritius.[8] Hoogstraten, significantly, deplored that neither this fresco nor others made by Fabritius for private clients had been placed "in a durable

[h]That is, a picture of the size of a seven-stuiver panel. In Antwerp panels came in three-, six-, eight-, sixteen-, twenty-, and twenty-six-stuiver sizes. Hanns Floerke, *Die Formen des Kunsthandels, das Atelier und die Sammler in den Niederlanden vom 15–18 Jahrhundert,* Studien zur Niederländischen Kunst- und Kulturgeschichte (1905; reprint ed., Soest, Holland: Davaco Publishers, 1972), p. 198. On the size of panels in Dutch paintings see Josua de Bruyn, "Een onderzoek naar 17ᵉ eeuwse schilderij formaten, voornamelijk in Noordnederland," *Oud-Holland* 93 (1979):96–115.

[i]On Willem de Langue's contacts with Vermeer and his family as well as with other artists, see J. M. Montias, "Vermeer and His Milieu: Conclusion of an Archival Study," *Oud-Holland* 94 (1980):47.

royal edifice or a church," where they would have been better preserved and visible to a wider public.[j] Hoogstraten's comment on the private character of Fabritius's commissions corroborates other evidence about the relatively modest level of public patronage in Delft.

At the limit of our definition of patronage are steady client-artist relations cemented by contracts. Johannes Jordaens the Younger, for example, contracted on four separate occasions for the delivery of paintings to an attorney in The Hague named Johan Stans. Some of the pictures had already been painted in Italy, others were to be made especially for Stans. The first three contracts, dated 1659 to 1661, stipulated that Stans would pay for the paintings he was about to receive only when he got married;[9] the last, dated 1665, called for payment in sixty days.[10]

Only exceptionally did clients stipulate in a formal contract the precise subject for a given commission and a standard of quality. The contract between Bramer and Bronckhorst, as we have seen, specified the medium of the painting and named a third party as an arbiter of quality. The only other case I know of occurred in 1612. A dispute had arisen between the painter Peter Stael and a passementerie-worker named IJselsteyn concerning a barter arrangement of paintings for fancy trousers, described as "coral red, striped, and trimmed with passementerie."[11] The trousers had been delivered, but Stael had turned over only one painting—a Sodom and Gomorrah!—for them. The matter had been referred to three arbiters who ruled as follows. Peter Stael was obligated to deliver, before May 1613, two landscape paintings of a size corresponding to the frame that IJselsteyn had given him. These were to represent "a winter" and "a summer" of the same quality and worth as the piece Stael had painted for the burgomaster, Jacob Paeuw. If he failed to deliver the paintings on these conditions, he would have to pay IJselsteyn a fine of 100 gulden. If Stael were to die in the meanwhile, his widow and heirs would have to pay seventy-seven gulden eight stuivers to IJselsteyn, who would be entitled in addition to choose one piece out of twelve that Stael had on hand ready to be finished. If the two paintings were delivered on

[j]One contemporary document, dated 1660, tells us that the widow of a brewer for whom Fabritius had painted a mural which was slated for destruction after the brewery was sold had petitioned to save the mural by ripping out the wall on which it had been painted, but we do not know whether or not it was—at least temporarily— preserved.

time, IJselsteyn would have to give Stael forty-eight ells of imitation gold galloon and a pearl for his wife.[k]

Painters-in-the-rough are not counted in this brief survey. Exceptionally, however, these *kladschilders* had to carry out commissions of a clearly artistic character. Jacob Corsendonck was asked in January 1671 to paint a "perspective of trees" ("perspectijff van boomen") on a barn door in Vlaerding.[12] From another document involving this same painter, we learn that the outside walls of houses were sometimes decorated with figures (*personaje*), which again must have required some artistic skill.[13] Finally, as was already mentioned in Chapter 6, the painting of coats-of-arms could be entrusted either to a broad-brush or to an artist-painter. In 1674 Ary Corsendonck, the son of Jacob, earned twenty-eight gulden for the painting of the heraldic escutcheon of Isaac Spierinx.[14] In 1654, Fabritius was commissioned by the city of Delft to paint the armories cited in Table 7.1.[l]

A type of patronage that involved direct, if usually quite limited, contact between clients and artists was the portrait commission. By their very nature such commissions called for some adaptation to consumer demand. I would venture to guess that most newly married men with at least moderate assets—say, in excess of 500 gulden, which would include young masters in any of the artisan guilds as well as merchants and rentiers—had their portraits painted, usually along with their spouse. If they were of very modest means they sat for a workaday painter such as Jan Claesz. Harlaer (or Havelen) who charged only six gulden for a portrait he made of a tailor around 1620.[15] Rich burghers had their portraits painted by Miereveld or by one of his pupils. No receipts or vouchers for Miereveld's portraits have been preserved in Delft, but the amounts owed to him by clients after his death for commissions completed varied from eighteen gulden (1627) to sixty gulden (1639).[16] Doubtlessly, the amount charged depended on the format (full- or half-length) and on the extent to which the master's assistants contributed to the execution. In the case of Miereveld's pupil Willem van Vliet we have an entry in the estate papers of the notary Dirck de Haen, who died in 1638,

---

[k]The coral red garment, the galloon, and the pearl are luxuries that would hardly seem suitable for the orthodox Calvinist party to which Stael belonged in 1618 (see above, Chapter 6). In their sermons, Calvinist preachers deplored the wearing of ostentatious clothes and jewelry such as Stael obtained in exchange for his paintings.

[l]Likewise, the artist Cornelis Daemen Rietwijck received three gulden three stuivers to paint some "small escutcheons" (*wapentges*) (Orphan Chamber, *boedel* no. 1428 I).

claiming a total of twenty-nine gulden for a portrait of the deceased, including five gulden for the panel.[17] Harmen van Bolgersteyn charged twenty-six gulden for a portrait in 1628; Anthony Palamedes received thirty-three gulden for the portraits of a man and his wife (including the panels) in the 1660s. At an unknown date, Hubert Jacobsz. Grimani was able to cancel a debt for beer of fifty-seven gulden ten stuivers by painting the likeness of his creditor,[19] but it is unlikely that he received such high prices for normal commissions. The highest price by far that I found noted in a contemporary document or a portrait commission was obtained in 1669 by "Baans konstschilder in den Hage" for a portrait of Jacob Hogenhouck, captain of the Delft militia.[20] Baans, who is almost certainly Jan de Baen of The Hague (1633–1702), claimed the enormous sum of 175 gulden for this single picture. It is remarkable that so prominent a Delft citizen should have commissioned an out-of-town artist for his portrait.

Artists could also be commissioned to paint copies of family portraits so that each heir would have his parents' picture. No less distinguished an artist than Johan van Ravesteyn of The Hague received the commission in 1638 to paint such a set of copies, presumably from originals he himself had made, of the portraits of Cornelis Michielsz. Ring and his wife. Unfortunately the document does not record how much Ravesteyn was paid for the copies. (The original went to the oldest son; the other children received the copies.)[21]

WORKING THE MARKET

Artists in Delft had many outlets for ready-made works. They could sell paintings to private clients who visited their atelier or the exhibitions in the premises of the Guild of St. Lucas (after 1661) or some other gallery. They could hold a lottery or ask the official in charge of the disposition of estates (the *boelhuysmeester*) to auction them off. They could also consign them with a local dealer who might alternatively buy them outright. Examples of all these types of transactions can, and will be, documented with one important exception: I have not found a single reference in a contemporary document to an individual who visited a painter's atelier and bought a painting in cash. This of course reflects a bias in the nature of the written evidence; there was simply no reason to record such transactions. But even mention of debts owed to painters by estates—for works that were presumably bought directly from the artist—are rare.

A mention of twenty-five gulden due to Jacob Woutersz. Vosmaer by the widow of the Delft patrician Robbrecht Pietersz. van Schilperoort for one or more paintings, a debt due by a tailor in Monfort for paintings delivered, and the names of clients of Anthony Palamedes in Gorcum, The Hague, Rotterdam, and Haarlem who owed him anywhere from fourteen to fifty gulden each for paintings are about all the instances I could find.[22]

That direct sales from stock must have occurred frequently may be inferred from the large inventories of paintings in the estates of prominent Delft painters who, unlike Miereveld, worked primarily for the market, such as Willem Jansz. and Jan Willemsz. Decker, Hans Jordaens, Wouter Jacobsz. Vosmaer, and Cornelis Daemen Rietwijck.[m]

With the exceptions cited, the closest we come to records of direct sales by painters to their clients are the numerous mentions in contracts and in estate papers of paintings delivered to settle debts. The case of De Vlieger's working off a debt for the purchase of a house by painting for his creditor has already been mentioned. Egbert van der Poel was obligated to supply paintings valued at 100 gulden in payment of his debts.[23] Similarly Evert van Aelst owed paintings for 161 gulden[24] and Wouter Jacobsz. Vosmaer for 25 gulden.[25] Another Vosmaer, possibly Daniel or Niclaes, was in debt for nine gulden one stuiver for which he was committed to furnish one painting.[26] These debts were all owed to innkeepers. Emanuel de Witte undertook to paint two pictures, each worth 100 gulden, that were to be delivered to Adam Pick who, by this time, was also an innkeeper, as well as a painter. Pick had agreed to pay fifty gulden apiece for the paintings, the balance being due to him for a gambling debt.[27]

---

[m]Eight out of fifty-six paintings in Willem Jansz. Decker's inventory were attributed. Most of the attributed paintings—especially those listed among the frames, panels, and uncompleted pictures—must have been done by Willem Jansz. or his father Jan Willemsz. Decker. (Records of Notary Adriaen Rijshouck, no. 1817, 1 January 1625.) Only four out of 146 pictures sold by Hans Jordaens's widow after the artist's death were attributed. Many of the unattributed paintings had "historical" subjects typical of Jordaens's work. The great majority of the unattributed paintings must have been painted by the deceased. (Records of Notary Willem de Langue, no. 1686, 4 July 1630.) In the auction sale of Jacob Vosmaer's pictures and drawings after his death, there were 104 paintings, of which nine were attributed to Vosmaer himself, but at least another thirteen unattributed flower paintings were most probably by him (Orphan Chamber, *boedel* no. 1847, 8 and 9 April 1642). In the Cornelis Daemen Rietwijck inventory of December 1660, 183 pictures were mentioned, almost all anonymous, including "seventy small and large paintings of faces and others," presumed to be by Rietwijck. (Orphan Chamber, *boedel* no. 1428 I.)

[195]

Astonishingly little is to be found in the notarial archives regarding the public exhibition by artists of paintings available for sale. Abraham Bredius discovered two references to exhibits in The Hague in the 1620s, one by the dealer Pouwels Weyts and one by the painter Wellem Jansz. Decker. The States General authorized Weyts on 2 September 1622 to exhibit paintings twice a week in the gallery "between the Great Hall and the chamber of the States General." According to the receipt signed by the clerk of the Rentmaster General of North Holland, found in Decker's estate papers, six pounds (twenty-four gulden) had been paid from the funds in the estate for one year's rent of the "White Gallery of the Court" that Willem Jansz. Decker had leased in The Hague in 1624 "to stand with his painting(s)" ("als gestaen hebbende met syn schildery").[28] Exhibition in the court of the princes of Orange was a practice which, as we saw in Chapter 2, already went on in the beginning of the seventeenth century. As for exhibition space in Delft itself, however, the only information available, at least up to the renovation of the premises of the Guild of St. Lucas in 1661, concerns a large painting partially owned by Carel Fabritius, which was available for sale and hanging in the Town Hall in 1653.[29] It was probably this same painting, which later was said to have been painted by Daniel and Niclaes Vosmaer and retouched by Fabritius, that "had long hung in the Town Hall but now lay in the Prinsenhof [in Delft]."[30] There is no way to tell whether the scarcity of these references is a reflection of the lack of opportunities for artists to exhibit works in public places or of the failure of contemporaries to report these opportunities in the written records that have come down to us.

The evidence on the prices paid to painters for their works is too meager to uphold any generalization. The transactions that I have referred to, bearing no indication of a painting's size, beyond small or large, provide only a feeble basis for comparisons. The entries in *boelhuys* auction records, in the minority of instances where the items are attributed, may refer to paintings executed shortly beforehand or many years previously. By the time a painting came up for auction the artist may have become old-fashioned or his style may have changed, and the picture may bring a lower price than one of his contemporary products would have brought. This is likely to have been the case for a painting by Jan van der Meer, almost certainly Johannes Vermeer, that sold for twenty gulden ten stuivers in an estate auction in 1661, by which year the artist probably already received substantially higher prices for his works (he is said to have obtained 600 gulden for a painting with a single figure in or before 1663.)[31] One still can form only a very general idea of the prices different painters received from the odd quotations in estate papers and *contracedullen*. In the 1640s and early 1650s, starting at the lower end of the scale, paintings by run-of-the-mill artists such as Niclaes Vosmaer, Willem van den Bundel, and Pieter Vromans II typically fetched five to fifteen gulden; those by Gerard Houckgeest and Evert van Aelst sold for twenty to thirty-five gulden; Emanuel de Witte's works ranged from twenty (for early works) to one hundred gulden, Bramer's from ten or fifteen (perhaps for smaller works) to thirty to forty gulden; Couwenbergh, who painted chiefly large-scale, highly finished pictures with mythological themes that appealed to the upper class, thirty to one hundred gulden; flower paintings by Jacob Vosmaer went from ten to fifteen gulden to 130 gulden for large pieces. The prices of Hans Jordaens's works varied greatly but centered around thirty to fifty gulden. Pictures by Adriaen Linschoten could sell for as low as thirteen gulden (for a "face") and as high as one hundred gulden for a "history of King Nimus." No painter in Delft in this period, with the possible exception of Vermeer, received prices as high as those brought by paintings attributed to Rubens (500 gulden for a Venus and Adonis at the Boudewijn de Man sale of 15 March 1644), Baburen (605 gulden for a "school" at the same sale), or Bloemaert (600 gulden for a St. John the Baptist).[32] When the master baker Hendrick van Buyten proposed to take two paintings by Vermeer in lieu of a debt for 617 gulden 6 stuivers a year after his death (in 1676), the offer was quite exceptional.[n] Some of the disparities in prices reflected significant differences in production costs, due to size, number of figures, and degree of finish. They give only the vaguest notion of the scale of returns per unit of time of a painter's work, which is what we really should like to have. We can perhaps surmise that Hans Jordaens, Couwenbergh, Jacob Vosmaer, and Adriaen Linschoten did appreciably better in this respect than Niclaes Vosmaer, Willem van den Bundel, and Pieter Vromans II, but we have no solid evidence for saying so.

LOTTERIES

If we may judge by the written evidence, lotteries and raffles were an important outlet for artists wishing to sell their paintings, as well as

[n] On the Vermeer paintings, see Blankert, *Vermeer of Delft*, pp. 149–50.

for dealers and even for private individuals eager to cash in on this popular mode of gambling. The fashion for them seems to have hit a peak in the period 1615 to 1625 and then declined or even disappeared in later years.

I begin out of chronological sequence with a lottery organized by the master glass-engraver Claes Claesz. van Leeuwen in 1626, the only one described in sufficient detail in the source for us to make sense of its operation. The list of prizes and the conditions of this lottery were published in Bredius's *Künstler-inventare*.° The lottery was financed as follows: "The sum total of the above prizes according to their estimated value comes to 1,275 gulden; each lot at 25 gulden makes 51 lots; since there are 30 prizes, there must be 21 naughts (*nieten*)." The "naughts" drew a blank. A special provision reduced the maximum loss of unlucky participants: anyone drawing three or more blank lots was entitled to receive a painting estimated at three Flemish pounds (eighteen gulden). The most valuable lot—first prize—was a St. John the Baptist preaching in the wilderness by "Blommert of Utrecht" (Abram Bloemaert) estimated at 360 gulden. The next three prizes were all by Bartholomeus van Bassen with staffage by Esaias van de Velde: a large temple "wherein was represented the history of the adulterous woman for 162 gulden," a Church of St. Peter (150 gulden), and a hall or chamber with the story of the rich man and Lazarus (108 gulden). The fourth prize was a head (*trony*) by Cornelis van Haarlem (fifty-four gulden); and the fifth another Van Bassen-E. van de Velde collaboration representing a temple with St. John healing the cripple (fifty gulden). There were also three pictures by Groenewegen and E. van de Velde (one for forty-eight gulden and two for thirty-two gulden each); a landscape and a conflagration by Hans Jordaens (fifteen gulden and eight gulden respectively); two

°7 vols. (The Hague: Martinus Nijhoff, 1915-1921), 1:321-24. The original document is in the Records of Notary Adriaan van Twelle, no. 1654, 18 July 1626. Bredius omitted the following prizes: a Caritas for eighteen gulden, two small banquet pieces for four gulden, a banquet with a capon for five gulden, a Diana for five gulden, a banquet with figures for sixteen gulden, a kitchen with birds for fourteen gulden, a winter on a large canvas for thirteen gulden, a landscape on a large canvas for thirteen gulden, another landscape for eleven gulden, a winter for eleven gulden, another landscape for seventeen (the last three on canvas), and three copies after Frans Floris: one *trony* for seven gulden, another for six gulden, and another for five gulden. A note in the original manuscript (omitted by Bredius) indicated that the last few prizes were estimated by Van Leeuwen who was ready, if the need arose, to pay cash for the prizes at the estimated values. All other prizes were estimated by Hans Jordaens or Cornelis Jacobsz. Delff or both.

pictures by Blocklandt (twelve gulden and eight gulden); a kitchen piece by Dirck Govertsz. (forty-eight gulden); and one more Van Bassen-E. van de Velde collaboration (a temple with the story of Zacharias for forty-six gulden). In all there were twelve prizes worth more than the twenty-five-gulden cost of a raffle ticket. The estimations of the values of the more important lots were made by headmen of the Guild of St. Lucas (Hans Jordaens and Cornelis Jacobsz. Delff), the rest by Van Leeuwen himself. Since the lottery was fair, in the technical sense that the expected value of a lot (the probability times the average value of a prize) was equal to its purchase price (twenty-five gulden), Van Leeuwen could make a profit on it only if the appraised value of the thirty lots (1,275 gulden) was higher than what he had paid for them. It is notable also that neither the city of Delft nor the Camer van Charitate was entitled to any part of the gross receipts or profits from the enterprise, as was customary at the time. Neither did the town apparently insist on the local residence of artists represented in the sale. Van Bassen, who had six expensive pictures in the sale, had left Delft for The Hague in 1622. Dirck Govertsz. and Cornelis van Haarlem lived in Gorinchem and Haarlem respectively and were never members of the local guild. Only Groenewegen, who had come from The Hague to join the guild in Delft in March 1626, some three months before the sale, and Hans Jordaens himself represented the local artists' community.

The financial aspects of the lotteries staged by artist-painters are not known in the same degree of detail. On 25 April 1614, Jacob Vosmaer received consent from the Weth to raffle "a few pieces of painting" on the condition that twenty-four gulden be donated to the poor via the Camer van Charitate.[33] On 14 August of the same year, the painter Willem Jansz. Decker sold twenty paintings by lottery. None of the paintings were attributed in the notarial document giving an account of the lottery with the exception of a large landscape with staffage by Hans Jordaens. Since many of the paintings represented religious and mythological scenes of the type that were found in Willem Jansz. Decker's death inventory ten years later,[P] there is a good chance that a number of the lots were painted by Decker himself. Some of the landscapes with religious staffage may have been painted by Willem Jansz.'s father, Jan Willemsz. Decker. Unlike the Van Leeuwen raffle, which was supervised by headmen of the St. Lucas Guild, this lottery was run with the help of three assistants with no

[P]Referred to above, p. 130

obvious connection to the artistic community: Abraham Jacobsz., servant of the weavers' guild (*gilde knecht*), drew the lots; Cornelis Tonisz., tailor, read the names (inscribed on the drawn lots); and Cornelis Sijmonsz., baker, announced the prizes or blank lots. All three declared that everything had been done legally and in good faith, as did the notary Adriaen Rijshouck. The lottery had taken place at the house of Willem Jansz. Decker "with open doors and windows," anyone wishing to see or hear being freely admitted.

The names of the recipients of the prizes were written above the lots they drew. Six of the lots fell to the seller himself, three to Jan Willemsz., presumably Decker, the organizer's father; and two to the notary Rijshouck. Thus eleven out of thirty prices accrued to "insiders." Franchoys Tobias, who was registered in the 1613 master list of the Guild of St. Lucas among the illuminators and art dealers, received two prizes. None of the other buyers of lots and prize recipients seem to have been professionally linked to the art market.[q] One named Maritgen Jansdr. was identified in the document as the wife of *mynheer* the sheriff of Delft, Dirck Bruynsz. van der Dussen. Another was a "Dr. Valentius," perhaps the same person who many years later had Carel Fabritius decorate a ceiling in his house in fresco.

The lotteries so far described were confined to paintings. Other lotteries were organized to raffle off a wide variety of luxury goods including, besides paintings, silverware, firearms, mirrors, and fancy fabrics. Rogier Laurens (also named Laurensz. or Lauwersz.), a merchant who resided at various times in Amsterdam and Delft, specialized in setting up such lotteries in any city of the United Provinces that was willing to tolerate them, in an age when gambling and luxuries were both widely condemned by religious authorities. After his application to stage a lottery in Delft was turned down by the town authorities, Rogier Laurens, with the help of two second-hand dealers (*uytdraegsters*), one of whom happened to be Johannes Vermeer's grandmother, sought to obtain a consent from the bailiff of Vrouwenrecht on the edge of Delft to furnish the document. On the understanding that the States of Holland and West Friesland had also given their assent, Laurens rapidly marshaled prizes worth 22,735

---

[q]With the possible exception of the prize recipients named Gerrit and Jan Jacobsz. Mosger who may have been the sons of the painter Jacques de Mosscher, mentioned by Van Mander. This same artist was registered as "Jacob Musscher" (in the margin "Jacob Fransz. Muskel") in the 1613 master list of the guild (See Table A.1 of Appendix A).

gulden. Of this enormous sum, 800 gulden represented paintings and alabaster work supplied by the registered art dealer Pouwels Weyts and his mother. Goods worth much more—over half the total value of the prizes—were consigned by goldsmiths or sold by them to Laurens. Mirrors, copperwork, mantels, women's clothing, velvet-silk breeches, stockings, and costly firearms made up the rest. A good deal of the merchandise came from Haarlem, Amsterdam, The Hague, Dordrecht, Utrecht, and Rotterdam, as if barriers to intercity trade did not exist. When the assistant sheriff of Delft, on order from the States of Holland and West Friesland, stopped the lottery just as the first lots were being drawn, Laurens found himself in serious difficulty. Some consigners wanted their goods back plus compensation; others, whose goods he had purchased outright, did not want them back and sued him for a total of 4,300 gulden. Among those who brought suit were a silversmith, an armorer, a dealer in mirrors, and a maker of copper utensils. Some of the goods were damaged and had to be repaired at Laurens's cost. The remaining goods were impounded at the house of the art dealer Pouwels Weyts. Laurens estimated his losses to be in excess of 1,000 gulden. Laurens is known to have arranged several other lotteries in other towns between 1622 and 1624.[34] These enterprises were apparently profitable enough to risk large amounts of money and to sustain an occasional loss.

The love of gambling or whatever partiality to risk-taking drove Delft citizens in the 1610s and 1620s to spend their money on lotteries was also mirrored in their proclivity for betting. Bets were offered and taken on all manner of things: whether the birds in a nest up in a tree were ravens or rooks, whether a battle would be won or lost, or whether a painting was by one artist or another.[r] The single most valuable painting that I have found mentioned in a seventeenth-century document in Delft—a St. John the Baptist preaching in the wilderness by Bloemaert[s]—was sold for 620 gulden in 1628 by Edwaert Evertwijn, a rich burgher of Delft, to Cornelis Jansz. de Raedt and Heynrick Ronaert, then in Rome, on the following conditions. The stipulated price of 620 gulden would have to be paid six years hence if and only if: 1) Evertwyn became legally married; 2) his future bride had a first child at least seven months after the marriage; and 3)

---

[r] See below, Chapter 8, p. 235.

[s] This painting may be identical with the one of the same subject also by Bloemaert sold in Cornelis van Leeuwen's lottery in 1626, which was then estimated at 360 gulden. If so, the earlier estimate had been on the low side, compared with the nearly twofold price obtained only two years later.

the child, at the expiration of the six-year period, was sufficiently mature to go to the house of De Raedt to dun him for the debt or, in De Raedt's absence, to notify the neighbors that the debt had fallen due. If any of these conditions were not met, the buyers would get the painting for free.ᶜ Another important bet that determined the price at which two paintings would be sold was made in Schiedam, a few miles from Delft, and is included here because the paintings in question were the work of a Delft artist. On the 29th of May 1625 a company of Schiedam militiamen had gone out to a small town named De Cluyndert where the bookbinder and printer Jan Wolphertsz. had announced in front of the company "that he wished to sell a piece of painting—one of two at the choice of the buyer—made by the painter Hans Jordaens, worth four Flemish pounds (twenty-four gulden), on the wager that the town of Breda, which was then besieged, would not be won [by the enemy]." The petitioner, Pieter Dijertsz. Zevenhuijsen, took up the challenge. The two bettors finally settled on the following conditions. If Breda was freed, Zevenhuijsen would pay fifty gulden for the two paintings and he would treat the company to wine when the *schutters* were back in Schiedam. If the town fell, he would get both paintings free and Wolphertsz. would pay for the wine. Two witnesses then stated that when Wolphertsz. was presented with the bill for the wine on 6 July, he declared that he knew nothing about it.[35] In the meantime, of course, Breda had fallen to the Spanish troops (at the end of May), and the oversanguine bookbinder had lost his bet.

THE WEEKLY AUCTIONS AND THE SECONDHAND DEALERS

Gerard Versteegh held an important and lucrative position in Delft in the 1660s and early 1670s: as the *venduemeester* appointed by the town authorities he had responsibility for the weekly auction sales of the possessions of deceased residents as well as for occasional ad hoc sales organized for the benefit of the citizens. The pattern of these sales was only interrupted in 1672 "on account of the danger and bad

ᶜRecords of Notary Willem van Assendelft, no. 1855, 25 May 1628. In 1644, this same Evertwijn bet the equivalent in woodlands of 220 gulden that Dunkirk, which was then under siege, would be evacuated within four years by the French king or by the States General (Records of notary Cornelis Cornelisz. Brouwer, no. 1660, 8 July 1644). A similar bet was made by other individuals over the purchase of a cow in 1646 (Records of Notary Govert Rota, no. 1978, 19 September 1646).

times to which our dear fatherland has been subject,"[36] as a result of the war with France.

A great many works of art—but chiefly paintings—passed through these sales. The *contracedullen* or official records of these auctions represent by far our most important source of knowledge about the market prices of paintings in seventeenth-century Delft. These records, supplemented by a number of inventories assessed for inheritance purposes, will be analyzed in the next chapter. I do not think it possible to estimate the overall magnitude of these sales relative to other transactions in works of art, but I would guess from their size and frequency that they were a very important—perhaps the most important—source of supply, both for well-off collectors and for lower middle-class people buying pictures to decorate their homes."

To what extent could these auction sales be used as an outlet by artists seeking to market their works? The evidence here is sadly lacking. I have found only one *contracedulle* of works sold by an artist in his lifetime. Harmen van Bolgersteyn had seventeen works auctioned off by the *boelhuysmeester* on 23 May 1628. Only one of these works was attributed—a Venus by Frans Floris that went for thirty-six gulden. The rest, chiefly still-lifes and landscapes that brought prices from six to sixteen gulden, were very probably by Van Bolgersteyn himself. The sale totaled 216 gulden 5 stuivers, from which two deductions were made, one for 27 gulden 10 stuivers and one for 9 gulden, presumably for auction expenses and for the special levies on these sales (*boelhuysrecht*).[37]

Much more would be known today about collectors in Delft if the practice of naming the individual buyers at auction sales in the *contracedullen* had continued beyond the early 1620s. As it is, we have records of about a dozen sales where the buyers' names are indicated, from 1615 to 1622, and only an occasional citation of a buyer's name thereafter. But even this small sample is revealing. Frans Tobiasz., no

---

"It is probably significant in this connection that pictures mentioned in a notarial document not infrequently turned up at some other time in a sale. Two notable examples: pictures by Carel Fabritius, Couwenbergh, and (Evert) van Aelst belonging to Willem Jansz. Kronenburgh in 1667 were sold by auction after his widow's death in 1673 (Records of Notaries Jacobus van Berlecum, no. 2164, 28 September 1667; and of Testart van Hasselt, no. 2157, 25 October 1673); a picture of an angel by Giovanni del Campo sold by Leonaert Bramer to Dr. Johan Hoogenhouck in the early 1630s (Records of Notary Testart van Hasselt, no. 2157, 1 March 1672) turned up at the Hoogenhouck sale in 1647 (Orphan Chamber, *boedel* no. 810 I).

doubt identical with the Franchois Tobias whom we last saw as a participant in Willem Decker's lottery, purchased a map of India for one gulden seventeen stuivers at a 1618 sale.[38] He was probably a dealer both in prints and maps and in paintings. At this same sale the painter Van Bolgersteyn bought various household goods—but no pictures. The only name of a painter that cropped up in this small sample was that of "Mr. Hubert," probably Hubert or Huybert Jacobsz. Grimani, who bought a painting with figures for four gulden fourteen stuivers.[39] At the sale of the goods of Maritgen Coenen, the widow of the wealthy merchant Joris Claesz. Tristram, of 14 November 1617, a number of rich burghers bought paintings.[40] "Dr. Valensis," probably the same person who received a prize in Decker's lottery, bought a peasant wedding by "Jordaen" (almost certainly Hans Jordaens) for 130 gulden. Simon Heul bid eighty gulden for a painting of the *Preaching of Christ in the Little Ship*. Gerrit Beuckelsz. van Santen purchased a landscape with Juno, Pallas, and Venus by Bloemaert for thirty-five gulden ten stuivers. The future burgomaster Joost Jacobsz. van Adriechem bought a Preaching of St. John the Baptist by Hans Jordaens for fifty gulden, a panel of the story of Lot by Stael for eight gulden nine stuivers, and a landscape for twelve gulden.[v] In 1620, Cornelis Egbertsz. (Sas), an important early faiencier, acquired at an estate sale a "banquet of fruit" for six gulden nineteen stuivers, perhaps painted by Cornelis Jacobsz. Delff who later taught the orphan son of the deceased.[41] At smaller sales, artisans (a tailor, a maltmaker) also appeared as buyers.

One last category of purchasers at the auction sales consisted of secondhand dealers—usually women—who made a small-scale business of reselling all sorts of used clothing and furnishings, including an occasional inexpensive painting. Some of them apparently helped draw up inventories and carried out various odd jobs related to the ar-,disposal of estates. The names of Grietge Gerritsdr., Tryn Rochusdr., and Neeltge Gorisdr. (Vermeer's grandmother), who were all active in the early 1620s have come down to us. Grietge Gerritsdr., the illiterate wife of a carpenter, bought a painting of Lucretia for one gulden seven stuivers at the sale of Pieter Cornelisz. van der Wiel in March 1618.[42]

The most frequently cited of these *uytdraegsters* was Tryn Rochusdr., a good friend and partner of Vermeer's grandmother in

---

[v]The painting by Jordaens was still hanging in Van Adriechem's house when he died in 1653 (Records of Notary Willem van Assendelft, no. 1865).

the organization of the abortive lottery of April 1620. As early as 1615, she is recorded as having bought "a kitchen" (that is, a painting representing a kitchen scene) for one gulden ten stuivers.[43] In 1618 a certain Dirck Jansz. Rotteveel who was apparently the heir of the recently deceased widow of a rich butcher had a number of witnesses testify that Tryn Rochusdr., under various pretexts, had given away to the poor, distributed to friends, and taken for herself various silver items, clothing, and fabrics belonging to the estate. Some of these items had been returned and included in the auction sale but not in the inventory.[44] These allegations of wrongdoing did not prevent her from participating in the liquidation of estate of the painter Pieter den Dorst two years later.[*] Together with Vermeer's grandmother Neeltge Gorisdr., she had sold various items of clothing on behalf of the estate, had gone twice to Amsterdam to redeem goods that had been pawned by Den Dorst or his wife, bought items of clothing for the widow, and paid the undersheriff, on behalf of the trustees of the estate, for setting the widow in the stocks for her misbehavior (*quaet comportement*).[45]

These secondhand dealers, of lower-class background and illiterate, probably played a role in arranging and facilitating the sale of estates and thus in passing on works of art from one generation to the next, although their direct contribution was apparently restricted to the purchase and resale of cheaper items. The middlemen for transactions involving significant works of art were the professional art dealers who were normally registered—as the *uytdraegsters* were not—in the master books of the Guild of St. Lucas.

Before broaching the subject of the dealers, I should mention at least in passing that there were many transactions in paintings and other works of art that involved no middlemen of any kind. All sorts of barter transactions and sales contracted between parties that encompassed paintings are recorded in contemporary documents. Typical instances include a garden exchanged against two paintings, a "vanitas" and a picture of Joseph and Holy Mary, together worth forty gulden.[46] Or an artist might sell a painting that had not been painted by him to a collector, as in the case of Bramer's sale to Johan Hoogenhouck, some time in the 1630s, of a painting by Giovanni del Campo (Jean Ducamps) that he had brought back with him from Italy in the late 1620s.[47] One conclusion that I think can be drawn from the frequent references to these transactions is that paintings were

---

[*]On Den Dorst, see above, Chapter 6.

relatively liquid valuables at the time, perhaps because standards of quality were fairly uniform among large groups of people, at least among people of the same social class. In seventeenth-century Delft it may not have been harder to find a buyer for a painting than for a silver jug or a leather-covered "Spanish chair." The illiquidity of works of art in today's world is a reflection of the wide disparity of tastes even among individuals in a given income group, and of the difficulty of locating the rare customer willing to pay the highest price.

THE ART DEALERS

Franchois or Frans Tobiasz. is the first guild-registered art dealer about whom information has survived. We have already seen that he participated in a lottery for paintings organized by the painter Willem Decker in 1614 in which he won two lots and that he had purchased a map at a weekly auction sale in 1618. In 1612, he was referred to as "Frans Tobiasz. van den Bosch *bode van Delft op Parys*."[48] As *bode* (literally, messenger) from Delft to Paris, he was responsible for conveying mail, transferring money, and handling other affairs that Delft citizens might have had in Paris.[x] In this 1612 document, the notary Jan de Molijn lodged a "protest" on the part of Michiel van de Sande, painter in Rotterdam (c. 1583–after 1629)[y] against Frans van den Bosch living in Delft. Frans had bought an unspecified quantity of blue ashes (used in oil paint) at six gulden per pound. He had then refused to accept delivery of an additional consignment of three pounds three ounces of this material on the pretext that it was not worth as much as the foregoing deliveries. Van de Sande claimed that this batch was just as good as before and threatened to sue him if he persisted in his refusal. Frans responded to the protest by informing the notary that the ashes were not nearly as good as those that had been delivered previously. He was, however, willing to submit the dispute to three connoisseurs (*kenders*) ("master painters" crossed out). "The above-cited three master painters [sic]" would be asked to give their opinion on the question. This is one of the very rare instances where materials used by artist-painters are referred to in an

[x]The parents of the painter Joris Gerritsz. van Lier transferred money to their son in Paris via the *bode* of Delft to Paris (see above, Chapter 6).

[y]On this painter, who two years later moved from Rotterdam to Utrecht and, by 1623, was living in Amsterdam, see Bredius, *Künstler-inventare*, 5:1,486–89.

original source. In this case we have an art dealer purchasing colors, presumably for resale. In the late 1640s the Delft painters Jan Spangaert, Leonaert Bramer, Pieter Groenewegen, and Pieter Vromans II also bought colors from Rotterdam (from the dealer Crijn Hendricksz. Volmarijn); a decade later we find the painter Louis Elsevier trading in white lead color, which he also obtained from Rotterdam.[49]

Like Tobiasz., Jan Serange (c. 1566-1624) was also registerd among the illuminators and art dealers in the original master list of the guild, but there is no other evidence that he actually lived in Delft until the early 1620s. In January 1619 he was still "a dealer in paintings residing in Rotterdam." When he died in Delft in October 1624, he left many valuable tulip bulbs but so few paintings—and those few perhaps by his own hand—that he could hardly have been very active in the trade, at least at the time of his death.[50]

Our first full-fledged, Delft-based dealer is Pouwels Weyts who left Dordrecht for Delft in December 1618. By April 1620, as we have already seen, he was consigning paintings valued at 800 gulden in a lottery. He registered in the guild as a master painter in August 1620. In September 1622, as we have also seen, he was authorized to exhibit paintings in The Hague. His activity as a dealer from that time until his death in May 1629 is totally obscure. That he did reasonably well, however, is indicated by the donation of five gulden to the "Opperste Kleed" at the time of his death.[51]

I referred in Chapter 3 to a dealer named Hendrick Jansz. Vocke-staert who had apparently omitted to pay his full admission dues to the Guild of St. Lucas but was considered a member, with a member's obligations, by the headmen. His estate papers and the records of his *boelhuys* sale give us a glimpse into the nature of his business.[52] He sold, in addition to paintings, silver objects, gold belts, and gilded mirrors. His specialty seems to have been paintings on alabaster, for which many customers in The Hague owed him money at the time of his death. He apparently imported some of these alabaster paintings, which were found in many inventories about this time, from Mechelen in Flanders, or so I infer from an entry in his estate papers for a debt to a certain Hans van Beeck in Mechelen for such goods. The paintings that were sold in his estate auction, which may or may not have been part of his stock, were mainly inexpensive pictures selling for two to seven gulden, including three flower vases (two to three gulden), a crab or lobster (seven gulden), four breakfast pieces (from two gulden six stuivers to six gulden sixteen stuivers), a landscape (four gulden nineteen stuivers), a preaching of Christ (six gulden), five alabaster paintings (one to two gulden apiece) and thirteen *lacke bordekens*—perhaps Oriental pictures made with lacquer enamels—for one to two gulden per pair. The wide variety of objects sold by Vockestaert takes us back to the very first reference in Delft to paintings in a notarial deposition where they were found conjoined with mirrors and silver utensils.

I have found one other document about the sale of paintings by a merchant who was not registered in the guild: Hendrick Stiers, English merchant in Delft, sold five pictures to an English barber in 1627, to be paid partly in cash installments and partly in barbering services.[53] But English citizens, whose activities were governed by the English court, seem to have been exempt from guild membership rules, and, in any case, an occasional sale of an art object was likely to escape guild controls.

In the early 1630s two dealers set themselves up in Delft who, by virtue of their extensive contacts with painters in Delft and elsewhere, began to play an intermediary role between painters and collectors that went beyond the essentially mercantile activities of their predecessors. The first to register in the guild, on 18 October 1631, was Reynier Jansz. Vermeer, the father of Johannes Vermeer. The second was the many-sided painter-dealer Abraham de Cooge, who joined the guild on 11 June 1632.

Reynier Vermeer probably first became acquainted with the art trade when his mother Neeltge Gorisdr. organized lotteries and worked as a secondhand dealer. His father-in-law Balthasar Claes Gerritsz. worked as a counterfeiter of domestic and foreign coins in 1619 and early 1620. By 1627 Balthasar was said to own a collection of paintings worth "thousands of gulden" (a claim which may well have been exaggerated).[54] Reynier was trained in Amsterdam for four years, from 1611 to 1615, as a *caffawercker,* a weaver of satin damask fabrics. In 1623 he nominally transferred household goods valued at 965 gulden 11 stuivers to his father-in-law, among which were paintings worth seventy-one gulden ten stuivers, all unattributed. In 1641 he bought the inn called Mechelen for 2,700 gulden, which he operated until his death in October 1652. From 1631 on, the year of his inscription as an art dealer in the guild, his contacts with prominent painters of his day can be traced, first with the flower-painter Jan Baptist van Fornenburch, domiciled in The Hague, later with Pieter Steenwijck ("vanitas" paintings), Balthasar van der Ast (still-lifes), Pieter Groenewegen, and Egbert van der Poel who painted barnyards, townscapes, and ice scenes.[55]

In March 1643, Reynier Vermeer asked the *ebony* framemaker Gerrit Jansz., the father of Anthony van der Wiel (also framemaker), who later married his daughter Gertruy, to testify regarding a painting which the still-life painter Evert van Aelst had given him (Reynier) to sell some time previously. Van Aelst apparently owed him some money and hoped to repay it by the sale of the painting. But the painting was not sold. Van Aelst, claiming that he was now able to sell the picture himself, had sent Gerrit Jansz. to Reynier's house to reclaim it. The picture had now been back with Van Aelst for two years, but the debt apparently still had not been repaid. From this we learn that Reynier Vermeer accepted pictures on consignment, which he was not always able to sell.[z]

Reynier Vermeer must have apprenticed his son Johannes to one or more painters in the late 1640s and early 1650s. If, as is generally believed, Johannes's teacher was a Delft master—perhaps Leonaert Bramer or Evert van Aelst—his father's ties to the artistic community of his native city can only have been strengthened. Early in the 1650s, drawings were made after some of Reynier Vermeer's pictures by Leonaert Bramer, who also drew sketches of paintings belonging to Adam Pick, Abraham de Cooge, and a few well-known private collectors. Finally, in 1654, two years after Reynier's death, a debt of twenty-five gulden for a painting or paintings that the dealer had purchased was recorded in the inventory of Cornelis Saftleven in Rotterdam.

Reynier Vermeer's activities as an art dealer were a natural complement to his innkeeping business. An inn was a good place to meet artists, many of whom no doubt lived up to their contemporary reputation as avid consumers of beer and spirits; it was also a fine place to hang and show pictures.[aa] Yet, when all the evidence is weighed, it appears that Reynier Vermeer carried on only a modest trade in pictures. It is probably significant that in the numerous

[z]The document of 24 February 1646 (cited in note 24 above) in which Evert van Aelst committed himself to paint pictures to settle a debt for food and drink incurred with another innkeeper suggests the possibility that the painting consigned by Van Aelst with Reynier Vermeer was also in lieu of payment for food and drink. It is interesting that in this case the creditor did not accept the picture outright in payment of the debt but was only willing to sell it on Van Aelst's behalf.

[aa]The painter Adam Pick owned and managed an inn in the early 1650s. He too may have bought and sold pictures. (As a painter registered in the guild he was entitled to

notarial documents where he appears he is never called *konstverkoper*. He was primarily an innkeeper who probably traded more or less exclusively in paintings by artists with whom he was personally acquainted.

Abraham de Cooge was a dealer of wider scope and probably of greater significance for the art market in Delft. Unlike Reynier Vermeer, his primary concern was with the fine and applied arts, first as an engraver, later as painter, then as an art dealer, and finally, from the early 1660s on, as a faiencier.[bb] It may well be, as Hanns Floerke once suggested, that his early work as an engraver, working after diverse pictures and drawings and producing prints on a large scale requiring wide dissemination, predisposed him to dealing in art works.[55] In one aspect he resembled the early dealers in pictures: he too, in addition to paintings, dealt in luxury objects, including tulip bulbs at the time of the great speculation (1637), clocks (1655), and organs (1655).[57] Nonetheless, he sold principally paintings, both in Delft and in other cities, at least until he became a faiencier. Perhaps the earliest mention of De Cooge referring specifically to painting may be dated some time in the early 1650s (in any case before the death of Reynier Vermeer in October 1652) when his name is cited, along with nine private collectors and his fellow dealer Vermeer, on the back of a sheet in the set of drawings by Bramer after paintings in Delft collections.

On 18 October 1652, De Cooge gave his correspondent in Antwerp power of attorney to collect 690 gulden from Johan Rhenen arising from the sale of paintings.[57] An entry in the journal of the important Antwerp dealer Matthijs Musson, dated 8 July 1653, indicates that De Cooge soon afterwards came to Antwerp himself, perhaps to collect the debt.[58] Translated from the Flemish, the entry reads:

> Monsieur Koeghen spoke to me about his desire to have me sell a piece that stands in the Prekerenpant, painted by Blocklant, to wit an Ascension with two side wings, one representing an Annunciation, the other a Nativity. And if I can sell the piece at the price of

---

do so.) Other innkeepers (Ary Jansz. van Straten, Jacob Helm, Johannes Cordy) in Delft are known to have had collections of paintings. However, there is no way of knowing whether they, legitimately or otherwise, engaged in the trade.

[bb]In 1630 he was arrested in Gorinchem for having made a libelous political engraving (Bredius, *Künstler-inventare*, 7:36-37). He first registered in the Guild of St. Lucas as a painter in 1632 and reregistered as a faiencier in 1666.

800 gulden, anything above 800 gulden we shall share half and half. In Antwerp, the 8th of July 1653, we have both signed this as an *aide-mémoire*.

[*signed*, MATTHIJS MUSSON and ABRAHAM DE COOGE]

The arrangement is not entirely clear but it seems that De Cooge wanted 800 gulden for the triptych and anything above that amount would be shared equally between the two merchants. The triptych was displayed in Antwerp's Prekerenpant, a court on church premises where paintings had long been exhibited.[cc]

Our next entry, dated 16 September 1653, finds Abraham de Cooge in Amsterdam where, at his request, the dealer H. van Uylenburgh, two "amateurs and experienced connoisseurs of the art of painting" (Marten Kretzer and Lodewijck van Ludick), and some of Amsterdam's most famous painters (Breenberg, Van der Helst, Simon Luttichuysen, Pouwels Hennekijn, Philip de Koninck, and Willem Kalf) gave their opinion that a certain landscape, three feet, four inches wide and two feet, four inches high, must have been painted by Paulus Bril. Rembrandt van Rijn testified separately to the same effect, two of his pupils witnessing the document.[59]

Among some loose papers of the aldermen of Heemstede, Bredius found a reference dated 25 April 1654 to "a large drawing of Rafel Urbyn (Raphael Urbino), representing Herod's Massacre of the Innocents, purchased from Abram de Koogen art dealer in Delft for the sum of 300 gulden."[60]

On 27 May 1661, De Cooge named Gerrart Suijer to represent him in Amsterdam in an affair concerning a painting by Porcellis purchased by a hat merchant named Louweris Doucy. The power-of-attorney was witnessed by William Jansz. Kronenburch, a rich merchant and collector in Delft. On 9 June 1663 De Cooge constituted himself guarantor against any claims and pretensions that "Gerrit Zuijr" (presumably the same man as was cited in the previous document) might have against Dirck Schade regarding a painting of a barber's shop by Brouwer that he, Schade, had sold Zuijr. A month later, on 10 July Dirck Schade, merchant in French goods in Utrecht, drew up a blank power-of-attorney to summon Gerrit Zuijr, baker, to pay 525 gulden that the latter had promised him in a barter of

---

[cc]The word Prekerenpant probably stems from Preeckherrenpand, or preachers' court. In Antwerp, the Pand of the Lievevrouwkerck had been used since 1481 to exhibit and sell artworks during the biannual kermesses (Floerke, *Die Formen des Kunsthandels* p. 8).

paintings, two that he had delivered to Zuijr—a barber's shop and the other called *the monk*, both originals by Brouwer—against two pieces—one being *Jupiter's Golden Rain* and the other the *Holy Virgin's Ascension*, both by (Cornelis) Poelenburg—and, over and above this, the annulment of all previous acts and claims that either one might have had against the other.[61] What had presumably happened is that Abraham de Cooge had sold Schade a Brouwer painting representing a barber's shop. This painting had been sold to Suijer or Zuijr who had questioned its authenticity. De Cooge had "covered" Schade against any claims that might arise from the transaction. Finally Schade and Suijer had agreed to swap the contested Brouwer and another painting by the same artist for two paintings by Cornelis Poelenburg and the promise of 525 gulden. If the Poelenburgs cost, say, seventy gulden a piece, each Brouwer was worth over 330 gulden, a high but not unreasonable price for this rare master, who was already highly esteemed in the seventeenth century. Suijer registered as an art dealer in the guild in Delft five years later, 29 March 1666.[62]

From the 1660s on, De Cooge was increasingly occupied with the faience works of which he was part owner. He apparently delegated to his son Meynard de Cooge, who himself never joined the guild, the day-to-day management of his picture business.

In June 1666, Meynard bought from Daniel Vosmaer, who had done the landscape in a picture that he had painted with his brother Niclaes, Daniel's "entire share" in the property, which amounted to one-third. Before his death in 1654, Fabritius apparently had also claimed a third for "retouching the picture." On 12 and 13 July, Meynard arranged to have testimony given by the painters Jochum de Vries and Pieter van Asch to establish that Fabritius 1) had only retouched the seascape and the ships in the picture, 2) had not earned even one-fourth of the value of the picture, and 3) had little experience in painting seascapes. They also testified that the landscape painted by Daniel Vosmaer in the picture was worth fifty gulden more than Niclaes's seascape.[63] (Daniel Vosmaer's view of Delft seen through an imaginary loggia is illustrated on the jacket of this book.) Finally testimony was given that Fabritius had wanted to get one-third of the sales price but had also expressed his willingness to bear one-third of the expenses. On the 31st of August, witnesses declared before a notary in Amsterdam at the request of Abraham de Potter that they had been present by the side of Daniel Vosmaer and Abraham de Cooge when De Potter had asked Vosmaer what share he had in the large painting hanging in the Prinsenhof and how much he transferred to De Cooge. Vosmaer had answered that he had transferred only his share, which was a fourth, and that his brother was also owner of a fourth share. Abraham de Potter, who had bought the picture, had his brother-in-law Jan Baggelaer sue De Cooge for the share that De Cooge claimed to own in the picture.[64] There is not enough information here to form a precise image of the differences involved, beyond the evident fact that De Potter had acquired Fabritius's share, which he claimed to be larger than De Cooge was willing to allow, whereas he thought that the share claimed by Daniel Vosmaer and sold to De Cooge was too large. Who had rights to the late Niclaes Vosmaer's share is not clear. Since Meynard de Cooge was one of the trustees of Niclaes's estate, we should perhaps assume that he had control of it, but this would contradict his attempt to have witnesses deprecate the value of the marine painter's contribution.

In September 1667, the painter Pieter van Asch testified that, some time after the explosion of October 1654, Meynard de Cooge had repaired and varnished a number of damaged paintings by "Couwenburg, Carel Fabritius, Van Aelst, and others" belonging to the collector Willem Jansz. Kronenburgh. Van Asch declared that when he heard that De Cooge had asked so much for the repairs, he felt that Kronenburgh would have done better to ask him to do the job, but when he had seen how much work had been done he opined that he would not have been willing to do it for fifty gulden. The housemaid of Abraham de Cooge testified that she too had helped repair the pictures on Meynard's order.[65] It is less surprising that a dealer who was also a painter should have repaired pictures than that a housemaid who had presumably no art training should have been mobilized to help.

Our last document related to Abraham de Cooge's activity as art dealer is a sale of paintings, dated 28 March 1680, to the heirs of Arent Jorisz. Pynacker. Since De Cooge is identified as *plateelbacker* in Delft, we cannot be sure that the paintings were not from his own collection rather than from his dealer's stock. The paintings and their prices were:

A Dead Christ by Tintoretto	250 gulden
Abraham's Exodus by [Frans?] Wouters	120 gulden
A Crossing [of the Dead Sea] by Schoonhoven[dd]	30 gulden

[dd]Could this be Jan Cornelisz. Schoonhoven, painter in oil, registered in the Delft St. Lucas Guild's Master List of 1613? I have found no other mention of this painter's works in a Delft source.

A St. Jerome by Bloemaert	50 gulden
A Landscape by [Hans] Jordaens [II]	50 gulden
A Vase of Flowers by [Hans] Bolongier	30 gulden
An Old Man's Face by Bloemaert	30 gulden
Two small gray Seascapes by Porcellis	50 gulden
A *trony* of a Shepherdess by Hoogstraten	50 gulden
Swans by [Louis] Elsevier	50 gulden
A round Landscape by [Adriaen] Muylties	50 gulden
A Landscape by [Albert] Cuyp	20 gulden

The Tintoretto, which was too expensive for an ordinary copy, is one of the very few paintings in any Delft inventory attributed to an Italian master.[66]

If we are willing to assume that our sample of the paintings that are known to have gone through Abraham de Cooge's hands is not too badly biased, we must conclude that his stock in trade was of exceptionally high quality. An important Blocklandt triptych, a large landscape by Pouwels Bril, an original drawing by Raphael, a genre scene by Brouwer, a Porcellis, a major work to which Fabritius had contributed, and a painting attributed to Tintoretto—these were by no means run-of-the-mill commodities in the United Provinces or in Flanders at the time. The fact that we find him dealing as far away as Antwerp and Amsterdam also adds to his stature as a dealer.

Johannes de Renialme, the last professional dealer of interest for this study, was actually based in Amsterdam but, as "Johannis Rijalleme," he joined the guild in Delft in August 1644 as a *konstverkoper*. He owned a house in Delft, which his widow occupied after his death in 1657.[67] He was a close acquaintance of Abraham de Cooge, according to the latter's own testimony.[68] He must have been a real art lover, judging by a deposition made in Haarlem in 1637. Cornelis de Bruyn and the painter Jan Miense Molenaer referred to a painting by Govert Jansz. in De Renialme's possession which a certain Govert van den Heuvel wanted to acquire in exchange for some smaller pictures: De Renialme had refused to sell the picture to Van den Heuvel saying that "he first had to have his pleasure for a while longer from the painting" ("hy van de voorsz. schilderij eerst syn plaisier noch wat moste hebben").[69]

The only evidence of De Renialme's selling anything in Delft is of a (sculptured) stone slab (*steen taefel*) that the notary Willem de Langue had paid for with a debt acknowledgement, the value of which was later contested.[70] An inventory of ninety-one paintings in the dealer's possession taken four years before he joined the guild in Delft contained only one painting by a Delft artist, a "Robbery" by "Jordaens," which was probably by Hans Jordaens the Elder. The inventory made after his death in June 1657 shows that, in the meantime, he had bought a number of pictures by Delft artists, presumably on his frequent trips to Delft. One of these, I have argued elsewhere, was the earliest recorded picture by Johannes Vermeer, a *Visit of the Holy Women to the Tomb*, estimated at twenty gulden.[71] Out of 248 attributed paintings, many of which were attributed to Italian and Flemish painters, fifteen were by Delft artists: eight by Bramer alone, two by Miereveld, and one each by [Hendrick] van Vliet, Palamedes Palamedesz., [Willem or Jan] Decker, and Jacob Pynas. This may not seem like very many, but we must keep in mind that Delft was only beginning to tell as an artistic center when De Renialme died.

Nothing is known about Johannes Vermeer's sideline business in picture-dealing beyond a highly significant statement by his widow, four months after his death in December 1675, to the effect that "her husband during the war with the king of France and in the next ensuing years had been able to earn very little or almost nothing and that the artworks that he had bought and in which he dealt had to be dumped [literally, 'cast from his hands'] at very great losses in order to feed his children."[72] It is generally believed that the "twenty-six pieces, large as well as small paintings" that were sold to the Haarlem painter and dealer Jan Coelenbier after Vermeer's death for 500 gulden[73] must have represented his stock in trade, since the average price of less than twenty gulden was far too low for paintings that he himself would have painted.[74]

Another art dealer already cited in Chapter 3 was Vermeer's brother-in-law Anthony Gerritsz. van der Wiel, whose main occupation was making ebony frames. He joined the Guild of St. Lucas as a dealer in 1656. Making frames, like innkeeping, was a business that went hand in hand with selling pictures.[ee] Nicholas Breda, another frame-maker, had joined in the preceding year as an art dealer.

Although a number of documents about both Van der Wiel and Breda have come to light, not one relates to their side occupation as dealers. They perhaps sold inexpensive pictures for cash, along with

---

[ee]It is possible that Van der Wiel joined the guild in 1657 because some of the pictures owned by Reynier Vermeer had passed to Johannes Vermeer's sister Geertruy after Reynier's death and he needed to have guild membership to sell them in his shop.

the frames they made. Little or nothing is known about the other *konstverkopers* in the guild—Christoffelina Assendelft (registered 1629),[f] Jan Legous (1634), Mathis Hendricksz. (1641), Jan Jacobsz. Goeree (1644),[gg] Mateus de la Croes (1649), and Jacomijntge van der Gocht (1670). Jocomijntge, who registered in the guild as *kunst en boekverkopster*, must have sold prints as well as books. Several of the other dealers probably sold both prints and cheap panel pictures. It is doubtful whether any of them operated on a larger scale, at least in the sale of paintings.

With all the dealers active in Delft, we still find an occasional mention of an artist selling a picture directly to or consigning it with a dealer in another city. In 1636, Balthasar van der Ast, the excellent flower and still-life painter, named a jeweler in Antwerp to collect fifty-two gulden from Pieter de Neff (Pieter Neffs the Elder), also painter, for "one piece of painting" that he had apparently sent to him and for which Neffs had failed to pay.[75] It is probable (but not certain) that Pieter Neffs acted as a dealer in this transaction. In the inventory drawn up after the death of Anthony Palamedes's wife, there was inscribed a small debt of eight gulden owed by the Rotterdam and Leyden art dealer Leendert Volmarijn. On 12 April 1675, Pieter Jansz. van Ruyven, master painter, gave power-of-attorney to Gerard Klinck, also master painter,[hh] to act as his correspondent in Amsterdam. Klinck was instructed to demand from the curator of the insolvent estate of [Gerard] Uylenburch, also painter and art dealer, that "he deliver to him two paintings painted by Van Ruyven, one representing Cain and Abel, the other a Ceres, being a candlelight picture, which he, Van Ruyven, had brought to Uylenburch to sell on his behalf" ("omme ten dienst van hem compt. te vercopen ende beneficieren").[76] Gerard Uylenburch was a very important Amsterdam dealer who went bankrupt in early 1675.[77] One of the few known paintings by Van Ruyven (perhaps a self-portrait) is illustrated in figure 11.

[f]A few years after entering the guild she sold table and chair coverings to the Hoogheemraadschap of Delfland.

[gg]Goeree, by the time his wife died in 1651, seems to have become a leather merchant. A collection of his paintings (or was it his stock in trade?) was sold at auction on 26 June 1652 and brought 584 gulden (Records of Notary Cornelis Georgin, no. 2083).

[hh]This is almost certainly "Gerrit Claesz. Clijnck" who registered in the St. Lucas Guild as a painter in 1663 but then was crossed out without having paid his entrance fee. On 10 December 1671 he was called "meester konstschilder" in Delft (Records of Notary Roelandus van Edenburgh, no. 2244) when he was already living in Amsterdam, where he may have joined the guild.

FIG. 11 Pieter Jansz. van Ruijven, Self-portrait (?) (1679), 14⅜ x 20 in. Art
Trade (1978), Amsterdam

Our last document bearing evidence of contracts between Delft artists and out-of-town dealers concerns Maria van Oosterwyck, the only female professional painter in seventeenth-century Delft (though not a member of the guild). On 26 January 1673 the "famous lady artist-painter" (*vermaert konstschilderesse*) asked two witnesses to testify that "they had been present, had seen and had heard when she had handed over to Melchior Lidel, a merchant in Amsterdam, in the month of April of the preceding year, two pieces of painting, painted by the aforesaid Juffrou van Oosterwyck, one being a festoon [of flowers] with a blue ribbon hanging from a nail and the other a bouquet of flowers in a jug on which was drawn the birth of our Lord Jesus Christ." She had directed Lidel to take them to Munich in Germany so that they could be sold on her account.[78]

SUMMARY AND ANALYSIS OF THE EVIDENCE

The vivid impression that emerges from the scattered data and anecdotal evidence collected in this chapter is that artists in Delft faced a competitive, diversified market for their output. They could sell directly or through dealers, to local or to out-of-town clients. Raffles and special *boelhuys* sales provided them with alternative outlets. State and municipal patronage was hard to come by but could provide an important source of earnings for highly reputed artists like Bramer, De Vlieger, Fabritius, and Couwenbergh. This lively market for works of art operated with a minimum of collateral information: exhibits were in their infancy; there was virtually no literature to guide customers' tastes—no catalogues or books about artists,[ii] no advertising, nothing that would have helped, objectively or otherwise, to establish or puff up an artist's reputation. In the early years of the seventeenth century most paintings were judged by their visual impression alone, much like silverware or furniture. Later, the names of artists began to matter more: attributions, as we shall see in the next chapter, appeared with increasing frequency in inventories. By the mid-century point, artists' signatures were accepted by a wide circle of consumers as a signal of quality.

The fact that more specialized and larger-scale dealers were active in Delft as the decades passed may reflect both the growth of the Dutch art market as a whole and the increasing importance of Delft as an

---

[ii]The exception is of course Karel van Mander's *Schilderboeck*, published in 1604, in which connoisseurs could look up most of the Netherlandish artists active before that date.

outlet and as a source of supply for out-of-town buyers. Prior to 1620, Franchoys Tobiasz. had carried on a small-scale business in the city. In the early 1620s, Jan Serange, Pouwels Weyts, and Hendrick Vockestaert came from Rotterdam, Dordrecht, and The Hague to exploit local possibilities on what would appear to be a larger scale than their predecessors; but all died before they had much time to establish their trade. In the 1630s Reynier Vermeer depended on his personal contacts with painters and, we conjecture, on the exposure given their works on his premises facing the market square to combine art-dealing with innkeeping. A little later Abraham de Cooge, together with his son Meynard, raised art-dealing in Delft to a higher level, trading in expensive paintings and drawings in Amsterdam and Antwerp as well as locally, doing business with distinguished collectors, artists, and other important dealers. Johannes de Renialme, who joined the guild in 1644, probably dealt on an even larger scale than De Cooge. Since Delft was relatively unimportant market in the 1650s compared with Amsterdam, Leyden, Antwerp or Paris, I suppose that he may have been more interested in buying pictures from local artists there than in developing a local clientele. In the early 1670s, as the testimony of Vermeer's widow indicates, Delft was suffering from a war-induced depression: pictures were not selling; even the *boelhuys* sales were no longer held. It is perhaps significant that in the mid-1670s Vermeer's widow was selling her late husband's stock to a dealer in Haarlem while Pieter van Ruyven and Maria van Oosterwijck were consigning their works with dealers in Amsterdam rather than selling them outright to local dealers. This was perhaps another aspect of the pull of larger towns and of the decline of Delft as a *ville d'art* in the last quarter of the century.

EIGHT

Art Collections in Seventeenth-Century Delft

In mid-seventeenth-century Delft, perhaps two-thirds of the population, estimated at twenty-eight to thirty thousand inhabitants,[a] lived in
households possessing paintings.[b] All in all, as many as forty to fifty
thousand paintings hung in the city's four thousand-odd houses at the
time.[c] I doubt whether one hundred of the paintings are left in Delft
today. Some found their way into museums and private collections
outside Delft. Almost all the cheap ones, which cost a few stuivers
when they were first bought, have disappeared, burnt in fires or
thrown away with the rubbish when they were no longer worth
keeping, before they had acquired the value age and scarcity confer on
even the poorest daubs.

DELFT INVENTORIES

The inventories preserved in notarial archives and in the estate papers
of the Orphan Chamber are the only record left of these tens of
thousands of pictures. Even though only a minority of these invento-

[a]Estimated from the population count of 1622 (22,769 inhabitants), on the
assumption that the total population increased in proportion to the number of deaths
from the early 1620s to the 1640s.

[b]In my sample of 442 Delft inventories of household possessions dated in the
1640s, 80 percent contained one or more paintings. I have made an approximate
adjustment to take into consideration the underrepresentation of the poorest
households in the sample (cf. below).

[c]There were about eleven paintings per inventory (or household) in my sample for
the 1640s (see Table 8.2). The number of households probably exceeded the number
of houses by 40 to 50 percent. However, I arrived at the total number of paintings in
Delft by multiplying the number of *houses* by eleven. I made allowance for the fact
that a substantial fraction of households possessed no paintings, a fraction that is
underestimated in my sample of inventories. Thus the two biases offset each other. If
the true number of paintings per household was seven or eight—a reasonable
correction—then the number of paintings per house may have been about eleven as I
have assumed.

ries and estate papers have survived, there are still enough left to form a fairly good impression of the range and contents of contemporary collections. More importantly, there is enough evidence to trace changes in the makeup of collections in the seven decades, 1610 to 1680, that mark the rise, the apogée (in the 1650s) and the subsequent decline of Delft as an artistic community.

My sample of 1,224 inventories spanning this period forms the core of my analysis. I have classified all paintings itemized in these sources by artist and subject to the extent that they were attributed and their subject was described. In addition, for all inventories based on auction records or on assessments, I have noted the price of all artworks, including prints and sculptures, and computed their share in the total value of movable goods sold, assessed, or appraised. This close study of a relatively large sample of inventories yielded, as a byproduct, some observations on contemporary connoisseurship and on the changing character of collections through time.

The seventeenth-century inventories of Dutch paintings that have been published so far in modern times, including the very useful compilation in Abraham Bredius's *Künstler-inventare*, were selected for their intrinsic interest—because they belonged to artists or because they contained works of art attributed to artists worthy of attention— but they were hardly representative of the broad range of contemporary collections in the Netherlands. Published inventories tend to overrepresent very significantly the collections of wealthy burghers featuring a great many attributed paintings. They may have given students of Dutch art the unwarranted impression that most of the pictures in the inventories recorded by notaries were identified by subject and had some painter's name attached to them. This is no more true of inventories in Amsterdam or Leyden than of those in Delft. In most inventories of poor and lower middle-class people in Delft (and of many better-off burghers as well), artworks are summarily described as "a panel" (*een bort*), "a painting" (*een schilderij*), a portrait or "a face" (*een tronie*); when the notary or his clerk was a little more interested in the item, he would write down "a landscape," "a kitchen," "a pot of flowers," "a Lot" (Lot and his daughters), or "a Sacrifice of Abraham." Records of estate auctions, called *contracedullen*, contain especially poor descriptions. Few of the items listed in these bare-bones inventories and *contracedullen* are attributed. Often several pictures—the number is generally but not invariably indicated—are lumped together in one lot. Inventories

[221]

evaluated or appraised by notaries as a basis for dividing the assets of an estate among the heirs, as collateral, or as a contribution of one party or the other to a marriage where the assets will be held in common, usually contain more information on the subjects of the paintings that comprise them than do the *contracedullen,* but still only a minority have any paintings in them that the notary or clerk took the trouble of attributing (assuming that he would have been able to do so had he wanted). Inventories where a majority of paintings are attributed usually occur in estates of movable goods evaluated at 2,000 gulden and up that belonged to relatively wealthy Delft citizens.

Unfortunately, I cannot claim that my sample of over 1,200 inventories is either exhaustive of all the inventories that have come down to us in the records of notaries or of the estate settlements of the Orphan Chamber, or even that they represent an unbiased sample of the entire population of these inventories. My "data base" for all decades except the 1640s is perhaps best described as a 20-25 percent sample of all extant *contracedullen* and inventories significantly biased toward the upper end of the wealth distribution. They overrepresent inventories with attributed paintings, since I systematically recorded all inventories containing attributions. For the decade of the 1640s, I initially sampled ninety-seven inventories on a first pass (as I did, more or less, for the other decades) and then combed through all surviving notarial records for inventories of movable possessions whether or not they contained works of art. As a result of this search, I was able to add 345 inventories to my original list of ninety-seven.

The supplementary list increased the number of paintings in my original sample two-and-a-half-fold but only contributed 80 percent more "titled" paintings, whose subject was in any way described, and less than one-fifth as many attributions as the original sample. Twenty percent of all inventories in the new sample contained no paintings at all.

The low incidence of titles and especially of attributions in the second sample is of course a reflection of the bias toward richer inventories in my first sample, which picked up a disproportionate share of all the titles and attributions in extant inventories. I would venture to guess that my samples for the decades of the 1620s, 1630s, 1650s, and 1660s covered between a quarter and a half of all "titled" paintings and 70-80 percent of all attributions in extant inventories.

These samples, ranging from 119 to 187 inventories per decade, give an adequate representation, in my view, of the attributions in inventories that have survived.[d] With regard to subject, the samples for these decades are satisfactory only for the study of broad trends in major categories. My samples for the years 1610-1619 and for the 1670s are even less adequate: the first because few inventories are left dating from this period, due in part to the Town Hall fire of 1618 that destroyed most Orphan Chamber estate papers, the second because I did not exploit all the notarial records of the late 1670s.

The samples I collected may be biased due to the existence of two types of nonrandom gaps in coverage. First it is likely that many of the original collections—particularly those of the poorer strata of citizens—were never notarized in the period covered by the present study. Secondly, many inventories described in contemporary notarial records have disappeared.

Losses due to the gradual disappearance of documents through fire, water damage, or sheer neglect are a serious cause of understatement. To give only one example, the inventories of estates drawn up by Notary Willem de Langue—one of twenty active in the 1640s—were virtually all destroyed. Only very few inventories and *contracedullen* (not recorded in his own handwriting) are to be found in his records. Those that did survive, however, reveal his great connoisseurship.

We can make an approximate comparison of the size of our samples with the "universe" of all collections in each decade as follows. There were about 600 deaths a year in Delft in the 1640s, according to the burial records. Of these some 250 to 300 may have been adults, or 2,500 to 3,000 per decade. The overwhelming majority of deceased adults were married or had recently lost their spouse. In any event, since I have dropped from my sample the few instances I found where an inventory of the same collection was drawn up twice, once after the death of one spouse and once after the other's, I should eliminate any such duplication from my potential universe of inventories as well. I think I can safely assume that the number of potential households whose movable goods might have been inventoried at least once in each decade (if an inventory had been made each time either partner to a marriage died) should not exceed 1,500-1,600. My sample of

---

[d]The slightly larger percentage of attributions in these decades than in my original sample for the 1640s is due to the fact that I made a second search for inventories with attributions—less systematic however than for the 1640s—which enlarged my original samples by 20 to 30 percent.

TABLE 8.1
Measure of Sample Bias of Inventories (1640s)

	Original Sample (N = 97)	Additional Sample (N = 345)	Sample from the Book of Death Donations (N = 692)
Number appearing in the book of death donations	14	31	692
Number making donation	12	14	268
Average donation in gulden (exclusive of nongivers)	54.0	34.8	28.8

SOURCES: Delft MA, Camer van Charitate, "Opperste Kleed Boeken" for 1640s; notarial records; estate papers of the Orphan Chamber.

about 400 inventories of individuals who died in Delft in the 1640s should then cover about a quarter of all existing collections.[e] In other decades (except the first and last covered in this study), where my samples average about 100 to 150 inventories, I probably recorded one inventory for every ten to fifteen households. In the span of seventy years covered by this search, I should think that only a small percentage of collectors—chiefly individuals living in the 1660s and 1670s—died after the terminal date of my investigation (1680).

An instructive way to get a measure of the bias in my sample of inventories is to match it against the registered death donations to the Camer van Charitate.[1] These donations may be taken as a rough measure of the economic status of the deceased. I did this for my original and additional samples for the 1640s with the results shown in Table 8.1.

The sample of names selected at random from the book of donations to the Camer van Charitate consisted of 692 individuals out of a total of 1,849 names recorded in the book for the decade of the 1640s. These in turn represented a little over 30 percent of all the individuals who were buried in Delft in this period, including children and other persons not living in separate households. Out of the 692 names in the sample from the book of donations, I was able to find only forty-five individuals (6.3 percent) whose inventories of movable goods were included in my total sample for the 1640s. This low

[e]Some 10 percent of my sample of 443 inventories are records of the possessions of brides or bridegrooms drawn up as part of their marriage contract, of debtors pledged to their creditors, and of individuals who did not die in Delft.

percentage I attribute in part to the difficulty of matching names: many of the women in the book of donations are referred to by the name of their husbands or their fathers only ("the wife of Niclaes Nieustadt," "the daughter of the burgomaster"); a number of individuals are called by their patronymic in one sample and by a last name in the other; commonly occurring names such as Jan Jansz. or Grietje Cornelisdr. were particularly difficult to pair with certainty in the two sources, especially when the burial date of the person whose inventory was included in the sample (and whose name seemed to match one of those in the book of donations) was unknown.[f]

It is remarkable that almost all the individuals I was able to match in my original sample of inventories with names in the book of donations actually left some money or valued possession to the Camer van Charitate, whereas only a little more than a third of the individuals named in the book (in my "full sample" of 692 names) did so. About half the individuals in my additional sample of inventories, which picked up a great many more poor estates than the first, made donations to the Camer. The average value of donations in the original sample was significantly greater than in the additional sample; the difference between the additional and the full sample does not appear to have been statistically significant.

All these statistics confirm the serious bias in my original sample of inventories dated in the 1640s in the direction of individuals with above-average wealth, which was largely, but not fully, corrected by the additional sample. The bias for the other decades was probably roughly comparable. I would venture to guess that the individuals whose inventories I noted may have been about twice as wealthy as the average inhabitant of Delft with a separate household. What this implies for my analysis of paintings by subject and by artist is that I collected far too few inventories with no paintings at all and far too many with attributed paintings, as compared to a truly representative sample. These defects notwithstanding, a sample containing perhaps 70 to 80 percent of all the attributed paintings in extant inventories should still have considerable value for the study of art collections in Delft.

Table 8.2 summarizes the information available in the sample of inventories collected for all decades from 1610 to the end of 1679.

Inventories with price data, consisting chiefly of the records of

[f]Whenever there was any doubt whether a name in the sample of inventories was identical with a name in the book of donations, I excluded it.

TABLE 8.2
Summary of the Information Available in Sample of Delft Inventories

	Number of Inventories in Sample	Number with Price Data	Number Containing Any Attributed Paintings*	Total Number of Paintings*	Number of Paintings Itemized by Subject*	Number of Paintings Attributed†
1610–1619	49	30	1	536	473	110
1620–1629	147	93	10	2,016	1,225	178
1630–1639	140	98	21	2,290	1,338	159
1640–1649						
Original sample	97	61	42	2,155	1,226	392
Additional sample	345	77	10	2,905	967	68
Total	442	138	52	5,060	2,193	460
1650–1659	202	115	59	3,814	1,888	489
1660–1669	123	70	50	2,617	1,640	402
1670–1679	121	73	33	2,636	1,176	263
Total	1,224	617	226	18,969	9,933	2,061

SOURCES: Delft, Municipal Archives, notarial records and estate papers of the Orphan Chamber.
*Including itemized drawings.
†Including monogrammed paintings.

auctions, sales, and estate appraisals, together with a few transfers, sales, and records of possessions held as collateral for debt, represented almost exactly half of the total sample collected in all decades.

If we leave out of account for the moment the additional sample of inventories collected for the 1640s, we find that the percentage of the total number of inventories containing attributed paintings and the percentage of attributed paintings in the total number of paintings listed in the 1640s and in the next two decades increased dramatically compared to the 1620s and 1630s. Whereas only 6.9 percent of all paintings in our sample were attributed in the 1620s, this proportion rose to 9.2 percent in the 1640s (original sample), 12.8 percent in the 1650s, and 15.4 percent in the 1660s. It then fell back to 10 percent in the 1670s, possibly due to sampling fluctuation.

I am confident, despite the varying size and the biased character of the samples in each decade, that the rise in the relative importance of attributions in the 1640s and 1650s represents a real phenomenon. My argument for the plausibility of this increase rests on my earlier claim that these samples probably covered some 70 to 80 percent of all extant inventories with attributed paintings.

If my surmise is correct, notaries and their clerks became distinctly more conscious of the importance of appending an artist's name to a painting in the 1640s and 1650s. This represents a significant change in attitude toward the painted objects described in inventories. There is no greater step in the metamorphosis of craft into art than the recognition that an object is the unique creation of an individual and that its worth to potential amateurs will depend, at least in part, on the information they have about its maker. It is remarkable that makers of furniture and silverware, with no known exceptions in the case of Delft-based artisans, remained anonymous in inventories during the period, apparently unable to gain recognition as artists transcending their craft.[8]

Paintings represented by far the most numerous and valuable works of art in Delft inventories; yet sculptures, pen drawings, prints, needlework and embroidery pictures, and other types of decoration at the limit between art and craft were by no means rare. Sculptures are

---

[8]In a few inventories, the mark or the initials of the silversmith or goldsmith are reproduced. But this seems to be more a matter of authenticating the object's having been made by *some* registered silversmith or goldsmith than of crediting the name of a particular maker.

almost never attributed.[h] They are described as "a St. George in stone," "two lions made of plaster," or, most commonly, just as "a Maria sculpture" (*een Marien beeld*). Some early inventories cite sculptures "cast in lead" (*van lood gegoten*).[i] Coats of arms are common objects in inventories. Some of them were sculpted, others painted; but they are usually not described in sufficient detail to tell which were painted and which sculpted. Similarly most alabaster boards or slabs were probably painted—some of them with only a lozenge (*ruytgewys*) design—but others were probably incised in low relief. Again there is no way to tell which was which. All armories and alabaster boards are included in the total value of works of art in my statistical analysis (but not in the breakdown by subject).

If we may judge from the contents of earlier inventories of the 1610s and 1620s almost all the better-off households had at least one or two sculptures. Later their number seems to decline. In any case, they are rarely appraised or sold for more than two to three gulden and they represent only a very small fraction of the value of works of art in collections, either at the beginning or end of our period.

Pen drawings, especially of ships (a genre made popular by Willem van de Velde the Elder but also frequently practiced by Delft artists), occur fairly often in inventories. Red chalk drawings are less frequently cited. I have chosen to include both in my sample of attributed paintings when they are actually itemized in an inventory, as distinguished from a folio volume of prints and drawings attributed to an artist. They are also included in my breakdown by subjects.

Prints are found in all types of households, from the humblest to the richest. They may serve as decoration, as religious symbols, or even as a source of subject matter for certain craftsmen. A few wealthy, artistically inclined individuals collected them, often together

---

[h]I can cite only one exception. On 23 October 1624 a silversmith named Thomas Cruse "transferred and sold" his entire inventory to the rich amateur Aper van der Houve (See above, Chapter 2.). Besides two unattributed paintings and one print by Goltzius, the inventory contained thirty-five sculptures, all but three of them attributed. The sculptors were Hendrick de Keyser (eight pieces), Giovanni da Bologna (ten pieces), Willem van Tetrode of Delft (twelve pieces), Michael Angelo (one piece), and Arent van Bolten (one piece). The inventory is reproduced in Abraham Bredius, *Künstler-inventare: Urkunden zur Geschichte der Holländischen Kunst des XVI[ten], XVII[ten], XVIII[ten] Jahrhunderts*, 7 vols. (The Hague: Martinus Nijhoff, 1915-1921), 4:1,456-58.

[i]Many of these, including some lead "riders" and "knights," are contained in the inventory of Dr. Jacob Thielmans van der Eynde who died on 2 August 1625 (Orphan Chamber, *boedel* no. 551).

with drawings, in portfolio volumes for their own sake: in such rare cases they are identified by the artists who created them.[j] An early instance of a craftsman in an art trade who owned prints that he presumably employed in his work is the glassmaker and glass-engraver Dirck Reyniersz. van der Douw who owned a book of "the Passion by Aelbert Duyre," another book of the Passion by Lucas van Leyden, and a "little book with twenty Roman gods."[2] Similarly the embroiderer Franchois van Ruymelaer owned a number of prints and cartoons in 1620 which he used to "embroider and to engrave."[3] The mapmaker Pieter van der Lande, who died in 1637, kept a book of Dürer prints, perhaps for his enjoyment but also possibly as a source of designs for the decorative figures he may have inserted in his maps.[4]

In auction sales anonymous prints were rarely valued above a few stuivers a piece (e.g., "fourteen prints for thirty stuivers" in the same Van der Lande inventory). The most valuable prints were actually maps that were hung on walls either in frames or in rollers. These maps, which are never attributed, typically cost fifteen stuivers to two gulden. I have included prints and maps in the value of works of art contained in inventories sold or estimated but not in my sample of paintings classified by subject and artist.

At the limit between craft and art, we find an occasional paper cutout or a framed leather pattern (e.g., "2 gelyste goude leeren").[5] We also encounter in many inventories "written panels" (*geschreven borts*), some of them with the Ten Commandments or with "Solomon's prayer."[k] It is often impossible to tell whether a "Ten Commandments" (*een tien gebode*) is a painting representing Moses with the tablets or a written list or possibly both—that is, a list of the Commandments illustrated by a biblical picture. Specimens of fine calligraphy (many made by the Delft schoolmaster Felix van Sambix) are also to be found, normally hanging on the wall and framed. All these written boards and decorative writings are included in the value of the artworks contained in inventories, but not in any of my breakdowns by subjects (unless they are suspected to be actual paintings). Decorated clavecins are sometimes recorded in the posses-

[j]For example, in the inventory of Dr. Johan Hogenhouck, where portfolios of prints and drawings by Goltzius, Claes Moyaert, Esaias van de Velde, "Bolonge" (?), Francois Périer, and other artists were to be found (Orphan Chamber, *boedel* no. 810 I, 3 April 1647 and 16 May 1648).

[k]"Een borritge daerinne geschreven 't gebedt Salomonis" (estate papers of Jan Brouwers, Orphan Chamber, *boedel* no. 214, 30 January 1641).

sions of the wealthier individuals. In a rare instance where the clavecin was decorated with a specific subject ("a naked scene of Venus and Adonis"),[6] I have chosen to include it in the breakdown of paintings by subject; however, musical instruments such as these are normally omitted from the value of artworks as well as from the subject breakdown.

CONNOISSEURSHIP

Notaries and their clerks were most frequently responsible for drawing up inventories. Richer estates, however, especially those that contained many works of art, were appraised for a fee of two or three gulden by painters. In Delft, dealers, as far as I know, were not called in for such appraisals.[l] In some cases, the notary's clerk happened to be an artist—Joris Gerritsz. van Lier, Pieter Steenwijck—and was particularly qualified to inventory the paintings in estates or in transfers of possessions as collateral for debt.[m] Altogether I have found thirteen inventories appraised by painters, four of them by a pair of artists working in collaboration. These were Hubert Grimani and Hans Jordaens in 1605,[n] Gillis and Matheus de Berg in 1638, Gillis de Berg and Abraham de Cooge in 1659, and Pieter van Asch and Hans Jordaens the Younger in 1678. The individual appraisers were Joris Gerritsz. van Lier (two inventories), Cornelis Jacobsz. Delff, Willem van den Bundel, Corstiaen Couwenbergh, Anthony Palamedes, Daniel Vosmaer, and Cornelis de Man. The artists who were entrusted with these appraisals were all active and fairly successful. It is probably significant that less-successful Delft artists very rarely cited in inventories, such as Sybrant Balkenende, Adriaen Pelleman, Anthony Beauregart, or Willem van Kerckhoven, are never recorded as appraisers. Neither do they appear in any extant records as teachers or as headmen of the Guild of St. Lucas, whereas nine out of thirteen of the above-cited painters known to have appraised inventories

---

[l]The well-known dealer Abraham de Cooge appears once as an appraiser of an estate, but he is called "engraver" rather than dealer.

[m]Van Lier is known to have apraised the paintings in three estates in the 1620s, including those of Vermeer's father and of his uncle by marriage Jan Thonisz. Back (J.M. Montias, New Documents on Vermeer and His Family, *"Oud-Holland* 91 [1977]: 273-75). We also know that he appraised the paintings of the ex-burgomaster Cornelis van der Meer, but the inventory itself has disappeared (Records of Notary Herman Jansz. van der Ceel, no. 1641, 21 November 1630). Pieter Steenwijck was a notary's clerk in the 1640s. None of the inventories drawn up by him have survived.

[n]Orphan Chamber, *boedel* no. 1.

served as headmen of the guild at some time or other. (This proportion should be viewed as a minimum considering that the extant lists of guild officers, reproduced in Appendix C, are incomplete.) While the expertise demonstrated in the manuscript inventories appraised by painters is certainly much above average, a number of anonymous appraisals, probably prepared by the notary himself, are quite comparable in this respect. I shall advert to one example of this type, drawn up by the notary Willem de Langue, after a brief analysis of the various dimensions of connoisseurship.

Six attributes of paintings listed in inventories may be distinguished: size, subject, style (attribution to a painter or a school), authenticity (original or copy), quality, and monetary value. All but the first are bound up with the connoisseurship of the recorder—the notary, clerk, auctioneer, or artist-appraiser—who drew up the inventory. Size is the least important of the six since its specification was limited to the indication "small" or "large,"[o] while the actual dimensions of works were almost never recorded in the period covered in the present study.[p]

The subject matter of painting, other than "histories" (biblical, mythological, or historical pictures) and allegories, is so succinctly described in most inventories, in terms such as "a little winter" (a winter landscape), "a vase of flowers," or "a kitchen," that we are given no ground at all for judging how much the recorders understood of the artist's intention. A partial exception is the rather obvious description of still life as "vanitas" paintings, which occurs from the 1620s on, and the use of the term *perspectyf* to denote a temple or a church interior. Much more interesting in this regard are

[o]Diminutives are also used to denote small size (e.g., *een zeetge*, a small seascape). The shape of paintings (eight-sided, round, square) is also frequently specified. Many inventories mention the type of frame (whalebone, "ebony with a gilded inner frame," white wood, etc.), but this information is rarely helpful to the historian. A systematic distinction seems to be made by most clerks between a painting (*schilderij*) and a panel (*een bort*). (One clerk, for example, describing an Adam and Eve painting crossed out *schilderij* and wrote *bort* over it.) A *schilderij*, when the distinction is made, seems to mean a painting on canvas, but one cannot be sure that the distinction was always made.

[p]In the Netherlands and Flanders the size of panels was indicated by their price ("a seven-stuiver panel"), but even this measure hardly ever appears in Delft inventories. The failure to specify size in Delft inventories contrasts with the practice in Italy of citing dimensions in palms or in terms of standard canvas sizes (e.g., *tela d'imperatore*) in many of the richer inventories. On the size of paintings, see Josua de Bruyn, "Een onderzoek naar 17ᵉ eeuwse schilderij formaten, voornamelijk in Noordnederland," *Oud-Holland* 93 (1979):96-115.

biblical or mythological pictures. It should first of all be noted that the shortcut description of a painting as a "religious scene" or a "biblical story" is *never* used. The recorder either cites the appropriate subject (e.g., "the History of Noah," "Drunken Noah," "the Ark of Noah," etc.) or is satisfied to call the painting a "panel" or *schilderij*. Curiously enough, this taboo or inhibition does not apply to mythological scenes. While most of these are at least summarily identified, a number of them are simply called *een poëterie* or, to cite a particular example, "a painting with diverse figures among whom goddesses sitting in the water."[7] The care and detail with which many religious pictures are described betray their symbolic significance. One of the few instances of hesitation that I have found, which supports my assertion that the recorders were conscientious in their descriptions of religious scenes, is a painting in a 1650 inventory "where an angel brings the news either to Mary or to Sarah that she will be fruitful" ("daer een engel tsij aen Marye ofte Sara bootschapt zij bevrucht soude werden").[8] How many art historians today would consider the possibility that a picture of an Annunciation might represent Sarah rather than the Virgin Mary?[q] Allegories such as *The Five Senses* (sometimes masquerading as *Shepherds and Shepherdesses*), *The Broad and the Narrow Way*, and *Laziness and Industriousness* were frequently recognized that would generally be regarded as genre scenes or as undecipherable allegories today.

I can document only two mistakes in the titles given to paintings in Delft inventories, both of which ascribe as religious what should have been a secular or mythological subject. An *Allegory of Virtue* (*amor di virtú*) was called "an angel" in an inventory of the 1640s.[9] A *Dead Adonis* was mistaken for an "Abel" in the same decade.[r]

Among the six attributes of painting, I distinguished style from authenticity. When a clerk writes that a square panel painting with an ebony frame was made by "Ludolf de Jong(h) or a disciple thereof,"[10] he has clearly recognized the painter's style but he is hesitant to

[q]One of course would expect to distinguish the two subjects by the apparent age of the biblical personage: the Virgin was young and Sarah old. But perhaps, in this particular instance, the distinction could not be made (possibly because the woman's face was turned away from the viewer).

[r]"An Abel in foreshortening by Goltzius" ("Een Abel in't vercorten van Goltzius") appears in the rich collection of Boudewijn de Man (*contracedulle*, Records of Notary Willem van Assendelft, no. 1861, 15 March 1644). This is probably the painting by Goltzius (inspired by the Dead Christ of Mantegna) in the Rijksmuseum, properly titled *The Dead Adonis*. (The prominent anemone and the lance next to the dead youth are sufficient for this identification.)

attribute the picture to the master directly. In a small minority of inventories, originals (*principaelen*) are distinguished from copies or paintings made after (*naer*) a master. There are also a few inventories extant where the recorder, unable to attribute a picture, stated specifically that it was painted "by an unknown master." In the inventory of Dr. Johan Hogenhouck, who died in 1647, for example, sixteen out of forty-six paintings and drawings were ascribed to *een onbekent meester*. One of these, by a stroke of luck, can now be identified: the *Allegory of Virtue* mentioned above as having been misrepresented as an angel was almost certainly painted by the Walloon painter Jean Ducamps, alias Giovanni del Campo, some twenty years previously. It is no wonder that the notary or clerk had been unable to recognize the work of a rather obscure painter who had worked exclusively in far-off Italy. We should never have known the painter's identity if it were not for a deposition made many years later by Leonaert Bramer who had brought back the picture from Rome to Delft and sold it to Johan Hogenhouck some time in the 1630s.[11]

In the appraisal of the possessions of Anna van Middelhouck, two paintings, together appraised for eighteen gulden, were first given to Pieter Groenewegen, then the painter's name was crossed out and the words "by an unknown master" were inserted. Another painting in the same inventory, valued at twenty-five gulden, was first "believed to be" (*vertrout*) by Bramer, after which the *vertrout* was crossed out: the appraiser had apparently become more confident of his attribution.[12] Remarks of this kind, testifying to the hesitation of the clerk regarding an attribution, while fairly common, can on occasion be quite revealing. We find in the inventory of the late patrician couple Zieren Middelhouck and Aeltgen van der Dussen a small *corps-de-garde* scene "said to be by a master from Amsterdam named Duyster" ("soo men meent van een meester van Amsteldam genoemt Duyster").[13] It is more or less transparent that the recorder of this painting did not know who Willem Duyster was. The name of the artist had perhaps been suggested to him by a family member of the deceased or by a more knowledgeable colleague.

At times the recorder's hesitation reveals his connoisseurship rather than his ignorance. I am impressed by the clerk who first attributed a painting to Jan van Goyen, then crossed out the name and wrote "by Van Hulst."[14] It took a certain expertise to distinguish a painting by Frans (or Maerten Fransz.) van der Hulst from one by Van Goyen whose work he closely imitated. (I assume of course that the clerk did not detect Van Hulst's signature after he had given the painting to Van Goyen.)

In a few instances a copy can be recognized, when it has not been explicitly cited as such, by its low sales price or assessment. There is little doubt that a panel representing a cardinal in an ebony frame "by Mr. Quintyn of Antwerp,"[15] which sold for one gulden ten stuivers cannot have been an original by Quentyn Metsys. Flemish Old Masters were generally far more valuable than that.

Normally pictures that were explicitly stated to have been copied after a certain master sold for one to five gulden, although a few examples can be found of copies that brought ten to twenty gulden at auction or were appraised at these relatively high prices.

It may be relevant at this point to summarize two documents (the first previously unpublished) shedding light on the contemporary attitudes toward originals and copies. According to a deposition dated 16 February 1621, Master Hubert Grimani, the portrait painter active in Delft from 1598 until his death in 1631, had undertaken to copy a painting for a master *caffa*worker named Cornelis Michielsz. Zoetens.[16] Grimani was given six weeks to copy the painting. On a certain day in December of the preceding year Grimani had boasted in front of witnesses that he could paint a better copy than the original and that he would do so for fifty gulden. Zoetens had agreed to this condition. There was also present in this gathering Jan Mathysz. de Been, a jeweler for the Medicis in Florence in later years, who offered Grimani 100 gulden if he could paint a copy better than the original on condition that the painter would give him 100 gulden if he failed to do so. But Grimani would not accept this last condition. Zoetens later delivered an original painting for Grimani to copy, as had been agreed. When Grimani was through copying the painting, both the original and the copy were brought to the house of one of the witnesses, a cloth merchant named Thonis Jansz. van Alenburch, in order for the copy to be examined and to be judged as to whether it was indeed superior to the original as had been stipulated in the agreement. With Grimani's consent, "Mr. Michiel Miereveld, assisted by Willem Willemsz. van Vliet," were invited to compare the original with the copy. When Miereveld was asked by the witness whether the copy was "better or even as good" as the original he answered that it was "by far not so good as the original, adding many other words besides." It is unfortunate that the deposition omitted to mention by whom the original had been painted. The omission is probably symptomatic of the premodern attitude toward copies that prevailed in this early period. It did not matter so much who painted the original and whether his idea or conception had been imitated or purloined; what really mattered was whether an artist had the craft and skill to do a "better job" than the original.

The second document, published by Bredius in 1888,[17] dates nearly twenty-five years later (6 July 1644). It subtly reflects a new attitude toward originality. According to two witnesses to a deposition Claes Bronckhorst, painter, a certain Wessel Hogedoorn, and Adam Pick, also painter, on a visit to the house of the petitioner Sijbert Cornelisz. Dogger, the town drummer, had noticed a large painting hanging in the front hall. Pick had said, "This is a piece done by Aelst." Dogger, pointing to another somewhat smaller piece hanging there, said, "This one is also by Van Aelst," to which Pick retorted that this was not true. After a discussion on the subject, Pick said: "Give me a pound of tobacco, I shall give you twenty-five gulden in cash for it; I say that Evert van Aelst did not make this piece nor had any hand in it, but I shall bring the man to your house or say who has made it." The petitioner then said that Van Aelst had painted it and that his name stood under the painting ("ende de selfs naem onder de schildery was staende"). Pick persisted and the bet was agreed on. When Bronckhorst pointed to Van Aelst's name under the painting, Pick said that even though the name did stand there, Van Aelst had not made it. Bronckhorst bore witness to the fact that the bet did not hinge on whether or not the painting was an original by Van Aelst. It hinged on Pick's assertion that he could show the painting was *not* painted by Van Aelst but by another person and that Van Aelst had had no hand in it.

The sequel of the affair is not known. It may be surmised that the deposition was drawn up to compel Pick to pay his wager after he had failed to show the painting was not by Van Aelst. Since Pick had been Evert van Aelst's pupil,[18] he might have known something about the authenticity of the painting that Dogger and his witnesses did not. In any case, what distinguishes this deposition from the one from which we learned about the copy made by Grimani is that here the exclusive concern was with authenticity. None of the parties to the dispute expressed an opinion as to whether the piece was well-painted or not. The only visual evidence invoked was the alleged signature.

Since signatures are very infrequently mentioned in inventories containing attributions, we seldom have any way of knowing whether a clerk or an artist-appraiser attributed a painting after reading an artist's signature or monogram or by recognizing the master's style. In one inventory, a landscape was said to be "signed (*geteckent*) F. Benier."[19] Perhaps the obscurity of the artist, who is also unknown to me, prompted the recorder to invoke his signature. Elsewhere in the same inventory, the same clerk cites a pair of seascapes "signed bvp." Here he apparently read off the letters of the monogram on the painting (which may have been that of Bonaventura Peeters). Altogether I found forty-three paintings, mostly dated in the 1660s and 1670s, that were identified by the monogram of the artist. The fact that the clerk in these instances noted down the monogram when he could not attribute a name to a painting—a practice virtually unknown in the first half of the century—testifies to the enhanced significance of attributions from the 1650s on.

In a few cases, I found it possible to assign a monogram to a particular artist, especially when the subject of the work was typical of his specialty. Thus a "still life signed F van S" was almost certainly painted by Floris van Schooten,[20] while a flower-piece monogrammed A.M.B. is likely to have been made by the Delft artist, Anthony Marinisz. Beauregart. Such instances are clearly indicative of the original recorder's limited expertise.

I conclude this section by summarizing the contents of an inventory drawn up by Notary Willem de Langue, whose connoisseurship was probably inferior to none in Delft in his time, at least among all but professional artists. The possessions belonged to a wealthy indigo merchant named Niclaes Gael who had died on 30 October 1638.[21] Besides originals by Karel van Mander (probably the Elder), Pieter Stael, Cornelis Kittenstein, Maerten van Heemskerck, Jochum de Vries, Jan van Goyen, "Scheele Neel" (Cornelis Molenaer), Pieter Claesz., Claes Hondecoeter, Pieter Molijn, and Cornelis Claesz. (Wieringa), our notary recognized sixteen copies, after Van Goyen, (Salomon) Ruysdael,[*] Groenewegen, Esias van de Velde, Pieter Molijn, Van Heemskerck, "Scheele Neel," and Pieter van Asch. With the exception of a number of family portraits, only a few paintings remained anonymous. It is no coincidence that so many painters were Willem de Langue's clients or witnessed deeds for him (Evert van Aelst, Balthasar van der Ast, Harmen van Bolgersteyn, Leonaert Bramer, Willem van den Bundel, Jacob van Geel, Hans Jordaens, Willem van Vliet, and Abram Vromans as well as the out-of-towners

---

[*]This is the only mention of Ruysdael's name (Salomon or Jacob) that I have found in a Delft inventory between 1610 and 1679. It is remarkable that copies of the works of Molijn, Van Goyen, and Salomon van Ruysdael had reached Delft by 1638.

Gerard ter Borch and Moses van Uyttenbroek) and that he was well-acquainted with the dealer Reynier Vermeer and his son Johannes.[f] De Langue was himself a collector—one of the eleven after whose paintings Bramer made drawings between 1648 and 1652— and he must have enjoyed the company of artists. A good deal more would undoubtedly be known about painting and collecting in Delft in the period 1620 to 1650 if many other inventories made by Willem de Langue had survived. (The portraits of De Langue and his wife by Willem van Vliet are reproduced in fig. 12.)

Remarks on the quality of paintings—our fifth attribute—were occasionally made by inventory-takers. Such remarks are always deprecatory. I have never come across a remark in an inventory about a picture's beauty, attractiveness, or curiosity. Negative comments are sometimes made about a batch of poor-quality paintings which the clerk did not wish to itemize separately, as a set of nineteen panels "both large and small, painted by no artful masters" ("soo groot als cleyn van geen constige meesters geschildert").[22] One appraiser opined that a painting of the Five Senses was "very bad" (*geheel slecht*) but still valued it at one gulden ten stuivers (a day-and-a-half's wage for a faiencier's adult apprentice). He then went on to assess "a few bad paintings" (*wat slecht schilderyen*) for the same price.[23] (I have not tried to guess at the number of paintings in such lots, which are not counted in Table 8.2). One notary's clerk characterized two land-scapes and one banquet scene as *slecht*, and "one landscape and one [sea] with ships" as *heel slecht*.[24] One occasionally finds the expression "work by the dozen" (*dosijn werk*), also denoting coarse production.[u] These deprecatory remarks unfortunately tell us very little about these works—whether they were badly drawn, poorly colored, or just old-fashioned.

The last dimension of connoisseurship that I want to make some observations about is the ability to evaluate paintings. How realistic were the assessments made by notaries and painters? We rarely have a chance to check on these appraisals because very few inventories were

[f] De Langue was Reynier Vermeer's family notary. On 5 April 1653, he witnessed a document drawn up by another notary in which Johannes Vermeer's future mother-in-law declared she did not approve but would not put an obstacle to his marriage with her daughter. On 22 April 1653, the young Vermeer and Ter Borch both signed as witnesses to a deposition notarized by De Langue (Montias, "New Documents," p. 281).

[u] As in "5 groot als kleyne stuckges synde dosynwerck" estimated for nine gulden (Inventory of Eduwaert Locking, Records of Notary Jacob van Santen, no. 2017, 18 December 1651).

both assessed *and* sold at auction. The estate of Joris Cornelisz. van Houten represents one of these rare cases.[25] Its twenty-three paintings were estimated to be worth 151 gulden 10 stuivers in April 1672. When these same paintings were sold at auction in June of the same year they brought 190 gulden 11 stuivers. Two landscapes by (Pieter) van Asch estimated for sixty gulden the pair went for forty-two gulden each. A fruit basket by the Middelburg master Bartolomeus Assteyn estimated at ten gulden sold for twelve gulden ten stuivers. Other paintings cannot be identified in the *contracedulle*, the items in which, as usual, are more summarily described than in the *taxatie*. The estimates seem to have been some 20 to 30 percent below market values, but there is no reason to believe that the bias was intentional. The two Van Asch paintings, in any event, were both the most highly valued in the estimate and in the sale.

On the basis of this very slender evidence, I shall assume that prices of appraised paintings were reasonable approximations of market value and make no distinction between the prices culled from the two types of inventories. My main use of evidence from prices concerns attributed and unattributed paintings, discussed after the next section.

SUBJECT MATTER

In my collection of 1,224 inventories spanning the years 1610 to 1679, the subject matter of paintings was specified in a little over half the pictures listed in the sources. Altogether I classified 9,623 paintings according to the following principles.[v] My more detailed breakdown consisted of fifty-six subject groups, such as "monks, hermits, and confessions," "seascapes and river landscapes," "barn scenes," "dogs, cats, live birds, and other small domestic animals," "family portraits," "portraits of kings, queens, and princes," "portraits of other famous persons," "faces" (*tronyen*), and "self-portraits." I then aggregated these fifty-six groups into ten major categories: 1) Old Testament; 2) New Testament; 3) other religious paintings, including religious allegories; 4) mythology; 5) other "histories" and allegories;

---

[v]The difference between this number and the total number of paintings for which some information about subject matter was available (9,933) represents paintings drawn from additional inventories for the period 1650 to 1680 that I did not classify by subject.

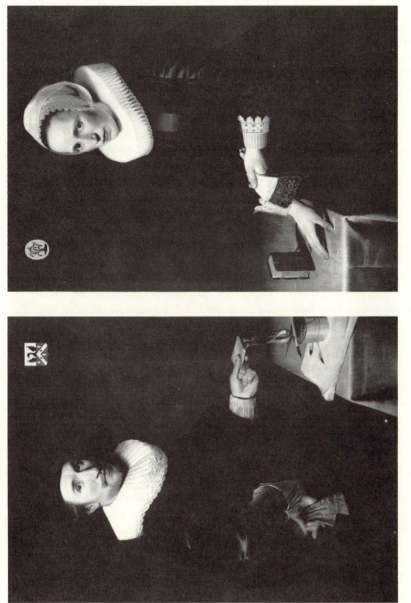

FIG. 12 Willem van Vliet, Portraits of Willem de Langue and his wife, Maria Pynacker (1626), 44¾ x 34½ in. Sir George Leon Collection, London (Photo: Iconographisch Bureau, The Hague)

6) landscapes; 7) genre; 8) still-lifes; 9) portraits and faces; and 10) others, including small domestic animals, children (other than portraits), "naked persons," and candlelight scenes.

There were very few paintings in each decade (less than 1 percent) that I could not classify satisfactorily, either because I was not able to understand the subject or because I was not sure to what it referred (e.g., "een angniet," "een quartier," "een contrefeytsel met de eene handt in den arm." "Een angniet" may be a lamb; "een quartier" may be a representation of the quartering of soldiers in a town; the portrait with one hand in the arm may be a person missing a hand.). In a few cases also the subject was not specified with sufficient accuracy in the source to allow me to classify the painting in one or another of my fifty-six groups. Thus a "painting of fowl" (*vogeltgen* or *gevogeltje*) could be a still-life with dead birds or a picture of live birds à la Melchior d'Hondecoeter. In several of these cases, the name of the painter provided a clue to a proper classification. "A painting with fowl by Lelienberch," for example, is much more likely to have been a still-life than a scene with live birds. A fair number of paintings belonged simultaneously to two groups or even to two broad categories. The most common were the religious or historical-mythological landscapes, such as "a landscape with Tobias," "a landscape with the pilgrims going to Emmaus," "a conflagration of Sodom," or "the Burning of Troy." In all such cases, I have classified the painting in a religious, historical, or mythological group. I also segregated a group of "religious landscapes" that I included among the religious pictures but not among the landscapes (to avoid duplication).

Finally, a couple of groups did not fit comfortably in any broad category; yet I included them in one category or another because I thought they came close enough to warrant stretching a definition. "Monks and hermits" more or less belong to the category of genre; "barns" (*schuren*) and slaughtered animals—subjects that were first introduced in the 1640s—fit, albeit uneasily, in the still-life category.[*] Where peasants in an interior or at a kermess are mentioned, I classified these scenes in a genre group. One important group that created problems are the numerous "kitchen" paintings (*keucken*). In the 1620s and 1630s, most of these were still-lifes with prominent pots, pans, dead poultry, vegetables, and fruit, with perhaps a woman

---

[*]I recorded nine paintings of barns and slaughterings in the 1640s, seven in the 1660s, and two in the 1670s.

or a boy working alongside these objects. The works of Cornelis Jacobsz. Delff offer many typical examples of such scenes. Some of these may have had a religious significance, Jan Emmens has shown,[26] whether or not an explicit religious subject, such as "Christ in the House of Martha and Mary," appeared in the background. In the 1650s these "kitchens" shift in emphasis; instead of a virtuoso display of objects, we now get a moralizing story (e.g., about a maid neglecting her duties, as in paintings by Vermeer and Rembrandt or an old woman praying, as in the work of Nicolaes Maes). To put all such "kitchens," including three where a maid is mentioned, in the still-life category (as I have) severely stretches my definition of this category. Another difficult group to classify were the "perspectives," which can denote inside or outside views of churches and palaces. I placed them in the landscape category for want of a better pigeon-hole.

While I recognize that these taxonomic decisions are arbitrary and debatable, they affect such a small fraction of all paintings classified that I can claim they have no significant bearing on my analysis of broad trends in the ten categories.

The results of my classification into major categories are shown in Table 8.3. Profound changes in the relative importance of subject matter took place in the seventy years of the period investigated. In the first decade (1610-1619), 46 percent of the paintings for which I found an indication of subject were "histories"—religious, allegorical, or mythological—or devotional pictures of Christ, the Virgin Mary, Evangelists, Apostles, and other saints. By the 1670s, the share of these categories had dropped to less than 17 percent. The importance of landscapes grew as the share of histories shrank from 23-28 percent in the first four decades[x] to 34 percent in 1650-1659, and about 40 percent in the period 1660-1679. The share in the total of still-life paintings rose even faster than that of landscapes; however, most of this increase occurred from the first decade to the second and in the last two decades. The proportion of genre paintings was remarkably steady up to the 1660s, then rose sharply in the 1670s. Portraits and faces, as a percentage of all paintings classified by subject, fluctuated without a clear trend over the entire period; the very high percentage uncovered in the additional sample for the

[x]The percentage of landscapes in the decade 1610-1619 is inflated by the presence of thirty-three landscape drawings in a single collection. If we exclude these drawings the share of landscapes declines from 25 to 20 percent.

TABLE 8.3

Classification of Paintings by Broad Subject Categories
1610-1679

Subject Category	1610-1619		1620-1629		1630-1639		1640-1649		1650-1659		1660-1669		1670-1679	
	No.	%	No.	%	No.	%	No.	%	No.	%	No.	%	No.	%
Old Testament	71	15.0	184	15.0	150	11.2	186	8.5	122	6.8	103	6.6	42	4.1
New Testament	75	15.9	205	16.7	227	17.0	287	13.0	184	10.2	186	11.9	78	7.6
Other religious (incl. allegory)	29	6.1	74	6.0	62	4.6	110	5.0	45	2.5	51	3.2	26	2.5
Mythology	20	4.2	39	3.2	52	3.9	62	2.8	36	2.0	37	2.4	9	0.9
Other "history" (inc. secular allegory)	23	4.9	45	3.7	59	4.4	109	5.0	83	4.6	34	2.2	15	1.5
All landscape	121	25.6	290	23.7	369	27.6	573	26.1	610	33.9	606	38.6	419	40.9
All still-life	20	4.2	137	11.2	133	9.9	256	11.7	247	13.7	242	15.4	171	16.7
All genre	18	3.8	56	4.6	61	4.6	82	3.7	88	4.9	76	4.8	76	7.4
Portraits and *tronyen*	80	16.9	166	13.6	185	13.8	479	21.8	329	18.3	192	12.2	154	15.0
Other	16	3.4	29	2.4	40	3.0	49	2.2	58	3.2	39	2.5	35	3.4
Totals	473		1,225		1,338		2,193		1,802		1,566		1,025	

SOURCE: See Table 8.2

1640s leads me to suspect that sampling error may account for most of these fluctuations.[y]

Within the broad category of "histories," it would seem that the relative importance of Old Testament paintings underwent the greatest decline: they were nearly as numerous in the sample of the first two decades as New Testament paintings, but only a little more than half as numerous in the 1660s and 1670s. The share of mythology paintings held its own at 3 to 4 percent in the first decades then more or less steadily declined from the 1640s on, dropping to less than one percent of the total by the 1670s.

The fairly sweeping changes in the proportions of the various subject categories that these reasonably large samples reveal could only have occurred if there were a substantial turnover in Delft collections. The following hypothetical calculation, based on educated guesses about the numbers involved, give some idea of the turnover necessary to bring about the structural changes observed. Suppose that there were altogether some 30,000 paintings in Delft houses in 1620 and 45,000 in 1660; in the first period 50 percent of the total were histories, 25 percent landscapes; in the second, these proportions were reversed. Thus we posit that there were altogether 15,000 landscapes and 7,500 histories in 1620, 22,500 landscapes and 11,250 histories in 1660. The compound rate of growth of the landscapes was 2.75 percent per year; the number of histories declined at the rate of 0.72 percent per year. Suppose the rate of discard had been one percent for landscapes and 1.5 percent for histories. Then the rate of accretion, before discard, would have had to be 3.75 percent per year for landscapes, 0.78 percent per year for histories. At the midpoint of the forty-year period, that is, in 1640, about 562 landscapes and 102 histories would have had to be added per year to Delft collections. These figures appear reasonable, though perhaps somewhat on the low side.[z] (If so, our hypothetical rates of discard were probably understated.)

[y]While the share of "histories" and landscapes were broadly similar in the original and the additional samples for the 1640s, those of still-lifes, genre, and portraits differed appreciably. I suspect these differences reflected differences in the distribution of wealth categories among the households whose inventories I collected in the two samples. Compared to other subjects, portraits probably were more frequently to be found in poorer than in richer households, while still-lifes and genre paintings were rarer in the former.

[z]In the next section I conclude that 40 to 50 percent of all attributed paintings in Delft collections were executed by Delft-registered painters. Suppose these proportions held for all paintings itemized by subject in Delft inventories. Then Delft

Note also that not all the changes in the relative importance of subjects need correspond to new paintings with "modern" subjects. I suspect (but cannot prove by any concrete examples) that many paintings painted in the 1610s or 1620s were first recorded in inventories as "a Tobias" or "Burning of Troy" and were later called "a landscape" or "a conflagration." If my surmise is correct, the structural changes I have analyzed reflect both changes in actual subject matter and in perception, and the rate of turnover in collections needed to bring about the observed percentage changes in their composition by subject may have been smaller than my rough calculations indicate.

Some notion of the subject matter of newly acquired paintings—at least if they had been painted by Delft-based artists—can be gained from the primary specialization of newly registered painters in the guild (Chapter 6, Table 6.2). The breakdown of artists by their primary specializations is broadly consistent with the changes in the composition of inventories by subject matter that we have analyzed, both reflecting relative gains in landscape at the expense of histories and the rise of still-life and genre.

The (relative) decline of portrait-painting, however, emerges clearly from the analysis of painters' specialities, whereas it cannot be established from the breakdown by subject in Table 8.3. The reason for this, in my view, is that some artists who specialized in other types of painting, including the church painter Hendrick van Vliet and the genre painter Heyndrick van der Burch, produced portraits on order when they had a chance, so that the proportion of portraits to the total number of paintings may not have dropped as sharply as the (relative) number of painters whose *primary* specialization was portraiture.

Important changes also occurred within some of the ten broad categories of Table 8.3. Because the samples in individual groups are smaller and the statistical significance of small differences is subject

---

painters would have contributed some 225 to 250 landscapes a year to local collections around 1640. Ten artists in Delft specialized in painting landscapes, seascapes, and "perspectives" at that time. If half of their output was sold outside Delft, each artist would have had to produce and sell about forty-five to fifty pictures a year to arrive at the total additions to collections that we have estimated. I should have guessed that a full-time specialist in landscape, aided by one or two apprentices, would turn out *at least* one medium-sized painting a week and thus could easily market forty-five to fifty pictures per year.

to considerable doubt, I will only dwell on the most salient trends within categories.

In the second decade of the century, what may be called "allegorical landscapes"—the four seasons (chiefly summer and winter), the four winds, the sun and the moon—represented just under 10 percent of all landscapes. Their relative importance steadily declined until, in the 1670s, they were reduced to 3 percent of the total in this category. Religious landscapes[aa] represented 5 percent of all landscapes in 1610-1619 (12 percent exclusive of drawings), 4 percent in 1620-1629, and one to two percent in all succeeding decades. Ships, seascapes, and river scenes represented some 15 percent of all landscapes from 1610 to 1639, about 20 percent from the 1640s to the 1660s and 27 percent in the 1670s. Battle scenes, skirmishes, and robberies achieved their greatest relative importance in the 1630s and 1640s (5 to 6 percent of all landscapes) when Palamedes Palamedesz. and Isaac Junius were producing these scenes in Delft. Beach scenes and cityscapes were of negligible importance in the earlier part of the century; by the 1660s and 1670s they represented small but distinct genres (1 to 3 percent of all landscapes each). "Perspectives," presumed to be mainly church interiors, made up one to two percent of all landscapes until the 1660s when they shot up to 4 percent, their proportion subsiding again to 2.5 percent in the 1670s. These modest percentages of course understate the share of some of these groups in the entire landscape category because many of the paintings simply called "landscapes" might have been more accurately titled "a skirmish," "a beach scene," or even "a winter."

In the genre category, peasants together with peasant kermesses and dances (*boerendansen*) play a prominent role in all decades, but particularly in the first two and in the last two decades of the period covered (about 40 percent and 35 percent respectively). The decade-to-decade fluctuations, however, may not be significant. Society pieces (*geselschapjes*), brothels, and card players make up less than 10 percent of all genre pieces from the 1610s to the 1640s. In the 1650s they reach a share of nearly 30 percent, dropping again to 24 percent in the 1660s and 21 percent in the 1670s. There can hardly be any doubt that the importance of this group was greater in the second half of our period than in the first. *Corps-de-garde* scenes, virtually nonexistent in the first two decades, became fairly common from the

---

[aa]As I have already mentioned, religious landscapes were included in the religious categories and excluded from the broad category of landscapes.

1640s on, representing 5 to 10 percent of all genre paintings in the last decades. Musicians and dancers (other than *boerendansen*) vary greatly in importance from decade to decade, reaching a high point of nearly 25 percent of the genre group in the 1640s (for the entire sample collected in this decade). One difficulty when we get to fairly narrowly defined groups such as this is that they may not have been perceived in the same terms at different times: a scene described as "musicians" in the 1640s may have been regarded as a *geselschap* ten or twenty years later.

In the still-life group, fruit pieces and flowers occupy an important place throughout the period 1610-1679. In the first three decades they both represent about 20 percent of the entire category. From the 1650s on fruit pieces forge ahead, reaching about 25-30 percent. "Kitchens" make up 15 to 20 percent of all still-lifes up to the 1630s, then recede in importance to 10 to 12 percent in the period 1640 to 1670. The share of the heterogeneous group consisting of "break-fasts" (*ontbijtjes*); "banquets" (excluding open-air scenes); "vanitas" pieces; fish, crabs, dead birds; and undifferentiated "still-lifes," hovers around 50 percent up to the mid-century point then declines to about one-third. (The term "still-life," incidentally, makes its first appearance in the first half of the 1640s.) "Banquet" is the most common designation for a variegated still-life in this composite group, especially during the first half of the seventeenth century. "Barns," as I have already mentioned, emerge as a new genre in the 1640s, representing 3 to 5 percent of all still-lifes from 1640 to 1660 but only a little over one percent in the 1670s. Curiously enough, I could not find a single "still-life interior"—a room without persons—in my entire sample, either because such representations were very rare in Delft or because they were called something else that I did not recognize.

Among the portraits and faces, one group should be singled out: the portraits of the princes of Orange and of their families, of kings, queens, religious leaders, and admirals were important in all decades, but especially in the first half of the century when they represented as much as 20 to 30 percent of the entire portrait category. Displaying a portrait of His Excellency Prince Maurice or Prince Frederick Hendrick was a token of one's loyalty to the House of Orange. A large percentage of all the households in Delft, rich and poor, seem to have hung portraits of the reigning *stadhouder* and his family on their walls.

[246]

ATTRIBUTIONS

Altogether I found 1,962 paintings and 56 drawings in Delft inventories to which some artist's name had been attached, plus 43 monograms. Included in the total above were 505 paintings said to be copies after the artists cited, including three Flemish paintings said to be by or after a master. In Table 8.4 I have classified, insofar as possible, all these paintings (including copies) and drawings according to the origin or residence of the painters to which they were attributed. Since many artist moved from town to town, I had to use a rule of thumb to assign each artist to one town only. In the case of artists who were registered in the Delft guild at any time in their life, I assumed that they were "Delft artists." If an artist was registered at some time in his career in the guild in The Hague, I assigned him to that city. Most other entries were unambiguous. Dutch artists who could not be classified were either those whose name was not recorded with sufficient precision in the inventory (e.g., "Saftleven" could be Cornelis or Herman: the former lived chiefly in Rotterdam, the latter in Utrecht; "Karel van Mander" the Elder lived in Haarlem, the Younger lived in Delft) or an artist whose residence could not be ascertained (e.g., Wouter Hoop).[bb]

A glance at the table suffices to recognize the preponderance of local painters in Delft inventories. Attributions to Delft-based painters, almost all of whom were registered in the guild, make up 71 percent of all attributions in the small (and somewhat unreliable) sample for 1610-1619, 40 percent in the 1620s, one-half in the 1630s, and around 60 percent in the remaining decades. Delft's population at mid-century probably did not represent more than 5 percent of the total urban population of Holland[cc] and its artists were probably no more important or numerous than in other large cities. If the share of paintings attributed to Delft-based painters in surviving inventories were representative of the actual composition of all

[bb]I found five paintings and one drawing by the seascape painter Wouter Hoop in the Delfshaven inventory of Willem Verhoeff, surgeon, who died 27 May 1658 (Orphan Chamber, *boedel* no. 1776). It is possible that he was a resident of this dependency of Delft. The only known painting by this artist (in the Utrecht Museum, where he is called Wouter Hool) represents a view of Dordrecht on the Merwede river.

[cc]I base this rough calculation on an interpolation between the urban population figures for 1622 and 1660-1670 given in Jan de Vries, *The Dutch Rural Economy in the Golden Age* (New Haven: Yale University Press, 1974), p. 90.

TABLE 8.4

Origin or Residence of Painters Represented in Delft Inventories, 1610–1679

Origin	1610–1619	1620–1629	1630–1639	1640–1649	1650–1659	1660–1669	1670–1679
Delft	78	71	76	278	307	245	161
Other Dutch							
Amsterdam	—	4	4	15	20	16	9
Haarlem	—	16	29	30	24	6	11
Leyden	—	3	3	1	3	2	3
Rotterdam	—	3	—	3	10	6	3
Dordrecht	—	—	—	—	2	1	8
Utrecht	1	6	6	12	22	15	4
The Hague	—	13	11	38	37	44	15
Gorcum	—	1	1	3	3	2	—
Middelburg	—	—	—	—	2	1	1
Schiedam	—	—	—	2	3	1	—
Other	—	1	3	9	11	11	2
Total	1	47	57	113	137	105	56
Non-Dutch							
Flemish	29	18	—	26	8	5	3
Italian (all)	—	—	4	4	—	—	—
Old Masters							
Delft	—	8	7	9	4	2	2
Other Dutch	—	10	—	2	1	—	—
Flemish	2	—	5	4	4	4	4
Total	2	18	12	15	9	6	6
Amateurs	—	17	3	3	1	1	2
Unknown	—	7	7	15	20	16	27
Monograms	—	—	—	6	5	24	8
Grand Total	110	178	159	460	487	402	263

SOURCE: See Table 8.2.

inventories, then we should have to conclude that Delft collectors were quite provincial in their tastes, given to buying mostly local products irrespective of quality. While this conclusion is likely to be generally valid, it is potentially weakened by what may be a serious bias in the data: it is very probable that the notaries and their clerks who drew up the inventories, appraisals, and *contracedullen* on which we base our samples recognized the works of Delft painters much more readily than those of "foreigners." Two comparisons at least help to place an upper bound on the extent of this bias. In a sample of fifteen priced inventories in which the attributed paintings made up at least half of all paintings recorded, I found that Delft-based artists represented 55 percent of all the attributions—a satisfactory coincidence with my overall sample. On the other hand, in the album of Bramer drawings after paintings in Delft collections conserved in the Rijksmuseum, only seventeen attributions out of fifty-one, one-third, were by Delft-based artists (including Abram van Beyeren and Pieter Groenewegen, who spent a good part of their career in The Hague). This album, however, is evidently far from complete: over half of it seems to have disappeared,[dd] and it is quite conceivable that a larger proportion of Delft artists were to be found among those that are now missing.[ee] Taking these various samples into consideration, I would suggest, that, if the bias due to the lack of knowledge or misperception of notaries and clerks were corrected, the proportion of Delft-based artists for the entire period would still not fall below 40-50 percent.

When we come to analyze subgroups of artists—breaking down the non-Delft contingent by origin—we have to deal with smaller samples that are more exposed to chance fluctuations. Still, some characteristics of these subgroups are so pronounced that they deserve mention.

It is clear, for instance, that there cannot have been many Italian paintings in Delft. I found only five paintings by or after Italian masters, of which at least three—and perhaps all five—were copies: a "Last Judgment by Michel Angelo," surely after a print, copies after Raphael and Titian, one painting (a kitchen scene) by "Bassan," and

[dd]Written on the back of the drawing numbered 107 are the names of the eleven collectors who owned the paintings from which the drawings were copied. It was probably the last of 107 drawings in the original album.

[ee]If I am right in assuming, as I did in the previous note, that the album originally contained 107 drawings, I can safely infer that Bramer only copied a fraction of the paintings in the eleven collections represented in the album (since important collections typically contained fifty or more paintings). I have not a clue as to how Bramer selected the paintings he chose to copy.

one (a "Jacob and Esau") by the "Young Bassan."[ff] There were no
works by Italian masters among the fifty-one paintings in Delft
collections copied by Bramer, or at least among those that have
survived. Two paintings by Adriaen Brouwer, one by Pieter van Mol,
and one by Elsheimer exhausted the list of non-Dutch masters in the
album of drawings by Bramer. The question this apparent poverty
raises is whether there were enough original Italian paintings in local
collections for young artists to study the art of the masters *sur place*.
How did Vermeer, for example, acquire the expertise necessary to
testify on the authenticity of Italian paintings, as he did when he was
called to The Hague, together with Johannes Jordaens the Younger
who had recently returned from Italy, to testify on the authenticity of
paintings in the Reynst collection?[gg] Since it is improbable that he
ever visited Italy, I can only guess that he studied Italian originals in
Amsterdam where it is known that there were many such paintings to
be seen.[hh]

Other foreign schools were also very poorly represented. I did not
find a single French painting in the entire period.[ii] Even contemporary
Flemish masters seem to have been rare in Delft. I came across only
four paintings *by* Rubens, plus one copy *after* Rubens and one "by or
after" his work, one by Anthony van Dijck and one that may have
been by or after Jacob Jordaens (in Vermeer's death inventory), which
is not included in the table because it was left unattributed by the

[ff]I counted among the "unknown" masters, a painting by "Baro," one after a print
by "Barsant," one by "Bertius," and another by "Boratius," one or more of which may
have been by or after Barocci or Bassano. It is conceivable also that a painting said to
be by "Momeri" was by an Italian master. The original by Tintoretto sold by
Abraham de Cooge in 1680 (Chapter 7) was not included in my count.

[gg]The document, discovered by Bredius, is summarized in Albert Blankert, *Vermeer
of Delft: Complete Edition of the Paintings* (Oxford: Phaidon, 1978), p. 148. Vermeer
and Jordaens, incidentally, testified that the paintings were not originals by great
Italian masters but poor copies and imitations.

[hh]For example, in the 1657 inventory of the Amsterdam merchant Johannes
Renialme (who was also registered as an art dealer in the Delft guild), there were ten
paintings by Italian masters (and a few by *Italiénisant* French masters such as Valentin
de Boulogne and Claude Lorrain). These, judging by the prices, were probably
originals. Since Renialme was acquainted with Willem de Langue, the Vermeer family
notary, it would have been easy for young Vermeer to get to see his pictures in
Amsterdam (unless Renialme had at least a part of his stock-in-trade to show in
Delft). The Renialme inventory is reproduced in Bredius, *Künstler-inventare*, 1:230–
39.

[ii]There were seven paintings by "Loron" in an inventory of the 1670s. These may
have been, but probably were not, by Claude Lorrain.

FIG. 13 Willem van den Bundel, Landscape (1620s), 28¾ x 41⅛ in. Art Trade (1978). Amsterdam

clerk recording the inventory. One would have expected to find some genre paintings by popular Flemish masters such as David Teniers and Frans Francken the Younger, but only one by each of these masters cropped up.

More paintings by the landscape painter Joost de Momper were found in Delft inventories than by any other contemporary Flemish master. In the rich collection of the grain merchant Joris Claesz. Tristram who died in 1617 there were six paintings by De Momper and nineteen landscape drawings on paper by the same artist.[27] The collection of Frans Jaspersz. Mesch who died in 1627 featured seven landscapes by De Momper.[28] In the works that have survived by early landscape painters in Delft including Willem van den Bundel (fig. 13) and Jan Willemsz. Decker we can detect the influence of the Flemish master.

Flemish masters of the sixteenth century—classified among the Old Masters in Table 8.4—were also represented in inventories of the first quarter of the seventeenth century. Among these we find Pieter Aertsen ("Lange Pier"), with three originals and one copy; five paintings by Sebastiaen Vranks; one copy after Willem Key; and one original by Frans Floris, all in the 1610s and 1620s. Anthonie Blocklandt was virtually the only Delft Old Master that I encountered in my sample of inventories, but his name came up fairly often: altogether fourteen of his paintings and seventeen copies after his works are cited (the majority in the 1620s and 1630s).

Among Dutch contemporary painters who lived and were registered in the guilds of other towns in Holland and Zeeland, by far the greatest numbers represented were found in Haarlem and The Hague. It is probably significant that Haarlem contributed the greatest number in this group in the 1620s and 1630s when the Haarlem school had the greatest *rayonnement*. From the 1640s on it was gradually displaced in local inventories by The Hague, a city only a few miles from Delft, with which Delft had the closest ties. Here Jan van Goyen played a predominant role with forty originals and five copies (twenty of the originals cited in the 1660s alone); but Moses van Uyttenbroek, Dirck Dalens, Frans Knipbergen, and especially Adriaen van der Venne (eighteen paintings) also contributed to this preponderance.[jj] It

---

[jj]The close artistic ties between The Hague and Delft manifested themselves in 1) master-pupil relations (Jan van Ravesteyn of The Hague was Miereveld's most successful pupil); 2) business dealings (e.g., Jan van Goyen's contracting of a 1,000-gulden loan from Simon G. van der Made in Delft, the rental of a brewery by Jan Steen, the sale of frames by Anthony van der Wiel to Hubert van der Venne in

FIG. 14 Jacob Vosmaer, Vase of Flowers (1615), 33½ x 24⅝ in. The Metropolitan Museum of Art, Purchase, 1871 (Photo: Museum)

is remarkable that Utrecht painters (e.g., Bloemaert, Van Bylert, Uytewael, Terbruggen, and Droochsloot) were as well-represented in Delft inventories as Amsterdam artists until the 1660s and much better represented throughout than were Leyden artists. This also shows that artists from these far larger cities were underrepresented in local inventories relative to their population and artistic importance. In view of the influence of the Middelburg school on Delft flower-painting —on such artists as Wouter Jacobsz. Vosmaer (fig. 14) and Balthasar van der Ast—I should have expected to find many more works by Middelburg painters. It is of course possible that paintings by Delft artists influenced by the Middelburg school of flower-painting were considered acceptable substitutes for pictures by genuine masters of the school and thereby reduced the demand for works by these out-of-town artists. Indeed, this remark can be extended to comparisons involving the works of artists stemming from other towns: the chance an artist had of being "imported" into Delft where there were a number of local painters working in a variety of popular Dutch styles may have depended on his ability to produce works that had no close substitutes on the local market. Van Goyen's special advantage on the Delft market may have owed to the fact that, with the possible exception of Pieter van Asch (fig. 15), he had no close imitators or tolerable substitutes working there in the 1640s and 1650s, after Simon de Vlieger had left town.[kk]

The "amateurs" cited in Table 8.4 are generally painters who are identical with or are somehow related to the person in whose inventory their name occurs. Jacob Jansz. Helm, for instance, was a rich collector and former councilman of Delft who died in July 1626.[29] No less than sixteen pictures in his estate were said to be by his hand, including a self-portrait and various "histories." He was not registered in the guild, and I have found his work nowhere else. Anthoni van der Houve, who painted a fruit piece in the inventory of Geertruyd Gerrit Camerling (1663),[30] received this same painting as a bequest from the deceased. He was most probably an amateur who was a friend or relative of Geertruyd Camerling.

The "unknown" painters generally contributed only one or two

The Hague); and 3) artists who at one time or another were members of the Guilds of St. Lucas in the two towns (e.g., Willem Luyts, Abram van Beyeren, Paulus Potter).

[kk]It would be interesting to study the effect on Van Goyen's sales in Haarlem of his numerous imitators working in that city (Frans and Maerten van der Hulst, Jan Coelenbier, and Van Goyen's close competitor in the 1630s, Salomon Ruysdael).

Fig. 15 Pieter van Asch, Wooded Landscape (1650s), 19 x 26⅜ in. Art Trade (1975). London

pictures each. In a few cases I suspect that their name is a garbled version of a known artist (e.g. Pelt for Cornelis Beelt, Daniel Vos for Daniel Vosmaer, Uyler for den Uyl, Van Gotien for Van Goyen), but, to narrow the range of uncertainty of my estimates, I forebore from linking these names with the putative artists in question.[ll] Many other painters ring no bell at all: "Gregorio," "Caspar van Goyer," "F. Benier," "Olivenne de Bocq," "Arent van Brussel," "Button," "Belgij," "Yeman de Potter," "Carel de Leeu," "Adriaen van Nuys," "Van de Mers," "Christiaen van Mereu," and "Broer Cornelis."

In Table 8.5 are listed the twenty most popular, or at least the most frequently cited, artists in Delft inventories.

Of the nineteen contemporary artists listed in Table 8.5, all but two (Van Goyen and De Momper) were registered in the guild of Delft; with the exception of Van Beyeren and Adriaen van Linschoten who both moved to The Hague, they all spent most of their lives in Delft. Several of these painters are all but unknown today, including Hans Jordaens the Elder, perhaps the best-selling painter in Delft until his death in 1631, Pieter Vroomans, Evert van Aelst, Gillis de Berg, Adriaen Linschoten, and Pieter Stael. A few paintings have survived by Hans Jordaens the Elder (fig. 4), Pieter Vroomans, Evert van Aelst, and Gillis de Berg, none securely by Linschoten. Miereveld, who was certainly the most famous painter of Delft during his lifetime, would stand higher on my frequency list if it were not that very few portraits in inventories are ever attributed. We would also recall that Miereveld painted many if not most of his portraits for prominent personages outside Delft.[mm]

Painters such as Hans Jordaens, Jacob Woutersz. Vosmaer, Evert van Aelst, Leonaert Bramer, Pieter Vroomans, Peter van Asch, and Pieter Stael were not only common in Delft in the seventeenth century in the sense that a large number of paintings were attributed to them in extant inventories but also in that they occurred in many different inventories. It was quite frequent for a clerk drawing up a middle-class inventory—corresponding to an estate with movable goods valued at

[ll]On the other hand, I did consider "Moreel" and "Heynsberger" close enough to Moreelse and Haensbergen to put them both in the Utrecht group. I thought it reasonable to include a landscape by "Dalon" with paintings by the fairly common landscape painter Dirck Dalens in The Hague group. Also, because I frequently found his name singularly distorted in archival sources, I identified "Mr. Boringa" as Anthony Beauregart (flower piece).

[mm]I have not included in the count the finished and unfinished portraits found in his inventory after his death.

TABLE 8.5

Twenty Most Frequently Cited Artists in Delft Inventories
1610–1679

Artist	1610–1619	1620–1629	1630–1639	1640–1649	1650–1659	1660–1669	1670–1679	Total
Hans Jordaens the Elder*	15	25,1[c]	10	19	23,1[c]	13,1[c]	21	126,3[c]
Leonaert Bramer	—	—	4	16,5[c]	12,1[c]	24	10,1[c]	66,7[c]
Jacob Woutersz. Vosmaer†	—	7	11	13	10	17,2[d]	4	62,2[d]
Pieter Vroomans‡	—	—	—	12	20	15	12	59
Evert van Aelst§	—	—	—	13,1[c]	20	21	1	55,1[c]
Pieter Stael	14,14[d]	11	9	6	11	1	3	55,14[d]
Herman Steenwijck‖	—	—	—	6,1[c]	13	14	16	49,1[c]
Pieter van Asch	—	—	2[c]	12,5[c]	16	10	7	45,7[c]
Jan van Goyen	—	—	3,4[c]	7	8,1[c]	20	2	40,5[c]
Cornelis Jacobsz. Delff	—	7	4	15	10	4	1	41
Pieter Groenewegen	—	1	3,4[c]	13,1[c]	7	6	1	31,5[c]
Gillis de Berg#	—	—	2	3	12	8	12	37
Egbert van der Poel	—	—	—	—	10	11	10	31
Jochum de Vries	—	—	7	16	4	2	1	30
Corstiaen Couwenbergh	—	—	2	12	5	8,1[c]	2,1[c]	29,2[c]
Adriaen Linschoten	—	—	—	16,4[c]	7	1	1	25,4[c]
Joost de Momper	6,19[d]	9	—	9,1[c],1[d]	2	—	—	26,1[c],20[d]
Abram van Beyeren	—	—	—	3	5	12	3	23
Michiel Miereveld	7	6,1[c]	—	4,4[c]	3	—	—	20,5[c]
Anthony van Blocklandt	—	5,8[c]	4[c]	2,5[c]	4	1	2	14,17[c]

SOURCE: See Table 8.2.

NOTE: The superscript c denotes a copy after the master, the superscript d a drawing by the master.

*Includes all paintings by "Jordaens" that, from their date or their subject, can be attributed to Hans Jordaens the Elder.

†Including all flower paintings by "Vosmaer."

‡Includes all paintings by "Vro(o)mans" and "Vroomans the Younger."

§Includes paintings attributed to "Van Aelst," two or three of which may have been painted by Evert's nephew Willem.

‖Includes all still-life paintings attributed to "Steenwijck," some of which may have been painted by Herman's brother Pieter.

#Includes all still-life paintings attributed to "de Berg" (Mattheus de Berg was a figure painter).

500 to 1,000 gulden—to attribute a painting to one or two of these artists and leave all other paintings in the inventory unattributed.

In contrast to these relatively high frequencies, it is instructive to cite the attributions in Delft inventories to the masters who created the glories of Holland's Golden Age. The attributions to Rembrandt were, one in the 1640s, two in the 1650s, and four in the 1660s; to Frans Hals, one in the 1640s; to Vermeer, one in the 1660s;[31] to Gerard ter Borch, none; and to Jacob Ruysdael, none. The well-known artists who spent some time in Delft are better-represented: Pieter de Hooch with eleven attributions in the 1650s, most of them in the inventory of Justus de la Grange in whose employ he spent some time before moving from Delft to Amsterdam; Carel Fabritius with ten attributions; and Jan Steen with three attributions, two in the 1660s and one in the 1670s.

The only popular artist in Delft listed in Table 8.5 whose reputation can be compared with any of these now-famous masters was Jan van Goyen. Of the Delft-based artists in the table, only Blocklandt, Bramer, and Miereveld occupy a secure—though hardly a preeminent—place in the history of Dutch painting today.

The earlier generation of Mannerist artists was better represented than most of the great "modernists." We have already seen that Cornelis van Haarlem and Anthonie Blocklandt were popular artists in Delft from the 1620s to the 1640s (six originals and ten copies, fourteen originals and seventeen copies respectively). Karel van Mander the Elder (with ten originals plus three paintings and one copy that can be given either to him or to his son Karel van Mander the Younger) and Goltzius (six originals and two copies) did fairly well also. It is remarkable incidentally how frequently these Mannerist artists were copied (at least in earlier decades). One indication that the contents of inventories tended to reflect contemporary tastes, rather than the tastes of earlier generations, and hence that there was a significant rate of turnover in collections, is that very few Mannerists are found in inventories from the mid-century point on. Nevertheless, the fact remains that the modernists who spread the fame of Dutch painting far and wide are poorly represented, even at the end of the period under study.

Much work remains to be done on attributions in inventories in other Dutch towns to determine whether, and if so to what extent, Delft collectors were provincial, conservative, or both in their apparent lack of interest in the painters now thought to be the most outstanding in the Dutch school.

THE VALUE OF WORKS OF ART

The prices assigned in appraisals and auction records may shed light on a problem that came up in the preceding section in connection with the representativeness of attributed paintings. Did notaries and clerks attribute paintings that they selected more or less at random from all the paintings they inventoried or was there something special about these pictures that moved them to single these pictures out? I analyzed the prices of paintings in fifty-two inventories in which both attributed and unattributed paintings were to be found. Since I could find no significant differences in average prices through time, I decided to pool all fifty-two samples, ranging from 1617 to 1672 (as I will do throughout this section). The average price of an attributed painting—across all fifty-two inventories—was 16.6 gulden, of an unattributed painting 7.2 gulden. A test of the difference showed that it was statistically significant at the 99 percent probability level.[nn] The average price of an attributed painting was higher than the average price of an unattributed painting in fifty out of fifty-two inventories. Because most of the inventories containing both attributed and unattributed paintings were fairly rich—averaging in excess of 2,000 gulden—even the average value of unattributed paintings was fairly high, reflecting the better-than-average quality of pictures owned by wealthy citizens.

In Table 8.6 I have assembled data from a small number of more modest inventories (with a total value less than 1,000 gulden) that contained both attributed and unattributed pictures.

It is remarkable that the prices of the attributed paintings in these more modest estates are about on a level with the unattributed paintings in the more wealthy estates. However, the prices of unattributed pictures average around two to three gulden, appreciably lower than in the richer inventories. Prices of attributed pictures rarely go down as low as the landscape painting given to Willem van den Bundel (one gulden fifteen stuivers). The work of Van den Bundel, a painter respected enough to have been elected to the board of the guild three times in the 1620s and 1630s, may have been considered passé a generation later when this inventory was recorded.

[nn]The standard deviation of the attributed sample was 11.7, of the unattributed 4.3. The estimated standard deviation of the two samples combined was 8.81. The *t*-value of the difference between sample means was 5.45. It is clear, in any event, that the paintings the clerks attributed were more valuable than the others. This still does not tell us whether these "others" were originals by less expensive painters or good copies after fashionable artists.

TABLE 8.6
Value of Attributed and Unattributed Paintings
in Seven Inventories Valued at Less Than 1,000 Gulden

Owner	Value of Total Inventory of Movable Goods (gulden)	Number of Attributed Pictures	Average Price of Attributed Paintings (gulden)	Number of Unattributed Pictures	Average Price of Unattributed Paintings (gulden)	Standard Deviation
Geertgen Gysbrechts (1647)	416	1*	5.75	13	2.6	4.0
Tryntge Heyndrix (1648)	627	1†	8.0	10	2.6	1.5
Pieterneletge Aelbrechtsdr. (1655)	972	2‡	8.0	22	5.3	4.4
Jacob Manryque (1658)	840	1§	1.75	11	1.3	1.2
Appolonia Jacobs van Ouwerdyck (1668)	292‖	3#	12.9	4	2.8	2.4
Margareta van der Burch (1672)	836	1**	7.25	21	2.9	2.1
Samuel Spa (1676)	937	6††	6.3	42	2.7	2.6

SOURCE: See Table 8.2.
*"An original by Claes Vosmaer." †Leonaert Bramer.
‡"Jordaen the Elder" (Hans Jordaens the Elder) and "Sachtleven" (Herman or Cornelis Saftleven).
§Willem van den Bundel. ‖Perhaps an incomplete inventory. #All by Cornelis Jacobsz. Delff. **Bramer.
††Pen drawings by "Koesermans" (Johannes Coesermans, registered in the Guild of St. Lucas in 1661).

Very few estates that brought less than 300 gulden at auction contained attributed paintings. In one instance (auction sale of Barbertgen Fransen, total 286 gulden),[32] we know from the inventory drawn up before the sale that it contained two paintings by (Pieter) Vroomans, but we do not know which these were because the *contracedulle* only listed the paintings without attribution or description.

Next I chose at random ten inventories with total value of movable goods between 87 and 313 gulden including seventy-one paintings, all unattributed. The average value of a painting for this group of inventories, all dated in the 1660s, was 0.88 gulden (standard deviation 1.44 gulden). In general, however, even in these poorer inventories most of the paintings whose subject was specified cost one to three gulden. A large panel painting (*groot bort*) was seldom valued at less than four gulden.

From these disjointed bits of information, I would very tentatively conclude that inventories of movable possessions valued at over 2,000 gulden contained chiefly paintings by guild masters, from Delft or elsewhere, or good-quality copies costing five gulden and up. Inventories valued at less than 500 gulden may have contained a few pieces by masters—though probably no masterpieces—but most of the pictures they contained were copies or imitations made by apprentices and journeymen or by specialists in "work by the dozen." I know of no guild master in Delft who specialized in *dozijn werck* but I suspect that some of the rarely cited painters, including those known mainly as *kladschilders*, were of this type. Less well-off citizens may also have owned pictures painted some time ago by masters whose works had lost market value because they were now considered old-fashioned (e.g., Willem van den Bundel in the late 1650s).

Finally I attempted to ascertain whether there might be a difference between the prices of pictures by Delft-based and out-of-town artists. My hypothesis that the latter should be more expensive had to be rejected: there was virtually no difference between the averages for the two groups in my sample of fifty-two inventories. Of course, this does not rule out a significant difference in price for equivalent size and quality—attributes that I had no way of controlling for.

My second principal use of value-of-inventory data was to gauge the effect of differences in wealth—as measured by the total value of movable goods—on the value of works of art collected. To introduce this topic, a few words on the available statistics are in order.

I have already mentioned that priced inventories consisted of appraisals (*taxatien*) and auction records (*contracedullen*). When an appraisal was made it often covered all the possessions—movable goods, real estate, and financial investments—of the decreased, the bride or bridegroom, or the debtor in default. Auctions, on the other hand, generally disposed only of movable goods. The difference between the value of the entire possessions of an individual and his movable goods was often very large, especially in the case of rich merchants with considerable business assets. The wealthy grain merchant Pieter Willemsz. Dusseldorp left an estate worth 18,366 gulden, including houses, boats, and debentures, but his movable goods were valued at only 1,725 gulden 10 stuivers.[33] When Judickgen Gerrits, the wife of the eminent faiencier Lambrecht Gysbrechtsz. Kruyck, died in 1641, the couples' movable possessions were appraised at 1,135 gulden, including clothing worth 235 gulden. This was only a small part of their total assets valued at 22,626 gulden or even of their net worth (assets minus debts) estimated at 11,381 gulden. (The house where they lived was priced at 4,000 gulden, the former brewery used by Kruyck for his faience works at 6,000 gulden.)[34]

In many cases, the contents of the *contracedulle* are such as to suggest that not all personal belongings had been put up for sale. When no items of clothing wound up in the sale or when artworks or any other category of assets represented a suspiciously high proportion of the total value of goods sold, I concluded that the sale did not cover the entire estate of an individual and excluded the inventory from my sample.

While I have not made a systematic study of *taxatien* comprising the value of houses and gardens, I can offer the rule-of-thumb that, for middle-level inventories valued at 500 to 1,000 gulden in movable goods, real estate—usually the value of the house of the deceased—was worth anywhere from 150 to 250 percent of the value of the inventory.

Clothing was very expensive in the seventeenth century. In small- and medium-level estates a couple's clothes frequently cost 60 to 80 nercent as much as all the furnishings of their house, including the works of art. In households with movable possessions worth 1,000–1,500 gulden, clothes were proportionally less important, representing around 40 percent of the value of furnishings. Among the furnishings, bed and bedding were often the most costly items, valued at 30 to 50 gulden per set. Silver and gold objects were generally absent from estates valued at less than 500 gulden (the majority of which comprised *some* works of art), but their value rose as a percentage of total assets in larger estates. Even though the value of silver and gold exceeded the value of works of art in many of the larger estates, the relation was reversed in the richest households where there was a strong interest in collecting. Thus the movable possessions of Receiver General Boudewijn de Man that sold at auction for a total of 13,081 gulden consisted of 6,139 gulden of paintings, 3,927 gulden of silver and gold pieces and 3,014 gulden of furniture and other goods.[35]

The results of my statistical study of the value of works in art in inventories of movable possessions are summarized in Table 8.7.

The median value of the inventories of movable possessions in my

TABLE 8.7
Value of Artworks in Inventories, 1610–1679: Summary Results

Value of Total Inventory (In gulden)	Number of Inventories	Percentage Share of Artworks in Total Inventory
0–99	61	1.53
100–199	48	2.23
200–299	47	3.78
300–399	49	3.72
400–499	37	2.89
500–599	23	3.36
600–699	30	4.62
700–799	22	3.69
800–899	15	5.76
900–999	10	5.83
1,000–1,099	13	4.62
1,100–1,199	8	6.90
1,200–1,299	8	6.20
1,300–1,399	3	4.30
1,400–1,499	8	5.29
1,500–1,999	21	7.60
2,000–2,999	23	8.78
3,000–3,999	12	3.67
4,000–4,999	5	16.30
5,000–6,000	1	3.00
10,000–15,000	2	25.90

SOURCE: See Table 8.2.

sample of 461 inventories was 531 gulden, the mean 938 gulden. The median value of art works collected was 14.4 gulden, the mean 76.7 gulden. The very large differences between the median and the mean for both total inventories and value of works of art suggests that the distributions are highly skewed toward high values of inventories and art collections.[oo] The median value of movable possessions for the more representative sample I collected for the 1640s (including my supplementary sample) was 488 gulden (mean 927 gulden). For this same period, the median value of art works collected was 12.5 gulden (mean 104.7 gulden).[pp]

For the sample of all six decades in Table 8.7, there appears to be a sharp rise in the percentage share of the value of works of art in the total value of movable possessions from the poorest group of inventories (0 to 99 gulden) to the 200 to 299 gulden group. A good part of this rise is due to the sharp decline in the percentage of inventories containing no works of art (from one-third in the former to 10 percent in the latter). From this point on, the percentage share of the value of works of art fluctuates without a trend around 3 to 4 percent to the 800 to 899 gulden group when it rises again to 5 to 6 percent and again to 7 to 9 percent between 1,500 and 3,000 gulden. There is then a sharp drop between 3,000 and 4,000 gulden (which may be due to sampling fluctuation). Since the standard deviations of observations within group averages were quite high (typically 1.5 times to twice as high as the group average), differences between any two averages of successive value-of-inventory groups should not be considered significant.

To estimate the "wealth elasticity of art collections"—that is, the statistical relation between percentage changes in the value of art collections (y) and percentage changes in the total value of movable goods (x)—I regressed the natural log of y on: 1) the natural log of x, and 2) the year in which the inventory was recorded. (The introduction of the time variable is needed to gauge the independent effect of time on the dependent variable, since, if time were conjoined with the wealth variable, it might bias our estimate of the wealth elasticity.)

[oo]When the top decile of the observations was eliminated from both samples, the mean was reduced to 649 gulden for the value of inventories and to 25.6 gulden for the value of art collections.

[pp]After elimination of the top decile, the mean of the inventory values was reduced to 570 gulden, the mean of the artworks to 23.9 gulden. The inventories so eliminated ranged from 1,584 to 13,309 gulden, the collections of artworks from 97 to 6,139 gulden.

Because my samples for the different decades were of different size and were subject to varying degrees of suspected bias, I also ran the regression not only for the entire period 1610-1679 but for each decade separately. The results are shown in Table 8.8.

For the period as a whole, the wealth elasticity of art collections (γ_1) is estimated to be 1.23 with a standard error of 0.052. There is therefore a 99 percent probability that the true elasticity is greater than unity. On average, a 1 percent increase in the value of total inventories is associated with a 1.23 percent increase in the value of art collections. The time variable has a slight positive trend, but it is not significant. The constant is not significantly different from zero. R^2, the fraction of the total variance in the dependent variable explained by the two independent variables, is equal to 0.55, which is quite satisfactory for this sort of specification.

The decade-by-decade analysis gives results that are extraordinarily homogeneous, given the biases in our samples. The elasticities are closely bunched around the average for the entire period of 1.23, with a range extending from 1.15 in 1670-1679 to 1.36 in 1630-1639. However, only the elasticities for the 1630s and 1640s are significantly in excess of unity at the 95 percent probability level. The time variable and the constant do not differ significantly from zero in any decade.

Next I divided my entire sample in two equal parts, the first containing the inventories above the median value of all inventories, the second those below the median. My hypothesis was that the wealth elasticities should be higher in the richer set of inventories, on the basis of the following reasoning. Individuals with modest inventories ranging from 50 to 500 gulden may be thought to have bought paintings and prints much as they bought furniture. Walls had to be covered, if possible with attractive decorations or morally instructive "histories," but there was no need, if one got a little better-off, to spend a greater percentage of one's income or to invest a larger portion of one's wealth in artworks. On the other hand, for a certain category of individuals, almost all of whom were in the two top deciles of the wealth distribution, collecting works of art became an end in itself. Some of them may have been patrons of Delft painters. Their investment in art was likely to represent a substantially larger portion of the value of their movable goods than for less wealthy individuals (though still above the median) who looked on art as decoration or as religious illustration.

The wealth elasticity is indeed higher for the subsample of richer inventories (1.235 versus 0.92 for the below-median sample). This

TABLE 8.8
Results of Regressions, 1610–1679

	Coefficient of LOGINV (γ_1)	Standard Error	Coefficient of t (γ_2)	Standard Error	Constant (c)	Standard Error	R^2
Entire period	1.23	0.052	0.0024	0.0033	−8.93	5.43	0.55
1610–1619	1.23	0.25	0.016	0.105	−31.3	169.5	0.63
1620–1629	1.11	0.14	0.054	0.057	−91.6	92.3	0.46
1630–1639	1.36	0.12	0.051	0.051	−89.5	83.6	0.64
1640–1649	1.26	0.11	−0.014	0.046	18.6	76.3	0.60
1650–1659	1.21	0.13	0.022	0.038	−41.0	62.0	0.53
1660–1669	1.22	0.18	0.033	0.058	−60.8	97.3	0.46
1670–1679	1.15	0.15	−0.075	0.062	−130.8	104.0	0.55

NOTE: Basic equation: LOGART = γ_1 LOGINV + γ_2 log t + c, where LOGART is the log of the value of the artworks, LOGINV is the total value of the inventory, t is the year, c is the constant intercept, and γ_1 and γ_2 are respectively the coefficients of LOGINV and log t.

TABLE 8.9

Regressions Based on Subsamples of Above- and Below-Median Inventories

	Above-median			Below-median			Size of Total Sample
	Coefficient of LOGINV (γ_1)	Standard Error	R^2	Coefficient of LOGINV (γ_2)	Standard Error	R^2	
Entire period	1.235	0.121	0.31	0.92	0.11	0.25	462
1610–1619	1.541	0.357	0.72	1.045	0.98	0.15	22
1620–1629	0.934	0.271	0.28	0.952	0.306	0.22	74
1630–1639	1.40	0.294	0.41	0.783	0.251	0.23	72
1640–1649	1.256	0.107	0.35	1.21	0.238	0.32	100
1650–1659	1.49	0.221	0.56	0.795	0.424	0.10	80
1660–1669	1.420	0.480	0.25	1.024	0.314	0.31	60
1670–1679	1.363	0.309	0.45	0.838	0.429	0.14	54

NOTE: The regressions have the same specification as those in Table 8.8. The coefficients of the time variable and the constants are not reported because in no case did they differ significantly from zero.

superiority holds true, as shown in Table 8.9, for all decades except the 1620s, where the two elasticities are essentially identical. For the sample covering the entire period and for all decades (except, again, for the 1620s) all the wealth elasticities of the above-median groups exceed unity (significantly so in the 1640s and 1650s). In the below-median sample, none of the wealth elasticities (for the entire sample or for the individual decades) differs significantly from unity. It is interesting to note that the R^2 statistics are almost invariably higher for the above-median than for the below-median regressions. Relative differences in wealth were apparently better predictors of relative differences in the value of art collections at higher than at lower levels of wealth.

A SUMMING UP

The relatively large sample of inventories I have sifted through in this chapter is biased toward the upper end of the distribution of household wealth (though much less so than the inventories of paintings that have been published by Abraham Bredius and other specialists in Dutch art of the period). Despite this upward bias, I was still able to draw certain conclusions grounded on the following line of reasoning. Inventories below the median of the sample distribution of inventories of movable goods—531 gulden—contained mainly "work-by-the-dozen," paintings costing a gulden or two apiece. If the median of the entire population of Delft inventories were, say, 250 gulden—a reasonable figure[99]—this would imply that the vast majority—perhaps two-thirds—of all inventories consisted more or less exclusively of such artisanal products. The bulk of works by master painters would be found in the top third of the (unbiased) wealth distribution (say, above 500 gulden). But even inventories of movable possessions worth 500 to 1,000 gulden—the range in which we would find the estates of most handicraft masters, from builders to weavers—would normally contain very few paintings costing more than five to ten gulden, a price for which one could buy a Vroomans, a small Bramer, or a Nicolaes Vosmaer, corresponding to the lower range of paintings by guild masters (Cf. Table 8.6). Most of the paintings that hang in museums today—the Van Goyens, the Vermeers, the Rembrandts, the Fabritiuses—would have been owned

[99]I suggested earlier that the average wealth of households in my entire sample of inventories might be about twice the average wealth of all households in Delft.

by merchants, printers, successful innkeepers, notaries, and patrician-rentiers with inventories of movable goods starting at 1,000 gulden but occurring most frequently in the 3,000 to 10,000 gulden range. The fact that the "wealth elasticity of works of art" was above unity only in the class of citizens whose wealth was above the sample median also suggests that serious collectors were in the upper range of this group.

These inferences allow me to speculate on two contemporary stereotypes about the market for Dutch art in the seventeenth century. According to the first, most Dutch houses were "full of paintings"; the second, already cited in Chapter 6 in connection with the economic status of painters, claims that "most of Holland's painters no longer worked for a few patrons but were dependent on shopkeepers, bakers, butchers, and even peasants, roughly the same stratum of society into which most painters were themselves born."[36]

The first generalization, frequently based on a broad interpretation of an entry in John Evelyn's diary in which he marveled at the abundance of paintings in the houses of Dutch people and particularly of peasants,[37] has limited validity, at least for Delft. Most poor households—the houses of the apprentices and the journeymen who made up a majority of the population's wage earners—possessed few if any paintings. Inventories in the 50 to 150 gulden range contained anywhere from one to ten little "boards" of very little value. At least a third contained no paintings at all. French and English visitors to Holland (e.g., B. de Monconys, René Descartes, Sir William Temple, and Evelyn) who themselves stemmed from the nobility or from the high bourgeoisie had little opportunity to visit poorer houses. Their impression of the relative abundance of paintings in Holland, compared to their own country, was probably correct, but it was exaggerated due to the bias in their observations."

The second stereotype, which assigned the bulk of the clientele for Dutch artists to the lower middle-class, is also misleading, if not totally false. The evidence in this chapter suggests that the buyers of master painters' works were mainly in the top third of the wealth distribution. A few clients, doubtless, were (master) "bakers and

"John Evelyn is also frequently quoted to the effect that the Dutch were given to speculating in artworks on a broad scale in the first half of the seventeenth century. Unfortunately, I have found nothing in my analysis of inventories and of notarial depositions regarding purchases and sales of works of art either to substantiate or to impugn the validity of this observation.

butchers,"⁵⁵ but the majority belonged to higher-status occupations. These exaggerations aside, the fact remains that paintings by guild-registered masters did penetrate into the middle and lower strata of Delft society, as had probably not been the case before the seventeenth century and still was not the case in France, England, or Italy at that time.

On the contents of inventories themselves, we found that the subject matter of the paintings collected underwent a gradual but profound change in the course of the century. Religious and mythological "histories," as well as allegories, receded in importance; landscapes, which gained most of the ground "histories" had lost, were gradually shorn of their earlier religious or otherwise symbolic significance.ᵗᵗ I take these trends to be evidence of the secularization of Dutch, or at least of Delft, society after it had recovered from the religious turmoil of the half century preceding the Synod of Dordrecht (1618), but also of a turning away from the humanistic preoccupations of the previous century. A landscape, a still-life (without manifest symbols), or a "society piece" may well have been more interesting to look at and easier to live with by 1660 than an Esther before Assuerus, an Allegory of the Broad and the Narrow Way, or a Diogenes.

Finally we come to the apparent provincialism of Delft collectors who concentrated their purchases on paintings by Delft-based artists, the most popular of whom are now judged to have been inferior to their best out-of-town competitors (e.g., in the painting of woods and streams, Pieter van Asch from Delft compared to Salomon or Jacob Ruysdael from Haarlem). Was Delft more inward-turning than other cities? Only a systematic comparison of attributed artworks in inventories in Delft and in other cities of more or less the same magnitude (Rotterdam, The Hague, Utrecht, Haarlem) might be expected to supply an answer to this question. My conjecture, based on published inventories in these other cities, is that Delft was not

---

⁵⁵It is well known that the baker Hendrick van Buyten bought a number of Vermeer's paintings at high prices. But it is only recently that information has come to light showing not only that he was at one time a headman of the bakers' guild (most of whom were fairly well-off) but that he had inherited considerable amounts of money which he lent out at interest. He died a rich man. (Montias, "Vermeer and His Milieu: Conclusion of an Archival Study," *Oud-Holland* 94 [1980]: 57).

ᵗᵗIt might be added, on the basis of visual rather than archival evidence, that in the course of the century still-lifes were gradually emptied of their spiritual content (cf. the "vanitas" paintings of Pieter Claesz. versus the displays of finery—"*pronk*" still-lifes—of Willem Kalf).

atypical in this regard. Most collectors in Holland were inclined to buy works from local artists because they knew them personally, because they had seen their works hang in public places or in their fellow citizens' collections, or simply because these artists were better able to adapt their products to the town's tastes and fashions. To some extent also, the Guild of St. Lucas placed restrictions on sales by out-of-town painters that added to the cost and trouble of securing their works. Last but not least, civic pride—at a time when the cities of the United Provinces were largely autonomous—helped steer local demand toward the artists who spread abroad the fame of their city.[uu]

The value of art collections by the middle of the seventeenth century consisted overwhelmingly of paintings. There were few sculptures in Delft collections and fewer still of any importance. Prints were relatively inexpensive. Tapestries, which were very costly, by and large were not collected by the burghers in our sample. One form of applied art that virtually every one did collect, but which I have neglected so far, was decorated ceramics—Chinese porcelain for those that could afford it; delftware dishes and tiles, which occupied an increasingly important place as the century wore on, both in modest and in relatively wealthy homes. This book would be incomplete if I omitted to discuss the other arts and crafts whose creators fell under the authority of the Guild of St. Lucas. I shall do so in the next chapter, concentrating on the printing trades, tapestry-making and the delftware industry, where I not only look at the demand for their products on the part of patrons and collectors but at the supply side as well—at the artists and artisans who collaborated to make these goods and at the capital they required for their manufacture, in contrast to the artist-painters who could do with almost no capital at all.

[uu]Pride in the painters of Delft is a conspicuous feature of Dirck Evertsz. van Bleyswijck's *Beschryvinge der Stadt Delft* (Delft, 1667), *passim*, but especially pp. 850-57.

NINE

The Minor Arts: The Printing Trades, Tapestry-Making and the Delftware Industry

CAPITAL INTENSITY IN THE ARTS

In these days of fully automated plants, the capital requirements of seventeenth-century printers, tapestry-makers, and faienciers may appear trifling. Yet relative to the resources that people had at their disposal at the time, these requirements presented a considerable hurdle. Unless a man's family had already amassed wealth or he had married money, there was not much chance of starting one of these businesses. He could try to borrow funds—500 gulden here, 1,000 gulden there—either directly from a would-be lender or, via a notary, from an anonymous rentier who was willing to entrust his capital under suitable guarantees, but this was uphill work for anyone who was not already well-established. There were no investment banks to facilitate the process of capital accumulation. The masters of faience kilns, who were the most pressed for capital, lived frugally, built up capital by marriage whenever they could, saved as much as they were able to from the proceeds of their sales, and borrowed heavily. When they suffered heavy reverses, they folded or sold out.

Beyond the fixed-capital costs of printing presses, weaving looms, or kilns, one also had to have a good deal of working capital to keep one's establishment afloat. Stocks of raw materials—paper and ink for the printers; wool and silk yarn, silver and gold thread for the tapestry-weavers; wood for fuel, clay, sulfur, soda, lead, and tin for the faienciers—had to be kept on hand. Inventories of finished goods, especially in the case of books, were large and costly to carry. Because transportation was still fairly slow, goods sold out of town remained in transit for days; but even after delivery took place, clients often delayed payment, so that money remained tied up in lengthy pursuits through "factors" and other persons who were given powers of attorney to collect from dilatory customers. We would not know nearly so much about the more capital-intensive art industries if it were not for the numerous notarial deeds in which creditors dunned their debtors in the hope of turning their "accounts receivable" into cash.

An artist-painter, by contrast, had only very small capital needs. His atelier occupied a room in the house he owned or, as in the case of Emanuel de Witte when he first arrived in Delft,[a] of the part of the house he rented. An easel, some panels and canvasses, colors, and a rubbing stone or two made up the artist's equipment and stock in trade. He carried the bulk of his capital in his head, in the form of the training costs that his family had incurred. To be sure, his output was not always easily marketed, and he had to accumulate some working capital in the form of pictures ready to be sold in his own house or consigned at a dealer's, but these immobilized products of his own labor did not have to be financed with cash outlays in the same manner as purchased inputs.

Master sculptors had larger capital requirements than artist-painters, though probably not so large as most printers, tapestry-makers, and faienciers. The few notarial documents dealing with the sculptor's trade bear on the problems of procuring good-quality stone in appropriate quantities. In a deposition of 1647, Heynrick Swaeff, master stonecarver, testified that, on one occasion, being short of stone while he was waiting for a shipload to come in, he had tried to borrow five or six blocks from Master Corstiaen (van Hulst) who was awaiting delivery of a ship laden with stone presently docked in Leyden. Master Corstiaen, after an initial refusal, had consented to let Swaeff have a few blocks.[1] The cost of stones that had to be imported from fairly far away—the merchant with whom Swaeff had a contract for delivery came from Zutphen in Gelderland to the east of Amsterdam—must have been quite significant.[b]

In the following sections devoted to three relatively capital-intensive arts industries (printing, tapestry-making, and faience),

[a]See above, Chapter 5.

[b]From a dispute over the quality of marble delivered, which arose in 1660, we learn that a piece of white marble for a sculpture had been purchased for fifty-four gulden by Pieter Rycx, who was carrying out an important commission for the city at that time (above, Chapter 7, Table 7.1). Because the block was fissured and had wormholes, arbitrators rebated the price to twenty gulden. It is not clear whether the blocks bought by Master Corstiaen and borrowed by Swaeff were of marble or of ordinary sandstone (Records of Notary Christiaen van Vliet, no. 2034, 16 July and 6 August 1660).

special emphasis is placed, wherever possible, on the expenditures in fixed and working capital sustained by enterprises. However, for the sake of providing a more rounded picture of these industries, I have also included some information about their labor force, product prices, and stylistic trends.

THE PRINTING TRADES

Most publishers of books also printed and distributed engravings. They bought the original copperplates from the artists and printed as many copies as the market would bear. The value of the plates owned by a major dealer, such as Nicolaes (or Niclaes) de Clerck, was considerable. De Clerck seems to have been the most active publisher of prints in Delft in the first quarter of the seventeenth century. A few words about his career provide the background for the subsequent analysis of his stock in trade at the time of his death.

In 1608, as we saw in Chapter 2, De Clerck applied for and obtained permission to exhibit books, maps, and paintings in the Chamber of the States-General in The Hague. From 1614 to 1617, he rented space in the Town Hall in Delft for his exhibits (for twelve gulden for three years).[2]

In 1614, the town of Delft gave Nicolaes de Clerck and Johannes van Londerseel, engravers living in Delft, a present of eighteen pounds Flemish (108 gulden) for a map of The Hague which they had "dedicated and presented" to the magistrates.[3] On 13 February 1618, De Clerck dissolved "a society or company" he had formed some three years previously with a merchant named Louys van Somer for the express purpose of printing and distributing a book called *Het toneel der deurluchtige personagien* (The theater of illustrious persons).[4] His partner, who had supplied 200 gulden for the project, had died in the meantime. De Clerck now undertook to reimburse the sum to the widow by December 1618, including the interest that had accrued since 1615. The book had apparently not been printed. This type of temporary association—which economized on capital—remained a characteristic feature of the publishing industry in Delft.

Nicolaes de Clerck died in September 1623. Some of his activities as a print dealer can be reconstructed from a series of contracts for the sale of plates made by his widow Catharina Zegers after his death. By the first contract, signed on 5 September 1624,[5] she sold to Ghysbrecht Huesden, attorney and notary, who had married her older daughter Sara, the following engraved copperplates: "*The Seven Wise Men among the Greeks*, a *Peter with a Paul*, *Sleep*, a *Hercules*, a *Triton*, the *Sleeping Mars*, all by De Gheyn, and two more plates engraved by David Vinckeboons, together for the sum of 100 carolus gulden."[c] The same day the widow sold Sara[6] "the *Laocöon* by De Gheyn, the *Triumph of Bachus* by Vroom, *Christ at the Column* by Matham, *Pomona*, the *Ship of Icarus*, the *Ship* by Vroom, the *Spanish Fleet*, the *Triumph of David*, fourteen plates by Wierix, the *Capture of Breda* and the *Battle of Thurenhout*, the *Twelve Articles of the Faith*, a *Shooter* by De Gheyn, the *Ten Commandments* in two sheets, the *Five Senses* in two sheets, twelve landscapes of which six by De Gheyn and six by Savery, and finally twelve plates of the embroidery book together for the sum of 500 gulden."[d] Two years later, on 17 June 1626, the heirs of Nicolaes de Clerck sold a number of copperplates at auction. As luck would have it all the buyers at this auction were cited (and are shown below in parentheses). I believe the document is of sufficient interest for our knowledge of art in Delft to reproduce in full the list of plates that were sold (Table 9.1).

It is remarkable that in all three sales of these copperplates not one name of a Delft-based engraver was cited and that all the buyers at the third sale were from out of town.

The mapmaker Floris Baltensz. and his son Balthasar Florisz. enjoyed considerable reputation for their work both in Delft and in

---

[c] All the plates by "De Gheyn" seem to have been engraved by Jacob de Geyn III, the son of Jacob de Geyn II. *The Seven Wise Men among the Greeks* bear the numbers 10-17 in the oeuvre of Jacob de Geyn III in F. W. Hollstein, *Dutch and Flemish Etchings, Engravings, and Woodcuts 1450-1700*, 18 vols. (Amsterdam: M. Herberger, 1949-1974), the *Hercules* no. 19, the *Peter and Paul* nos. 20 and 21, the *Sleeping Mars* no. 22, the *Sleep* no. 24, and a *Triton Blowing on a Conch* no. 30. Of these, nos. 10-17, 20-21, and 22 bear inscriptions showing N. de Clerck at one time sold and distributed them. Several (20, 21, 22, 24, and 30) also indicate that they were later sold by (J.) Hondius. No engravings by David Vinckeboons are known; however, several engravers including J. Matham made prints after his work.

[d] The *Laocöon* was most probably the work of J. de Geyn III. In Hollstein, the engraving no. 18 of this artist has a first state bearing the inscription "N. de Clerck exc." and the date 1619, the second state "Hondius exc." and the date 1631. The *Christ at the Column* is presumed to be Jacob Matham's engraving no. 91 in Hollstein, "Dionisio Calvart pinxt," first state "N. de Clerck exc.," second "Hondius exc." The "*Shooter* by De Geyn" may be from the series, the *Exercise of Arms*, nos. 146-262 in Hollstein, engraved by J. de Geyn III. The six landscapes, also by J. de Geyn II, are probably identical with nos. 287-292 in Hollstein. The *Triumph of Bachus* by Vroom and the "six landscapes by Savery" are almost certainly after the works by Hendrick Vroom and Roelant Savery.

TABLE 9.1
Engraved Plates Sold at Auction by the Heirs of Nicolaes de Clerck
(In Gulden and Stuivers)

Item	Price
Eleven poor plates (*slechte plaetgens*) bought by Broer Jansz., *courantier** in Amsterdam.	3 gld. 10 st.
Four copperplates (Broer Jansz.)	3 gld.
An unengraved copperplate (Broer Jansz.)	3 gld. 2 st.
Three copperplates (Henricus Hondius, in The Hague)	4 gld.
The governors (*de gouverneurs*), eighteen plates, (Broer Jansz., in The Hague [*sic*])	18 gld. 5 st.
Six small plates (Broer Jansz., in Amsterdam)	22 st.
Seventeen chief heretics (*hoofdketteren*) (Jan van Waesbergen, in Rotterdam)	24 gld. 2 st.
Three antiques (*antycque*) [ancient personages] (Henricus Hondius, in The Hague)	9 gld.
Two copperplates of the funerals of the prince of Orange (Claes Jansz. Visser)	30 gld.
A plate consisting of the heads of "the *trenes* [?] masters" (Jan Jansz., in Amsterdam)	10 gld. 19 st.
Four plates of Swiss [guards] (Broer Jansz., in Amsterdam)	4 gld.
A plate of a peasant kermess and another plate (Henricus Hondius, in The Hague)	6 gld. 5 st.
Two copperplates (Broer Jansz., in Amsterdam)	3 gld.
Two small plates, Andromeda and the Heathens (Henricus Hondius, in The Hague)	6 gld. 10 st.
The Last Supper (*avontmael*) of Heemskerck (Henricus Hondius)†	5 gld. 15 st.
A plate, The Owl, by de Gheyn (Claes Jansz. Visser)‡	5 gld.
Two copperplates (Broer Jansz., in Amsterdam)	4 gld. 11 st.
Three small plates: a vase of flowers, a Ten Commandments, and a kitchen (Broer Jansz.)	4 gld. 13 st.
Three plates (Jan van Waesbergen).§ In the margin: "taken over by Henricus Hondius in The Hague."	5 gld. 1 st.
Eighty-one plates of Metri (Emanuel van Meteren?) at two gld. four st. apiece (Jan Jansz., in Amsterdam)	178 gld. 4 st.
123 small plates, at two gld. one st. apiece (Broer Jansz., in Amsterdam)	252 gld. 3 st.
Forty-eight small plates being heads (*tronien*), at three gld. two st. apiece (Jan Jansz., in Amsterdam)	148 gld. 16 st.
Eight small plates of heads at twenty st. apiece (Broer Jansz., in Amsterdam)	8 gld.

TABLE 9.1 (continued)
Engraved Plates Sold at Auction by the Heirs of Nicolaes de Clerck
(In Gulden and Stuivers)

Item	Price
Two small plates of the princes of Orange, Maurice and Hendrick (Jan van Waesbergen, in Rotterdam)	15 gld. 15 st.
Two faces (Claes Jansz. Visser)	8 gld.
Total	772 gld. 13 st.

SOURCE: Records of Notary Jan de Roon, no. 1627, 17 June 1626.
*Publisher of a *courant* or newspaper.
†Perhaps Heemskerck's engraving no. 26 in Hollstein.
‡No engraving of an owl by J. de Geyn II or III is listed in Hollstein.
§The name of the buyer "Sara de Clercq" was first written and then crossed out before the name of Jan van Waesbergen was inserted.

the rest of Holland. They frequently received "presents" from the Delft burgomasters for the maps they had donated to the city and from the States-General for the maps that the States ordered. Shortly after the death of his father in 1620, Floris Baltensz. removed to Amsterdam where he sold the copyright to his maps of Reynland, Delftland, and Schieland to the famous cartographer Willem Blaeuw.[7] The sale of plates and copyrights for maps to dealers in Amsterdam and The Hague is symptomatic of the attraction that these larger markets exercised on artists and on the works of art they sold.

After the death of Nicolaes de Clerck in 1623, Willem Delff (1580-1638) developed a successful business turning out reproductive engravings after paintings by Miereveld and other artists. Few documents concerning Willem Delff's activities have survived.[c] He was the last Delft-based engraver of real importance. From the 1640s on, Delft's role in the publishing trade was chiefly limited to book-printing.

In the seventeenth century the "curious printing of Holland" was said to "merit the greatest applause." According to a contemporary English source, "from the cutting of the steel punches to the pulling off at the press, [it is] managed with greater curiosity than hitherto any

[c]On 19 January 1628, Willem Jacobsz. Delff gave power of attorney to a correspondent in Amsterdam to collect sums owed to him by Jodocus Hondius and Franchois van Hoeje, booksellers in Amsterdam (Records of Notary Johan van Beest, no. 1664). For Willem Delff's death inventory (1638), including a list of the prints he owned, see Orphan Chamber, *boedel* no. 73a.

[277]

nation has performed it."[8] The English printer Joseph Moxon who· wrote these words had good knowledge of the matter since he had learned the trade in Delft with his father James Moxon, who appears in some of the documents cited below.

A price-fixing contract dated 15 January 1627[9] bears the signatures of all the important book-printers and dealers active in Delft at that time: Jan Andriesz. Cloeting, Felix van Sambix de Jonge, Adriaen Gerritsz. van Beyeren, Jan Pietersz. Waelpoth, Cornelis Jansz. Timmer, and Barbartgen Heyndricks, the widow of Joris Andriesz. Cloeting. These worthy people declared that the parties to the contract should not sell at prices other than those set by the printers "any Latin books for boys to learn from according to the list proclaimed by the magistrates of Delft last Sunday at the Town Hall." Wholesale rebates· from printers' prices accorded to retailers were listed for each type of book. Fines were to be imposed on violators. It is noteworthy that this price-fixing agreement—the only one of its kind that I have come across in Delft—makes no mention of the Guild of St. Lucas. The guild was less involved in the control and restriction of trade in the crafts under its jurisdiction than is commonly supposed.

The scope of the printing, binding, and book distribution business in seventeenth-century Holland transcended the boundaries of individual cities. Contracts were frequently made by book dealers in Delft for printing in Amsterdam or in Rotterdam for delivery of the products to England or elsewhere. The English business community or "Court," which enjoyed certain privileges including freedom from guild membership in the 1620s and 1630s, participated in many of these complex deals.

We first learn of an English printing shop in 1631[10] when Arent Korsz. Hoogenaer, typesetter of the academy (i.e., the university) in Leyden declared at the request of Middleton Cooper in Delft that he had made and delivered a year ago on behalf of the petitioner 237 pounds of letters of nonpareil roman type of English height ("letters non paril romeyn engels hoochte"). He also testified that he had seen some of this type last August in the printing shop of Joan Nutten (Newton) who at the same time the letters were delivered was still in Cooper's employ and continued to work for him for some time afterwards. Two days later Arthur Woodward, a well-known English merchant in Delft, made another deposition at the request of Middleton Cooper.[11] He stated that he had been in Cooper's house in the presence of Joan Nutten (Newton), who had been Cooper's servant or employee (*knecht*). When Woodward asked Newton why he had conducted himself so disloyally when he had been so trusted by the petitioner, Newton answered roundly that he had indeed stolen the type and that he was willing to make restitution but that he did not know how much. On being asked further whether he had a share in the printing shop in which he was working presently he answered in the negative, declaring that he had sold the type to his new masters. This last claim is hard to square with the fact that Newton, as early as April 1631, had hired an apprentice typesetter, named Claes Symonsz. for a period of three years, which suggests that he must already have been in business for himself by that time.[12] A few months later he was in partnership with two men when we find him selling to his landlord Hendrick Gerritsz. Ervervelt a third share in a lot of 6,000 books together with a third of the stock of type and printing equipment that he owned with Jan Voet (Foot) and Willem Herentlyff.[13] A stock in trade of at least 6,000 books, which may have tied up a working capital of ten to fifteen thousand gulden, implies that the business was of significant size. Ervervelt resold Newton's share to another Englishman named Thomas Cowper, who signed a contract in May 1632 with the father of the same apprentice Claes Symonsz., whereby Cowper replaced Newton as the boy's master.[14]

In September 1632 the name of Jan Foot, Newton's former partner, turns up in another contract. He now agrees to exchange with Thomas Crawford three gold and diamond rings for "230 new Bibles containing the Old and the New Testaments together with an annotated psalmbook which he, Crawford, declares had already been printed for him in Amsterdam."[15] For each Bible that was not delivered in time, Crawford would pay six-gulden penalty. In November 1633 Thomas Craefordt (Crawford) sold Jan Foot 696 newly printed unbound Bibles and 696 New Testaments for 800 gulden.[16]

Calvinist Geneva Bibles[f] printed by English printers in Holland in the 1630s were imported into the England of Charles I as contraband "weapons against episcopacy" (i.e., against the established Church of England). Bishop Laud tried unsuccessfully to stop their importation. Some English printers, including James Moxon, who makes his first appearance in one of the next documents, were "prosecuted and fined at the instance of the English king's resident" (in Holland).[17]

---

[f] The Geneva Bible contained notes on the authorized (Calvinist) translation, known as the "Geneva notes."

In 1633 Thomas Cowper, now living in England, appointed Mr. Paulus Calmbach, bookseller in Leyden, to manage his printing shop in Delft.[18] Calmbach (c. 1607-1652), born in Groeningen, is the only Dutch master printer that we find associated with English printers and entrepreneurs in Delft.[19] According to the terms of the contract, Cowper gave Calmbach full power and authority to hire and fire servants and boy-apprentices. Calmbach agreed to deliver twenty-four reams of paper, consisting of 472 or 480 sheets, printed on both sides on two presses. He was to earn three gulden ten stuivers per week for supervising the shop plus 22 stuivers per ream of printed nonpareil.[g] For ink, leather, oil, and other supplies, he was promised three stuivers per ream. Costs over and above three stuivers per ream were to be reimbursed by Cowper on the basis of Calmbach's signature. For printing and reprinting in brevier type he was to receive twenty-eight stuivers per ream (presumably six stuivers above the normal rate of twenty-two stuivers per ream). In case Calmbach was able to produce more than twenty-four reams of printed matter, he would be paid four stuivers per ream. Cowper undertook to furnish Calmbach with clean white paper, type, presses, and all other needs hereto unspecified and to compensate him for any damages due to the lack of any of these necessities. In case the proofs were not corrected in time due to Cowper's negligence, and the servants had to wait for the corrected proofs, Calmbach was authorized to hire a corrector at Cowper's expense. In the entire document wherever the name Thomas Cowper appeared, it had replaced the name of Willem Lee which had been crossed out. Cowper, however, was said to have been "assisted" by Willem Lee, merchant in London.

Willem or William Lee was the capitalist who stood behind Crawford in this contract. But he did not stand behind him for long. At the request of James Moxon and Matthew Simones, the notary Gerrit van der Wel went to Cowper's house on 27 November 1626—Cowper was apparently back in Delft from England—to inform him that Moxon and Simones had contracted with Willem Lee to do book-printing and that he, Lee, had promised to deliver all the machines (*instrumenten*), type, and other requirements for this purpose that were presently under the supervision (the words "and under the

[g]Calmbach was then able to earn a minimum of twenty-nine gulden eighteen stuivers a week (three gulden ten stuivers straight time plus twenty-four reams at twenty-two stuivers per ream). This was about six times as much as an adult *knecht* working for a faiencier or a carpenter earned.

[280]

custody" were crossed out) of Thomas Cowper.[20] In case Cowper refused, Moxon and Simones held him responsible for damages. The notary delivered this protest in the name of the two "insinuants." A few months after displacing Cowper, James Moxon put up "two printing presses with a thousand pounds of assorted type" as collateral for a loan obtained from Joris Turbel, merchant, who had supplied him with this equipment.[21] The creditor was empowered to sell the presses and the type at auction if he, Moxon, failed to repay the loan on the due date.

James Moxon, the father of Joseph Moxon whose words of praise for Dutch printing were quoted above, probably arrived in Delft in 1636, not long before he lodged with Cowper. The first book with his imprint appeared there in 1637. This was Henry Hexham's book, *A True and Brief Relation of the Famous Siege of Breda.*[22] According to one source he left Delft for Rotterdam in April 1638.[23]

A document of 10 April 1641 represents a rare instance where Dutch printers made a deposition with an English colleague. On this occasion Carel Warnaertsz. van Turenhout and Anthony Baerthoutsz. van Heusden[h] testified in the house of the important publisher Jan Piertersz. Waelpoth that James Moxon had promised to print fifty copies of the first part of *The Art of War* (*De oorlogs konst*) for Captain Heyndirck Hecksaen (Henry Hexham), a quartermaster.[24] Hexham was to have a few plates made at his own expense, but Moxon had committed himself to supply some printed sheets (signatures) that were missing. The costs of the operation were to be borne chiefly by the printer. The third part of Hexham's *Principle of the Art Military*, to cite the book's correct title, finally appeared in Rotterdam with Moxon's imprint in the same year. On 6 May 1641, a tobacco-pipemaker testified at Moxon's request that Captain Hexham had agreed to buy twenty-five copies of the book at three gulden a piece, while Moxon was to keep the rest. The nature of the disagreement does not transpire from the two documents. Unfortunately, no later documents bearing Moxon's name have been preserved.

In 1644 Arthur Woedwart (Woodward) and his brother-in-law Pouwels Callenbach (Calmbach), printer living in Delft, drew up an agreement settling a suit they had waged against each other concerning the printing of a number of Bibles by Calmbach.[25] Woodward promised to pay Calmbach 800 gulden in two installments. However,

---

[h]Van Heusden registered in the guild in 1642; Van Turenhout seems never to have joined the guild.

[281]

in case Calmbach demanded 1,000 English printed Bibles in counterpart for the 800 gulden, Woodward undertook to deliver this number of Bibles at Calmbach's pleasure. Furthermore, Calmbach was entitled to take out of Woodward's shop all the equipment belonging to him.

From about 1647 to his death in 1652 Calmbach lived in Rotterdam. In 1651 he sold to the notary Jacob Spoors a press and some type for 200 gulden. Spoors in turn lent the press to his son-in-law Abram Pietersz. Heuckelom.[26] In a deposition of 4 February 1652, a month before his death, Paulus Calmbach declared at the request of Gijsbrecht van Rhoon, bookseller in Rotterdam, that he had been present when van Rhoon had drawn up an agreement with Abram Pietersz. Heuckelom, book-printer in Delft, whereby the latter undertook to print a book called *Oprecht onderzoek* (A sincere investigation). Van Rhoon supplied Van Heuckelom with 168 pounds of type, presumably for the purpose of printing this book. When Calmbach died, a large number of unbound English Bibles and devotional books, as well as paper and all sorts of printing equipment (but no presses), were found in his estate.[27]

As I have already remarked, none of the printers named in these documents—Middleton Cooper, Jan Foot, Joan Newton, and James Moxon—let alone the entrepreneurs—Willem Lee, Thomas Cowper, and Thomas Crawford—ever joined the Guild of St. Lucas. These foreign entrepreneurs operated their printing shops as an enclave in the economy of Delft, producing chiefly English-language religious books for export.[i] They did, however, buy their principal raw materials in Holland, including type (from Leyden), ink, and paper, and they hired local apprentices. Calmbach, as we have seen, was a Dutch printer who worked for English employers. I have found no evidence that either the printers or the capitalists who backed them had contacts with Delft artists. As far as I can make out they also operated independently from local (guild-registered) printers and booksellers.

A 1649 contract signed by Michiel (Pietersz). Stael[j] of Delft and Johannes Breeckevelt of The Hague contains interesting details on the ten-year partnership they formed to print and sell books.[28] The two men had decided to live together, Stael with his wife and child, Breeckevelt as a bachelor (if he came to marry, his wife would be

---

[i] The odd job-printing of fifty copies of *The Art of War* for Captain Hexham appears to be an exception.

[j] Michiel was the son of Pieter Stael the Younger, baker, and the nephew of the painter Pieter Stael the Elder. He too failed to join the Guild of St. Lucas in Delft.

allowed to join). The partners were to contribute all the household goods in their possession for their joint use, "as behooves honest friends." Each would be empowered to make decisions regarding the business and each would hold accounts separately. All important decisions, however, would be resolved in common. Stael contributed his equipment as capital for the enterprise, for which he was entitled to draw interest at five percent per year of the capital's value. The capital was estimated as follows.

250 lbs. of Augustine cursive and roman at 10 st. per lb.	125 gld.
106 lbs. of Augustine [Gothic?] at 10 st. per lb.	53 gld.
10 lbs. of "flowers" [ornaments] at 10 st. per lb.	5 gld.
An A B C in wooden letters and figures.	7 gld.
175 lbs. of descandian [Gothic?] at 12 st. per lb.	105 gld.
44 lbs. of cannon [Gothic?] and large caps at 9 st. per lb.	20 gld. 5 st.
9 lbs. of double august caps at 9 st. per lb.	4 gld. 1 st.
A printing press with all that belongs to it.	112 gld.
85 lbs. of text [Gothic?] at 4½ st. per lb.	19 gld. 2 st. 8 pen.
122 lbs. of text roman at 4½ st. per lb.	27 gld. 9 st.
215 lbs. of descandian roman and cursive at 6½ st. per lb.	68 gld. 18 st. 8 pen.
Total	546 gld. 15 st. 8 pen.

The low ratio of machinery (112 gulden) to type (about 434 gulden) in the partners' capital stock is noteworthy. The contract further stipulated that, in case Breeckevelt should contribute any capital of his own to the partnership in the future, he too could draw interest on it. The contract said nothing about the purchase or lease of the premises where the printing would be carried out and where the books would be sold. The document was witnessed by Anthony Palamedes, master painter.

The Stael-Breeckevelt shop was modest in size but not exceptionally small. In 1641 the printer Anthony Barthoutsz. van Heusden, whom we have already encountered, bought a book-printing shop with all the ancillary equipment from the widow of the printer Aryen Cornelisz. (van Delff), active in Schiedam from 1605 to 1641,[29] for only 200 gulden.[30] In 1661 Heyndrick Rollaer, bookseller in Delft, borrowed 689 gulden at 4 percent interest from his widowed mother to buy a printing shop with all its equipment including presses.[31] He registered in the guild two-and-a-half months after he incurred this debt.

We unfortunately have no information about the value of the presses and the equipment owned by the most important printers in Delft. When we read, for instance, that the publisher Simon Jorísz. Cloeting borrowed 3,000 gulden in 1653 from his mother Barbara Heyndrixdr., the widow of the bookseller Joris Cloeting, we can be fairly sure that this money was put into the business, the capital requirements of which must have been vastly in excess of those invested in the printing shops we have learned about so far.[32] The Cloeting family owned the "Golden A B C" on the Market Place which was probably the largest printing and bookselling establishment in town. Around 1660, the business came into the hands of the Dissius branch of the family, Abram Dissius having married Maria, the daughter of Joris Cloeting, in 1648. The Dissiuses prospered. Abram's son Jacob was an important collector of paintings. Eight examples by Vermeer—the largest single collection of works by this painter ever owned by the same person—were found in his death inventory of 1682.[33]

Arnold Bon, who composed the poem about Fabritius and Vermeer in Dirck van Bleyswijck's *Beschryvinge der Stadt Delft*, was another prominent publisher in Delft. He appears with his principal colleagues in the industry, Jan Pietersz. Waelpoth, Anthony van Heusden, Simon Cloeting, and Abraham Dissius in a deposition dated 7 January 1656 in which they all attested at the request of Pieter van Waesbergen, bookseller in Rotterdam, that they had estimated a dictionary of the French and Flemish languages (*Le Gazophylage de la Langue Francoise et Flamande*) at thirty-three stuivers per copy. However, they declared themselves unwilling "to take 25, 50, or 100 copies, let alone 150 copies to be paid in cash."[34] In what appears to be a deposition from the opposing side in this affair, Jacob Pool, bookseller in Delft, declared a month later at the request of Jan Neranus, bookseller in Rotterdam, that he had bought on several occasions a dictionary of the *Frans ende deutsch* (i.e., Nederdeutsch or Netherlandish) languages printed by Neranus for three gulden (sixty stuivers) a copy.[35] The difference between the price of sixty stuivers and the estimate of thirty-three stuivers, assuming that the two attestations referred to the same dictionary, may have turned on the quality of Neranus's work. Four years earlier a deposition by a journeyman printer named Gillis de Haen already complained of the poor quality of the type that Neranus had sold to his (De Haen's) employer Hendrick Houthaeck, a registered printer and bookseller in Delft: some of the letters were too high, others too low, most were unfit for printing.[36]

All these notarial depositions give us only a fragmented image of the printing trades in Delft in the seventeenth century. They leave little doubt, though, that printers and booksellers were organized quite differently from artist-painters who generally worked alone or with apprentices. Printers operated in partnerships and "companies" to meet the relatively high capital costs of their activity. These associations were at times formed for the specific purpose of printing one or more books, after which they apparently were dissolved. The smaller printers (particularly the English) were very mobile, moving every few years from city to city, perhaps to satisfy a particular demand or to escape political or religious persecution. The Delft printers and booksellers seem to have had close ties with their colleagues in Rotterdam, Leyden, and to a lesser extent, Amsterdam. We know that some Delft printers bought their type from these other cities. It may be that all the type used in Delft was imported since none of the numerous documents about the industry cites any typecasting activity in Delft itself.

I could find little evidence of professional ties between the printers and booksellers of Delft and the other members of the guild (other than that provided by the engravers and printmakers who had links with the two communities). After the death in 1638 of Willem Jacobsz. Delff, who maintained very close relations with his father-in-law Michiel Miereveld (whose portraits he engraved), Delft could not boast of one single engraver or map-maker of any significance. The book people intermarried or chose their spouses among the town's merchants and professional men. The only painter I know of who was able to break into the exclusive circle of the rich printers and booksellers of Delft was Louis Elsevier, who married the daughter of Jan Pietersz. Waelpoth. But Elsevier was at least as much a business-man dealing in paints and colors as he was an artist; moreover, the marriage, given his ties with the famous family of publishers in The Hague, may have amounted to a dynastic alliance for the Waelpoths.

Prosperous booksellers were probably more involved with art as clients and patrons (as in the case of Jacob Dissius) than in their professional capacity.

TAPESTRY-MAKING

While painters in Delft were oriented primarily toward a bourgeois market, the weavers of tapestries were at first altogether dependent on the patronage of princes, patricians, and very wealthy individuals. The special character of the weavers' clientele goes a long way toward explaining the extreme concentration of the industry and its financial fragility, given the high capital requirements of the business and the sporadic demand of these few customers. Competition, when there was any, came from Flanders, whence most of the early weavers of Delft had immigrated, not from the rest of the Netherlands. The virtual domestic monopoly the Delft weavers enjoyed until late in the seventeenth century and the cautious, bureaucratic procedures by which "institutional buyers" acquired tapestries may also have had something to do with the conservative design and execution of the works themselves.

In Chapter 2 I briefly alluded to the tapestry works set up by the Flemish immigrant Franchoys Spierinx in the former St. Agatha convent in 1595. This enterprise, created with the help of the town authorities, was already greatly admired for the "Gobelins" it produced when Arnold van Buchell visited them in Delft in 1598.[37] Soon after the works in the St. Agatha cloister were launched, Spierinx received an order for a series of tapestries from Charles Howard, Lord of the (British) Admiralty. The tapestries, which were to represent the defeat of the Armada in 1588, cost the munificent sum of 7,115 pounds sterling.[38] Hendrick Cornelisz. Vroom, the Haarlem marine painter, designed the cartoons.[k] Soon afterwards Vroom designed a similar series representing the battle of Nieuwport for the Great Hall of the State of Zeeland in Middelburg. In 1600, Spierinx requested from the States-General the right to export to France six tapestries "on behalf of the king."[39]

From then on, the States-General regularly commissioned works from the master. Most of these were presented to princes and other

[k] Karel van Mander wrote in his *Schilderboeck* (Haarlem, 1604) that the commission was first given to him but that he had turned it down because drawing ships was not his kind of work. Van Mander adds that it was he who had introduced Vroom to Spierinx.

[286]

potentates to further the diplomatic aims of the fledgling republic. In October 1606, for example, eight tapestries representing the history of Alexander the Great were offered to the son of the French Foreign Minister Villeroy; in July 1609 the president of the French Parliament, Pierre Jeanin, was the recipient of a similar gift. Orders for the wife of the Great Elector of Brandenburg, for "Chalil Bassa" (Shalil Pasha?), and for Gustavus Adolphus of Sweden followed in 1613, 1614, and 1619. Soon afterwards samples were sent "to His Majesty the King of Great Britain who is curious to see them."[40]

But all this generosity began to weigh heavily on the States-General's finances. By 1620 the treasury fell short of funds to pay for the series of tapestries on the subject of "Orlando Furioso" that were to be presented to Lord Hey, the extraordinary envoy of the British Court to The Hague. After some delay, the required sum was found, but the States resolved that from now on all the provinces would have to contribute equally to such gifts.

Until 1615 Franchoys Spierinx was the sole producer of wall-size tapestries in Delft.[l] If we are to believe the report of a later competitor, Spierinx's monopoly was highly profitable: he sold his tapestries for thirty to thirty-three gulden the ell (about twenty-seven inches) that cost him fifteen to sixteen gulden to produce. According to this same source the principal painter he employed, Karel van Mander the Younger, had "slaved eleven years in Spierinx's house without being able to put his head above water" and had accumulated no savings to leave his widow in case of his death.[m] Spierinx's hold on his employees was not tight enough to prevent Van Mander and his fellow-painter Abram Bonaert from earning money on the side by occasionally painting cartoons for other entrepreneurs, such as Mathijs de Schepper in Delft who produced smaller tapestries for sale in Amsterdam.

In 1615 Van Mander sought the help of the Delft authorities to set

[l]Tapestry-like products, however, were produced in smaller workshops. In 1614, for example, a merchant from Rotterdam named Guillaume Papineau ordered forty mantlepiece coverings (*schoorsteencleeden*) from Joost Jansz., *tapissier*, of the same quality as Joost had made for the house "de Dubbelde Slootel" in Rotterdam. Papineau supplied the cartoon. Abraham Bredius, "De tapijtfabriek van Karel van Mander de Jonge te Delft," *Oud-Holland* 3(1885):2.

[m]This deposition by the painter Huybert Grimani is dated 19 January 1623 (Records of Notary Herman Jansz. van der Ceel, no. 1638). On 8 June 1623, Franchoys Spierinx declared that while Van Mander had worked for him, he had continually gotten into financial difficulties from which he, Spierinx, had had to rescue him.

up a competing enterprise; but the town refused to grant either financial support or any other privileges, perhaps because the authorities did not wish to undermine the Spierinx enterprise, whose international success reflected favorably on the town's reputation. Another source of capital had to be found. In September of that year Nicolaes Snouckaert, lord of Schrappla (near Hamburg in Germany), agreed to invest 85,199 gulden in a new "company for the making of tapestries," owned jointly with Van Mander and Hubert Grimani.[41] Van Mander was entrusted with the company's management. Snouckaert's investment was enormous for the time. None of the faience works of the first three quarters of the century had assets of this magnitude. Nor did I come across any other business in Delft of a comparable size.

Far more information has come down to us about the Snouckaert-Van Mander-Grimani manufacture than about Spierinx's. What we now know, however, comes chiefly from the numerous depositions that were made after the finances of the company had begun to flounder.

Van Mander needed a large place to weave his tapestries. Like Spierinx, he opted for a former convent. But St. Anna's convent, unlike St. Agatha's that the city had leased to Spierinx for a nominal rent, had to be acquired at the company's expense. The new atelier employed forty workers,[42] compared to twenty to twenty-five *knechts* for a large faience workshop. In the six years under Van Mander's management, the company produced a total of 2,323 ells of tapestries, coverings, and cushions.[43] We can safely assume that Van Mander never received a higher price than the $42\frac{1}{2}$ gulden per ell that he was able to charge for the series commemorating the victories of Christiaen IV of Denmark in the years 1616-1620.[44] If he averaged forty gulden per ell on all his deliveries (an estimate likely to be on the high side), the total receipts of the company under his direction came to about 93,000 gulden, or 15,500 gulden a year. The profits on these sales must have been very modest, if there were any profits at all, considering that the wage costs alone amounted to as much as thirty-eight gulden per ell for fairly routine work (such as the landscape segments).[45] According to one testimony, an ell of fine tapestry could easily be made "for sixteen or at most seventeen gulden" including all costs. Even if the sales prices were slightly in excess of variable costs, the overhead, which included Van Mander's extravagant expenses on his trips to Denmark, the nonreimbursement of loans to employees, and various other extraordinary outlays,[46] would have syphoned off any gross profits. By July 1621, Van Mander had already run through about 40,000 gulden out of the original capital sum of 85,199 gulden contributed by Snouckaert. To secure the rest of his capital, Snouckaert requested collateral in the form of tapestries in stock. About this time Maerten van Bouckholt, Snouckaert's brother-in-law, was placed in charge of the stores where the yarn and the cartoons were kept. Not even Van Mander could have access to these materials without Van Bouckholt's permission. A few months later, in November 1621, Van Bouckholt was entrusted with the direction of the company. Van Mander continued to work in the St. Anna convent, supervising the production of cartoons. Even this did not work out well: complaints were later made that an acute shortage of designs for the weavers to work from occurred because Van Mander, for several months, had only one painter working for him.[47] On 11 June 1623, Snouckaert sent a notary to Van Mander's house to ask him to choose neutral mediators to settle their financial differences. Van Mander must have died in the next two days—Bredius suggests the possibility of suicide—since, in a deposition dated two days later, on June 13th, the "sister of the late Karel van Mander" was accused of having insulted the wife of Maerten van Bouckholt, the new manager of Snouckaert's works.[48]

The depositions made after Van Mander's death testify chiefly to his extravagance and mismanagement, but they also reveal that the late artist, in order to reduce inflated production costs, had cut back on the quality of the company's products by introducing inferior silks and other materials in the manufacturing process. Mismanagement, profligacy, and an acute shortage of skilled labor (discussed below) are sufficient to explain the financial failure of the Van Mander-directed manufacture. It is not necessary, and it is probably incorrect, to invoke, as Max Eisler did, the "drive for profits" under the pressure of "large-scale capital alien to the business," that allegedly prompted the manufacturer to concentrate on merchandising at the expense of artistic quality.[49]

The new management of Van Bouckholt, a silk dyer by trade, could not save the enterprise. Thefts from the stores, a complicated and inefficient system of wage payments, and the refusal of the workers to repay the loans made by Van Mander created more financial difficulties. Finally on 26 November 1623, Aert Spierinx, son of Franchoys, joined the company. Competition between the rival manufactures of Spierinx and Snouckaert ceased. Snouckaert in an attempt to recoup his losses used the former convent increasingly for the sale of tapestries and other coverings from stock. In February 1624 Van Bouckholt was finally dismissed, and the premises were soon afterward leased to a silk merchant.[50]

The high wages of cartoon-painters and weavers that helped sink the enterprise could not be laid at Van Mander's door. Franchois Spierinx had a long-established work force. Witnesses asserted that Van Mander could not get "fine and artful workers" ("fraeij ende constige werkgasten") from out of town unless they were offered an advance of seventy to eighty gulden on their future wages to settle in Delft, which advances were rarely repaid. Higher-than-contractual wages had to be paid for all sorts of special tasks. There was talk also of the costs of the company's social security system: each employee paid one stuiver a week into a fund for the assistance of sick workers, which was matched by the management. This added only perhaps two gulden a week to the payroll, which could not have been less than 200 to 250 gulden (for forty employees), but this sort of social insurance was unusual at the time and was probably considered an unnecessary expense. Another fringe benefit were the frequent gifts of kegs of beer to the workers to celebrate various company events, such as Snouckaert's return from a trip to Germany.[51] It is clear in any event that skilled labor could only be had at premium wages. The profitability of the Spierinx enterprise when it enjoyed a monopoly in the manufacture of large-scale tapestries was no indication that a second establishment would be financially successful.

We have already seen that Van Mander only employed one painter of cartoons during the last phase of his career. This caused such a bottleneck that weavers, who had had to make do with odds and ends of designs for their borders, sometimes had to unravel the work they had completed and weave it over again. Even the manufacture of Franchoys Spierinx suffered from a shortage of cartoon-painters. On 26 March 1624, the painters Jonas van der Burch, twenty-eight years old, Pieter Mathijs (Pastenax), fifty-six and Jan Augustynsz. (van der Linden), thirty-one, testified at the request of Aert Spierinx that, along with Jacques de Groot, they all had painted cartoons for the petitioner. They had worked "since November 1622, Sundays and weekdays, in the winter and in the summer, as late as they could see" and they had been paid "above their daily wages for the extra hours." They further declared that "they had never painted all the parts that fitted into a complete design" ("noyt heele stucken aenmalcander hebbe geschildert") but that "each time the cartoon of a piece [of the design] was ready, it was immediately taken away for use by the tapestryweavers."[52] The shortage of cartoons helps explain why so many of the tapestries produced were "repeats" for which cartoons could be reutilized. One of the cartoons for the Alexander the Great series, for example, was used four times before it was sold to His Majesty the King of Bohemia when it was still worth 2,000 gulden.[53]

With the exception of De Groot, all the painters who made the deposition about the pressure under which they worked were registered in the guild, as were of course Karel van Mander, Huybert Grimani, Abram Bonaert, and Engel Rooswijck (Van Mander's brother-in-law), who often appears in documents concerning the tapestry manufacture in the St. Anna convent and may have produced cartoons for them. Some of the other painters in watercolors in the Master List of 1613, including Pieter Jansz. and Pieter Pietersz. Vromans (the father of the imitator of Bramer), and Adriaen Hondecoeter may also have been employed as designers.

But for Engel Rooswijck and Karel van Mander the Younger, a few of whose productions have survived, nothing is known of the works of the tapestry designers of Delft. Rooswijck, trained in Haarlem, was a moderately talented follower of Cornelis van Haarlem.[n] Karel van Mander the Younger is remembered chiefly for the tapestries he designed, for which the actual cartoons have disappeared. His most famous series, which he designed and manufactured for the Danish King Christiaen IV, are known only through a late seventeenth-century watercolor copy by F. C. Lund.

Eisler calls the younger Van Mander "a very gifted, but in no way original adept of the Rubens school".[54] His work may further be characterized as baroque, muted by conservative Delft taste. The influences on his work are Flemish: from their dynamic-heroic composition to their De Momper-like landscape backgrounds. This, after all, was the style popular in Delft in the late 1610s and early 1620s, in painting as well as in faience, as witness the popularity of Peter Bronckhorst, Peter Stael, and Hans Jordaens in painting and of polychrome dishes and tiles of the Antwerp type in faience. I dare say that no other city of Holland was as dominated by Flemish antecedents as Delft in this early period.

After the death of Franchoys Spierinx in 1630, Maximiliaen van der Gucht took over manufacture in the St. Agatha convent. While Van der Gucht in his long career, until his death in 1689, occasionally

---

[n]See the reproduction of *Adam and Eve* by Engel Rooswijck in *The Bible through Dutch Eyes: From Genesis to the Apocrypha* by Alfred Bader, exhibition catalogue (Milwaukee: Milwaukee Art Center, 1976), p. 13.

produced a battle scene of the Spierinx-Van Mander type for an aristocratic client, this was not his speciality. He concentrated on relatively simple landscapes or flower-strewn fields that he could sell at more moderate prices. The new note is struck in a 1637 order by the prince of Orange for six tapestries representing "fine landscapes for the *garde-robe* of His Excellency," the ell priced at eighteen gulden.[55] This was appreciably less than the thirty to forty gulden per ell obtained by his predecessors for "histories" in the period 1615–1625, when, if anything, the overall level of prices may have been slightly lower. In 1639, he received twenty-six gulden per ell for four pieces of tapestry depicting the House of Nassau, a more traditional subject and a more costly realization. In October 1640 the burgomaster of Delft contracted with Van der Gucht for a series of tapestries for the Town Hall. The city was to supply the cartoons, which could not be employed for any other project and must be returned to it after their use. (The name of the cartoon designer has not been preserved). The cost per ell was set at twelve gulden the square ell.[56] From Van Bleyswijck's description in his *Beschryvinge der Stadt Delft* we know that the tapestries gave Van der Gucht the opportunity of displaying the skill of his weavers in making landscapes filled with mythological-allegorical staffage and animated by numerous animals and plants. In 1645 Van der Gucht was given an order to produce two tapestries for a Polish nobleman named Estienne Oborski in the prince's household. The order called for "gold thread in the yellow parts, silver in the white, except for the flowers." The angels and some of the figures were to be woven in alternate silver and gold. Despite the extraordinary quality of the materials used, the price was only twenty gulden per ell, perhaps because the cartoons were supplied by the client.[57] In 1647 Van der Gucht executed an order for another Polish nobleman, Seweryn de Goluchowo. An exception in his known oeuvre, the subject represented a battle scene, the *Battle of Nieuwpoort* of 1600, in the tradition of Van Mander's Danish wars. The contracted price per ell was twenty gulden, with the possibility of a gratuity if the work turned out to be fully acceptable. The tapestry, conserved in the Brussels Musée du Centenaire, is a stiff but accurately drawn exercise in the topography of war. Its best features, Eisler argues convincingly, are the hanging floral wreaths of its borders and the cartouches of various towns viewed in profile that frame the battle itself, in the manner of contemporary maps.[58] In the 1660s Van der Gucht delivered a number of landscape tapestries and furniture upholsteries at eleven and twelve gulden for the Delft and Leyden Town Halls of a purely decorative character: forest landscapes with little or no staffage for the tapestries, flowers on a dark ground for the upholstered chairs.[59] These commercial products of the 1660s were the last step in a half-century evolution in the manufacture of tapestries: from the skillful realization by weavers of original artists' cartoons, they became a stereotyped product fit for the purse and for the taste of the rich bourgeoisie. The trend in subject matter—from mythological histories to landscapes and flowers—can be explained by the cost-cutting policy aimed at reaching a wider public (landscapes being less expensive to produce than histories), by the change in fashion that produced a similar shift in painting, or, most probably, by both. We shall see in the next section that the delftware industry underwent the same cost and price decline as tapestries with the effect of widening the market for its products.

THE DELFTWARE INDUSTRY

A few notarial depositions chronicling the early development of the faience industry in Delft were summarized in Chapter 2. For the period following the restructuring of the guild in 1613, the original documentation is quite abundant. Much of it already has been exploited in standard books on the delftware industry.[60] What has not been done is to piece together and aggregate the information available on economic aspects of the industry: the number of establishments, employment and wages, the prices at which the potteries were bought and sold, their working and fixed capital, and their finances. With the possible exception of the number of potteries operating at various dates, none of these magnitudes can be estimated with precision; but there are at least fragments of information bearing on all of them that deserve to be presented.

In Table 9.2 I have assembled available data on the names of the potteries and of their founders and the dates of foundation of all establishments that began operating before 1671.

The data in the table are not free of problems. Delftware potteries were generally not called by name until at least the 1640s. To assign a name at an earlier date to a pottery that eventually acquired one, the line of ownership and sometimes the location of the pottery have to be retraced. On occasion names changed in the course of time (e.g., "Rouaen," probably named after the birth place of the founder Pouwels Bourseth, later became "Het Lage Huys"). An old brewery

TABLE 9.2

Delftware Potteries in Operation, 1600-1679

Name of Pottery	Founder(s)	1600-1619	1620-1629	1630-1639	1640-1649	1650-1659	1660-1669	1670-1679
De Vier Helden van Room	Herman Pietersz.	pre-1600	—	—	—	—	—	—
De Porceleynen Schotel	Egbert Huygensz. Sas	pre-1600	—	—	—	—	—	—
De Romeyn	Cornelis Rochusz.	1600	—	—	—	—	—	—
Rouaen (later, Het Lage Huys)	Pouwels Bourseth	c. 1603	—	—	—	—	—	—
De (Porceleynen) Lampetkan	Abram Davidsz.	c. 1609	—	—	—	—	—	—
De (Vergulde) Boot	Egbert Huygensz. Sas	c. 1613	—	—	—	—	—	—
De (Vergulde) Bloempot	Cornelis Egbertsz. Sas	1616	—	—	—	—	—	—
De Twee Scheepjes	Cornelis Schipper		1628	—	—	—	—	—
De Metalen Pot	Dirck Jeronimusz. van Kessel			1638	—	—	—	—
De Ham	Frans Pouwelsz. van Oosten			1639	—	—	—	—
De Dissel	Lambrecht Kruyck				1640	—	—	—
De (Dubbelde) Schenkkan	Samuel Berevelt				1648	—	—	—
Het Oude Moriaenshooft	A. de Cooge-P. J. Oosterlaan				1648	—	—	—
Het Gecroonde Porceleyn	H. M. van Gogh				1648	—	—	—
Het Hoge Huys	Samuel Berevelt					1650	—	—

De Paeuw	Pieter Jeron. Kessel	1651	—	—	—		
Het Jonge Moriaenshooft	Jan Groenlant	1654	—	—	—		
De Porceleynen Flees	W. Eenhorn-Q. Kleynoven	1655	—	—	—		
De Drie (Vergulde) Astonnen	Jeronimus P. Kessel	1655	—	—	—		
Het Bijltje	Adriaen van Houten	1657	—	—	—		
De Grieksche A	Wouter Eenhorn	1658	—	—	—		
De (Porceleynen) Klaeuw	C. van der Hoeve-C. Schoonoven		1661	—	—		
De Twee Wilde Mannen	Sebastiaen Cuyck		1661	—	—		
De Witte Starre	W. Cleffius-G. Kruyck		c. 1661	—	—		
De Drie (Porceleynen) Flessen	Cornelis Bijlevelt		1661	—	—		
Het Fortuyn	Joris Mesch		c. 1661	—	—		
Het Hart	Joris Mesch		c. 1661	—	—		
De Roos	Widow A. van der Block-C. Schaep			pre-1667	—		
De Drie Klokken	Barbara Rottewel				pre-1671		
De Jeneverboom	Ary de Milde				pre-1671		
Total (by end of decade)		7	8	10	14	21	28	30

SOURCES: Ferrand W. Hudig, *Delfter Fayence* (Berlin: R. C. Smidt, 1929), pp. 294-323; C. H. de Jonge, *Delft Ceramics* (New York: Praeger 1970), pp. 151-156; René-Louis Delenne, *Dictionnaire des marques de l'ancienne faïence de Delft* (Paris; Richard Masse, 1957), pp. 253-262; Delft, Municipal Archives, Notarial protocols; Camer van Charitate, "Reckeningen van de deuijt op de gulden," 1598 to 1644.

NOTES: A dash in a column means that the establishment continued operating in that decade.

called "De Ham" on the east side of the Achterom apparently gave birth to two faience manufactures, one called "De Ham" and the other "De Metalen Pot." The former was founded by Frans Pouwelsz. van Oosten in 1639 and was sold to Jacob Jacobsz. Duckerton (or Ducarton) in 1653. The latter was started by Dirck Jeronimusz. van Kessel and was transferred or sold to his nephew Jeronimus Pietersz. van Kessel in 1655. The two remained separate at least to the end of the century. In spite of these problems, I believe that my estimates for the total number of delftware potteries operating at the end of each period are substantially accurate. It is reassuring to note that Dirck van Bleyswijck's estimate at the time he was writing (1667) of twenty-eight *plateelbackeryen* agrees with my total for that date.[61] In any event, there can be no doubt whatever about the overall trend in the size of the industry: slow steady growth in the beginning (from seven establishments by 1616 to eleven by 1640), followed by rapid acceleration (twenty-one establishments by 1658, twenty-seven by 1661), with a final slowdown in the last two decades. In the thirteen years of swiftest expansion, from 1648 to 1661, more than one delftware pottery was created on average each year.

Was the industry marked by restraints on competition, either on the marketing side or in the hiring of labor, or was it large enough to be competitive? The only attempt at collusion I am aware of dates from 1644 when there were eleven establishments in the industry. At that time Jan Gerritsz. van der Hoeve, owner of the "De Porceleynen Schotel," and Gerrit Willemsz. Verstraten, the owner of the most important pottery producing tin-glazed faience in Haarlem[o] contracted to "give all their *knechts* such wages as they had decided on, specified in a separate agreement, and not to hire any individual without first notifying the other contracting parties."[62] However, by the 1650s and 1660s frequent references to going rates of wages are found in notarial depositions.[P] On the retail side, something akin to perfect competition must have prevailed since we read in a contract dated 1663 that porcelain wares will be sold "at going market prices at the time of delivery ["ten prijse als de mart ten tyden des leveringe

---

[o]He was the son of Willem de Rieu (i.e., De la Rue, which he translated into Van der Straet or Verstraten), who lived in Delft in the early 1620s and may have briefly owned a pottery there (see above, Chapter 3).

[P]A contract to employ decorators on delftware (*plateelschilders*) in Paris specified that wages would be set one-third higher than such *knechts* "normally earn in Delft." (Records of Notary Adriaan van der Block, no. 2161, 13 September 1667).

cours lopen sal"] and at prices similar to those at which the principal shops sell their wares in Delft."[63]

In Chapter 4, I estimated the number of adult *knechts* working for delftware potteries at 150 at the beginning of 1640, with a possible underestimation of fifteen to thirty. There were in addition ten masters or widows of masters who owned faience works and three masters who were employed in other masters' establishments. Assuming, for lack of other information, that the numbers of employees per delftware pottery remained the same throughout the period 1650 to 1680, total employment may be estimated to have risen from 150 to 180 in 1640 to 300 to 360 in 1660 and 450 to 480 at the close of the 1670s. If we include the dependents of these *knechts* plus the masters and their families, we can easily arrive at some 1,600 individuals, or roughly 5-6 percent of the population of Delft at the time.

In Table 9.3 I have assembled all the information available to me on the prices at which delftware potteries were bought and sold, along with their equipment, stocks of raw materials and finished goods, and other assets.

The principal shortcoming of the data on the value of delftware potteries bought and sold is that it is frequently not known whether a price includes or excludes the value of equipment. In most cases, when equipment is not mentioned in the contract or in the Camer van Charitate record of real-estate transactions, I think we can safely assume that it was included in the purchase price. Working on this assumption, I arrived at an average price per pottery inclusive of equipment of 2,046 gulden in the period 1600-1619, 3,049 in 1620-1629, 3,735 in 1630-1639, 7,800 in 1640-1649, 8,762 in 1650-1659, 7,371 in 1660-1669, and 7,878 in 1670-1679. Needless to say, comparisons between successive decades are of doubtful significance, but it can hardly be denied that very substantial increases in the capital investment in faience works took place from the beginning of the period to the 1640s. The sharpest increases appear to have occurred in the 1640s and 1650s.[q] On the other hand, the industry, from 1672 to the end of the decade, was depressed. "Het

[q]As I have already mentioned in other connections, general wholesale and retail prices in the Netherlands increased up to about 1620 and then fluctuated without a clear trend for the rest of the period under consideration. No indexes or systematic observations of individual prices are available for Delft. In any case the substantial increases in the capital sums invested in the individual potteries should only be discounted to a minor extent, if any, for increases in the general price level.

TABLE 9.3
Sale Prices of Delftware Potteries and Accompanying Assets

Name of Pottery	Date Sold	Price of Pottery (gulden)	Value of Equipment Sold (gulden)	Value of Raw Materials, Semifinished and Finished Goods (gulden)
Rouaen	1606	2,050	—	—
	1623	2,000*	1,100*	—
	1653	5,400	—	—
De Romeyn	1606	3,400	—	—
	1621	3,500*	—	2,125*
	1636	2,200	900	—
	1638	2,714	900	—
	1668	5,100†	—	—
	1671	8,000	—	—
De (Porceleynen) Schotel	1613	1,180	—	—
	1614	1,300	—	—
	1647	12,000	6,000	7,088
	1671	15,000	—	—
De (Porceleynen) Lampetkan	1619	2,300	—	—
	1649	6,000	3,000	—
De Twee Scheepjes	1628	2,547	402	—
De Vier Helden van Room	1634	3,600	—	—
	1668	7,000	—	—
De (Vergulde) Boot	1634	3,600	1,000	—
	1666	5,525	—	—
De Ham	1640	2,100	—	—
	1653	6,500	—	—
	1663	6,500	—	—
	1672	6,000	—	4,720

Pottery	Year			
De Dissel	1640	3,800	—	—
	1648	6,000	—	2,650
	1666	9,000‡	15,950‡	—
De (Vergulde) Bloempot	1649	4,600	—	—
	1671	3,000	—	—
	1676	5,000§	—	—
De Paeuw	1652	12,700‖	—	—
	1662	12,000	—	—
De Bijltje	1657	n.a.	1,600	—
De Grieksche A	1658	10,450	—	—
De (Dubbelde) Schenkkan	1660	5,000	—	—
De Drie (Vergulde) Astonnen	1661	n.a.	—	1,047
	1667	6,000	—	673
Het Gecroonde Porceleyn	1662	10,250	—	—
	1676	9,000#	—	—
Het Oude Moriaenshooft	1663	3,000	—	—
De (Porceleynen) Klaeuw	1668	16,200**	—	—
De Roos	1669	4,500	—	—
De Metalen Pot	1670	6,000	—	—
De Drie (Porceleynen) Flessen	1665	5,150	—	—
	1671	5,000††	500††	2,000††
	1674	8,000	—	—
	1676	6,000	—	—

SOURCES: See Table 9.2.

*Assessment.

†The pottery was offered at this price in a rental contract at the option of the lessee.

‡Two-thirds share of pottery sold for 16,500 gulden including 6,000 gulden for premises alone.

§Option to buy the pottery given to C. J. Meschaert for this price.

‖Minimum. Debt owed for this amount arising from the purchase of the pottery.

#Offered at this price, unsold.

**Share of one-twelfth sold for 1,350 gulden.

††Debt remnants for purchase of pottery, equipment, and materials (Records of Notary Dirck Rees. no. 2146, 30 January 1671).

Gecroonde Porceleyn," which had changed owners at a price of 10,250 gulden in 1662 could not find a buyer at 9,000 gulden in 1676. The highest price bid at auction was 6,100 gulden, and the pottery was withdrawn from the sale.[64] "De Drie Porceleynen Flessen" sold for 2,000 gulden less in 1676 than in 1674.[65] It should be observed, however, that the variance in purchase prices was much larger in the 1660s and 1670s than in the 1620s and 1630s. In the latter period very large establishments, such as "De Paeuw," "De Porceleynen Klaeuw," "Het Gecroonde Porceleyn," and "De Grieksche A" coexisted with modest ateliers, of a size comparable to those that had flourished a generation earlier, such as "De Vergulde Bloempot" and "De Drie Astonnen." It is noteworthy that the oldest potteries in Delft—"De Vier Helden van Room," founded by Herman Pietersz.; "Rouaen," founded by Pouwels Bourseth; "De Romeyn," founded by Cornelis Rochusz. van der Hoeck; and "De Porceleynen Schotel" founded by Cornelis Egbertsz. Sas—all shared in the expansion of the 1640s and 1650s, although only the last of these four attained the size of the largest potteries operating in the 1650s and 1660s.

On the basis of the average price in the 1660s, which corresponds to our largest sample (thirteen sales or assessments), we may estimate the total fixed capital in the industry at about 190,000 gulden in that decade. If we add another 100,000 gulden for inventories of raw materials and goods in process, we reach a sum close to 300,000 gulden. This was quite a large amount of money for Delft, but it should be kept in mind that there were a number of very rich merchants in Holland whose assets were in excess of 100,000 gulden.[66] Niclaes Verburg, the director of the Netherlands East Indies Company in Delft and probably the richest man in the city when he died in 1676,[67] had assets evaluated at 530,302 gulden.[r]

The prosperity of the delftware industry coincided with the decline of the city's breweries. Out of 100 breweries that were in operation in the late sixteenth century it has been claimed that only fifteen were still open by 1680.[68] Many provided buildings for the new potteries, including "De Roos," "Het Bijltje," "De Witte Starre," "De Paeuw," "De Drie Klokken," "De Metalen Pot," "De Schenkkan," "De Ham," "De Dissel" and "De Grieksche A." This last brewery was bought by

---

[r]Verburg owned vast amounts of porcelain, mostly imported from the East. Only a few (Oriental) paintings were listed in his estate, but the inventory may not have been complete.

Wouter Eenhorn and Quiring Aldersz. Kleijnoven in 1655 for the very large sum of 10,000 gulden, to which the partners had to add a considerable investment in equipment, raw-material inventories, and goods in process.

The following story of the ownership of one major pottery shows how capital was typically built up in the industry and how intricate family ties developed among some of the owners. Hans de Wint, the first individual with no training in the craft to invest in a *plateelbacke-rij,* called himself a lance-maker (*spiesmacker*), which probably meant that he was an armorer. He had presumably prospered by supplying the Dutch insurgents in the war against Spain with armor, but the truce of 1609 must have reduced the profitability of his business. He first began to turn his lances into dishes in the first half of 1613 when he bought the pottery that was later called "De Porceleynen Schotel." In July of that year, he was admitted into the guild with special dispensation from my lords the burgomasters, seeing that he had not spent the requisite years in the trade.[69] He placed the pottery under the direction of Lenaert Jansz., his brother-in-law. On 5 December 1613, nine of the pottery's *knechts* complained about Lenaert's mismanagement.[70] Four days later, after the headmen of the guild had intervened, De Wint and Lenaert Jansz. signed a new contract laying down in great detail the latter's duties as *meesterknecht,* and stipulating his wage of one gulden a day.[71] In early 1614 De Wint sold "De Porceleynen Schotel" to Beuckel Adamsz. van der Burgh and his wife Catharine Jans for 1,300 gulden cash.[72]

Whatever might have been his true profession or craft, Beuckel Adamsz. (or Aemsz.) was surely not a faiencier by trade. He in fact never joined the guild. But his son, Hendrick Beuckelsz., within a week of the purchase of the pottery, did so. Soon afterwards, Hendrick married Catharina Pouwels, the daughter of Pouwels Bour-seth, the founder of the "Rouaen" pottery. When his father-in-law died in April 1620, Hendrick took over the management of "Rouaen." Less than a year later he had bought it, along with two smaller houses, for 2590 gulden.[73] He remained owner and master of "Rouaen" until his death in 1657.

In the meantime, Beuckel Adamsz. had died about 1617 and his widow Catharina Jans had remarried a certain Pieter Maertensz. Durven. After Hendrick van der Burgh had acquired Bourseth's pottery in 1620, "De Porceleynen Schotel" was left in the custody of Catherine Jans, who had by then become the widow of Pieter Maertensz. Durven, and of her stepson Gerrit Pietersz. Durven. The latter had been admitted into the guild as master in 1616. In 1618 he married Lysbeth Cornelis Carn, the sister of Hendrick Beuckelsz.'s second wife Josge Cornelis (Hendrick Beuckelsz. had married her in 1623 after the death of *his* first wife Catharina Pouwels). After Abram Gerrit Durven's death, Lysbeth Cornelis ran "De Porceleynen Schotel" with the help of Abram Pietersz. Durven, Gerrit's brother, who acquired a half interest in the works.[5] In 1626 she remarried with Hendrick Marcellis van Gogh. Hendrick Marcellis, a Mennonite, was born in Gogh (Goch) in the duchy of Cleves around the turn of the century. He became a citizen of Delft in 1631, but he only joined the guild in 1640. Several of the *knechts* of "De Porceleynen Schotel" declared in 1640 that they had worked with him for over ten years.[74] Both Abram Durven and Hendrick Marcellisz. presumably derived their right to manage the works without belonging to the guild from Lysbeth Cornelis, the widow of a registered master. Some time in the 1630s, Abram Durven apparently gave up his half share in the business. The exact date was of some importance since the pottery was prodigiously successful under Van Gogh's management and Abram Durven's heirs made very large claims after Durven's death, based on his share in these profits. In 1640 Van Gogh claimed that most of the profits of the preceding fifteen years amounting, according to his reckoning, to 38,000 gulden, has been earned after Abram Durven abandoned the partnership. Nevertheless, he was willing to turn over the grand sum of 40,000 gulden in free silver money to Abram Durven's heirs to be quit of their claims.[75]

Van Gogh, who was admitted to the guild in April 1640, remained sole owner of "De Porceleynen Schotel" until March 1647, when he sold the pottery to Dirck Jeronimusz. Kessel for 12,000 gulden plus 6,000 gulden and an estimated 7,088 gulden of equipment, raw materials, and goods in process.[76] He then bought "Het Gecroonde Porceleyn," apparently a new pottery that seems to have been constructed on his order. He died a few months later, in 1649. His widow Lysbeth Cornelis ran the new pottery until her death in 1661. This pottery, too, prospered under her management. When she died in 1661, she left a very large estate[77] including "accounts receivable" for faience wares delivered to many parts of the country and to Flanders

[5]Abram Durven never became a member of the guild. Technically, he did not have to join since Lysbeth Cornelis, as a former master's widow, was entitled to continue her management of the pottery. The sale of the pottery is documented in the Records of Notary Guillaume de Graeff, no. 1719, 25 February 1625.

amounting to 23,411 gulden.ᶜ No other estate papers of active faienciers show anything like this volume of business.

In August 1642, nearly twenty years before her death, Lysbeth Cornelis had married off her son Pieter Gerritsz. Durven to Maria Hendricks van der Burgh, the daughter of Hendrick Beuckelsz. . With this connubial knot, the family circle closed upon itself.ᵘ Later on Pieter Gerritsz. Durven played a pivotal role in the faience industry. In the 1660s he owned a mill that ground most of the colors and glazes that were used by delftware potters.

Besides Hans de Wint and Beuckel Adamsz., many other "capitalists" became owners without previous training in the craft. Lambrecht Gysbrechtsz. Kruyck (c.1599-1644) was a businessman with a variety of interests before he took up faience: he sold glass and porcelain in the 1620s; even after purchasing the former brewery "De Dissel" for 3,800 gulden in 1640 he continued to deal in flax and cloth.[78] He registered in the guild shortly after buying "De Dissel." His son Gysbrecht Lambrechtsz. inherited the pottery in 1644 and sold it in 1648 to P. J. Oosterlaan and Abram de Cooge, the well-known art dealer. Gysbrecht Kruyck at various times in the 1650s and 1660s owned important shares in "De Porceleynen Schotel," "De Witte Starre," and "De Paeuw." The younger Kruyck, who was clearly one of the pillars of the industry, was appointed headman of the guild in 1653, 1662-1663 and 1669-1670 and 1679-1680. It is interesting that his businessman father never acceded to the board of the guild, which was apparently reserved for masters trained in the craft.

Aelbrecht Cornelisz. Keyser, who became one of the most famous faienciers in seventeenth-century Delft,ᵛ entered the industry through a unique route. Originally an out-of-towner, he was employed in the 1630s, apparently as master-*knecht*, in the shop of Adriaen Cornelisz. Cater, the most important potter of ordinary lead-glazed wares in Delft.[79] (Makers of lead-glazed pottery, used primarily for kitchen utensils, were not members of the Guild of St. Lucas.) Keyser acquired the delftware faience works, "De Twee Scheepjes," in

ᶜAbout a third of the accounts receivable were for deliveries to Amsterdam. Debtors in Antwerp, Ghent, and Brussels also appeared for a few hundred gulden each.

ᵘMaria Hendricks was the granddaughter of Catharina Jans and Beuckel Adamsz.; Pieter Gerritsz. Durven was the step-grandson of Catharina Jans. His wife Josge Cornelis was also Catharina Jans's daughter-in-law.

ᵛHis name is the only one I have found specifically mentioned (on several occasions) in the ordinances of the guild (Appendix B).

January 1642 and joined the guild in November of that year. He was headman in 1652-1653, 1657-1658 and 1661-1662. After he died in 1667, he was succeeded by his son Cornelis Aelbrechtsz. in association with Jacob and Adriaen Pynacker, both of whom had married daughters of the elder Keyser and were thereby entitled to a part of the inheritance.[80] This pattern of acquisition by marriage was, as we have already seen, quite typical.

The route by which Willem Cleffius entered the industry is similar to Lambrecht Kruyck's, whose daughter Sara he married in 1646: he also dealt in faience wares. By 1660 he was in association with his brother-in-law Gysbrecht Kruyck in "De Witte Starre." He must have occupied himself chiefly with the sales end of the business since he called himself "merchant in Delft porcelain living in Amsterdam" in March 1662.[81] The next year we find him in Delft naming Cornelis Jansz. Brouwer as his master-*knecht* to release his establishment from the necessity of being run by a master faiencier.[82] He apparently never became a master himself. Typically, though, his son Lambertus did, in June 1667. Lambertus Cleffius was a skilled potter, who seems to have been one of the first two manufacturers of Delft's famous red teapots in the early 1670s.[83] The Cleffius family was allied by marriage with the Eenhorns, another key family in the industry. Wouter Eenhorn, a former dealer in flax, had married one of Lambrecht Kruyck's daughters. He was thus Willem Cleffius's broth-er-in-law. Since the foundation of "De Grieksche A" in 1655, Wouter Eenhorn owned this very distinguished pottery with his partner Quiring Aldersz. Kleynoven, who was the full-fledged master in the association. Finally, one supplier of capital transferred his assets from the book trade to the faience industry. Sebastiaen Cuyck registered in the guild as a bookseller in 1657 and as manager-owner of a *plateelbackerij* in 1662. By the end of the decade he was out of the faience business and was borrowing funds to acquire a concession for the collection of the tax on salt.

The increasingly mobile provision of capital, which, as in Sebastiaen Cuyck's case, moved in and out of different industries, presumably in response to changes in their relative profitability, became a character-istic feature of the late 1660s and 1670s. Such disparate individuals as Simon den Danser, a businessman in Delfshaven; Dancart van Verselewel, an attorney in The Hague; and the widow of the notary Adriaen van der Block all bought shares in delftware potteries as a financial investment, with no apparent intention of being otherwise involved in the business.[84] Mere financial participation marked the last stage in the process of separation of capital from skill, know-how, and management that had begun with the entrance into the industry of the lance-maker Hans de Wint in 1613. As the capital requirements for acquiring and running faience establishments grew, those who possessed the skills and the know-how had to marry an owner's daughter or form an association with investors if they wished to gain or to retain a hand in the business.

While the high profits made by a few prosperous faienciers such as H. M. van Gogh and his widow Lysbeth Cornelis held out great expectations of rewards for daring investors, a realistic assessment of the situation would also have required an awareness of the heavy overhead and working-capital requirements that exposed the manufactures to the risk of substantial losses. Even before the downturn of the early 1670s, which may be attributed to the war with France, some delftware potteries had already run into financial troubles. Jannetge Hendrix Verhaer, the widow of Jeronimus Pietersz. Kessel who had died in 1660, had tried valiantly to keep "De Drie Astonnen" afloat after his death. But the estate papers drawn up after her death in 1667[85] showed debts exceeding assets by 6,706 gulden.[w] "De Roos" was in serious trouble in the late 1660s. On 23 July 1669, fourteen of its employees—dish-turners, decorators, and ordinary workers— declared at the request of one of the co-owners, the master faiencier Jan Jansz. Culick, that "they had not been laid off, let alone been asked to quit their work for the pottery but had taken their leave voluntarily." They had "seen to it that another master would provide them with work during the slack period *(in de slaptyt)* and that they should suffer no losses."[86] The company, which was owned by Augustyn Cools, The Hague attorney Verselewel, and Jan Culick, did suffer losses, over the sharing of which they had some disagreement.[87] In 1671 Augustyn Cools, who had rented the pottery for some time, reported losses of 2,487 gulden over three years.

During the war with France, several potteries were forced to close or at least to wind down their operations.[x] The master faiencier Jan Jonasz. van der Burgh (c.1628–c.1676) after a fairly successful career as master-*knecht* and part-owner of "De Vier Helden van Room," the

---

[w]Already in 1660, the pottery's debts exceeded its assets (Orphan Chamber, *boedel* no. 2026, 24 November 1661).

[x]The question was raised of closing Martinus Gouda's pottery as early as 1672 (Records of Notary Roelandus van Edenburgh, no. 2256, 21 July 1673).

oldest delftware pottery in the industry, ran into financial trouble in the early 1670s. When he died in late 1675 or early 1676 his estate, loaded with debts, was repudiated by his heirs.

On the basis of this slim evidence, I tentatively conclude that the variance in financial performance was substantially greater toward the end of the period than in the beginning. This may be broadly explained as follows. At first, the scale of operations was modest, and the master received a competitive remuneration corresponding to his skills and experience. Later, the scale of operations expanded and financial problems arose. Large amounts of working capital had to be carried to pay current expenses, while clients delayed payment and "accounts receivable" piled up. The potteries became vulnerable to fluctuations in demand, suffering more acutely from episodes of "slack time" than they had previously when operations could more easily be curtailed. Given this variance in profits and the financial difficulties of the less well managed (or more unlucky) enterprises, one might have expected a classic concentration of the establishments in the industry in the hands of a few capitalist-owners. That this phenomenon did not take place, at least in the period under study, may perhaps be explained by the lack of financial intermediaries, such as investment banks, that would have made it possible to collect the large amounts of capital required for a successful merger. Guild restrictions on the number of *knechts* permitted in each establishment may also have played a role in curbing mergers.

These speculations aside, I would judge that the most profitable period for the *plateelbackers* in the decades 1610–1680 occurred between 1640 and 1665. What role the interruption of shipments of blue-and-white porcelain from China, due to the fall of the Ming dynasty and the internal troubles that followed it, is an important unresolved question. There can hardly be any doubt that sales of domestic substitutes benefited to some extent from the interruption in imports of Chinese products. We also know that the number of manufactures in operation rose at a rapid pace in the critical period that followed. The expansion of the industry to meet the presumed increase in demand would not have been possible, however, if various factors had not been present to exploit the windfall: an expandable skilled labor force (at least from the 1620s on),[y] entrepreneurial talent, and some supply of capital. As it turned out, the bottlenecks to

---

[y]We saw in Chapter 2 that skilled labor was in short supply in the first decade of the century. Later, enough boy-learners (*leerjongens*) were apparently hired to meet the demand for skilled workers. While I have not enough data to construct a reliable

expansion did not reside in human factors but in supplies of raw materials. By 1661, a very serious shortage of white glazes and colors (*schilderwit* and *veruwen*) had arisen. The mills that ground them were incapable of keeping up with the demand. Pieter Gerritsz. Durven, the most prominent miller, had to discriminate among his clients. The miller and those of his clients who felt disadvantaged heaped recriminations on each other, including claims of contract violations. The accusers alleged that they had suffered breakdowns in production by reason of the shortage. This led to a veritable deluge of notarial depositions and protests.[88]

The basic skills used in shaping tiles, dishes, and other faience on the wheel were probably developed by ordinary potters long before the birth of the delftware industry. The fact that master faienciers made use of the apprentices and journeymen in common potteries producing lead-glazed wares to step up their output when they were short of help certainly suggests this. How the dish-turners learned how to mold fancy objects like chandeliers and parrots is beyond my knowledge. It is doubtful whether the potteries employed sculptors to help them: no sculptor in Delft appears to have had any documented contact with the delftware industry.

The question that arises regarding the decoration of faience is the extent to which the training or the skills of the artisans who performed this task had anything to do with the artist-painters who were relatively so numerous in Delft. Some connections can be traced, but they are neither as many nor as close as one might have expected. Isaac Junius, a master in the guild, both painted easel pictures and decorated faience. His paintings were chiefly of battle scenes and encampments. The tiles that he is known to have decorated consist of

---

index of wages, the odd quotations at my disposal indicate that wages did not rise during the period 1645-1665. Four daily-wage quotations for various *knechts* in the employ of Lambert Kruyck, who died in 1644, average one gulden four stuivers (Orphan Chamber, *boedel* no. 418). In another pottery, in 1645 a *knecht* received eighteen stuivers a day. (Records of Notary Frans Boogert, no. 1993, 31 March 1645). In 1663 a kiln-stoker was paid one gulden ten stuivers a day for night work (seven gulden ten stuivers per week for daytime work) (Records of Notary Johan van Ruiven no. 1967, 9 March 1663). In 1667, the wage of one stoker was set at eighteen stuivers a day for daytime work and one gulden twelve stuivers for night work (Records of Notary Abraham Verkerck, no. 2202, 11 August 1667). A *plateelschilder*, normally one of the better paid *knechts*, was promised one gulden five stuivers a day in the same year (Records of Notary Jacobus van Berlecum, no. 2162, 2 July 1663). A master-*knecht* received only eleven gulden a week in 1673 (Records of Notary Dirck Rees, no. 2148, 27 July 1673).

six finely painted portraits of Reformed preachers based on prints (three of them after paintings by Anthony Palamedes and one by Cornelis Daemen Rietwijck) and two views of Hendrick de Kaiser's monument to Willem of Orange in the New Church, also after prints. Abraham de Cooge who, as we saw in Chapter 7, was an important art dealer in Delft from the 1640s to the 1660s, began his artistic career as an engraver and ended it as a faiencier. He seems to have had an interest in "De Dissel" in the mid-1640s, and he owned the pottery outright from 1666 to at least 1678.[89] We cannot document any decoration by his hand, although a few have been attributed to him.[90] It may be significant that "De Dissel" had an early reputation for its finely decorated "porcelain wares."

The case of the tile and plaque painter Frederick van Frytom (c.1632-1702) is virtually unique. An artist of great distinction, he painted in addition to easel pictures, wood and river landscapes on plaques, perhaps on orders that he was given to carry out for one or more of the Delft potteries. The fact that the master faiencier Lambert Cleffius owned one of his plaques and lent him some money makes Cleffius a chief candidate as one of his employers. There is no documentation at all about his early training. What can be said with reasonable certainty is that he was influenced by the Rotterdam landscape painter Adriaen Heyndricksz. Verboom (1628-1670).[91] Another painter on faience of more limited scope and talent named Gysbrecht Verhaast worked for the pottery "Het Jonge Moriaen-shooft," owned by Rochus Hoppesteyn. A plaque signed by Verhaast dated 1686 shows a lower middle-class interior genre scene of the type frequently associated with Rotterdam or Haarlem painters. The only other painter working on porcelain or faience of whom a visual record has survived is Michael van Eemst, who first registered in the guild as a *plateelbacker* in 1668 and registered again as a *meester schilder* in 1675. Two exterior views of the St. Bavo Cathedral in Haarlem bearing a signature "M. Eems" and the date 1662 were sold in 1867.[92] One of them is now in the Frans Hals Museum in Haarlem.[93] Judging by the date and the subject, they were painted in Haarlem before the artist moved to Delft.

Claes Jacobsz. (Spierinxhoek), inscribed among the painters on the original Master List of 1613 was almost certainly a painter on faience. By 1629, however, he had also become a merchant in silk cloth.[94] Jonas Jansz. Verburgh (c.1596-1660) registered in the guild as a watercolor painter about 1614. (The date is uncertain because he only appears in the master list, not in the dated register of new members.)

In the 1620s, we find him working as a painter, presumably as a cartoon-designer, for Franchoys Spierinx, the last time on 1 January 1627 when he signed with his peculiar mark.[95] On 15 July 1628 he reappears, as plain "Jonas Jansz." working as a *plateelbackersknecht* in the pottery of Abram Pietersz. (Durven), "De Porceleynen Schotel," signing with precisely the same mark.[96] His literate son Jan Jonasz. van der Burgh (c.1628-1676), who probably learned the craft from him, is one of the few sons of *knechts* who after years of employment in the same capacity was able to acquire an interest in a pottery and accede to the status of master. He registered in the guild in 1654 and was part owner of the "Vier Helden van Room" by 1657. As I have already related, he suffered financial failure at the end of his life.

All the other artist-painters who in one way or another collaborated with the delftware industry are only names today. Adriaen Hondekoete (or Hondecoeter), born in Mechelen, arrived in Delft in 1590, and was inscribed in the original Master List of the guild of 1613 as a painter in watercolors. He later reappears on the master list of the *plateelschilders* between Gerrit Egbertsz. Sas who registered in 1616 and Jan Loquefier who registered in 1617. It is likely (but not certain) therefore that he shifted his occupation some time between 1613 and 1617 from painting in watercolors, probably for a tapestry manufacture, to a delftware pottery. His son "Aryen Ariensz. de Honnecoeter," born around 1602, was for many years a *plateelbackersknecht*. Cornelis Marinusz. van der Plaet, son of the master painter Marinus Cornelisz. van der Plaet, called himself *plateelbacker* when he married in 1641;[97] he registered in the guild without mention of profession in 1643; in the 1650 Master List he appears among the painters. He must have been an artist-painter who at least occasionally was employed by a delftware pottery. There is no way to know whether the painting of a fruit piece by "Van de Plaat" in a Delft inventory was by him or by his father.[98] Joannes Hoendermans was a decorator on faience (*plateelschilder*) in 1673; three years later he registered in the guild as a master painter.[99] He is known to have painted still-lifes. Hugh Dircksz. van der Douw (or Dol), born about 1598, was admitted to the guild as a painter; he was still in Van Gogh's employ in 1640, after which we lose his trace.[100] Jan Hansz. de Milde was said to be a painter when he married the daughter of the master faiencier Cornelis van der Graef in June 1643. In December of that year he registered in the guild, also without mention of profession, with a guarantee by Cornelis van der Graef that he would pay the five gulden outstanding on his entrance fee. His family relation to a pottery owner has given rise to the supposition that he painted on faience for his father-in-law or for his brother the registered potter Ary de Milde,[101] but I have been able to find no direct evidence of this. He too showed up on the 1650 Master List of the guild as a painter.

This exhausts our list of artist-painters who decorated faience. In all we identified five individuals who were originally said to be painters and were later called *plateelschilders* (Claes Jacobsz. Spierinxhoek, Adriaen Hondecoeter, Hugh Dircksz. van der Douw, Jonas Jansz. van der Burch, and Isaac Junius). In addition we found three men who probably started out as faienciers but later registered as painters (Cornelis Marinusz. van der Plaat, Michiel Eemst, and Johan Hoendermans). We also know of one painter (Jan Hans de Milde) and one engraver, painter, and art dealer (Abraham de Cooge) who had close ties to the faience industry without necessarily having decorated any faience wares themselves.

That there were links between the two métiers is undeniable. But the influence of the painters as a group on the decoration of delftware appears slight. Not a single outstanding personality among the master-painters seems to have had anything to do with the potteries.[z]

While I have not made a systematic investigation of themes or influences on painted delftware, I am hardly impressed by the impact on the industry of the painters of the "school of Delft." With the exception of a few plaques copied after Anthony Palamedes, most of the works illustrated in standard texts on Delft faience show either copies after the Haarlem engraver Jacob de Geyn (chiefly of soldiers and *schutters*), or plaques imitating the work of Nicholas Berchem, Jan van Goyen, David Teniers, and other out-of-town artists.[aa] In general, the tiles were rapidly executed after engravings or even after tiles copied from engravings. That there were no Delft-based engravers— after the death of Willem Jacobsz. Delff—whose prints could have

[z]It was once believed that the important Amsterdam painter Werner van den Valckert was identical with the decorator on faience of the same name noted in Delft in 1635 and 1646 who worked for Cornelis Harmensz. Valckenhoff, the son of the founder of the industry Herman Pietersz. (See, for example, Rijksmuseum, Amsterdam, *Catalogue des tableaux, miniatures, pastels, dessins encadrés du Musée de l'Etat à Amsterdam* [Amsterdam: Roeloffzen-Hübner en van Santen, 1904], p. 312). It is now believed that Van Valckert died in Amsterdam in 1627–1628 (*All the Paintings in the Rijksmuseum* [Maarssen: Gary Schwartz, 1979], p. 553). A comparison of the signatures of the painter and of the *plateelschilder* also rules out any possibility of their being one and the same person.

[aa]See for instance the plaques illustrated in Fernand W. Hudig, *Delfter Fayence; ein Handbuch für Sammler und Liebhaber* (Berlin: R. C. Smidt, 1929), pp. 97–101.

FIG. 16 Anonymous, Two Delft Tiles, (third quarter 17th cent., first quarter 17th cent.), each 5¼ x 5¼ in. Author's collection, New Haven (Photo: Josef Szaszfai)

been used as sources by the *plateelschilders* may be one reason why established artists did not exert more influence on the decoration of faience.[bb]

The last topic I wish to turn to is the market and the clientele for delftware. My basis proposition is that the trend away from the polychrome products that predominated from the origins of the industry to perhaps the mid-1620s, toward blue-and-white goods, was accompanied by a significant decrease in costs and prices. This cheapening of the products of the industry enabled the manufactures to penetrate a new, wider public.

The evidence for the reduction in production costs rests in part on an examination of the products themselves. Anyone who has had in his hands a typical polychrome tiles of the period 1600–1625 and compared it with a blue-and-white tile of the 1650s will agree that the cost of painting the latter must have been a fraction of the former (fig. 16). The design in the first period is painted all over in free hand; in the second relatively few lines are traced on the surface of the tile with the aid of pouncing paper. The tile is now also thinner, probably because a better mixture of clays became available.[cc] This economized on the basic raw material of the tile and cut down on costs. The prices of the tiles confirm these visual impressions. In 1608 and 1610 Cornelis Rochusz., the owner of "De Romeyn," delivered several batches of glazed tiles to the city for one and two stuivers a piece.[102] Pouwels Bourseth, the owner of "Rouaen," who died in February 1620, sold tiles representing flower vases, which were undoubtedly polychrome at that time, at prices varying between 1½ stuivers and 3½ stuivers apiece or 75 to 175 gulden per thousand.[103] From various sources we learn that the prices of blue-and-white tiles were only twenty-one to twenty-seven gulden per thousand in the period 1649 to 1659.[104] The general trend of prices, as I have argued elsewhere in

[bb]The only engraver of any importance was Willem Jacobsz. Delff who specialized in portraits, a subject that was rarely executed in faience. Those I have mentioned by Isaac Junius were quite exceptional. I may note in passing that Junius copied the six portraits on faience signed by him from prints made by Crispijn van der Queborn, a Hague artist, after paintings by the Delft-based Anthony Palamedes and Cornelis Rietwijck. The two tiles representing the monument of Willem the Silent were after engravings by Cornelis Danckertsz., also working in The Hague.

[cc]On the discovery of special clays in 1627, see the Records of Notary Willem de Langue, no. 1685, 25 October 1627. Technical progress in the manufacture of delftware also seems to have taken place in the mid-1620s, but its nature is obscure due to the secrecy that surrounded new processes (Cf. Records of Notary Cornelis Coeckebakker, no. 1613, 30 January 1625).

this book, was rising till 1620 and then perhaps slightly upward or stable from 1620 to 1650. I am convinced therefore that the decline in the prices of tiles did not result from any general trend in prices but was the competitive outcome of a reduction in costs due to changes in decoration and production techniques.[dd]

Who were the consumers of delftware products? Virtually every family owned some tin-glazed wares. The difficulty with any statistical investigation is that it is not possible, in most inventories, to distinguish among five basic types of utensils: 1) those made from authentic porcelain imported from the Orient, 2) Italian majolica, 3) Antwerp imitations of Italian products, 4) delfware proper, 5) common lead-glazed earthenware that poor people ate from (and most people used as cooking utensils).

Only the richest inventories make any distinctions among the various types. To give the reader some ideas of the relative importance of the value of faience and porcelain wares that Delft citizens possessed, I have selected a small sample of twenty inventories, dated from 1615 to 1679, in which the total value of all these wares combined can be compared with the value of the owners' paintings and, in most cases, with the total value of their inventory of movable goods. These data are summarized in Table 9.4.

The value of faience and porcelain wares owned exceeded the value of paintings in only five out of twenty inventories in the sample. The percentage ratio of the two types of possessions for the eighteen cases where the value of paintings exceeded zero was 92.2, but the variance around this average was quite high. No clear trend can be made out in the ratio through time for this small sample with a characteristically large range of inventory values.

CONCLUSIONS

The relatively heavy capital requirements of the industries discussed in this chapter go far to explain the institutional arrangements that developed in the course of the seventeenth century. Master craftsmen contracted with wealthy partners outside their specialty to supply capital. Some of the principal instances cited were those of Willem Lee in printing, Nicolaes Snouckaert in tapestry-making, and the

---

[dd]I have not been able to carry out a similar comparison for dishes because the range of prices for different sizes and qualities in any one period was too large and my sample too small to make such a comparison meaningful.

TABLE 9.4

Value of Faience and Porcelain Wares Versus Value of Paintings in Selected Inventories, 1614–1679
(In Gulden)

Owner	Date	(1) Total Value of Inventory	(2) Faience and Porcelain Wares	(3) Paintings	Percent Ratio of (2) to (3)
Magdalena Williems	1614	96.2	2.0	3.2	62.5
Cornelis Voorstadt	1615	290.1	6.6	3.5	188.6
Cornelis [illegible]	1619	116.6	1.9	6.4	29.7
Willem Heyndricksz.	1621	n.a.	9.9	97.1	10.2
Maria van Starrenburch	1649	n.a.	49.1	7.1	691.7
Annetge Harmens	1650	190.1	2.2	3.9	56.4
Maertge Dirxdr.	1650	417.5	3.2	5.2	61.5
Geertgen Cornelis	1651	533.0	3.0	13.5	22.2
Ariaentge Jansdr.	1651	265.0	2.1	0	—
Lenart Vogelscam	1652	563.0	6.0	0	—
Neltge Cornelis	1653	162.4	1.4	7.9	17.7
Neltge van den Schult	1657	359.5	0.8	4.8	16.7
Abram Adriaensz. van Beyeren	1658	n.a.	20.0	67.3	29.7
Franco van Beest	1664	1,465.0	60.8	161.8	37.6
Jacob Beet	1665	1,616.0	84.4	89.1	94.7
Samuel van Broekercken	1671	425.0	5.9	228.0	26
Michiel Ball	1674	1,148.0	86.8	49.5	175.3
Maertge Vranckryck	1677	n.a.	4.1	5.5	74.5
Jasper van Dyck	1677	201.5	1.0	4.5	22.2
Cornelis Brouwer	1679	242.8	4.3	6.5	66.2

SOURCES: Delft, Municipal Archives, Notarial records, and Orphan Chamber estate settlements.

widow of Notary Adriaen van der Block in delftware manufacturing. In guild-regulated industries, such as delftware, the separation of capital ownership from mastery in the craft presented a problem that was only gradually solved in the 1650s when master-*knechts* who had been admitted as masters in the guild were permitted to manage shops in place of their owners. Marriage with the daughters of wealthy burghers—whether these burghers were already established in the industry or not—was another way for master craftsmen to get hold of capital. But the combination of competence in the craft and the availability of capital did not guarantee success. Poor management, in the case of the tapestry-maker Karel van Mander the Younger and most probably of the faiencier Jan Jonasz. Verburgh, brought on the eventual collapse of their enterprises. The main point to keep in mind is that the larger and the more capital-intensive the establishment was, the more difficult it became to manage successfully, especially when there was acute competition both for skilled labor and for markets.

There seemed to be no obstacle to entry in the printing and delftware industries. On the other hand, guild rules inhibited the expansion of employment in individual establishments. These two factors may help to account for the vigorous rise in the number of faience shops, especially in the period of 1640-1660. There was probably an increase in the number of printing shops as well, but here we are on weaker ground because we know nothing about the liquidation of unsuccessful ventures. On the other hand, the possibilities of setting up tapestry works in competition with those of Spierinx and Van Mander were nonexistent, given the high capital requirements of the business and the town's policy of protecting existing establishments from competition. In this industry, the only road to expansion was through the greater intake of *knechts* in each manufacture. This was legally possible after 1620 since the tapestry workers were no longer subject to the control of the Guild of St. Lucas, except for the trivial requirement of having to pay their death dues to the guild. The relatively large number of *knechts* in Van Mander's manufacture—about forty in the early 1630s—compared to perhaps twenty-five per faience shop, may have had as much to do with this legal and economic environment as it did with technological disparities between the two industries.

These differences aside, the ways the tapestry and faience manufacturers penetrated new markets by lowering production costs and prices are strikingly similar. From the 1600s until at least to the end of the first quarter of the century, the products of both ceramic and tapestry manufacturers were strewn with details in design. So much is going on in some of the early dishes painted "all over" and in the allegorical or historical tapestries that the general design is often hard to make out.ᵉᵉ Detail and anecdote were stressed at the expense of decorative effectiveness. By the mid-century point, in both industries decorative values had gained the upper hand. The result was a cheaper and more popular product. The difference of course is that tapestry, an inherently expensive commodity to begin with, could only descend from a product adapted to an aristocratic market to one suitable for town halls and great rooms of patricians and rich merchant dwellings. Only chairs upholstered with Maximiliaen van der Gucht's tapestries with their characteristic designs of flowers or landscapes on dark-blue backgrounds penetrated into more ordinary but still upper middle-class homes. Tiles and decorated faience dishes, on the other hand, were sold by that time to a very wide public that comprised a majority of urban dwellers and many of the better-off farmers as well.

Art historians will also recognize the counterpart of this evolution in the realm of painting, from the "additive" designs, laden with details, of late Mannerist artists (Marten de Vos, Cornelis van Haarlem, Abraham Bloemaert), via the well-focused but still "busy" and agitated pictures of the baroque, to the calm, simplified, crystal-clear conceptions of the so-called classicists, particularly of those who flourished in Delft after 1650, such as Vermeer, Carel Fabritius, and Pieter de Hooch.ᶠᶠ I suspect that the elimination of excess detail in

---

ᵉᵉHenry Havard, *Histoire des faïences de Delft, Haarlem, Rotterdam, Utrecht, etc. et des porcelaines de Weesp, Loosdrecht, Amsterdam et La Haye*, 2 vols. (Amsterdam: "Vivat," 1909), effectively stresses this point. Of a delftware charger signed by Thomas Jansz. around 1600-1615, he writes that it is covered with such an *"amoncellement de personnages"* and the 400 figures represented are so intertwined that it cannot be reproduced by a line engraving. Even in the 1630s, this confused "additive" quality still prevailed. Note also that polychrome tiles were painted "all over," far more densely than the later tiles. An interesting difference is that in the early tiles the corner design is "reserved," that is, the pattern is suggested by the solid blue color surrounding the design which is left in white (the color of the background). In the later tiles the design is painted in blue on the white surface. In time these corner designs tended to become smaller as tiles become ever cheaper and more decorative. The final reduction of this process is the entirely white wall tiles that were a popular variant of the blue-and-white tiles in the eighteenth century.

ᶠᶠI use the words "Mannerist," "baroque," and "classicist" in their conventional meaning. Until a more precise vocabulary has been developed by art historians, I consider these terms will do well enough to identify the stylistic traits with which I link these trends in this paragraph.

baroque paintings (accompanied by a more "painterly" handling of subjects) may have helped to produce less costly pictures that could be sold to wider circles of consumers; however, the final simplification associated with the classical phase of Dutch painting seems to have corresponded to a change in taste that cannot satisfactorily be explained in these economic terms.

TEN

A View of the Forest

The intensive archival work that I have done for this book yielded generally reliable and detailed information about small and disparate fragments of a total reality. I have tried to stitch a number of these fragments together by counting the number of artists and artisans of different types, by estimating the taxes they paid, the value of their houses they bought and sold, and their death donations; I have also laboriously computed the value, the subjects, and the attributions of thousands of works of art in inventories of movable goods recorded in notarial records and Orphan Chamber papers. Besides their intrinsic importance, these aggregates and the averages I derived from them were also surrogates for the data I could not hope to collect directly: the yearly incomes of guild members, the value of their output (paintings, faience, tapestry), the total costs of their training. In my view, the statistics I assembled, while imperfect, especially in the biases they introduced by overstating the average wealth of the owners of inventories, were still usable and instructive.

Conjoined with these totals and averages is an assortment of finely detailed miniatures collected in the archives—anecdotes drawn from the life of the participants in our story of artistic and artisanal life in Delft. It will be some comfort if the statistics and the odd facts I have marshaled about the arts in Delft turn out to reflect this teeming life more faithfully than any account published previously.

In the last analysis, my analytical approach will only gain approval provided it is considered at least as valuable—for the new insights it provides as well as for the confirmation or invalidation of previous hypotheses—as traditional work in this area. There happens to exist a previous study, carried out along traditional lines, of the arts in Delft that offers a sharp contrast to mine. This is the book that I have cited from time to time by the Austrian art historian Max Eisler, *Alt-Delft: Kultur und Kunst*, published in Amsterdam in 1923. Like mine, Eisler's study covers Delft painting, tapestry, and faience. It also includes a brief chapter on sculpture (as I do not). However, it omits all mention of other trades in the Guild of St. Lucas, such as glassmaking and embroidering, to which I occasionally refer. Eisler based his book entirely on archival research carried out by Abraham Bredius, J. Soutendam, and other scholars in the late nineteenth and early twentieth centuries. His study differs from the present investigation essentially in two ways: Eisler relied to a much greater extent on what he inferred from visual evidence (from paintings, tapestries, sculptures, and faience wares); he also laid special emphasis on the socio-political atmosphere of Delft and its influence on the arts. The evidence Eisler drew from the works of art that he described is colored by a strong commitment to traditional art-historical concepts centered on the antinomy of the baroque and classical styles.[a] The dialectic evolution from one style to the other plays a role in the structure of his thought similar to that played by the modes of production in Marx's *Capital*, the ineluctable historical development of which Marx described at such eloquent length. Eisler, like Hegel, believed in a world spirit that nudged forward the history of taste. He typically concludes a discussion of the precise linear style in still-life painting initiated by the Delft artist Evert van Aelst[b] by suggesting that "the slumbering classicism of the early generation had at last come awake" with this development.[1] What Eisler meant to convey was that the linear style and the clarity of design which he had already detected in late sixteenth-century Delft painting, in the works of Miereveld, Harmen van der Mast, and Jacob Willemsz. Delff, reemerged in the "classicizing" tendencies of the 1650s. The breakthrough of classicism in Delft had to wait until the world spirit was ready for its revival on a European scale in the second half of the seventeenth century.

Eisler linked the latent classical tendencies in Delft art to the socio-political atmosphere of the city. Precise drawing, good taste and measure, clarity and coolness of arrangement: these are in his words, "the form and expression of correct burgher-noblesse."[2] In Eisler's view, Delft was essentially a patrician city, jealous of its prerogatives and its autonomy, governed by turns by a few old families for

---

[a]The Mannerist style is glossed over by Eisler. He refers indirectly to the style when he refers to certain paintings as "Romanist." He belongs to that generation of art historians who held that the importation of the Italian manner into Dutch painting in the late sixteenth and early seventeenth centuries had been a retrograde step for art.

[b]Where did Eisler ever see a picture by Evert van Aelst? Two have recently surfaced (a fruit piece and a vase of flowers, both in the possession of dealers in 1975), but as far as I know none were known with certainty in Eisler's day.

centuries on end. The ardent support that Delft gave to the rebellion after the religious Alteration of 1572 could not change this: a few of the families lost ground or left town, but the principle of burgher oligocracy remained intact. Delft citizens, as Dirck van Bleyswijck wrote and Eisler quoted approvingly, were distinguished by sociability, restrained dignity, and sensual elegance ("Umgänglichkeit, gehaltene Wurde, sinnliche Hettigkeit"). Delft was the cleanest city of Holland. Neatness and dignity, restraint and stateliness were virtues of its citizenry and hallmarks of its art.[c]

Eisler also dwelled on the influence of city-sponsored humanistic education on Delft art. In his view, the Latin School, whose curriculum and books were made subject to city control in 1627,[d] the expansion of the public library in 1636, and the city-funded seminary for the preparation of future students at the theological faculty of Leyden University, while they contributed to the spread of education among the people of Delft, also helped to create artificially a climate of artificial humanism. This humanism tended to sever the taste of the educated upper class from the more earthy taste of the masses, which Eisler and most of the art historians of his time regarded as the nurturing ground for the homely virtues of Dutch art.[3] If Eisler is correct, and Delft was really different from other cities in this respect, we should find in Delft inventories more mythological, emblematic, and allegorical pictures of the type associated with humanistic conceits than elsewhere. The hypothesis should at least be worth keeping in mind for further research in other cities. At this juncture I can only say that the steady trend away from "historical" painting as the seventeenth century progressed, which I have documented in my study of the subjects of paintings in Chapter 8, suggests, if anything, a diminished influence of the humanities on the visual arts after 1630.

Whatever humanistic climate Delft might have fostered, it was not one that was very conducive to literary or musical expression. This town of twenty-five to thirty thousand inhabitants at the mid-century point was richly endowed with talent in the visual arts but produced next to nothing in other domains. Delft gave birth to the writings of the jurist Hugo Grotius and to the homilies and religious pamphlets of a number of eloquent Calvinist and Catholic preachers. One of the

[c]See particularly Max Eisler, *Alt-Delft: Kultur und Kunst* (Amsterdam: Elsevier, 1923) pp. 29-31. Eisler also cites the contemporary proverb, "Delft is statigh, Utrecht prelatigh" (Delft is stately, Utrecht ecclesiastic) to buttress his thesis.

[d]Recall the agreement of the booksellers on the fixing of Latin books' prices of January 1627 cited in Chapter 9.

latter, Stalpaert van der Wiele (1579-1630) even became a distinguished religious poet. Yet the more worldly aspects of literature were barely represented. The Chamber of Rhetoricians (*Kamer der Rhetorijkers*), called the "Turnip Flower" (*Rapen-bloeme*), which had enjoyed a lively reputation with its "dumb plays," charades, and poetry recitals until the last years of the sixteenth century, fell into desuetude in the seventeenth. It may be, as Van Bleyswijck suggests, that the opposition of certain Calvinist preachers who felt indignant over the license of the rhetoricians' performances brought about their decline. The attempt to resurrect the chamber in 1614 had no lasting results.[4]

In the 1620s, Gerard van Santen, the only Delft-based playwright whose works are still known, published a few comic playlets in Leyden and Amsterdam.[5] He may never have seen them performed in his home town.[e] Van Santen's importance for the history of art lies in his contacts with the rich patriciate of Delft, including the outstanding collector Boudewijn de Man to whom he dedicated a play; in his colorful descriptions of low-life taverns and whorehouse scenes in Delft, which offer a literary counterpart to similar scenes in the pictures of Heyndrick van der Burch, Anthony Palamedes, and other Delft-based painters; and in his detailed references to the art of painting, a craft that he may have practiced professionally after he left Delft for The Hague in the late 1620s.[f]

Music was the province of the organists of the Old and the New Churches, who achieved no great fame as composers, and of popular musicians (*speelluiden*) who played at marriages and other festivities but left no written record of their activities.

On the whole, it must be acknowledged that Eisler's ideas on the influence of the Delft environment on the arts are suggestive and plausible. Unfortunately, they can neither be affirmed nor validated by the information I have collected nor perhaps by any conceivable store of information. About all that can be said for them is that, by pointing to the ways in which Delft may have differed from other cities in the Netherlands, they may properly warn us against making unfounded

[e]Hitherto Van Santen's Delft origin was only inferred from internal evidence. Two documents that I have found (in the Records of Notary Willem de Langue, no. 1685, 26 August 1626 and 20 March 1627) concern a Captain Gerard Cornelisz. van Santen who is very probably identical with the playwright.
[f]Numerous references to painting in the plays are cited in A.C. Crena de Iongh *G. C. van Santen's Lichte Wigger en Snappende Siitgen; zeventiende-eeuwse gesprekken in Delfts Dialect* (Assen: Van Gorcum, 1959), pp. 27, 35.

generalizations about other Dutch art centers from the empirical material contained in this study. I hope that my statistical work on Delft will give an impetus to studies of other cities that will shed light on this point. For the time being it is my guess, based on published sources and very limited work in the Leyden, Hague, Schiedam, Gorinchem, and Amsterdam archives, that my Delft material is similar to what one would expect to find in cities of roughly the same size, such as The Hague, but differs in important respects, including the organization of the guild and the structure of the art market, from what one might encounter in Amsterdam or in a smaller town like Schiedam or Gorinchem.

It is one thing to speculate about the influence on art styles of the city patriciate, another to ask oneself what policies the Delft authorities actually pursued toward the arts. The importance that they assigned to the arts is suggested in part by the high rank of the deans that they appointed to supervise the Guild of St. Lucas. Hugh de Groot (Hugo Grotius's grandfather) in the middle of the sixteenth century, Simon Groenewegen van der Made in the second quarter of the seventeenth century, Sacharias Hofdijck van Beresteyn in the 1650s, and Dirck Meerman in the early 1660s—the only names of deans that have come down to us—are as distinguished a quartet of the "burgher-noblesse" as one could hope to find. It was under the tenure of Dirck Meerman that the guild was given the use, rent-free, of part of the chapel of the Old Men's House, which was city property. This was a modest subsidy but symptomatic of a positive attitude toward the guild and its members. My impression, nevertheless, is that the city fathers were not inclined to protect the guild at the expense of the arts. The Guild Letter of 1613 and its subsequent amendments and amplifications were not especially restrictive in their provisions about the importation of works of art from out of town. They had to be sold by dealers registered in the guild, and they could not be included in the estate sales that were held weekly by the *boelhuysmeester*, but otherwise I do not see what regulations would have prevented their being sold in Delft. That so many of the orders given by the city to artists went to outsiders (Hendrick Vroom, Simon de Vlieger after he had left town, Hendrick de Keyser) hardly betrays a strong commitment to trade restrictions. Neither do I see the city authorities bent on curbing the number of registered masters provided they had the proper qualifications. The size of the guild membership, we know, increased from 1613 to 1650. The only evidence of restrictive practices concerns the faience industry. From the 1620s to the 1640s, so few new masters were registered that I surmise there was an embargo on all new members who were not owners of potteries. The number of *knechts* that any faience establishment could employ at any one time was also nominally limited, but the regulation was apparently not strictly enforced. This evidence surely contrasts with the overtly restrictive practices of other guilds in Delft and elsewhere. The butchers of Delft, for instance, limited their numbers to thirty-two from time immemorial. When there was a vacancy the children of guild members enjoyed priority.[6] The bakers did not allow any bread baked in villages outside the city limits to be sold in Delft.[7] On an occasion when Delft frame-makers brought some frames and panels to sell in Rotterdam, which violated local guild rules, the headmen of the joiners' guild to which the frame-makers of Rotterdam belonged collected a substantial fine from their Delft colleagues and threatened, if this ever happened again, that they would burn the goods on the market place.[8] The fact, moreover, that about half of all attributed paintings in my sample of Delft inventories were given to out-of-town painters shows that imports were on a high level, though not as high as they might have been if Delft collectors had not been so provincial. I do not perceive any clear change in the policy of the authorities toward the guild in any of these respects in the course of the first three quarters of the seventeenth century.

For Eisler, a demanding craft tradition and good drawing were essential ingredients of what he regarded as the Delft school of fine and applied arts. What empirical support is there for this hypothesis? The working of silver and gold, an art trade that I have hardly touched on (because it did not belong to the Guild of St. Lucas), combined solid craftsmanship with precise drawing. The silversmiths and gold-smiths of Delft enjoyed a high reputation. The fine statuettes and dishes in *repoussé* silver of Adriaen de Grebber, one of the great artisans of the generation of the early 1600s, were known throughout the Netherlands. Claes Jansz. Bylevelt and Jan Mathysz. de Been were jewelers of the grand duke of Florence. A number of silversmiths and goldsmiths were connected with artist-painters by family or career links. Michiel Miereveld was the son of one of the most successful goldsmiths in Delft. The uncle of Gillis and Matheus de Berg was a silversmith and engraver; Anthony and Palamedes Palamedesz. were the sons of an agate polisher; Niclaes Bronckhorst, the son of the "history" painter Pieter Bronckhorst, was apprenticed to a silversmith when he was twelve years old, before he began his training as a painter;[9] his master, named Lieven van der Poel, was the father of the painter Egbert van der Poel. Both crafts must have profited from this interpenetration. (It is worth recalling that the Leyden painter Frans van Mieris, whose fine touch and precise drawing were widely reputed, also came from a family of goldsmiths.) We have seen that artists trained as painters went to work as cartoon-designers for manufacturers of tapestry and as decorators on faience for delftware potters. The art of drawing was probably the common denominator of all these fine crafts. Weavers of finely patterned silks (*caffawerckers*) learned drawing from Jacob Willemsz. Delff.[10] A contract for training an embroiderer stipulated that the master would teach his pupil how to draw.[11] Drawings and prints are found in the inventories[12] of glassmakers and sculptors.[g] Even painters-in-the-rough seem to have been taught the rudiments of art. Still-lifes are known by Willem van Odekercken; a signed copy after a painting by Adriaen van Ostade by Johan Molyn, who carried out decorating contracts for the city, now hangs in the Riga Museum.[h] A single document has survived testifying to the existence of a drawing academy in the 1650s. This academy, run by the portrait painter Cornelis Daemen Rietwijck, was a place where all sorts of young people, including a baker and a carpenter, received training in the rudiments of art which they could later use in their craft. Inventories reveal also that a fair number of amateurs drew and painted. However modest might have been their artistic achievements, their taste and connoisseurship can only have been refined by the training they received. Thus a basic knowledge of "portraying" was diffused, in part through traditional apprenticeship, in part through group instruction. I do not know how widely the teaching of art was spread in other Dutch cities, so that I cannot really maintain at this point how strongly this evidence supports Eisler's conjecture regarding the special appreciation of Delft burghers for sound drawing. All this said, what are we to make of the fact that so few drawings of the best-known Delft masters (De Hooch, Vermeer, Fabritius, Houckgeest, De Witte) have survived? Is it possible, as

[g]Inventory of the sculptor Christiaen van der Hulst (Records of Notary Joris van der Houve, no. 2023, 16 May 1650) contains a reference to "six books in-folio with diverse drawings by the deceased."

[h]I was doubtful whether the painting signed J. Molyn in the Riga Museum was really by this well-known *kladschilder,* but a comparison of the signatures confirmed the attribution. The signature is reproduced in W. Neumann, *Beschreibendes Verzeichnis der Gemälde der Vereinigten Sammlungen der Stadt Riga, des Rigaschen Kunstvereins und des Weil. Rigaschen Ratsherrn Fried. Wilh. Brederlo* (Riga: Rigaer Tageblatt, 1906), p. 77. For a deposition signed by Johan Jacobsz. Molyn, see the Records of Notary Willem van Assendelft, no. 1859, 20 December 1638.

[324]

Walter Liedtke suggests, that artists painted directly "from life," bypassing the preparatory work of drawing?[14] Eisler's thesis, if it has validity at all, would seem to be more pertinent to the decades of 1610 to 1640 before the "Delft School" flourished.

There is far more evidence in this book on the costs of training artists than on the nature of the instruction they received. I argued at some length that these costs were fairly high and could only be borne by relatively well-off parents. Children had to be taught how to read and write properly. They had to be apprenticed to a master painter for six years at a cost of some one hundred gulden a year if they lived with their master. There was also a heavy opportunity cost in the wages lost by the young apprentices as they underwent training. The fact that the fathers or guardians of virtually all artist-painters were masters in their craft—if they were not professionals or merchants—is certainly suggestive of the hurdles that a fledgling artist had to surmount if he did not stem from an established family. It is also worthy of note that the Camer van Charitate, Delft's welfare institution, did not assign any of its orphaned or otherwise impoverished wards to high-class crafts such as painting or silversmithing.

Because I had information on membership only in the Guilds of St. Lucas and St. Eloy (silversmiths), I could not make very meaningful comparisons of economic status across crafts (except for those subsumed under these guilds). The tax records on real estate that are available for 1620 and 1632 normally cite the craft of taxpayers but almost never specify whether or not they were masters in their guild. The "stonemason" Adriaen Willeborts van Weena was Delft's principal builder and architect in the 1620s. The "shoemaker" Pieter Corstiaensz. Hopprus (or Opprust) was an important tanner and leather merchant. This sort of "backward linkage," incidentally, was quite common: frame-makers dealt in ebony, stonemasons in marble, painters in lacquers and paints. The baker Hendrick van Buyten who took two paintings by Vermeer after the artist's death as collateral for a debt of 617 gulden that Vermeer owed him for bread was a prosperous moneylender in addition to being a master baker. Many of the other stonemasons, shoemakers and bakers were poor wretches, apprentices or journeymen who barely received a subsistence wage. The only comparisons of taxes paid that are at all meaningful are those that can be made with notaries and attorneys who were no doubt full-fledged professionals. These, as we have seen, paid higher taxes than master painters in the 1620s, but the sample is so small that the difference may not be statistically significant.

The problem of segregating the masters from their apprentices and journeymen in the tax registers and the notarial archives points up the major difficulty of this study that is alluded to in the Introduction: the virtual lack of any previous work on the economic history of Delft in the seventeenth century. It would have made my task much easier had I been able to compare my data on artists and artisans in the Guild of St. Lucas with wage and price statistics and lists of masters and servants in other crafts, or even with demographic data for Delft as a whole. I should have liked to have used a study of the beer or the textile industry as a basis of comparison for the art trades. An analysis of the socio-economic characteristics of the art community in Delft such as I have tried to provide should in principle follow, rather than precede, a general profile of Delft's economic activities. As it is, I was compelled to make my comparisons ad hoc, using samples that could have been larger and less biased if they had been constructed as part of a more general study. My comparisons of economic status within the community organized under the Guild of St. Lucas fortunately comprised a range of artists and craftsmen with widely disparate training and skills.

At the bottom of the guild were the furniture-makers, inscribed in the guild records as "chair-painters," who were primarily members of the Guild of St. Joseph. The list of their names is the next best thing to having a register of the masters in the furniture-making craft. Higher on the scale were the glassmakers, most but not all of whom were independent craftsmen. Until about 1650, the faienciers, as we saw in the last chapter, were almost all owners of potteries whose wealth depended on how well their business was going. Some, like Heyndrick Marcellis van Gogh, were richer than the most successful artist-painters. But the average of the taxes they paid, the prices of the houses they bought and sold, and the donations they left to the Camer van Charitate at their death seem to have been on a par with—or even somewhat inferior to—the comparable data noted for painters. At the top of the scale were the printers and booksellers who were apparently quite well-to-do, at least for the sample I collected. The economic characteristics of the *knechts* of the delftware potteries were significantly inferior to those of all masters in the guild except possibly for the furniture-painters. Detailed research into the estates left by these employees reveals that a minority among them, consisting chiefly of experienced and presumably talented decorators on faience, lived fairly comfortably—owning houses costing 500 to 700 gulden and movable goods worth up to 1,000 gulden—but the majority were poor. The economic indicators of wealth showed especially great variance for the painters. Like prestigious careers in show business or in the arts today, possibilities of success were virtually unbounded for the most lucky and talented—although they might have to go to The Hague and Amsterdam to take advantage of them. But there was also a good chance of dying poor as Evert van Aelst and Nicolaes Vosmaer did. Painting, as a high-risk occupation, probably attracted risk-prone individuals who were willing to accept a lower expected average income than they might have drawn from steadier occupations, in return for a chance to become famous or wealthy.

Just as I have tried to show that artist-painters generally came from a higher social stratum than they have been assigned to by most art historians, so my study of inventories indicates that the people who bought their paintings were themselves of above-average wealth. The great majority of the paintings that hung on the walls of Delft citizens were copies and other "work-by-the-dozen" that cost two gulden or less. The evidence I have collected suggests that contemporary masters in the guild—or at least those whose names were sufficiently familiar to be cited in inventories—normally sold their paintings for at least five to ten gulden. Collectors who bought paintings for these and higher prices were relatively well-to-do. The value of their movable possessions exceeded both the median of my sample of inventories and the arithmetical average. Most of the paintings that were once in Delft and hang in museums today, I suggested in Chapter 8, were owned by rentiers, merchants, professionals, and perhaps a few of the more successful craft masters.

THE RISE AND FALL OF DELFT

Sixteenth-century Delft had been of minor importance for painting or sculpture, yet enough competent painters worked there for young men to get their basic training, as did Maerten van Heemskerk from Jan Lucas and Miereveld from Blocklandt. There were also many works of art that an aspiring painter could look at. The two great churches and the city's convents were rich in art. Altarpieces by Van Scorel, Pieter Aertsen, Van Heemskerck, and Van Blocklandt graced their altars and refectories; the Italianate sculpture and decoration of Willem van Tetrode adorned the New Church just before the Alteration. At the close of the century, thirty years or so after the churches and convents had been stripped of their images by the Iconoclasts, there was little left of all this religious art. By that time the only specialty in which Delft still achieved distinction was portrait painting, regarded as low genre by Karel van Mander, the great theorist of Mannerism.[i] Huybert Jacobsz. Grimani, Harmen van der Mast, and the famous Michiel Miereveld himself were the foremost representatives of the genre.

The Flemish immigration quickened the pulse of Delft's artistic life. Many artists came to the city, some for only a short stay, others to establish a residence. In the last decade of the sixteenth century, Elias Lucasz. Verhulst, praised by Arnold van Buchell in his diary, introduced still-life painting to Delft. Soon after 1600 Willem van den Bundel from Brussels and Pieter Stael, son of an immigrant from Maastricht, began to specialize in landscape painting under the influence of the popular Flemish master Joost de Momper. Hans Jordaens the Elder brought with him from Antwerp a less austere, more intimate and decorative type of religious and mythological painting than had been known before, which rapidly became popular in Delft. Around the turn of the century Karel van Mander the Younger, whose father had immigrated to Holland from Kortryk, began painting cartoons for the tapestry manufacture of the Antwerp-born Franchoys Spierinx. Around 1610–1615, these immigrants were joined by the talented landscape and flower painter Jacob Vosmaer (a Delft-born citizen) and the specialist in architectural painting Bartolomeus van Bassen from Flanders. In 1621, Delft's first genre painter, Anthony Palamedes, son of Flemish immigrants, joined the guild. All the basic specialities were now represented. Technically competent masters could provide instruction in any category of painting. The number of artists-painters active in Delft increased from twenty-five in 1613, including four designers of tapestry cartoons, to thirty-five professional oil painters in 1650. It was not until the 1640s that the pull of Amsterdam and, to a lesser extent, of The Hague began to make itself felt seriously. By the 1650s more established artists were leaving Delft for these larger and more prosperous centers than were registering in the guild from all sources. Still, at the time of the explosion of the powder magazine of 1654 that killed Carel Fabritius, the city could boast of a veritable Pleiad of artists: besides Fabritius himself, Vermeer, Pieter de Hooch, Leonaert Bramer, Egbert van der Poel, Herman Steenwijck, Anthony Palamedes, and

---

[i]Van Mander argued in the section of the *Schilderboeck* devoted to Miereveld that this artist had been deflected from the righteous path of history painting by the need to earn money. (*Het Schilderboeck . . . der Edele Vrye Schilderkonst* (Haarlem, 1604), fol. 281.)

Daniel Vosmaer. By 1671, when Vermeer began his second term as headman of the guild, the only other painter of importance who was still active in Delft was Cornelis de Man.[j] A few departures, due mainly to the attraction of the larger cities to the north, may have been sufficient to reduce the community of artists working in Delft below a "critical mass," at which point the interactive forces holding together the community were loosened, and virtually everyone left town who did not have strong family ties to Delft itself (as Vermeer and De Man did). This was the hypothesis I advanced in Chapter 6. Another explanation, reinforcing the first, can be put forward that bears on the fate of painting in the entire Netherlands rather than just in Delft.

In Chapters 6 and 9, I reported on the simplification in design that took place in painting, tapestry, and decorated faience from about 1630-1640 onwards. Fashion increasingly favored simple, pellucid designs and decorative qualities over the additive, "busy" patterns of previous generations. The ultimate direction of this trend was a change in wall decoration that was necessarily averse to the cumulative display of pictures. By the 1660s already, the fashion for gilded leather hangings had begun to spread in more elegant interiors, as can be seen in the background of paintings by Pieter de Hooch and Cornelis de Man. Framed pictures clearly did not suit this decor. My hypothesis is that the trend toward "classical" qualities led to the diminished importance of paintings in the decorative schemes of upper-class rooms. Eventually, this change in fashion filtered down to less wealthy homes. The result was a shrinking in the market for paintings. A secondary hypothesis is that the number of paintings declined faster than the value of collections, as consumers began to collect fewer but better pictures (again as part of the process of simplification and clarification). These trends probably got their start in the 1660s when Vermeer in Delft and Frans van Mieris in Leyden, following the earlier lead of Gerard Dou, developed a clientele for minutely painted, highly expensive pictures. Statistical evidence capable of verifying these hypotheses would have to be sought in the inventories of wealthier citizens whose collections were formed in the 1660s and 1670s, most of whom did not die and leave estates until the late 1670s and 1680s, beyond the period of the present investiga-

[j]Johannes Jordaens the Younger enjoyed some reputation in the seventeenth century but is completely forgotten today. Bramer and Louis Elsevier were inactive by this date. Johannes Verkolje registered in the guild (coming from Amsterdam!) only in 1673.

tion. It is hardly necessary to add that the economic stagnation that followed the disastrous French invasion of Holland in 1672 also contributed to the final decline of painting in Delft.

It is not only the decoration of people's homes that had changed by the 1670s: the structure of society had also been altered since the time when the arts started blooming in the 1630s and 1640s. The records of Delft notaries were no longer filled with depositions by and about tailors, pinmakers, ship's carpenters, and other ordinary craftsmen. It is as if the role in society of common individuals had shrunk and the ranks of the lower middle class been depleted. I do not have sufficient data on estates or tax payments to prove the point, but it looks very much as if the distribution of wealth and privilege had become more unequal.

In the earlier period a loosely structured society in which talented individuals born in handicraft masters' families had easy access to educated upper-class people helped to create a favorable environment for the development of the arts. The Guild of St. Lucas itself was a microcosm of Delft society, where upper-class citizens (such as the painters Willem van Kerckhoven, Adriaen Fransz. van der Dussen, and Pieter Groenewegen in the 1620s) mixed with illiterate painters of furniture and glassmakers with calloused hands. That even the apprentices in the guild counted for something in this community is shown by their participation in the process of amending the guild letter.[15] There were of course obstacles to a man's rise in this society, but the obstacles to progress were less social than economic. (Women, on the other hand, probably suffered at least as much from social as from economic disabilities.)

Just as the generation of technical progress in industrial societies is favored by a competitive, open-ended social structure in which individuals are exposed to a variety of influences, so innovation in the arts feeds on a multiplicity of interactive contacts among carriers of ideas and on direct access to a wide variety of art products. Master painters in Delft had contacts with other trades not only through meetings of the guild but also, more directly, via the services they supplied to other crafts. The less talented or fortunate among them worked regularly as designers of tapestries in the works of Franchoys Spierinx and Karel van Mander the Younger or as decorators in the numerous delftware potteries. These opportunities provided a minimum level of earnings that reduced the risks of entering the profession.

Cross-fertilization took place both between crafts in Delft and among artists belonging to different guilds in more or less widely separated towns. Delft in its heyday was wonderfully situated to facilitate contacts among artists and to enable young people to view works of art in the other major towns of Holland at a moderate cost. It was connected by horse-drawn barges, called *trekschuiten,* directly to The Hague, Leyden, Maasluis, and Rotterdam, indirectly (after one or more transfers) to all the major towns of Holland. There were also easy connections, via sailboat across the Zuider Zee, with the *trekschuit* network of Friesland.[15] Rotterdam was three hours and Leyden four hours away by the same means of transport.[16] Fares were very low. In the 1660s it cost 3.6 penningen to go by barge to The Hague (a little more than one-hundredth of a gulden), 5 stuivers to Rotterdam (one-fourth of a gulden), and 7 stuivers 2 penningen to Leyden (about one-third of a gulden).[17] To travel all the way from Amsterdam to Rotterdam (via Delft), which took about thirteen hours, a passenger had to pay less than a gulden-and-a-half, roughly a day's work for a semiskilled *knecht* in a delftware shop.[18] No wonder the traffic of artists in and out of Delft was so intense.

Among the more important out-of-town artists who left a mark of their passage in Delft's notarial records may be cited the painters Adrian van der Venne, Moses van Uyttenbroek, Jan Baptist van Fornenburgh, and Jan Steen (all from The Hague), Hendrick Vroom and Pieter de Grebber (from Haarlem), Jan van Goyen (from Leyden), Adam Pijnacker (from Schiedam), and Gerard ter Borch (from an undetermined place),[k] the sculptors Hendrick and Pieter Keyser and Rombout Verhulst (from Amsterdam). Some of the artists who left Delft in the outward migration that depleted the ranks of the community in the 1650s and 1660s came back for an occasional visit (Pieter de Hooch, Heyndrick van der Burch, Simon de Vlieger). Delft artists also travelled, as far as France and Italy or as close to home as The Hague. Johannes Vermeer, to cite only one famous case, is known to have signed documents in Amsterdam and Gouda; he was also invited to The Hague to give his expert advice on Italian pictures (in 1672),[19] even though he could have seen only very few Italian originals in Delft and he had probably never visited Italy. The fact that artistic motifs and stylistic influences traveled so quickly from Delft

[k]On Ter Borch's visit to Delft in April 1653, perhaps to attend Vermeer's wedding, see J. M. Montias, "New Documents on Vermeer and His Family," *Oud-Holland* 91 (1977):281; and idem, "Vermeer and His Milieu: Conclusion of an Archival Study," *Oud-Holland* 94 (1980):47. The artist was last noted in Amsterdam in 1648. He probably spent some time in The Hague in the early 1650s.

to other places and back again also testifies to the intensity of the traffic in people and the trade in goods.[1]

So much for the factors that stimulated the supply of high-quality art. For art to flourish, there also had to be a vigorous demand for the products of the artists who were trained in Delft or immigrated there. Since traditional princely and ecclesiastic patronage was of minor importance, artists had to rely on a more or less anonymous market demand, on the clientele of master craftsmen and small merchants as well as the burgher-noblesse. One may quibble—I *did* quibble—about the precise status of craftsmen, such as the baker who bought paintings from Vermeer; the fact remains that this baker and others belonging to his social class did buy works of art. It is a commonplace in the field of Dutch art history that the importance of this clientele in shaping market demand steered the fashion in subject matter away from mythologies drawn from classical literature to realistic land-scape, still-life, and genre. The presently unanswerable question that has already been raised in the first part of these conclusions is whether this trend was perhaps less pronounced in Delft than elsewhere, owing to a legacy of humanistic traditions. However that may be, I am confident that the favorable conjunction of supply and demand factors that I have described accounts in large part for the creation, during a span scarcely exceeding one generation of a great deal of art that has withstood the test of time.

[1]All these cross-influences are only beginning to be studied. On the exchange of artistic ideas between Frans van Mieris in Leyden and Johannes Vermeer in Delft, for example, see Albert Blankert, *Vermeer of Delft: Complete Edition of the Paintings* (Oxford: Phaidon, 1978), p. 4 and Otto Naumann, *Frans van Mieris the Elder* (Doornspijk, Holland: Davaco Publishers, 1981).

APPENDICES

APPENDIX A

TABLE A.1
Painters Listed in the Master Book by 1613

Name	Specialty	Year of Birth	Year of Death	Origin
Oil Painters				
Michiel Jansz. Mierevelt	portraits	1567	1641	Delft
Huybrecht Jacopsz. [Grimani]	portraits	c.1563	1631	Delft*
Willem Willemsz. Luyt	*kladschilder*	n.a.	1625†	Delft*
Jan Gerbrantsz. de Jong	portraits	c.1573	1648‡	Delft*
Cornelis Jacopsz. Delft	still-lifes	c.1571	1643	Gouda
Pieter Heynderickx Molshoeck	amateur*	n.a.	1624	n.a.
Jacob Woutersz. Vosmaer	flowers	1584	1641	Delft
Hans Joordaen	"histories"	c.1560	1630	Antwerp*
Harman van Bolgersteyn	flowers	c.1585	1641	Delft*
Jan Willemsz. Decker	"histories"	c.1553	1632	Gouda
Reyer Isbrantsz. Crabmoes	amateur*	c.1578	1635	n.a.
Pieter Adriaensz. den Dorst	"histories"	n.a.	1620	Delft*
Abraham van der Hoef	"histories"	1576	1621	Delft*
Willem Jansz. Decker	landscapes	n.a.	1624	Rotterdam*
Sybrandt Balkenende	landscapes	n.a.	1627	Rotterdam*
Jacob Molyn	*kladschilder*	c.1575	1649	Delft*
Pieter Stael	landscapes	c.1575	1622	Maastricht*
Rochus Jacopsz. Delft	portraits	n.a.	1617	Gouda*
Karel Vermander	tapestry designs	1579	1623	Kortryk
Arent van Reijnoij	amateur*	c.1580	1624	Delft*

Name	Specialty	Birth	Death/active	Location
Jan Cornelis Schoonhove	n.a.	n.a.	1642§	n.a.
Olivier Willemsz. [Couwyn]	n.a.	n.a.	n.a.	n.a.
Claes Hals	n.a.	n.a.	1624*	n.a.
Marijnis Cornelisz. [van der Plaat]	artist-painter*	c.1592	1626*	n.a.
Aryen Barthelmeesz. Rypevelt‖	n.a.	n.a.	1644	n.a.
Jan Ghoosens van Dulleve	n.a.	n.a.	post-1628	n.a.
Jan Pietersz.	n.a.	n.a.	n.a.	n.a.
Cornelis Claesz. Schol	kladschilder	n.a.	pre-1623	n.a.
Bruijn Jansz.	n.a.	n.a.	n.a.	n.a.
Andries Corstiaensz. [de Coninck]	"histories"	n.a.	1630	n.a.
Abram Jansz.	n.a.	n.a.	post-1628	n.a.
Jan Pietersz. van Ghijlt	"histories"	n.a.	post-1625	The Hague
Cornelis Damen [Rietwijck]	portraits	c.1590	1660	n.a.
Sijmon Joordaen	landscapes	c.1585	pre-1640	Antwerp*.
Maerten van Tol	n.a.	n.a.	n.a.	Leyden
Willem Jacobsz. Delff	engraver	1580	1638	Delft
Pieter Bronckhorst	"histories"	1588	1661	Delft*
Jacob Fransz. Musscher	"histories"*	n.a.	1623	Antwerp*
Claes Jacopsz. [Spierinxhoek]	painter on faience	n.a.	post-1638	n.a.
Jan Augustynsz. [Verlinde]	tapestry designs	c.1593	post-1622	Mechelen
Watercolor Painters				
Pieter Jansz. Vroommans	n.a.	n.a.	1624	Mechelen*
Pieter Pietersz. Vroommans [de oude]	kladschilder	c.1578	post-1641	Flanders
Adriaen Hondecoter	n.a.	n.a.	n.a.	Mechelen*
Franchoys Verhulst	Tapestry designs	n.a.	1624	Mechelen*
Jan Jansz. Schotelmans	kladschilder	n.a.	pre-1624	Antwerp
Hans Verlinden	Tapestry designs	n.a.	1624	Mechelen*
Cornelis Pastinocx	n.a.	n.a.	c.1630	Flanders

SOURCES: Obreen, Archief I:4–11; U. Thieme and F. Becker, *Allgemeines Lexicon der Bildenden Künstler*, 37 vols. (Leipzig: F. Engelmann, 1907–1950). Additional sources of information not available (or incorrectly given) in Thieme-Becker follow. Huybrecht Jacopsz.: sixty years old,

19 January 1623 (Records of Notary Herman Jansz. van der Ceel, no. 1638). Jan Gerbrantsz. de Jong: forty years old, 23 May 1613 (Records of notary Henrick Vockestaert, no. 1577); death (?), Camer van Charitate, "Opperste Kleed Boek," no. 72, 1648. Pieter Molshoeck: death date, Delft, Municipal Archives, "Register van de doden begraven"; his birth year must have been before 1560 since he was apprenticed as early as 1572 (Thieme-Becker, 19:150). Herman von Bolgersteyn: forty-six years old, 9 January 1631 (Records of Notary Willem van Assendelft, no. 1856); died shortly before 13 April 1641 when his death donation was received (Camer van Charitate, "Opperste Kleed Boek," no. 71, fol. 68). Jan Willemsz. Decker: buried 6 August 1632 ("Register van de doden begraven"). Reyer Crabmoes: forty-four years old, 11 February 1623 (Records of Notary Gerard Camerling, no. 1650 II); he was buried 9 September 1635 ("Register van de doden begraven"). Pieter den Dorst: death *boedel*, with titles of his paintings, Orphan chamber, no. 500. Abraham van der Hoef: birth and death year are given in Dirck van Bleyswiick, *Beschryinge der Stadt Delft* (Delft, 1667). p. 845. Sybrandt Balkenende: a landscape by this artist was in the *boedel* of Arent Jansz. van Straten, dated 1 October 1651 (Orphan chamber, *boedel* no. 2016). Jacob Molyn: fifty-two years old, 13 July 1627 (Records of Notary Willem de Langue, no. 1685), buried on 2 May 1649 ("Register van de doden begraven"). Arent van Reijnoij: forty years old, 14 November 1620 (Records of Notary Gerard Camerling, no. 70, fol. 142). Martjnis Cornelisz. [van der Plaat]: slated to deliver paintings in 1621 to meet debt obligations (Orphan chamber, *boedel* no. 909 III); his death in 1626 is noted in the "Opperste Kleed Boek" for that year. Aryen Rypevelt: thirty-one yers old, 21 October 1623 (Records of Notary Herman Jonsz. van der Ceel, no. 1638); buried 25 March 1644 ("Register van de doden begraven"). Jan Ghoosens van Dulleve (alias Dulmen): painter and glass-engraver, *boedel*, Orphan chamber, no. 516; still alive, as painter in Leyden in 1628 (Records of Notary Jan de Roon, no. 1629). Cornelis Schol: his widow, who "continued" [the business], according to a note next to her late husband's name in the master list, is mentioned in 1623 (orphan chamber, *boedel* no. 1263). Andries Corstiaensz. [de Coninck]: buried 10 October 1630 ("Register van de doden begraven"). Abram Jansz: witness, 29 November 1628 (Records of Notary Henrick Vockestaert, no. 1574). Jan Pietersz. van Ghijlt: remarries as widower, 24 May 1625 (Delft, Municipal Archives, "Legger van de persoonen die haer begaven in den H. echtenstaat"). Cornelis Damen [Rietwijck]: fifty-eight years old, 29 September 1648 (Records of Notary Cornelis Pietersz. Bleiswijck, no. 1901); died on 29 September 1660 (Orphan chamber, *boedel* no. 1428). Maerten van Tol: probably not identical with Maerten Hendricksz. van Tol who registered on 18 April 1625 (Appendix A, Table A.2); this Van Tol became a citizen of Delft coming from Leyden in 1612 Delft, Municipal Archives, ("Poyrter regyster"). Jacob Fransz. Musscher: believed to be identical with the painter "Jacques Francois" who died 29 August 1623 ("Register van de doden begraven"). Claes Jacobsz. [Spierinxhoek]: painter and silk merchant, sold a house on 31 December 1638 (A. Bredius handwritten notes, R.K.D.). Jan Augustynsz.: thirty-one years old, 26 March 1624, working for Aert Spierincx, tapestry-maker (Records of Notary Herman Jansz. van der Ceel, no. 1639). Pieter Pietersz. Vroommans [de oude]: fifty-nine years old, 13 March 1637 (Records of Notary Willem van Assendelft, no. 1859); drew up his testament on 11 June 1641, mentioning his sons Pieter and Abraham (Records of Notary Willem de Langue, no. 1690); in 1625, Pieter

Pietersz. *schilder* was paid six gulden for painting a mantelpiece (Orphan Chamber, *boedel* no. 1815); this in all likelihood was Pieter Vroommans the Elder. Franchoys Verhulst: sponsored the tapestry designer Pieter Pastinocx (Table A.2 below) when the latter entered the guild on 5 May 1613 and is believed to have been a tapestry designer himself; buried on 25 November 1624 ("Register van de doden begraven," as "Franchois van Hulst"). Jan Jansz. Schotelmans (alias Schooten or van der Schoot), illiterate, died before 13 December 1624 when his widow is mentioned (Records of Notary Cornelis Coeckebakker, no. 1613). Hans Verlinden, apparently recorded twice in the master list, was buried on 7 February 1624 ("Register van de doden begraven," as "Hans van der Linden"); it is possible (though not likely) that Jan Augustynsz. (Verlinde), listed among the oil painters, is identical with Hans Verlinden; in the counts for Tables 6.1 and 6.2, I have assumed they were distinct individuals. Cornelis [Mathysz.] Pastinocx: painter and later baker, bought a house in the first half of 1629 on behalf of his wife (Camer van Charitate, "Reckeningen van de duijt op de gulden," vol. 56, fol. 32); she in turn, already as a widow, sold the house on 6 February 1634 (Records of Notary Willem van Assendelft, no. 1858).

NOTE: Names are spelled as they are in the original document, transcribed in F.D.O. Obreen, *Archief voor Nederlandsche Kunstgeschiedenis*, 7 vols. (Rotterdam, 1877–1890), 1:4–7.

*Inferred from a source but not known with certainty.

†Said to be "formerly painter" (*eertyts schilder*), records of Notary Cornelis Ingelo, no. 1634c, 8 February 1618.

‡Became an attorney (*procureur*) by 1617 and seems to have ceased to paint. It is not certain that the entry in this name in the "Opperste Kleed Boeken," no. 72, January 1648, refers to the former painter.

§A contribution was made to the "Opperste Kleed" on behalf of the late organist Jan Cornelisz. Schoonhoven on 20 August 1622. I have presumed that this was the former painter of that name.

‖Became an innkeeper in the 1630s. He was innkeeper of De Oranjenboom on 12 May 1640 (Records of Notary Govert Rota, no. 1976).

TABLE A.2

Painters Inscribed in the Guild, January 1613–June 1649

Name	Date of Inscription	Specialty	Year of Birth	Year of Death	Origin
Pieter Pastinocx	5 May 1613	tapestry designs	c.1568	1641	Mechelen
Bartelmees van Bassen	21 Oct. 1613	"perspectives"	c.1590	1652	Flanders*
Abram Bonaert	21 Oct. 1613	tapestry deisgns	n.a.	post-1630	Oudenaerden (Flanders)
Jan Daemen Cool	7 Mar. 1614	portraits	c.1589	1660	Rotterdam
Hans Claesz. Hondekoete	c.1614	tapestry designs	n.a.	1620	Flanders
Steven Willemsz. van Oudenhuijse	c.1614	n.a.	n.a.	n.a.	n.a.
Jonas [Jansz.] Verburcht	c.1614	tapestry designs	c.1595	1660	Delft*
Jan Claesz. van Havelem†	7 Apr. 1615	portraits	n.a.	post-1627	not Delft*
Willem Jansz. Ploij‡	14 Oct. 1615	portraits	c.1584	post-1665	Delft*
Willem Willemsz. van der Vliet	c.1615	portraits	c.1584	1642	Delft
Rytsert Jansz.	3 July 1615	kladschilder*	n.a.	post-1627	Dordrecht*
Enghel Jansz. Rooswijk	c.1616	"histories"	c.1583	post-1649	Haarlem*
David [Fransz.] van Hoorenbeeck	18 Oct. 1617	kladschilder*	c.1595	post-1629	Delft*
Jan Dircksz. van Nes	10 Oct. 1618	portraits	n.a.	1650	Delft
Gerrit Jacobsz. Molijn	24 Oct. 1618	kladschilder	n.a.	post-1644	Delft*
Dirck Cornelisz.	1 July 1619	n.a.	n.a.	n.a.	Delft
Pouwels Weyts	18 Aug. 1620	art dealer	n.a.	1629	Dordrecht
Jan Jansz. Valckenier	28 Oct. 1620	kladschilder*	c.1592	post-1650	Delft*
Abram Pietersz. Vroomans	13 Sept. 1621	artist-painter*	n.a.	pre-1662	n.a.
Anthonis Palmedes	6 Dec. 1621	genre	1601	1673	Delft*

Name	Date	Subject			Place
Adriaen Fransz. van der Dussen	8 Aug. 1622	n.a.	n.a.	n.a.	Delft
Willem Arensz. [or Adamsz.] Kerckho(o)ven	8 Aug. 1622	still-lifes	c.1597	post-1647	Delft*
Solomon Tonisz.	5 Sept. 1622	n.a.	n.a.	n.a.	Delft*
Pieter Hovenaer	15 Oct. 1622	portraits	n.a.	post-1637	Rotterdam*
Joris Gerritsz. [van Lier]	29 May 1623	flowers	c.1589	1656	Delft
Abram Woutersz.	24 July 1623	painter in Delfshaven	n.a.	n.a.	Delft*
Huyg Dircksz. van der Douw	24 July 1623	painter on faience	c.1598	post-1640	Delft*
Pieter van Nas [van Asch]	24 July 1623	landscapes	1602	1678	Delft
Maerten Ariensz.	16 Oct. 1623	painter in Delfshaven	n.a.	n.a.	Delft*
Willem [Willemsz.] van den Bondel	c.1623	landscapes	c.1575	c.1653	Brussels
Heyndrick [Heyndricksz.] Tol	9 Nov. 1624	artist-painter*	n.a.	1635	Delft*
Jiless Jilesse de Berch	15 Nov. 1624	still-lifes	n.a.	1669	Delft*
Boudewijn Ferdinandisz.	15 Nov. 1624	n.a.	n.a.	1625	Delft*
Claes Engelsz.	18 Apr. 1625	tapestry designs	n.a.	n.a.	Delft*
Jacob Jansz. van Velsen	18 Apr. 1625	genre	c.1597	1656	Delft*
Maerten [Hendricksz.] van Tol	18 Apr. 1625	artist-painter*	n.a.	post-1637	Delft*
Pieter Pietersz. Bemont	27 Oct. 1625	artist-painter*	n.a.	n.a.	Delft*
Willem Jansz. [Halleman]*	29 Oct. 1625	n.a.	c.1605	post-1636	Delft*
Pieter Groenewegen	30 Mar. 1626	landscapes	c.1600	1658	Delft*
Abram Lambrechtsz. Stulling	21 Sept. 1626	artist-painter*	n.a.	1639	Delft*
[Adriaen Jaspersz.] Pelleman	16 Oct. 1626	landscapes	n.a.	post-1651	Delft*
Dirck van der Mast	30 Aug. 1627	flowers	n.a.	1662	Delft*
Corstiaen Coubergen [Couwenbergh]	25 Oct. 1627	"histories"	1604	1667	Delft

TABLE A.2 (continued)
Painters Inscribed in the Guild, January 1613–June 1649

Name	Date of Inscription	Specialty	Year of Birth	Year of Death	Origin
Palmedes Pallamedes	25 Oct. 1627	battles	1607	1638	Delft*
Servaes Nouts	29 Oct. 1627	n.a.	n.a.	post-1640	Delft*
Jochum [Aelbrechtsz.] de Vries	10 Nov. 1628	seascapes	n.a.	1670	Speeck (Vrieslandt)
Jacob Fransse [van der Merck]*	11 Nov. 1628	genre	c.1610	1664	SGravendeel
Jacob van Geel	1628*	landscapes	c.1585	post-1638	Middelburg*
Leendert Bramer	30 Apr. 1629	"histories"	1596	1674	Delft
Pieter Aelbrechtsz. Schoonhave[n]	3 June 1630	engraver	n.a.	post-1649	Delft
Andries Pietersz. van der Linde	5 Sept. 1631	landscapes	n.a.	1664	not Delft
Jan Spangaert	18 Mar. 1632	genre	c.1590	pre-1664	Amsterdam
Evert van Aelst	15 Apr. 1632	still-lifes	1602	1657	Delft
[Balthasar] van der Ast	22 June 1632	still-lifes	c.1593	1657	Middelburg*
Aberam de Coege	11 June 1632	art dealer	pre-1600	post-1680	Haarlem
Heinderick Willemsz. van Vliet§	22 June 1632	"perspectives"	1611–1612	1675	Delft
Pieter Finson	12 Nov. 1632	artist-painter*	n.a.	n.a.	Schiedam*
[Jacob] Pynas	12 Nov. 1632	"histories"	c.1585	post-1648	Haarlem*
Symon de Vleyger	18 Oct. 1634	seascapes	1601	1653	Rotterdam
Pieter Gerritsz. [Vijg]	23 Oct. 1634	painter in Delfshaven	n.a.	post-1650	not Delft
Adryaen Lynschoote[n]	c.1635	"histories"	c.1608	1677	Delft
Willem van den Landen	30 May 1635	battles	n.a.	post-1650	Delft*
Pieter Pietersen Vroomans de Jonge	16 Oct. 1635	"histories"	n.a.	post-1654	n.a.
Jan Heyndericxs [Verpoort]*	1 Sept. 1636	kladschilder	n.a.	post-1650	Delft*
Harme[n] Eeverts [Steenwijck]	18 Nov. 1636	still-lifes	c.1612	post-1656	Delft
Gabriel Alderhuysen	28 May 1638	n.a.	n.a.	post-1660	Delft*
Mateus de Berg	20 Dec. 1638	"histories"	n.a.	1687	Delft*

		painter in Delfshaven			Delfshaven*
Joris Ariensz. Besaen	21 Dec. 1638	n.a.	n.a.	n.a.	n.a.
Geeraert van Hoeckgeest	22 July 1639	"perspectives"	c.1600	1661	The Hague
Henderick Jillesen [van Beijeren]	10 Oct. 1639	n.a.	pre-1600	post-1642	Delft*
Abram Vosmaer	31 Oct. 1639	still-lifes	1618	post-1660	Delft*
Jan Haels	23 Apr. 1640	n.a.	n.a.	n.a.	not Delft*
Isack Junis	7 Oct. 1640	battles	n.a.	post-1663	Delft
Wterant [Post]	4 Oct. 1640	kladschilder	c.1603	1670	Delft*
Jacob Pouwelsz. [van Schooten]	17 Dec. 1640	kladschilder	n.a.	post-1674	Leyden
Claes Bronckhorst	26 Mar. 1641	still-lifes	1611	post-1651	Delft*
Jacobus Delft	15 Oct. 1641	portraits	1619	1661	Delft
Esaias de Lint	25 Oct. 1641	faiencier	n.a.	n.a.	n.a.
Pieter Marijnijs Plaet	c.1642	n.a.	n.a.	n.a.	n.a.
Tomas Tomasz. [van Esch]	14 Apr. 1642	"perspectives"	c.1617	n.a.	not Delft
Emanewel [de] Witte	23 June 1642	still-lifes	c.1622	1692	Alkmaar*
Adam Pick	16 Oct. 1642	still-lifes	n.a.	pre-1666	Delft*
Pieter [Evertsz.] Steenwijck	10 Nov. 1642	genre	1621	post-1654	Delft*
Cornelis de Man	29 Dec. 1642	kladschilder	n.a.	1706	Delft
Willem van Odekerken	12 Oct. 1643	portraits	n.a.	1677	The Hague*
Cristiaen Kaeskooper	12 Oct. 1643	kladschilder	n.a.	n.a.	Delft||
Adrijaen Cornelisz. Delff	16 Oct. 1643	n.a.	n.a.	post-1663	Delft*
Pieter Clansius#	26 Oct. 1643	still-lifes*	c.1620	n.a.	not Delft*
Cornelis Marynse van der Plaet	9 Nov. 1643	still-lifes	1627	post-1658	Delft*
Willem van Alst	9 Nov. 1643	faiencier	n.a.	1679	Delft
Jan Hanse de Milde	12 Dec. 1643	kladschilder	c.1620	n.a.	Delft*
Jan Molyn	4 Jan. 1644	seascapes	c.1605	post-1688	Delft*
Heerman Witmont	27 June 1644	seascapes	n.a.	1674	not Delft
Nijclaes Vosmaer	12 June 1645	n.a.	n.a.	1664	Maeslandt*
Jakob Pieterse van der Burgh	15 Oct. 1645	artist-painter	c.1627	n.a.	Delft*
Pieter Leenderse van der Vin	7 Nov. 1645			1655	

Name	Date of Inscription	Specialty	Year of Birth	Year of Death	Origin
Ary Jacobsz. Kortendoeck	14 May 1646	*kladschilder*	n.a.	post-1659	not Delft
Antonij Marynisse [Beauregard]	11 June 1646	still-lifes	n.a.	n.a.	not Delft
[Paulus] Potter	6 Aug. 1646	landscapes	1625	1654	Enkhuysen
Jan Gabrielsz. Songe	3 Sept. 1646	landscapes	n.a.	n.a.	Delft
Louwijs Elsevijer	3 Sept. 1646	landscapes	c.1618	1675	Leiden
Simmon Fanger[t]	16 Oct. 1047	portraits	1625	1665	Delft*
Cornelis van der Voort	5 Oct. 1648	n.a.	n.a.	post-1674	not Delft
Heyndrick van der Burgh	25 Jan. 1649	genre	1627	post-1664	Naaldwijk
Jan Denijs [or Danijse]	12 June 1649	painter in Delfs-haven	n.a.	n.a.	not Delft

SOURCES: See Table A.1. Only sources are given below for information not contained (or inaccurately supplied) in Thieme-Becker. Jonas Verburcht (or van der Burch): Thirty-two years old, 26 June 1627 (Records of Notary Adriaan van Twelle, no. 1654) when he worked for the tapestry-maker Aert Spierinx; became a faïence-painter by 1628; was buried on 30 June 1660 ("Register van de doden begraven"). Jan Claesz. van Havelem (or van Havelaer): "Jan Claesz. *schilder*" claimed six gulden for making a portrait (Orphan Chamber, *boedel* no. 1352; no other painter by the name of Jan Claesz. is known); drew up his testament 15 December 1627 (Records of Notary Adriaen Rijshouck, no. 1818), by which time he had probably given up painting (*schilder* crossed out after his name, 26 September 1626, Records of Notary Guillaume de Graeff, no. 1714). Willem Jansz. Ploij: pair of portraits signed by his name and dated 1665 in photographic files of the Rijksbureau voor Kunsthistorische Documentatie in The Hague; sixty-two years old on 10 April 1646 (Records of Notary Schalkius van der Walle, no. 1971); mentioned in Delft 8 September 1661 (Records of notary Cornelis Pietersz. Bleiswijck, no. 1903); he is frequently called Willem Jansz. *schilder*, whence confusion arises with Willem Jansz. Decker and Willem Jansz. Halleman, whose last names are also frequently omitted. Rytsert Jansz.: inventory on his wife's death, 14 August 1625 (Records of Notary Jan de Roon, no. 1626); whereupon he apparently moved to Schiedam (ibid., no. 1628, 3 December 1627). Enghel Rooswijk: fifty-seven years old, 22 August 1640 (Records of notary Gerrit Adriaensz. van der Wel, no. 1939); died before 2 August 1649 when his widow testified (Records of Notary Nicholaes Vrienbergh, no. 2051). David van Hoorenbeeck, made and sold lacquers for paints (Records of Notary Henrick Vockestaert, no. 1585, 7 August 1621); twenty-eight years old on 6 March 1623 (Records of Notary Cornelis Adriaansz. de Roon, no. 1698); apparently became drummer (*tamboryn*) by 1628 and French schoolmaster in Haarlem by 1629 (Records of

Notaries Willem de Langue, no. 1686, 7 June 1628 and Cornelis Coeckebakker, no. 1614, 17 February 1629). Gerrit Molijn: worked with his father Jacob Molijn on painting of and repairs to house of late Michel Miereveld (Orphan Chamber, *boedel*, no. 1197 I, 11 April 1644). Pouwels Weyts: activities as an art dealer are documented in J. M. Montias, "New Documents on Vermeer and His Family," *Oud-Holland* 91 (1977): 272–73. Jan Valckenier: probably not an artist-painter; fifty-eight years old, 30 June 1650 (Records of Notary Adriaen van der Block, no. 1750). Abram Vroomans: connections with Leonaert Bramer and Abram Stulling and his election as headman of the guild in 1652 suggest he may have been an artist-painter. Willem Kerckho(o)ven: cited as *schilder*, twenty-four years old, 31 July 1621 (Records of Notary Jan de Roon, no. 1024); called Willem Adamsz. in master list and Willem Arensz. in "Register van alle de niewe meesters" but the latter is probably correct since the only known Adam van Kerckhoven was born circa 1599, whereas Adriaen (Adamsz.) Kerckhoven was born circa 1562, which would be consistent with Willem's birth year; Willem Adriaensz. Kerckhoven (no profession cited), forty-six years old, was a witness on 2 February 1647 (Records of Notary Adriaen van der Block, no. 1747); a still-life by Kerckhoven was listed in the inventory of Willem Verhoeff in Delfshaven (27 May 1658, Orphan Chamber, *boedel* no. 1776). Joris Gerritsz. [van Lier]: painted flowers (Orphan Chamber, *boedel* no. 1847); fifty years old, 18 July 1639; sixty years old, 8 September 1647 (Records of Notary Adriaen van der Block, no. 1739); buried 8 January 1656 ("Register van de doden begraven)." Hugh Dircksz. van der Douw: bethrothed 24 March 1629 ("Legger van de persoonen die haer begaven in den H. echten staat"); by 1630 he had become a painter on faience, and is noted in his craft until 1640 when he was said to be forty-two years old (Records of Notary Guillaume de Graaff, no. 1719, 25 February 1640). Heynderick Tol: was buried on 2 April 1635 ("Register van de doden begraven"). Boudewijn Ferdinandisz.: was buried in Delft on 3 March 1625 ("Register van de doden begraven"). Jacob van Velsen: "Jacob Jansz. *schilder*" (signs Jacob Jansz. Velss), twenty years old, 3 October 1617 (Records of Notary Cornelis Ingelo, no. 1634c.). Maertin van Tol: was a member of the guild in Dordrecht in 1637 (Obreen, *Archief*, 1:200). Pieter Bemont: probably an artist-painter, in view of his relatively wealthy origin and of the fact that his brother Franck Pietersz., who never registered in the guild, apparently worked with or for the painter Hubert Grimani (Records of notary Guillaume de Graeff, no. 1714, 9 May 1629 and Willem van Assendelft, no. 1856, 19 July 1630); confusion on the death date of Pieter Pietersz. is possible due to the fact that his father and perhaps his own son used the same name. Willem Jansz. [Halleman]: *schilder*, was twenty-nine years old on 2 April 1634 (Records of Notary Willem van Assendelft, no. 1858); and witnessed a document on 3 February 1636 (Records of Notary Cornelis Adriaansz. de Roon, no. 1700). Abram Stulling: died on a ship in the Pacific Ocean circa 1639 ("three years ago," according to a document of 13 August 1642, Records of Notary Jacob Spoors, no 1673). [Adriaen Jaspersz.] Pelleman: witnessed the testament of the widow of the painter and merchant Adriaen van Rypevelt, 18 January 1652 (Records of notary Melchior van der Borcht, no. 2040); two landscapes by Pelleman were noted in an inventory dated 11 February 1632 (Records of Notary Guillaume der Graeff, no. 1715); and another in the inventory of C. van der Heuvel who died on 15 February 1631 (Records of notary Willem van Assendelft, no. 1856). Dirck van der Mast: signed flower piece, dated 1656, in manner of Balthasar van der Ast, illustrated in Laurens J. Bol, *Holländische Maler des 17. Jahrhunderts nahe den grossen Meistern: Landschaften und Stilleben* (Braunschweig: Klinkhard and Bierman, 1969), p. 47. Buried 24 August 1662 ("Register van de doden begraven"). Servaes Nouts:

witness, 7 February 1640 (Records of Notary Willem de Langue, no. 1689). Jochum de Vries: was buried in Delft on 25 January 1670 ("Register van de doden begraven"). Jacob Franszen [van Sgravendael]: probably identical with Jacob Fransz. [van der Merck], born in Sgravendeel c.1610. Van der Merck is known to have been in Delft in 1631, when, according to the master list of 1613–1649, he actually left town. Pieter Aelbrechtsz. Schoonhave (or Schoonhoven): engraver (plaetsnyder), yet in the master list of painters; last cited 9 May 1649 (Records of Notary Willem de Langue, no. 1694). Andries van der Linde: painter and pastor of the Lutheran Church in Delft; noted in Delft from 1625 on; was buried on 29 April 1664 ("Register van de doden begraven"). Aberam de Coege: probably born before 1600 in view of his marriage in Haarlem in 1620. Pieter Finson (Vinson): active in Delfshaven at least since 1631, presumed to have been an artist-painter on the basis of a contract published in Oud-Holland 31 (1913):264–65. Adryaen [Cornelisz.] Lynschoote[n]: born in 1607–1608 according to Van Bleyswijck, Beschryvinge der stadt Delft, Delft, 1667 p. 859; buried 26 July 1677 ("Register van de doden begraven"); his death inventory, dated 2 August 1677, was published in Abraham Bredius, Künstler-inventare, 7 vols. (The Hague: Martinus Nijhoff, 1915–1921), 6, 1924–25. Pieter Pietersz. Vroomans de Jonge: drew up his testament on 15 April 1654 (Oud-Holland 12 (1894):170). Jan Heyndricxs [Verpoort]: paid three gulden as entrance to the guild as a master's son; presumed to be the son of Heyndrick Jansz. [Verpoort] who registered in the guild as a bookseller; he is the first painter to be called kladschilder in the register of new members of the guild; he was still listed as an active member in the 1650 master list. Harme[n] Eevertsz. [Steenwijck]: the entry in the register of new masters reads "Harme Eevertsz. brillemaecker" (Obreen, Archief, 1:32); the spectacle-maker Evert Harmansz. van Steenwijck is frequently noted in Delft from the 1590s to his death in 1654 (e.g., the important family document on the secession of Evert Harmansz. van Steenwijck, dated 28 April 1654, signed by Pieter Steenwijck, in the Records of Notary Jan Jorisz. van Ophoven, no. 1951); the last document in which Harman Steenwijck appears is dated 6 January 1656 (Records of Notary Cornelis Pietersz. Bleiswijck, no. 1902). Gabriel Alderhuysen (or Elderhuysen): mentioned in The Hague, 12 November 1660 (Bredius, handwritten notes in the R.K.D.); he already lived in The Hague when he drew up his testament in Delft on 29 January 1640 (Records of Notary Adriaen van der Block, no. 1740). Henderick Jillesen [Gillisz.] [van Beijeren]: paid rest of his entrance dues as "Heijnderick van Beijeren, living in 't booter huys," on 26 March 1640; called glassmaker in 1637 (Bredius, Künstler-inventare 4:1,165); and bought ebonywood May 1640 (Records of Notary Cornelis Pietersz. Bleiswijck, no. 1907); father of the painter Abraham van Beyeren who was born in 1620. Isack Junis: son of the Protestant minister Isack Junius; apparently identical with the individual of this name said to be living in Amsterdam on 6 September 1663 (Records of Notary Gerard van Assendelft, no. 2130); and who became a notary's clerk in Delft in 1664 (e.g., Records of Notary Frans Boogert, no. 2005, 18 April 1664). Wterant [Post]: called kladschilder, 4 April 1660 (Records of Notary Johannes Ranck, no. 2105). Jacob Pouwelsz. [van Schooten]: mentioned from 1635 (witness, 8 December, Records of Notary Willem van Assendelft, no. 1858) to 10 May 1674 when his wife (not widow) is cited (Records of Notary Cornelis Pietersz. Bleiswijck, no. 1916); from the fact that he was illiterate it may tentatively be inferred that he was a kladschilder. Esaias de Lint (or Linde): faiencier in Delfshaven, by error (?) included in master list of painters of 1650. Adam Pick: thirty-two years old, 12 May 1654 (Records of Notary Johannes Ranck, no. 2113); the painter Matteus de Berg testified about the son of the "late Adam Pick," 25 June 1666 (Records of Notary Abraham van der Velde, no. 2175). Adriaen Cornelisz. Delff: painted armories, mantelpieces and doors (*Oud-Holland* 42(1925):65). Jan Molijn: about eighteen years old, 20 December 1638 (Records of Notary Willem van Assendelft, no. 1859); fifty-six years old, 7 August 1675 (Records of Notary Roelandus van Edenburgh, no. 2258); painted armories and various types of rough work for the Hoogheemsraadschap of Delfland from 1670 to 1688 (Delft, Archives of the Hoogheemsraadschap van Delfland, Elfde Reckening, no. 798). Jakob Pieterse. van der Burgh: said to be living in Maeslandt when he registered; perhaps the son of Pieter Hendricksz. van der Burgh, mason in Honselaersdijk, presumed uncle of the painter Heyndrick van der Burch (see testimony of Pieter Hendricksz., dated 14 November 1647, Records of Notary Frans Boogert, no. 1994). Pieter Leenderse van der Vin: twenty-eight years old, 27 January 1655 (Records of Notary Johannes Ranck, no. 2113); died before 28 April 1655 (Records of Notary Frans Boogert, no. 2000, 14 May 1655). Ary Jacobsz. Kortendoeck: testament, 30 August 1659 (Records of Notary Johannes Ranck, no. 2104); illiterate (hence probably *kladschilder*). Antonij Marynisse [Beauregard]: his full name is mentioned, as owing six gulden for his entrance fee in the Master List of 1650 (Obreen, *Archief*, 1 p. 48). Heyndrick van der Burgh: baptized as the son of Rochus van der Burgh, in Naaldwijk, in 1627 (communication of Mr. P. Flippo).

NOTE: See Table A.1.

*Inferred from a source but not known with certainty.

†Not "Harelem" as in the Obreen transcription.

‡Not "Verloij" as in the Obreen transcription.

§The patronymic "Willemsz." (instead of Cornelisz.) was set down by the clerk, probably on the assumption that Hendrick was the son of the painter Willem Willemsz. van Vliet (who was actually his uncle).

‖The new entrant was not sure whether he was born in Delft or not but was allowed to pay the lower dues anyway.

#Spelling based on original of master book of 1650.

TABLE A.3
Painters Inscribed in the Guild, 1650-1679

Name	Date of Inscription	Specialty	Year of Birth	Year of Death	Origin
Pieter Ophoven	7 Feb. 1650	n.a.	1628	n.a.	Delft*
Pieter van Tooren	10 Sept. 1650	n.a.	n.a.	n.a.	not Delft
Geertie Moer	c1650	n.a.	n.a.	n.a.	n.a.
Daniel Vosmaer	14 Oct. 1650	landscapes	1622	post-1666	Delft*
Egbert van der Poel	17 Oct. 1650	landscapes	1621	1664	Delft
Coenrat Harmansz. Brouck-man	30 May 1651	clock painter	n.a.	post-1675	Delft*
Dirck Rietwijk	16 Oct. 1651	n.a.	pre-1630	c.1659	Delft*
Aelbrecht Teunisz. Ver-meulen	18 Oct. 1651	compass painter	n.a.	n.a.	Rotterdam*
Pieter Born	30 Sept. 1652	artist-painter	n.a.	post-1675	Delft*
Niclaes Van Rijck	30 Sept. 1652	still-lifes	n.a.	1666	Waelwijck
Kaerel Fabricijus	29 Oct. 1652	"histories"	1622	1654	Middenbeemster
Willem Verschoor	6 Jan. 1653	"histories"	n.a.	1678	Delft*
Johannes Druyf	13 Oct. 1653	kladschilder	n.a.	1664	Delft*
Johannes Vermeer	29 Dec. 1653	genre	1632	1675	Delft
Wilhem Sandersz. Delen	23 Mar. 1654†	kladschilder	n.a.	post-1676	Delft*
Pieter de Hooch	20 Sept. 1655	genre	1629	1684	Rotterdam
Nijkolaes Breda	24 Sept. 1656	art dealer	n.a.	n.a.	Delft*
Adriaen de Stout	12 Oct. 1656	painter in Delfshaven	n.a.	n.a.	not Delft
Johannes van Loo	19 Mar. 1657	artist-painter*	n.a.	post-1676	Delft*
Hans Jordaens [II]	1 Oct. 1657	landscapes	1616	1680	Delft*
Abram van Beijeren	15 Oct. 1657	still-lifes	1620	1690	The Hague

Name	Date	Specialty			
Jasper Seroth	10 Jan. 1661	n.a.	n.a.	n.a.	not Delft
Jacop Corsendonck	4 Apr. 1661	*kladschilder*	n.a.	1675	Delft*
Gedeon Jacobsz‡	2 May 1661	n.a.	n.a.	n.a.	not Delft*
Heinderick Jansz. Verpoort	25 July 1661	*kladschilder**	1635	1671	Delft*
Johannes Coesermans	22 Aug. 166	seascapes	n.a.	n.a.	not Delft
Maerten van der Fuijck	Jan. 1663	n.a.	n.a.	n.a.	Den Briel
Gerrit Clijnk§	24 Sept. 1663	*kladschilder**	n.a.	1681	n.a.
Joris van Cleef	26 Mar. 1665	n.a.	n.a.	post-1668	Delft*
Pouwels Jacobsz. van Schoten	26 Mar. 1665	n.a.	n.a.	n.a.	Delft*
Kornelys Gillysse van der Kloot	26 May 1665	n.a.	n.a.	n.a.	Delft*
Gijsbrecht van der Brugge	20 July 1665	portraits	1633	1730	Leyden
Gerrit van Rinckxhoven	17 Oct. 1665	painter in Delfshaven	n.a.	n.a.	not Delft
Joris Cornelisse van der Block	16 July 1667	n.a.	n.a.	post-1700	n.a.
Abraham Corssendonck	16 July 1668	artist-painter*	n.a.	post-1713*	Delft*
Daniel Verlouw	10 Sept. 1669	n.a.	n.a.	n.a.	not Delft
Gerret Pietersz. Vijg	23 Oct. 1669	n.a.	n.a.	post-1675	Delft*
Antonij Isendoorn	9 Dec. 1669	portraits	c.1625	n.a.	not Delft
Isaac van Wessel	8 Nov. 1670	portraits	n.a.	post-1675	not Delft
Jacobus van Cleef	27 Apr. 1671	n.a.	n.a.	n.a.	Delft*
Jan Verschure	22 June 1671	artist-painter*	1649	1674	not Delft
Adriaen Heindrickse Bouda	14 Sept. 1671	*kladschilder**	n.a.	post-1680	Delft*
Cornelis Adriaensz. van der Kuijt	12 Oct. 1671	n.a.	n.a.	post-1686	Delft*
Jan van der Korst	9 Nov. 1671	n.a.	n.a.	n.a.	Delft*
Pieter Janse van Ruijve[n]	23 May 1672	"histories"	1651	1719	Delft
Johannes Verkolje	19 June 1673	genre	1650	1693	Amsterdam
Jan Kranenburgh	10 Sept. 1674	n.a.	n.a.	n.a.	not Delft
Michiel van Eemst	12 Aug. 1675	painter on faience	n.a.	1684	Haarlem

TABLE A.3 (continued)
Painters Inscribed in the Guild, 1650-1679

Name	Date of Inscription	Specialty	Year of Birth	Year of Death	Origin
Johnannes Elsevier	30 Dec. 1675	artist-painter*	n.a.	1687	Leyden
Jan Willemse van der Spriet	30 Dec. 1675	portraits	n.a.	post-1690	Delft*
Marynes van Vlijet	17 May 1677	n.a.	n.a.	n.a.	Delft*
Arijen Jacobs Corssendonck	9 Aug. 1677	n.a.	c. 1657	post-1680	Delft*
Samuel Baroen	2 Oct. 1679	n.a.	n.a.	n.a.	not Delft*
Joannes Hoendermans	5 Oct. 1679	still-lifes	n.a.	n.a.	Delft*

SOURCES: See Table A.1. Additions and corrections to Thieme-Becker follow. Pieter Ophoven: confusion arises between Pieter Lenertsz. Ophoven, silk merchant, who was born circa 1637 (Records of Notary Frans van Hurck, no. 2097, 13 July 1651) and the painter Pieter Ophoven. It is assumed that the earlier baptismal date in the "Doopboek" (Delft, Municipal Archives, 15 October 1628) was that of the painter. Geertie Moer: in master list of 1650; the only woman listed among the painters in the entire seventeenth century; perhaps the widow of a *kladschilder*; a "Geertsen Moer," midwife, was mentioned on 1 December 1638 (Records of Notary Adriaen van der Block, no. 1738). Daniel Vosmaer: baptized 13 October 1622 ("Doopboek"); in Den Briel, 12 June 1666 (Records of Notary Cornelis Pietersz. Bleiswijck, no. 1911). Coenrat Harmansz. Brouckman: frequently mentioned as a clockmaker from 1640 to 1675, both for his work on clocks in Delft and in The Hague. Dirck Rietwijk: his father, the painter Cornelis Damen Rietwijk, paid five gulden for pen and paper and twenty gulden for board and lodging to a French schoolmaster, presumably for Dirck, in 1637 (Orphan Chamber, *boedel* no. 1274); he was married on 27 April 1652; his widow was mentioned on 12 September 1659 (Records of Notary Cornelis Georgin, no. 2085). Johannes [Marcusz.] Druyf: in November 1661 painted the rough work of the new chamber of the Guild of St. Lucas (J. Soutendam, "Eenige aanteekeningen betreffende Delfsche Kunstenaars," *Nederlandsche Spectator* (1870):11; on 11 February 1665 (Records of Notary Testart van Hasselt, no. 2155), both Druyf and his wife are said to have died "fourteen or fifteen weeks ago in the pesthouse." Wilhem Sandersz. Delen: in the estate papers of Anthony Nieulandt, who died 11 August 1669, a debt of ten gulden owed to the painter is recorded for wages for painting work ("over arbeitsloon van schilderen"); he was also paid for painting work on the house *d'claeuw* in 1671 (Records of Notary Roelandus van Edenburgh, no 2246). Johannes [Aerse] van Loo (or Loon): perhaps a pupil of Louis Elsevier, whose testament he witnessed on 3 October 1650 (Records of Notary Jacob van Santen, no. 2016); as servant of the Guild of St. Lucas (*gildeknecht*), he received the death dues of the bookseller Simon Cloeting who died October 1676 (Orphan Chamber, *boedel* no. 1010). Jacop [Ariensz.] Corsendonck: first registered in the guild (1655) as glassmaker; contracted on 21 October 1656 (before joining the guild as painter but possibly on the strength of the membership of his father, Arijen Jacobsz, who was still active as a *kladschilder* at the time) to paint the inside and the outside of a house (Records of Notary Cornelis Pietersz. Bleiswijck, no. 1909); buried on 13 April 1675 ("Register van de doden begraven"). Heinderick Jansz. Verpoort: thirty-three years old, 15 August 1668 (Records of Notary Johannes Ranck, no. 2121); buried 8 March 1671 ("Register van de doden begraven"); probably continued the business of his father (Jan Heindricksz.) as painter-contractor. Johannes Coesermans: four drawings of seascapes "done with the pen by Coestermans" in one inventory (12 October 1672, Records of Notary Roelandus van Edenburgh, no. 2246); and two seascapes "done with the pen by Coestermans" in another (Records of Notary Roelandus van Oderkercken; painted armories in 1677 (Obreen, *Archief*, 3:200); buried 5 son-in-law and presumed associate of the painter-contractor Willem van Oderkercken; painted armories in 1677 (Obreen, *Archief*, 3:200); buried 5 March 1681 ("Register van de doden begraven"). Pouwels Jacobsz. van Schoten: son of the *kladschilder* Jacob Pouwelsz.; probably identical with the painter "Poulys Jacobsz." who was a pallbearer for Cornelia van Santen (30 November 1668, Records of Notary Frans van Hurck, no. 2101); may have been a genre painter (see the index register of photographs in the Rijksbureau voor Kunsthistorische Documentatie (R.K.D.) in The Hague under this name). Gijsbrecht van der Brugge: recorded, with correct birth and death dates in Thieme-Becker under the name Gysbrecht Verbrugge, with date of entry in the guild omitted. Abraham [Ariensz.] Corssendonck: even though a number of his relatives were *kladschilders*, his testamentary bequest to his nephew Jacob Ariensz. (II) of "drawings, models, and prints" (28 January 1677, Records of Notary Testart van Hasselt, no. 2156) suggests he may have been an artist; he was also headman of the guild (for the second time) in 1700, an office to which normally only artist-painters were elected. Daniel Verlouw: frequently mentioned from 1659 to 1674 when his wife died; the second wife of "Daniel Verlou" was buried in 1713. Isaac van Wessel: portraits signed by this artist are dated from 1670 to 1675 (notes in photographic files of the R.K.D.); a note after his name in the master list of 1650 indicates that he left Delft. Jan Verschure: buried 6 June 1674 ("Register van de doden begraven"); four paintings by an artist of this name are recorded in a Rotterdam inventory (Thieme-Becker). Adriaen Bouda: an individual of this name was baptized 16 March 1649 ("Doopboek"); his testament is dated 24 August 1680 (Records of Notary Jacobus van Berlecum, no. 2166); the estate of Adriaen Gouda owed him four gulden four stuivers for wages and paints "for the house" (20 January 1674, Records of Notary Roelandus van Edenburgh, no. 2249). Cornelis van der Kuijt: Headman of the guild in 1678 and 1685–1686. Pieter Janse. van Ruijve[n]: Died on 17 May 1719 (not 1716 as in Thieme-Becker), according to R. Boïtet, *Beschrijvinge der stadt Delft* (Delft, 1729), p. 790. Michiel van Eemst: buried on 13 September 1684 ("Register van de doden begraven"). Aryen Jacobs Corssendonck [II]: grandson of Arijen Jacobsz. Kortendonck (or Corssendonck) I, said to be twenty-one years old on 8 September 1678 (Records of Notary Gerard van Assendelft, no. 2132); drew up his testament 30 August 1680 (Records of Notary Willem van Ruyven, no. 2283).

NOTES: Neither the painters of furniture nor the *wittwerkers* (painters on white wood) are included in this table. See also the note to Table A.1.

*Inferred from a source but not known with certainty.

†Crossed out in the original. Registered again on 27 July 1655.

‡Former glassmaker.

§Crossed out in the original. Left town without paying entrance dues.

APPENDIX B
Guild Regulations

GUILD LETTER OF 1611[1]

"Ordinance of the Guild of St. Lucas, whereunder are comprised all those earning their living here with the art of painting, be it with fine brushes (*pencelen*) or otherwise, in oil or watercolors; glassmakers; glass-sellers; dishbakers (*plattielbackers*); tapestry-makers; embroiderers; engravers (*plaetsnijders*); sculptors working in wood, stone or other substance; scabbard-makers (*scheemaeckers*); art-printers (*konstdruckers*); booksellers;[a] sellers of prints and paintings, of whatever kind they may be, all of whom together are to be regulated by this ordinance, subject to the fines and punishments hereafter set forth.

[Marginal note in the original] "On 19 October 1619, my lords of the Weth[b] ordained that the tapestry-makers shall henceforth remain outside the guild except that the master tapestry-makers shall pay their death or separation dues according to the specifications in this guild letter.

"1. First: that no one in this city, jurisdiction, or free territory (*vryheijt*) shall exercise mastery in the guild unless he be first a citizen of this city[c] and pay for his entry dues six carolus gulden of forty Flemish groot apiece, and twelve such gulden for a foreigner, but a master's son three gulden; on the understanding that these same masters must first have learned with a master in the aforesaid guild for two years, whereof they will be obligated to show proof to the headmen of this guild; except that the painters who do not use a brush shall pay twenty-five stuivers for their entry dues.

"2. And all this subject to the fine of ten carolus gulden.

"3. But in case there were some individuals of small means who should wish to be received in this guild as guild brothers, they shall pay for their entrance dues a fee that will be at the discretion of the burgomasters.

[a]Marginal addition: "and the book-printers; this was amplified by the lords of the Weth on 1 July 1630."
[b]The Weth, or "law," consisted of the sheriff, the burgomasters, and the aldermen of Delft.
[c]Marginal note: On 29 November 1649, the Weth interpreted this provision to mean "having become a citizen" (*poorter*). In other words, a foreigner could not enter the guild unless he had already paid his fee to become a citizen.

"4. The masters at present in this guild or who will henceforth be received and come into the guild shall be obligated to pay six stuivers yearly to the profit of the guild.

"5. The masters who take on any boy-apprentices (*leerjongens*) in order to teach them any of the aforesaid trades or crafts shall pay for each such boy as an entrance fee one gulden, and for a foreign boy two gulden, which entrance fee the masters will be obligated to advance and to claim for reimbursement from the parents of these same boys, it being understood that the aforesaid boys will have two months free of charge for a trial period (*tot een prove*); and the boys at the end of two years shall pay two stuivers yearly as guild dues, and a foreigner four stuivers.

"6. All foreign young men (*gesellen*) who shall come from outside to work as servants (*knechts*)[d] for any masters or shopkeepers (*winckel-houders*)[e] shall pay ten stuivers as an entrance fee and four stuivers yearly as guild dues, which money the masters or shopkeepers, in case the servants should be unwilling to pay, shall be obligated to deduct from their wages and to pay to the headmen. It is well understood that the servants are allowed to work for the duration of one month free of charge but no longer.

"7. The headmen of this guild shall keep a suitable register of all the guild brothers, as also of the servants (*knechts*) and the boys (*jonghens*), inscribing the same with their names and last names and their addresses so that they can conveniently be found and be known.

"8. No one at any time shall make with his own hand a painting or any other work comprised under the aforesaid guild of this town unless he be a guild brother in the same city, subject to the forfeiture of ten gulden of forty Flemish groot apiece and, in addition, that the aforesaid work shall be confiscated and forfeited to the profit of the guild, which fines shall have to be sought and collected from those who have made the work.

"9. And also nobody at any time coming from outside shall set any glasses[f] within this town or its jurisdiction, subject to a fine of twenty-four stuivers for every glass and the forfeiture of the same glasses; but in case the glasses should have been set in the holes before

[d]The word *knecht* may also be translated helper or apprentice. All the adult employees in a shop were called *knechts*.

[e]A *winckelhouder* was an individual who kept or managed a workshop or an atelier (e.g., to produce delftware).

[f]Reference here is to diamond-shaped or round glass sections set in windows, frequently within a trellis or lead mullions.

this was discovered, they[g] shall pay the correct value of the glasses set, which fines and values of the glasses set must be sought and collected from the individuals who set the glasses[h]; and no masters or servants here shall be allowed to set in the holes such glasses coming from outside, subject to a fine of six gulden.

[Marginal note] "Except that everyone shall be free to have glasses engraved and baked (*gebacken*) as he wishes; however the glass shall be broken up here and set as hereabove stipulated. Added by the Weth, 18 October 1627.[i]

"10. No one shall bring here from outside any painting or other work comprised under this guild unless he be a guild brother of the same guild, of the same trade (*amboicht*), subject to a fine of ten gulden that shall be forfeited by those who sell these, with the exception of the weekly free-markets (*vrije weeckmarckten*) and the yearly free-markets (*vrije jaermarckten*), upon which weekly and yearly free-markets this will be permitted without forfeiture. Besides the weekly and yearly free-markets, selling paintings and other works here will also be permitted during a period of twice twenty-four hours, provided that those doing the selling shall pay to the profit of the guild a daelder of thirty stuivers, and no longer than twice twenty-four hours, unless with the consent of the headmen of this guild.

"11. No foreigner coming into this town from outside with paintings shall be allowed to sell, or cause to sell the same at public auction, without first obtaining the permission and consent of the lord burgomasters of this town, and if nonetheless they should proceed with such sales without prior permission or consent from the lord burgomasters, then the headmen of this guild are authorized by the present to stop these public sales.

"12. The four headmen serving at the time shall be obliged to appear every four weeks on Mondays at three in the afternoon at an appointed place in order to do business there (*besoigneren*) and to take cognizance of any disputes (*questien*) that may have arisen in the aforesaid guild, subject to a fine of twenty-four stuivers to be forfeited by any headmen who should be absent.

"13. At which time and hour all the masters who have hired a

[g]That is, the guilty parties.

[h]"Or by those who have ordered or caused them to be ordered," amplified by the Weth on 1 March 1632.

[i]In other words, everyone was allowed to import glass for subsequent engraving or reworking, but any glass imported for windows must first be cut up in the appropriate sizes and shapes in Delft and set in the holes by masters in the guild.

[352]

servant or boy shall be obliged, within a period of two months following the hiring of the servant or boy, to appear before the headmen in the place where the headmen are holding their meetings and there let the servants or boys be inscribed and state for how long they are bound to the masters *and for what wage or price and on what conditions,* and this subject to a fine of two gulden to be forfeited by the masters.

[Marginal note] "On the last day of October 1611, the words in the text *and for what wage or price and on what condition* were eliminated by the Weth meeting among themselves and it was enjoined and ordered that the masters shall only inscribe their servants and boys and for how long they are bound to their masters.

"14. For which inscriptions, the masters shall be liable to the payment of six stuivers for each servant or boy.

"15. And in case the masters should not have registered their servants or boys within the two months following their engagement, then they shall not be able to invoke any legal bond between them (*geen actie van verbant te pretenderen hebben*).

"16. Servants or boys having completed the time during which they are bound are obliged to appear before the headmen with their masters and to extract from the register an act showing that they have satisfied their masters, for which act the servants or boys whose emancipation (*vrijmakinge*) is taking place shall pay the headmen fifteen stuivers once for the benefit of the guild.

"17. The servants or boys shall not be allowed to work for another master before and until they have satisfied the master to whom they were formally bound, whereof they shall have to show the act drawn up for them by the headmen, subject to the forfeiture of thirty stuivers for each day that they shall have worked for another master, to be forfeited by the servant or boy. The master who will have hired such a servant or boy without his having shown the foregoing act shall also forfeit thirty stuivers for each day that the servant or boy will have worked for him.

"18. Any disputes (*questien*) arising among the guild brothers, whether about their servants, boys, or any other matters concerning the guild, shall be settled by the headmen during their above-mentioned gathering. For each appearance before a gathering, these same headmen will receive one gulden, to be paid by the parties that the headmen will have found to be in the wrong or to be guilty; and the parties [to the dispute] may have a record drawn up of all the business the headmen shall have transacted in their affair, and they may further address and refer it to my lords the burgomasters of this town.[j]

"19. Whenever a guild brother comes to depart from this world, or while alive desires to leave the guild, he or his heirs shall pay for his death dues thirty stuivers.

"20. The ordinary (*gemeene*) guild brothers shall be obliged to appear at the appointed place and time for the burial of a deceased guild brother, subject to a fine of three stuivers, unless someone was away from home or was prevented from attending through great sickness, whereof notice must be communicated to the guild servant.[k]

"21. In case someone among the guild brothers should become impoverished and require a subvention, the headmen serving at the time shall support him out of guild receipts, as far as the latter may allow (*zal mogen strecken*), on condition that, if he should come into means, he should be obliged to make restitution; to this end he shall draw a deed acknowledging the amounts he shall have received as subvention from the box. And in case any poor fellow (*schamel gesel*) should need help and could not find any work here, the headmen shall be allowed to endow him according to his need and to the means that are in the box.

"22. The aforesaid guild shall be governed by four headmen, of whom each year two will retire, which two retiring headmen must stay out of office the following two years; the two ongoing (*anblijvende*) headmen shall choose instead of these [retiring headmen] four men out of the aforesaid guild and deliver their names to the lord burgomasters of this town, from among which names these same burgomasters shall select two new headmen who shall serve for the period of two years; and the selection shall take place yearly on St. Lucas Day.

"23. In case a headman in office should come to depart from this world, one of the last retiring headmen shall be chosen to replace him by my lords the burgomasters, with the proviso that he cannot be chosen again in the four succeeding years.

"24. The receipts of the guild from infractions (*breukens*,)[l] as well as from guild dues, shall be deposited and preserved in a locked box

[j]That is, they may refer the act to the burgomasters for the purpose of appealing the headmen's decision.

[k]This is the first mention of a guild servant. The guild letter does not specify by whom he should be appointed. On his duties and emoluments, see articles 28 and 29.

[l]Presumably, from fines and other forfeitures.

(*bosse*), of which box the headmen in office shall each have a key, such that no one without the other will be able to go into the box when there shall be a need to open it.

"25. The aforesaid headmen shall keep a suitable register of the receipts and set down in the books from whom, from where, and for what cause the respective sums shall have been collected or received, and they shall make an accounting thereof once a year and this in front of the dean,[m] which accounting shall be made precisely six weeks after St. Lucas Day, subject to a fine of six gulden to be forfeited by the headmen who shall have failed to make their accounting within this period.

"26. All the aforesaid fines collected by virtue of these articles shall be turned over to the town, to the officer,[n] and to the guild, each to the extent of one-third.

"27. And one-third of the receipts of the guild shall be spent to cover necessary expenditures and the sittings (*vacatien*) of the aforesaid guild and the yearly gatherings of the headmen, and the rest of all the receipts shall be levied and deposited in the aforesaid box for the upkeep of poor guild brothers, as has been related.

"28. The servant of the guild shall receive for each general announcement he shall make throughout the town twelve stuivers and for a private one (*een particuliere*) three stuivers, which shall be paid to him by those who will have set him to work.[o]

"29. The guild servant shall receive three gulden once for the services that he shall render to the headmen during the course of an entire year.

"30. Any individual chosen to be headman who should be found unwilling to serve will forfeit eight gulden to be allotted as above.

"31. The headmen of the guild in office shall be empowered to collect the aforesaid entrance dues and any fines to be levied from

[m]No provisions are made in the guild letter for the appointment of the dean or specifying his duties. However, it appears from Dirck van Bleyswijck, *Beschryvinge der Stadt Delft* (Delft, 1667), p. 652, that the dean was appointed by the burgomasters to supervise the guild and make sure that the headmen complied with its rules.

[n]The responsibilities and functions of this officer are nowhere defined. From the amendment of 2 July 1612 below, it may perhaps be inferred that he was appointed and delegated by the Weth to enforce the rules of the guild letter.

[o]This may be interpreted as follows. The guild servant was to be paid twelve stuivers for general, guild-related announcements and three stuivers for private announcements that he was asked to circulate throughout the town. A private announcement might concern a public auction or a lottery for the benefit of those staging it.

unwilling payers with all such rights as one may use in collecting debts from sealed letters, that is, on the third day after summons to a lawsuit (*op een gastdinck*).

"32. My lords the burgomasters henceforward reserve the rights to the interpretation, amplification and amendments of this ordinance.

"Thus proclaimed with the great clock of the Town Hall on the 29th of May of the year 1611, and the sheriff, burgomasters, and aldermen of this town have affixed the seal to this document hereunder.

Signed, J. GROENOUT, 1611"

AMPLIFICATIONS AND AMENDMENTS CONTAINED IN THE ORDINANCE BOOKS OF THE WETH

6 November 1611: "As complaints and doleances have been received by my lords of the town of Delft about glass coming from outside into this town without first being publicly advertised (*geen ommeleg gedaen en wort*), to the detriment and damage of the glassmakers and others comprised under the Guild of St. Lucas, so my lords the burgomasters have ordered and ordained, order and ordain by the present, that henceforth no glass brought into this town, together with the free territory and jurisdiction thereof, may be sold unless the guild servant has made beforehand a circular announcement, subject to a fine of twelve gulden, to be forfeited each time, both by the buyer and the seller.

Thus promulgated with the great clock of the Town Hall on the 6th of November anno 1611.

Signed, J. GROENEWEGEN"

2 July 1612: "On the second of July anno 1612 my lords of the Weth meeting among themselves (*collegialiter vergadert*), at the request of the headmen of the guild of the painters, granted the latter permission to collect all the fines falling due for violation of their guild letter by *parate executie*,[P] and the individual contesting [the fine] in law (*den opposant in rechte*) shall not be admitted [before the judges] unless and until the fine shall have been placed in the hands of the headmen (*genamptizeert sal hebben in handen van den hoomans*), except that the

[P]Such a fine may be collected immediately, irrespective of any pending suit or appeal.

headmen in office at the time shall be held responsible before the officer for any fines that they may collect by *parate executie* and shall pay him any shares of the fines accruing to him according to the guild letter; and, to this end, they must open their register for his inspection (*tot dyen eynde heure register den selven te openen*)."[q]

14 June 1614: "[My lords the sheriff and aldermen with advice of the burgomasters] further ordain that from this date forward all those wishing to engage and set themselves up in *(doen ende opstellen)* the craft of glassmaking shall have to make the following proof (*maecken desen navolgende proeffe*),[r] to wit, a lantern with prunts or a glass with a stem, at the option of the individual making the proof, and in case the proof should be approved by the headmen (*voor ghoet gekent*), then he shall be admitted into the guild, and otherwise not. It is further ordained that henceforth no dishbakers (*plateelbackers*) or claybakers (*geleybackers*)[s] will be allowed to put to work any servants or boys outside their shop or house or to cause any work related to dish- or clay-baking to be done in someone's house in any manner whatsoever, except in case of urgent need, as by reason of sickness, impotence, or other compelling causes, which will be subject to the judgment and discretion of the headmen in office at the time; subject to a fine of ten gulden of forty Flemish groot apiece to be forfeited, and, in addition, to the forfeiting and confiscation of the work so made, for the profit of the guild. The fine shall be sought and collected from those who have made the work.

[They further ordain] that the master dish- and claybakers shall henceforth keep and engage (*annemen*) no more than two boy-apprentices at the same time to paint or learn painting (*te doen ofte leeren schilderen*), each of whom they must make known to the headmen and inscribe in the register, with the understanding that when the boys will be within a year of having completed the period of their servitude (*verbonden tyt*), then the master shall be allowed to hire

[q]The words "for his inspection" (instead of "for him") have been inserted for clarification. On the share of guild receipts accruing to the officer, see article 26 above.

[r]To "make a proof" may also, less literally, be translated "to make a masterpiece." "Proof" carries the double sense of the test that the candidate must pass and the piece he must make to do so.

[s]Both the words *plateelbacker* and *geleybacker* denote an individual practicing the craft of faiencier.

two others in anticipation of the expiration of the period (*teygens dat de zelven tyt expireren sal*), but these shall not be set to work before and until the two years of the first boys shall have expired, subject to a fine of twelve gulden, if anyone should be found in violation. Published *in dato utsupra*."²

8 February 1615: "Concerning the painters and glass-engravers: My lords sheriff and aldermen with the advice of my lords the burgomasters have ordered and ordained, order and ordain by the present, that no one henceforth shall be allowed to set someone to work in his house to engage in a trade or activity of the Guild of St. Lucas unless he be of the same art-craft or trade (*kunstambacht ofte neringe*) and that he himself should have been received master.ᵗ

And this subject to the forfeiture of the work made or the value thereof, together with a fine of ten carolus gulden, so long and as many times as someone shall be found to have acted in violation, and the servants or boys shall forfeit thirty stuivers for every day that they shall be found to have worked for an individual who was not himself a master.

They order further that no painters or glass-engravers shall be received or recognized as masters unless they first have practiced (*geoeffent*) or learned the art of painting or glass-engraving for a full six years with one or more masters of the same art, which they must clearly give proof of (*doen blijcken*), except if by giving evidence of their work before the six years are up, they should show they are masters, which shall be left to the judgment and discretion of the headmen.ᵘ

Published with the great clock, the 8th of February 1615."³

19 October 1620: "Considering that the guild letter of the St. Lucas Guild, whereunder are comprised the glassmakers, states that no glassmaker may be received as master in the aforesaid guild unless he first have made an appropriate proof, to wit, a lantern with prunts or a glass with stem, without making any particular mention of what sort of lantern or what glass with stem, and considering that there are various types of glasses with stems, the headmen of the aforesaid

ᵗMarginal note: "No one allowed to keep boy-painters (*schilders-jongens*) to engage in the painting trade except that he himself be a master painter."

ᵘMarginal note: "No one may be *master painter or glass-engraver* who has not worked six years with a master or made a masterpiece (*prouff stuck*) within the aforesaid period." Emphasis is in the original.)

Guild of St. Lucas, with the approval of some guild brothers, had ordered a glass with stem to be made for the candidate's proof, of the type that young masters make; and the headmen having sought the approval of the proof, so my lords the magistrates of this city have approved the proof and likewise approve it by the present, ordering that the aforesaid glass that has been shown to the aforesaid lords and no other whatsoever shall be made for a proof and that the same shall be inspected by the headmen of the St. Lucas Guild and by the last retiring headman of the glassmaker's craft.

[Interlinear insertion in the original text] The lords of the Weth of the town of Delft, in amplification of the foregoing article, ordain and stipulate by the present that if someone's proof should turn out bad and that it should be failed by the headmen of the guild, the same glassmaker shall have to work for one year and six weeks as a servant before and until he may again begin his proof. Done on 16 August 1655."[4]

[42] "Order and ordain further that henceforth no one shall exercise the craft of claybaking unless he have first learned six years with a master, in conformance with the article of the guild speaking of the painters and glass-engravers. Also that no masters shall be allowed to hire more boy-learners than every two years one[v] *unless the boy within the two years*[w] were to die or run away, in which case the master may hire another boy for two years.

[v]Marginal insert in text: "Painter or (dish) turner (*drayer*), amplified by the Weth on 19 October 1648." (These words were crossed out). Marginal note under this insert: "For pregnant reasons, the lords of the Weth have considered advisable to erase the above marginal amplification and order that everyone concerned comply with the article of the guild letter and follow the old practice as was done prior to this, the 7th of December 1648." It is not clear why the words "painter or (dish) turner" should have been inserted or why they should have been crossed out a month-and-a-half later. One explanation is that the faienciers hired extra boys whom they set to work molding the clay, preparing "cover" for the tiles, or doing other auxiliary jobs, which could not be defined either as dish-turning or decorating, so that the Weth was soon compelled to plug this hole in the regulations which permitted some faience-making shops to expand more than the authorities desired.

[w]Insertion at top of folio: "At the suggestion and request of Aelbrecht Keyser, headman of the Guild of St. Lucas, and of a few faienciers' servants addressed to the lords of the Weth, the said lords of the Weth have resolved to alter the words underlined in the article standing next to this [insertion] (*within the two years*) and, by form of approbation, have deemed it desirable in their place to write *within his initially contracted time* [i.e. during the period in which the apprentice originally contracted to be bound to his master], the rest of the text remaining in force in its entirety; thus altered on 8 July 1658."

[Insertion at bottom of folio] The lords of the Weth of the town of Delft after deliberation over a resolution of 12 July 1666 concerning the above-standing forty-second article resolved, in conformance with this resolution and the guild letter, that the hiring of boys shall be allowed without limitation of time, and this until such time and while as their honors [the lords of the Weth] shall enact otherwise. Actum, 31 January 1667.

In consideration of the letter of the Guild of St. Lucas which states that all disagreements arising among the guild brothers should be settled by the headmen of the guild, and as some disagreements and disputes have at times arisen concerning the work of claybaking whereof the headmen had no full knowledge or science, so my lords have ordered that a master claybaker shall be appointed by the burgomasters who shall serve with the same headmen in order to help settle and compose all such disputes. Actum, the 19th of October 1620.

Amplification: The lords of the Weth of the town of Delft in amendment to the foregoing article order and enact that the aforesaid guild henceforth shall at all times be administered (*bedient*) by six headmen, to wit: two painters, two glassmakers, and two claybakers. Done October 19, 1648.

And that, in pursuance of the foregoing, the headmen of the claybakers, along with the others, shall also have a key to the box. Done October 2nd 1651."

12 May 1641: "Considering that complaints have been made before magistrates of this town about the abuses and violations that have occurred in the last few years in putting to work several boys simultaneously (*veelvoudige opsetten van jongens*), contrary to the forty-second article of the guild letter which states that no masters shall be allowed to hire more boys than one every two years, and so forth, my lords the sheriff and alderman with advice from the lord burgomasters, all having been heard previously in the matter, as well as the dean and the headmen of the aforesaid St. Lucas Guild who were also heard, together with the ordinary masters and the servants of the faienciers respectively, with a view to averting the abuses and violations, have ordered and ordained, likewise order and ordain, by the present [as follows]:

With respect to the masters: concerning the boys that they have too many of according to the forty-second article, for each [such excess] boy, they must desist for two years before they may hire any others, subject to a fine of twelve gulden to be forfeited.

With respect to the ordinary servants: they shall be obliged, in case any master should set to work any boys in violation of the forty-second article, to pay careful attention thereto, and to report the same at the next session of the headmen, subject to the same fine of twelve gulden as is to be forfeited by the masters.

And in case such a boy or boys, contrary to the forty-second article, should have been hired, henceforth they must be dismissed within a period of eight days, on pain of a double fine.

Also [it is ordained] that no masters shall set to work any servants coming from out of town without their having shown theretofore *that they have honestly and loyally satisfied their master,* subject to a fine of thirty stuivers.

[Marginal amplification] At the suggestion and at the request of Aelbrecht Keyser, headman of the St. Lucas Guild, and of some faienciers' servants addressed to the lords of the Weth, the said lords of the Weth have altered the words in the article standing next to this [alteration] [*that they have honestly and loyally satisfied their master*] and, by form of approbation, have found it desirable to set in their place *that they have satisfied their master for the period of six years,* the remaining part of the article remaining entirely as it stands. Thus altered, on the 18th of July 1658.

Published with the great clock of the Town Hall of Delft on 12 May 1641."[5]

20 April 1654: "Amplification [of the guild letter]:

The lords of the Weth of the town of Delft, at the request of the headmen as well as of the ordinary master clay- and dishbakers under the Guild of St. Lucas addressed to these honorable lords, have ordered and ordained, order and ordain by the present, that henceforth no one shall be admitted as master of clay or porcelain dish-baking who shall not have been apprenticed six years with masters in this town or have shown an appropriate attestation from other towns that he had been a master there or that he had been apprenticed with masters there for six years, in which case the aforesaid persons, before being admitted, shall be obliged to make a proof either as dish-turners or as painters in the following manner.

That those wishing to do their proof in turning dishes (*draijen*) shall be obliged to make a syrup-pot, a commercial (*winckel*) salad dish, and a round saltcellar, hollow inside, and made of one piece.

And those wishing to do their proof in painting shall be obliged to paint in free hand (*uytterhandt*) a half dozen of the largest dishes (*grootse grooten*) with *fine poorten*[x] and a large fruit dish decorated all over.

And regarding the proof made by the turners and the painters respectively, over and above the special proof of turning and painting, both shall be required to stack a pile of small (dishes) thirty high (*te zetten een cap cleynen van dertich hogh*).[y]

Regarding the use and preparation of materials, the candidate master (*aencomende meester*) shall endure the examination of two proof-masters who are to be appointed by the headmen.

Which aforesaid proof together with the examination [of the materials] must be made in the house of the oldest headman, under the supervision of the other headmen. The other headmen of the St. Lucas Guild may also be present for the making of the proof, but they may not examine the materials.

The aforesaid materials needed for the proof shall be delivered by the aforesaid headman at whose house the same [proof] will be made, and in case the proof should not be approved, the individual submitting to the proof shall be obliged to pay its value to the aforesaid headman, as it will have been estimated by the other headmen and proof-masters. In case it should be approved, he may either leave the proof-piece there or take it with him [paying its value] as estimated above.

However, if it happened that someone intended to apply any extraordinary art in making or preparing the materials needed for the

---

[x]This term is not clear. Henry Havard, *Histoire des faïences de Delft, Haarlem, Rotterdam, Utrecht, etc. et des porcelaines de Weesp, Loosdrecht, Amsterdam et La Haye*, 2 vols. (Amsterdam: "Vivat," 1909), 1:93, was informed by an older worker in the 1870s that *fine poorten* referred to small dots (*fine punten*). This is very unlikely since, in a deposition of 1651, reference is made both to *poorten* and *dubbelde punten* (Records of Notary Simon Mesch, no. 2048). The word *poorten* may be a distortion of *boorden* (lace borders), in which case it might refer to lacelike decoration. Note also that the gateways painted on the vertical sides of some seventeenth-century Delft tiles are also called *poorten*.

[y]This may mean that the candidate was required to stack a pile of thirty small dishes in the kiln before firing, which probably called for some skill to prevent the individual dishes from sticking to each other or the decoration from "running" in the process of firing.

proof which he did not wish to reveal to the proof-masters, in such cases he shall be allowed to bring the raw materials (*materialen int' gros*) to the house of the headmen where he will be making his proof, and a place apart shall be designated for him to prepare it. If the proof is approved, he will be allowed to take it with him, provided that he pay the headman for the use of his kiln where his proof will have been fired, subject to the estimation [procedure] described above.

With the exception and on the understanding, however, that the widows of masters after the death of their husbands may continue to exercise the trade without making a proof. [They may do so] their life long, but if they should remarry and, being remarried, die, then their husbands wishing to continue in the trade shall be obliged to make their proof within six weeks after their wife's death, in the manner specified above.

Thus done and confirmed by the lords of the Weth on the 20th April 1654 and announced with the great clock on the 21st following."[6]

4 November 1658: "The lords of the Weth of the town of Delft, at the request of the ordinary booksellers within this town by petition addressed to the honorable lords, have ordered and ordained, order and ordain by the present, that henceforth no one within this town or its jurisdiction shall engage in bookbinding, bookselling or book printing or be admitted into the guild unless he have previously learned his craft for two years with a master and have paid the right [of admission] to the Guild of St. Lucas, subject to a fine of fifty gulden.

Also that no one henceforth shall be allowed to sell, by auction or by public sale, any books unless they be public booksellers or shopkeepers, subject to the same penalty as above; however, the resolution of the said lords of the Weth of 22 October 1657 (according to which these same public auctions or sales of books or of paintings may not be held unless they have first been approved by the same lords) remains fully in force. Done the 4th November 1658."[7]

1 March 1661: "The lords of the Weth of the town of Delft, at the request of the headmen of the faienciers falling under the St. Lucas Guild addressed to the honorable lords, have ordered and ordained, order and ordain by the present the following points.

First that all porcelain-bakers as well as porcelain and faience sellers will fall under the faienciers' guild.

Furthermore that henceforth anyone wishing to carry on the trade of faiencier or porcelain-baker under and through the direction of a master-*knecht,* shall only be allowed to do so provided that the latter has been admitted to master's status by having done his proof and moreover that he shall have been registered as a shopkeeper (*winckel-houder*) in the guild. He [the shopkeeper] shall be obliged to pay the entrance fee and yearly guild dues as other guild brothers do, and although the latter thereby[z] obtain the right to employ servants and boys according to the forty-second article of the guild letter neverthe-less the shop manager shall not be allowed, in addition to the foreign boys (*vreemde jongens*)[aa] already hired by virtue of the forty-second article, to employ his own children as painters (*tot het schilderen*), which former masters and still others by virtue of becoming masters by doing the proof and exercising the trade for themselves, have of old been permitted to do and, by the present, may continue to do.[bb]

In addition, no more than one master shall be recognized and enjoy the right of master in each shop, even though several participants therein might have acquired master status by doing their proof or by transfer (*overdragte*).[cc]

Thus done and confirmed by the lords of the Weth of the town of Delft on 21 March 1661 and promulgated on the 29th of the same month."[8]

6 February 1662: "Amplification of the guild letter of the St. Lucas Guild.

Whereas the headmen of the St. Lucas Guild have pointed out and complained to the lords of the Weth that the members of this guild have had to sustain great expenditures in connection with the setting up and installation of the new guild hall in the old Drapiers' Hall in this city, as a consequence of which they have not only been forced to

[z] That is, by becoming members of the guild and remaining in good standing.

[aa] From the context it appears that by a "foreign boy" is meant a boy-apprentice not belonging to the shop manager's family.

[bb] According to a marginal notation of 26 July 1694 (beyond the period covered in this survey of guild rules) the headmen, the ordinary master faienciers, and the shopkeepers had asked the lords of the Weth to interpret the clause allowing masters to employ their own children as painters. The lords of the Weth ordained that the word "children" should apply to boys only and not to daughters or other women.

[cc] For example, by virtue of being the wife of a deceased master.

employ some funds belonging to the guild but also, in order to defray these expenditures, to raise certain sums, and [wishing] to be relieved of this obligation, with a view to lightening the burden of the common guild brothers for the greatest benefit of the guild, the aforesaid headmen acting in assembly have drawn up a few propositions, seeking that the same be laid down and confirmed by my lords of the Weth. These same lords having examined and considered this petition together with these propositions have found it proper to ordain that:

First, all out-of-town young men who have come here to be hired as servants by any masters or shopkeepers under this guild's jurisdiction, in order to work with the aforementioned, in place of ten stuivers in conformity with the sixth article of the guild letter, will henceforth be obligated to pay as entrance fee, to the benefit of the guild, two gulden ten stuivers [fifty stuivers].

Secondly, in amplification and amendment of the thirty-seventh article, that henceforth all the proofs must be made in the rebuilt guild hall and that the candidate during the time of his examination will be locked up in the same hall and released daily by the oldest headman in office and that the candidate shall pay to the benefit of the guild six stuivers, in addition to all the materials and equipment he will need to produce his proof, with the exception, in the case of the examination of the dish-turners and porcelain-bakers, that a potter's wheel be installed at the expense of the guild, and that all such proofs shall be approved and accepted by all the headmen in office and by the last retiring headmen, along with two proof-masters. The candidate shall pay the aforementioned headmen and proof-masters three stuivers for each inspection, except for inspections in excess of three which shall be free.

Thirdly, in line with the amplification dated 16 August 1655 concerning the proof requirement for the glassmakers, that henceforth any faience- or porcelain-makers having failed their examination and their proof having been rejected by the headmen, they must work a year and six weeks as *knechts* before they can again begin their proof.

Fourthly, that all public sales and auctions of paintings, books of prints (*konstboeken*) or other goods comprised under the guild shall henceforth be held exclusively in the new guild hall, where the guild servant may give amateurs a suitable opportunity to view them, with the proviso that the auctioneers shall pay to the guild servants without abatement of the auction masters' fees, for his services and attention, for each day that the hall or halls shall be used, two gulden ten stuivers to the benefit of the guild, as long as these goods are exhibited or auctioned off, on the understanding however that the guild will have to take care of the goods exhibited and auctioned off and to bear responsibility for any loss thereof.

[Marginal addition]: On 8 November 1683 the fees for use of the guild hall were raised by thirty-six stuivers.

Fifthly, whereas it has been discovered that many paintings at the weekly auction-master's sales have been brought in from outside and auctioned off and sold either openly or among other goods to the marked prejudice and detriment of the painters living in this city, it has been ordained that no one shall henceforth proceed to sell or cause to be sold any paintings stemming from outside at the weekly sales of the auction masters, on penalty of a fine of thirty stuivers for every painting, levied for the benefit of the guild.

Sixthly, whereas, according to the twelfth article of the guild letter stating that all disagreements concerning the guild should be settled (if possible) during the ordinary monthly meetings of the headmen, except if, on the request of someone, an extraordinary meeting should be held, the headmen shall henceforth receive for each convocation, instead of one gulden following the eighteenth article, one gulden sixteen stuivers, to be paid by the person who will be understood by the headmen to be in the wrong or to owe the payment.[10]

3 July 1673: "The lords of the Weth of the town of Delft upon request of the ordinary porcelain- and clayturner servants[dd] (*porceleyn ende geleydraeijers knechts*), already subordinate with respect to doing their proof under the St. Lucas Guild in this town and desirous of being brought under its supervision and governance in all respects, having seen in this regard the written report and advice of the headmen in office at the time of the same guild, have seen fit and resolved, see fit and resolve by the same, that the aforesaid porcelain- and clayturner servants will henceforth exclusively fall under the supervision and the governance of the aforementioned St. Lucas Guild; at the same time it is especially ordered and ordained that henceforth no dish- and claybakers in this town shall be allowed to order any handmade work belonging to the dishturner's craft made outside their home or shop, except through pressing need, through sickness, impotence or other necessary cause, which shall be left to the

[dd]The "turners" shaped the pots and dishes from clay. The word "porcelain" is used here inaccurately to denote earthenware or faience.

judgment and discretion of the headmen serving at the time, subject to a fine of ten gulden each time to be forfeited by anyone who shall be found in violation of this [article], in addition to the forfeiture of the work so made to the profit of the aforesaid guild. However, the aforesaid master dishbakers in conformity with the contents of the aforesaid report and advice, with the consent of the aforesaid porcelain- and clayturner servants pursuant thereto, shall be allowed to have potters' wares (*pottebackers goet*) made at their pleasure in potters' shops and, in addition, to set as many boy-apprentices to work turning dishes as they like, provided that they shall be obliged to register all such [boys] [among the servants inscribed in the guild books], in conformity with the guild letter. Thus done and resolved today the 3rd July 1673.

[Marginal note of 21 August 1673]: The lords of the Weth of the town of Delft, upon the request of virtually all (*meest alle*) the master dishbakers, having been apprised that the request mentioned in this [article] and the consent of the headmen of the St. Lucas Guild in office at the time [were made and obtained (?)ᶜᶜ] without the knowledge of the ordinary master dishbakers, have found fit and resolve by the present that the resolution standing next to this [marginal addition] shall remain unexecuted (*sal blyven buyten executie*) until further order and that the headmen shall communicate this [to the membership].

Actum given the 21st August 1673, me present [signature illegible].

[Insertion after the resolution of 3 July 1673]: The lords of the Weth of the town of Delft, by way of recapitulation (*bij wegen van resumptie*), having looked over and examined the above-standing resolution dated 3 July 1673, have found fit and agreed that this resolution shall not be carried out or put to execution but that in the future the matters to which it refers shall be left in all manners and ways as they were before the date of the resolution.

This done and confirmed the 23rd of October 1673, with my knowledge and signed by me, A. Hensius."[10]

2 July 1674: "The lords of the Weth of the town of Delft having obtained knowledge that, contrary to the contents of the ordinances of the St. Lucas Guild, under which the porcelain bakers are subsumed, for some time now it has been the practice that some

ᶜᶜPart of this line is illegible.

porcelain bakers' shops open here in Delft were not managed in conformity with the ordinance by and under the direction of a master-*knecht* who had properly done his proof and who at the same time effectively was carrying on this business (*de selve hantteringe effective als nog was doende*), but by other persons, who while they had done the ordinary proof, as a result of their getting involved in other offices and occupations had been severed from the same business (*hantteringe*) and consequently had only in effect lent their names and the property of having done their proof to the release of the same shops (*bevrijdinge van den selve winckels*),[ff] all of which is notoriously inciting [?] (*styeende*) against the contents of the aforesaid ordinance as well as the welfare of the aforesaid trade, so Their Honors [the lords of the Weth] considering it of the highest necessity that this should be seen to, after taking into cognizance the report of the lord dean and of the headmen of the aforementioned guild in office at the time, have found fit and ordered, find fit and order by the present, that henceforth no porcelain bakers' shops in this town may be released or be kept in operation by any one but a master-*knecht* having done his proper proof and, outside of any other employ, is working in Delft daily in the shop that he is releasing or [by a person] owning at least a fourth part in the same [shop].

And with regard to the persons mentioned previously who presently in the manner described are merely lending their names and the property of having done their proof to the shops that they are releasing, Their Honors for [good and valid] reason have found fit and resolved, find fit and resolve by the present that they shall be allowed to continue to release these same shops for the period during which they shall be hired to do so, in such way that once this period shall have expired, they shall never be allowed to release any shop, unless it be such that they come to work in it in effect every day or they participate to the extent of at least a fourth [in its ownership].

And also as it has been found, to the noteworthy prejudice of the aforesaid business and against the contents of the guild letter, that it happens daily more and more frequently that a master-*knecht*, having been hired and registered for the release of a shop, this same individual does not stick precisely to working in the shop that he has released but also engages in work outside it in another shop, so Their

---

[ff] A faiencier's shop was "released" (*bevrijdigt*) from the necessity of being run by an owner who had done his proof when a foreman (*meesterknecht*) having done his proof was appointed by the owner to manage the shop on his behalf.

Honors, to prevent this [practice], have found fit and ordered, find fit and order by the present, that henceforth all master-*knechts* shall not be allowed to work, now or ever, in another shop except one for the release of which they have been engaged and registered, subject to a fine of thirty stuivers per day, to be forfeited by the [master]*knecht* as well as by the boss shopkeeper (*baes winckelhouder*) who shall have set the master-*knecht* to work, for the benefit of the guild.

And in order to see to it that a master-*knecht* hired and registered to release a shop shall not come to leave it at his own volition to the marked prejudice of the shopkeeper and immediately to go to work and into service for another shop and be hired there, Their Honors, after taking cognizance of the aforesaid report, have seen fit to order and to enact and so order and enact by the present that a master-*knecht* having undertaken to release a shop in the manner above [described] shall be obliged to continue [to work there] for the stipulated period and in the meanwhile to engage in no other work or service in another shop, nor shall any other master or shopowner be allowed to hire him or put him to work, without having shown proof to the headmen of the Guild of St. Lucas in office at the time that the keeper (*houder*) of the aforesaid first shop was well satisfied with the aforesaid master-*knecht*, subject to a fine of thirty stuivers as before per day, to be forfeited by the *knecht* as well as by the master or shopkeeper respectively for the benefit of the guild. This done and confirmed by the lords of the Weth of the town of Delft on the second of July 1674."[11]

APPENDIX C

TABLE C.1

Headmen of the St. Lucas Guild, 1611-1680

Year	Name	Craft	Year of Birth	Year of Death	Date of Registration in the guild*	Place of Origin
1611	Michiel Miereveld	Painter	1567	1641	1587	Delft
1616	Pouwels Bourseth	Faiencier	n.a.	1620	1613	Rouen†
1619	Willem Jacobsz. Delff	Engraver	1580	1638	1613	Delft
	Ritsert Janszoon	Painter	n.a.	c. 1627	1615	Delft†
1622	Hans Jordaens	Painter	c. 1560	1630	1613	Antwerp†
	Huybrecht Grimani	Painter	c. 1563	1631	1613	Delft†
	Cornelis van Linschoten	Glassmaker	c. 1571	n.a.	1613	n.a.
1625	Willem van den Bundel	Painter	c. 1575	c. 1653	1623	Brussels
	Jan Cornelisz. Pool	Glassmaker	c. 1580	n.a.	1613	n.a.
1626	Cornelis Jacobsz. Delff	Painter	c. 1571	1643	1613	Delft
	Hans Jordaens	Painter	c. 1560	1630	1613	Antwerp†
1633	Jacob Vosmaer	Painter	1584	1641	1613	Delft
	Dirck Blaenoker	Glassmaker	c. 1573	1647(?)	1613	n.a.
	Willem van Vliet	Painter	c. 1584	1642	1615	Delft†
	Jan Dircksz. van der Laen	Glassmaker	c. 1600	post 1663	1622	Delft†
1634	Willem van den Bundel	Painter	c. 1575	1655	1623	Brussels
	Aerent van Saenen	Glassmaker	n.a.	post 1655	1625	Delft†

1635	Anthony Palamedes	Painter	1601	1673	1621	Delft†
	Claes van Swieten	Glassmaker	n.a.	n.a.	1613	Delft†
1637	Cornelis van Ryetwijck	Painter	c. 1590	1660	1613	Delft†
	Jan Dircksz. van der Laen	Glassmaker	c. 1600	c. 1663	1622	Delft†
1638	Willem van den Bundel	Painter	c. 1575	c. 1655	1623	Brussels
	Jan Edewaertse Bulonge	Glassmaker	c. 1599	1656	1627	Delft†
	Harmen van Bolgersteyn	Painter	c. 1585	1641	1613	n.a.
1640	Engelbrecht van Velde	Glassmaker	n.a.	post-1650	1627	Delft†
1648	Mattheus de Bergh	Painter	n.a.	1687	1638	Delft†
	Frans van der Fijn	Glassmaker	n.a.	post-1674	1633	not Delft
	Aelbrecht de Keyser	Faiencier	n.a.	1667	1642	Delft†
1649	Adriaen Delff	Painter	n.a.	post-1663	1642	Delft†
	Engebrecht van de Velde	Glassmaker	c. 1606	post-1650	1627	Delft†
	Frans (Pouwels) van Oosten	Faiencier	n.a.	pre-1675	1640	n.a.
1650	Pieter Vromans	Painter	n.a.	1654	1635	Delft†
	Jan Bokkevelt	Glassmaker	n.a.	post-1654	1631	Delft†
	Evert van der West	Faiencier	c. 1598	post-1652	1633	Delft†
1651	Cornelis Rietwijk	Painter	c. 1590	1660	1613	Delft†
	Jan Dircksz. van der Laan	Glassmaker	c. 1600	post-1662	1622	Delft†
	Gysbrecht Kruijk	Faiencier	1623	1681	1645	Delft†
1654	Leendert Bramer	Painter	1596	1674	1629	Delft
	Jan Bockevelt	Glassmaker	n.a.	n.a.	1631	Delft†
1655	Pieter van Kessel	Faiencier	c. 1603	1661	1634	Delft†
	Pieter Bronckhorst	Painter	1588	1661	1613	Delft†
	Arent van Sane(n)	Glassmaker	n.a.	post-1666	1625	Delft†
	Dirck van Kessel	Faiencier	c. 1605	c. 1662	1638	Delft†
1656	Willem Jansz. Ploij	Painter	c. 1584	post-1665	1615	Delft†
	Arij van de Velde	Glassmaker	n.a.	post-1666	1652	Delft†

Table C.1(continued)
Headmen of the St. Lucas Guild, 1611–1680

Year	Name	Craft	Year of Birth	Year of Death	Date of Registration in the guild*	Place of Origin
1657	Jan van der Hoeve	Faiencier	n.a.	1668	1649	Delft†
	Cornelis de Man	Painter	1621	1706	1642	Delft†
	Jan van der Laen	Glassmaker	c. 1600	post-1663	1622	Delft†
	Aelbrecht de Keijser	Faiencier	n.a.	1667	1642	not Delft†
1658	Antoni Palamedes	Painter	1601	1673	1621	Delft†
	Frans van der Vijn	Glassmaker	n.a.	post-1663	1633	Delft†
	Quijringh Kleijnove	Faiencier	n.a.	1695	1655	not Delft†
1659	Cornelis Rietwijck	Painter	c. 1590	1660	1613	Delft†
	Jasper Sarot	Glassmaker	n.a.	1693	1655	not Delft†
	Jakop Dekerton	Faiencier	n.a.	1675	1653	not Delft†
1660	Leendert Bramer	Painter	1596	1674	1629	Delft
	Arijen van der Velden	Glassmaker	n.a.	post-1666	1652	Delft†
	Quieringh van Kleynen-hoven	Faiencier	n.a.	1695	1655	not Delft†
1661	Cornelis de Man	Painter	1621	1706	1642	Delft†
	Arent van Saenen	Glassmaker	n.a.	post-1666	1625	Delft†
	Aelbrecht Keyser	Faiencier	n.a.	1667	1642	not Delft†
1662	Johannes Vermeer	Painter	1632	1675	1653	Delft
	Jan Dirckse van der Laen	Glassmaker	c. 1600	post-1663	1622	Delft†
	Ghysbrecht Kruijck	Faiencier	1623	1681	1645	Delft†
1663	Anthonij Pallemedes	Painter	1601	1673	1621	Delft†
	Frans van den Fijn	Glassmaker	n.a.	n.a.	1633	Delft†

Year	Name	Occupation				
1664	Jan Gerritse van der Houven	Faiencier	n.a.	1668	1649	Delft†
	Leendert Bramer	Painter	1596	1674	1629	Delft
	Sybrant van der Laen	Glassmaker	c. 1637	post-1692	1661	Delft†
	Isack Soubre	Faiencier	n.a.	n.a.	1661	Delft†
1665	Abraham de Kooge‡	Art dealer	c. 1600	post-1680	1632	Alkmaar
	Arijen van der Velden	Glassmaker	n.a.	post-1666	1652	Delft†
1666	Jacob Kerton	Faiencier	n.a.	post-1675	1653	not Delft†
	Cornelis de Man	Painter	1621	1706	1642	Delft†
	Arent van Sanen	Glassmaker	n.a.	n.a.	1625	Delft†
	Pieter Oosterlaen	Faiencier	pre-1630	1666	1652	Delft†
1668	Pieter Born	Painter	n.a.	post-1675	1652	Delft†
	Pieter Haringh	Glassmaker	n.a.	n.a.	1661	Delft†
	Quierinck Kleijnhooven	Faiencier	n.a.	1695	1655	not Delft†
1669	Louys Elsevier	Painter	1618	1675	1646	Leyden
	Michiel van den Houck	Glassmaker	n.a.	post-1703	1657	Delft†
	Gijsbert Kruyck	Faiencier	1623	1681	1645	Delft†
1670	Joannes Vermeer	Painter	1632	1675	1653	Delft
	Jasper Serrot	Glassmaker	n.a.	post-1693	1655	not Delft†
	Jakob Kerton	Faiencier	n.a.	post-1675	1653	not Delft†
1671	Cornelis de Man	Painter	1621	1706	1642	Delft†
	Cijbrant van der Laen	Glassmaker	c. 1637	post-1692	1661	Delft†
	Claes Metschert	Faiencier	n.a.	n.a.	1651	Delft†
1672	Anthonij Palamedes	Painter	1601	1673	1621	Delft†
	Arent van Sanen de Jonge	Glassmaker	n.a.	n.a.	1662	Alkmaar
	Abram de Cooge‡	Faiencier	c. 1600	post-1680	1666	Leyden
1673	Louijs Elsevier	Painter	1618	1675	1642	Delft†
	Michiel van der Hoeck	Glassmaker	n.a.	post-1703	1657	Delft†
	Quiringh Kleynoven	Faiencier	n.a.	1695	1655	not Delft†

TABLE C.I(continued)
Headmen of the St. Lucas Guild, 1611–1680

Year	Name	Craft	Year of Birth	Year of Death	Date of Registration in the guild*	Place of Origin
1674	Pieter van Ruijven	Painter	1651	1719	1672	Delft†
	Frans van der Fijn	Glassmaker	n.a.	n.a.	1633	Delft†
	Jan Klaesse van Straaten	Faiencier	c. 1634	n.a.	1659	Delft†
1675	Cornelis de Man	Painter	1621	1706	1642	Delft†
	Jasper Sarotte	Glassmaker	n.a.	post-1693	c. 1655	not Delft†
	Quieringh Cleijnhoven	Faiencier	n.a.	1695	1655	not Delft†
1677	Johannes Verkolje	Painter	1650	1693	1673	Amsterdam
	Maggiel van der Hoeck	Glassmaker	n.a.	1695	1655	not Delft†
	Cornelis Keyser	Faiencier	c. 1650	1684	1667	Delft†
1678	Cornelis van der Kuyt	Painter	n.a.	post-1686	1671	Delft†
	Seybrant van der Laan	Glassmaker	c. 1637	post-1692	1661	Delft†
	Lambertus Kleffius	Faiencier	n.a.	n.a.	1667	not Delft†
1679	Pieter van Ruijven	Painter	1651	1719	1672	Delft
	Jan van der Poel	Glassmaker	n.a.	post-1713	1667	Delft†
	Gijsbrecht Cruyck	Faiencier	1623	1681	1645	Delft†
1680	Cornelis de Man	Painter	1621	1706	1642	Delft†
	Jasper Sarot	Glassmaker	n.a.	post-1693	1655	not Delft†
	William Kleffius	Faiencier	c. 1626	post-1681	1666	not Delft†

SOURCES: All headmen's names are taken from F.D.O. Obreen, *Archief voor Nederlandsche Kunstgeschiedenis*, 7 vols. (Rotterdam: Hengel en Eeltjes, 1877–1890)1:12–43, 50–86; with the exception of the following years: 1611, 1614, 1616, 1619, and 1622 from J. Soutendam, "Eenige aanteekeningen betreffende Delfsche kunstenaars," *Nederlandsche Spectator* (1870):13; 1626 from Abraham Bredius, *Künstler-inventare: Urkunden zur Geschichte der Holländischen Kunst des XVI^{ten}, XVII^{ten}, und XVIII^{ten} Jahrhunderts*, 7 vols. (The Hague: Martinus Nijhoff, 1915–1921), 5:322.

NOTES: Only the "incoming," or newly elected headmen are listed in the table. Since the incoming headmen of one year became the retiring headmen of the next, for a few years where no other information was available, the names of the incoming headmen of one year have been inferred from the names of the retiring headmen of the next. All names are written precisely as they appear in the source.

*If a member's name appeared in the master book of 1613 and no earlier date of registration was known, the year 1613 is assumed to be his year of registration.

†Place of origin inferred from the amount paid as entrance fee.

‡De Cooge registered for the second time, as a faiencier, in December 1666.

Notes

NOTES TO INTRODUCTION

1. F. D. O. Obreen, *Archief voor Nederlandsche Kunstgeschiedenis*, 7 vols. (Rotterdam, 1877-1890), 1:1-119.

2. R. W. Scheller, "Nieuwe gegevens over het St. Lukasgilde te Delft in de zestiende eeuw," *Nederlandsch Kunsthistorisch Jaarboek* 26 (1972):41-48. These sixteenth-century accounts are discussed in Chapter 1.

3. Published as "New Documents on Vermeer and His Family," *Oud-Holland* 91 (1977):267-87; and "Vermeer and His Milieu: Conclusion of an Archival Study," *Oud-Holland* 94 (1980):44-62.

4. N. W. Posthumus, *Inquiry into the History of Prices in Holland*, 2 vols. (Leyden: E. J. Brill, 1946).

NOTES TO CHAPTER 1

1. D. P. Oosterbaan, "Kroniek van de Nieuwe Kerk te Delft; inleiding en aantekeningen," *Haarlemse Bijdragen* 65 (1958):9-18.

2. Ibid., p. 80.

3. Ibid., p. 192.

4. Ibid., p. 196.

5. Ibid., pp. 204-5; and L. H. H. van der Kloot Meijburg, *De Nieuwe Kerk te Delft* (Rotterdam: W. L. J. Brusse, 1941), p. 35.

6. *Beschryvinge der Stadt Delft* (Delft, 1667).

7. On early Dutch illustrated manuscripts, see P. J. Vermeeren, "Delftse verluchte handschriften ter Koninklijke Bibliotheek," in *Oud-Delft: Een Serie van Historische Publicaties*, ed. B. van't Hoff (Rotterdam and The Hague: Nijgh en van Ditmer, n.d.). On the master of Virgo inter Virgines see K. G. Boon, "De meester van de Virgo inter Virgines," in *Oud-Delft*, ed. van't Hoff.

8. Van Bleyswijck, *Beschryvinge der Stadt Delft*, p. 164.

9. Ibid., p. 290.

10. Ibid., pp. 210-11.

11. Ibid., pp. 256-57.

12. Ibid.

13. Delft, Municipal Archives, Reformed Community (*Kerk voogdy*), "Dit is alsulck uytgheef als die meesters der fabrike van die nieuwe kerck vuijtgegeven hebben" (n.d., ca. 1536-1560), fol. 56. Hereafter cited as "Uytgheef."

14. Ibid., fol. 76v.

15. Ibid., fol. 134.

16. Ibid., fol. 37v.

17. Ibid., fol. 99v, 135.

18. Karel van Mander, *Het Schilderboeck ... der Edele Vrye Schilderkonst* (Haarlem, 1604), fol. 245.

19. Delft, Municipal Archives, First Division (1ᵉ *afdeeling*), "Rekening-boekje (van de deken) van het sint Lucas gilde te Delft over de jaren 1537-1593," fol. 1, 1v. Hereafter cited as "Rekeningboekje."

20. Van Mander, *Het Schilderboeck,* fol. 226.

21. "Uytgheef," fol. 99.

22. Ibid., fol. 104, 104v.

23. Ibid., fol. 128.

24. Ibid., fol. 247v.

25. Ibid., fol. 150.

26. Oosterbaan, *De Oude Kerk te Delft gedurende de Middeleeuwen* (The Hague: J. N. Voorhoeve, 1973), pp. 77-78.

27. Van Bleyswijck, *Beschryvinge der Stadt Delft,* pp. 257-58.

28. Ibid.

29. "Uytgheef," fol. 135.

30. "Rekeningboekje," fol. 1.

31. Oosterbaan, *De Oude Kerk,* p. 78.

32. "Rekeningboekje," fol. 2.

33. Ibid.

34. Ibid., fol. 2v.

35. R. W. Scheller, "Nieuwe gegevens over het St. Lukasgilde te Delft in de zestiende eeuw," *Nederlandsch Kunsthistorisch Jaarboek* 26 (1972):42.

36. Van Bleyswijck, *Beschryvinge der Stadt Delft,* p. 165.

37. Van Mander, *Het Schilderboeck,* fol. 246.

38. Van Bleyswijck, *Beschryvinge der Stadt Delft,* pp. 254-55.

39. Ibid.

40. Ibid.

41. Ibid., p. 255.

42. Ibid., p. 248.

43. J. Soutendam, "Beeldstormerij te Delft in Augustus en Oktober 1566," *Bijdragen voor Vaderlandsche Geschiedenis en Oudheidkunde,* n.s., pt. 9 (1877):*passim.*

44. Van Bleyswijck, *Beschryvinge der Stadt Delft,* p. 413.

45. Ibid., p. 416.

46. Ibid., pp. 249-50.

47. "Rekeningboekje," fol. 5v.

48. Ibid., fol. 6.

49. Ibid., fol. 7.

50. Ibid., fol. 7v.

51. Ibid., fol. 6.

52. Ibid., fol. 8v.

53. Oosterbaan, *De Oude Kerk,* p. 265.

54. "Rekeningboekje," fol. 8v.

55. Ibid., fol. 9v.

56. Oosterbaan, *De Oude Kerk,* p. 34.

57. Ibid., p. 35.

58. Ibid., p. 262.

59. "Rekeningboekje," fol. 10.

60. Ibid., fol. 10v.

61. Ibid., fol. 24.

62. Rechterlijk Archief van Delft, No. 26ᵉ, *Contreboek,* cited in the handwritten notes of Abraham Bredius preserved in the Rijksbureau voor Kunsthistorische Documentatie (hereafter R. K. D.) in The Hague. Hereafter cited as "Bredius Notes."

63. "Rekeningboekje," fol. 10v.

64. Max Eisler, *Alt-Delft: Kultur und Kunst* (Amsterdam: Elsevier, 1923), pp. 138-39.

65. Cf. J. G. C. Briels, *Zuidnederlandse boekdrukkers en boekverkopers in de Republiek der Verenigden Nederlanden omstreeks* 1570-1630 (The Hague: Nieuwkoop and B. de Graaf, 1974), pp. 38-39.

66. On Vennecoel, see ibid., p. 39.

67. On the substitution of private for undersupplied public goods, see Burton A. Weisbrod, "Toward a Theory of the Voluntary Non-Profit Sector in a Three-Sector Economy," in *Altruism, Morality, and Economic Theory,* ed. Edmund Phelps (New York: Russell Sage Foundation, 1972).

NOTES TO CHAPTER 2

1. Delft, Municipal Archives, Justice Archives (O. R. A.), 168, "Camerbouck" fol. 372v. (16 July 1602). Hereafter cited as "Camerbouck."

2. G. J. Hoogewerff and J. Q. Regteren Altena, *Arnoldus Buchelius "Res pictoriae,"* Quellenstudien zur Holländische Kunstgeschichte, vol. 15 (The Hague: M. Nijhoff, 1928), pp. 42-43.

3. G. Brom and L. A. Langeraad, *Diarium van Arend van Buchell,* in *Werken* ser. 3, no. 2 (Utrecht: Historisch Genootschap, 1907), p. 460.

4. Quoted in Abraham Bredius, "De tapijtfabriek van Karel van Mander de Jonge te Delft," *Oud-Holland* 3 (1885):2; on tapestry manufacture, see also Chapter 9 below.

5. Delft. Municipal Archives. Orphan Chamber, *boedel* no. 1.

6. Records of Notary Vranck van Uytenbrouck, no. 1534, 24 May 1596. This severely damaged document cannot be made out in its entirety.

7. Delft O. R. A., "Camerbouck," 168, fol. 65v.-68v. The text is based on the excellent summary of the document by Bredius in F. D. O. Obreen, *Archief voor Nederlandsche Kunstgeschiedenis,* 7 vols. (Rotterdam, 1877-1890), 3:283-86.

8. Delft O. R. A., "Camerbouck," 169, 22 March 1605.

9. G. J. Hoogewerff, *De geschiedenis van de St. Lucasgilden in Nederland* (Amsterdam: P. N. van Kampen en Zoon, 1947), p. 31.

10. J. G. C. Briels, *Zuidnederlandse boekdrukkers en boekverkopers in de Republiek der Verenigden Nederlanden omstreeks 1570-1630* (The Hague: Nieuwkoop and B. de Graaf, 1974), p. 241.

11. Records of Notary Adriaen Rijshouck, no. 1764, 9 February 1612.

12. Records of Notary Pieter Adriaensz. de Roon, no. 1618, 24 and 28 June 1613.

13. Records of Notary Cornelis Westerbaen, no. 1523, 2 July 1593.

14. Delft. Municipal Archives. Van der Burgh handwritten notes.

15. Camer van Charitate, "Reckeningen van de deuijt op de gulden," no. 28, fol. 2.

16. A. H. H. van der Burgh, "Aanteekeningen betreffende de oudste Delfsche plateelbakkers," *Oud-Holland* 21 (1903):35.

17. Camer von Charitate, "Reckeningen," no. 29, fol. 22v.

18. Records of Notary Jan de Molijn, no. 1559, 6 March 1611.

19. Van der Burgh handwritten notes.

20. Records of Notary Adriaen Rijshouck, no. 1758, 9 October 1606. This document is transliterated in Van der Burgh, "Aanteekeningen," p. 24.

21. Records of Notary Adriaen Rijshouck, no. 1763, 28 January 1611. This document is transliterated in part in Van der Burgh, "Aanteekeningen," p. 39.

22. Records of Notary Jan de Molijn, no. 1559, 11 March 1611; and Van der Burgh, "Aanteekeningen," p. 45.

23. Records of Notary Jan de Molijn, no. 1560, 7 June 1611.

24. Records of Notary Jan de Molijn, no. 1563, 6 January 1612.

25. J. H. Kernkamp, *De handel op den vijand 1572-1690,* 2 vols. (Utrecht: Kemink en Zoon, n.d.), 2:335-50.

26. *Berichten van het Historisch Gezelschap te Utrecht,* vol. 1/2 (1846), p. 36.

NOTES TO CHAPTER 3

1. G. J. Hoogewerff, *De geschiedenis van de St. Lucasgilden in Nederland* (Amsterdam: P. N. van Kampen en Zoon, 1947), pp. 104, 162-64.

2. *Ibid.,* p. 171.

3. F. D. O. Obreen, *Archief voor Nederlandsche Kunstgeschiedenis,* 7 vols. (Rotterdam, 1877-1890), 1:48.

4. Ibid., p. 52.

5. Ibid., p. 53.

6. Ibid., p. 40.

7. Abraham Bredius, *Künstler-inventare; Urkunden zur Geschichte der Holländischen Kunst des XVI^{ten}, XVII^{ten}, XVIII^{ten} Jahrhunderts,* 7 vols. (The Hague: Martinus Nijhoff, 1915-1921), 6:2,232, 2,235.

8. C. H. de Jonge, *Dutch Tiles* (London: Pall Mall Press, 1971), p. 59.

9. Records of Notary Engelbert van der Vloet, no. 2067.
10. Records of Notary Willem de Langue, no. 1696.
11. Records of Notary Testart van Hasselt, no. 2155.
12. Records of Notary Willem de Langue, no. 1695, 27 July 1653.
13. Obreen, *Archief,* 1:12.
14. Ibid., p. 13.
15. Ibid., pp. 53, 63.
16. See Appendix B.
17. Obreen, *Archief,* 1:64-65.
18. Records of Notary Cornelis Coeckebakker, no. 1610, 17 March 1618.
19. See Appendix B.
20. Ibid.
21. Obreen, *Archief,* 1:73.
22. Ibid., p. 83.
23. Records of Notary Nicholaes Vrienbergh, no. 2054, 4 April 1656.
24. Records of Notary Dirck Rees, no. 2138, 11 November 1663.
25. Obreen, *Archief,* 1:32.
26. See Appendix B.
27. Obreen, *Archief,* 1:58, 65.
28. Ibid., p. 29.
29. J. Soutendam, "Eenige aanteekeningen betreffende Delfsche Kunstenaars," *Nederlandsche Spectator* (1870):12-13.
30. See Appendix B.
31. Ibid.
32. Dirck van Bleyswijck, *Beschryvinge der Stadt Delft* (Delft, 1667), p. 652.
33. Soutendam, "Eenige aanteekeningen," p. 18; Obreen, *Archief,* 1:57.
34. Van Bleyswijck, *Beschryvinge der Stadt Delft,* p. 646.
35. Appendix B.
36. Ibid.
37. A. J. J. M. van Peer, "Rondom Jan Vermeer van Delft," *Oud-Holland* 74 (1959): 243-44.
38. Soutendam, "Eenige aanteekeningen," pp. 10-11.
39. Records of Notary Willem van Assendelft, no. 1868, 19 October 1661.
40. Records of Notary Cornelis Coeckebakker, no. 1610, 17 March 1618.
41. Obreen, *Archief,* 1:61.
42. Soutendam, "Eenige aanteekeningen," pp. 16-17 and Chapter 7 below, p. 189.
43. Records of Notary Christiaen van Vliet, no. 2037, 27 May 1669.
44. See Chapter 2.
45. Appendix B.
46. Ibid.
47. Chapter 8, Table 8.4.
48. See Chapter 7, Table 7.1.

NOTES TO CHAPTER 4

1. Chapter 9, Table 9.2.
2. Records of Notary Nicholaes Vrienbergh, no. 2055, 31 August 1656.
3. Dirck van Bleyswijck, *Beschryvinge der Stadt Delft* (Delft, 1667), p. 646.
4. Delft, Municipal Archives, First Division, "Rekkeningen St. Lukas gilde beginnende den jare 1723," fol. 1 and 2.

NOTES TO CHAPTER 5

1. Johannes G. van Dillen, "Summiere staat van de in 1622 in Provincie van Holland gehouden volkstelling," *Economisch-historisch Jaarboek* 21 (1940):175.
2. Max Eisler, *Alt-Delft: Kultur und Kunst* (Amsterdam: Elsevier, 1923), p. 17.
3. Records of Notary Frans Boogert no. 1993, 31 March 1645; and estate records of Lambert Kruyck (Orphan Chamber, *boedel* no. 418).
4. The carpenter's wages are from a deposition in the records of Notary Adriaen van der Block, no. 1740, 13 November 1640.
5. On the price of brown bread in 1676 (eighteen stuivers for twelve lbs.), see the depositions of 21 and 23 October 1676 in the records of Notary Abraham van der Velde, no. 2178. For the other prices, see Eisler, *Alt-Delft*, p. 26.
6. Delft, Camer van Charitate, "Register van Ambachtsjongens," no. 52, fol. 84.
7. Ibid., fol. 213.
8. Ibid., fol. 167v.
9. Records of Notary Adriaen Rijshouck, no. 1760.
10. Contract of 2 February 1621, records of Notary Herman Jansz. van der Ceel, no. 1636.
11. Contract of 4 February 1629, records of Notary Adriaan van Twelle, no. 1654.
12. Records of Notary Willem van Assendelft, no. 1858.
13. Camer van Charitate. "Reckeningen van de duijt op de gulden," 1598–1644.
14. Orphan Chamber, *boedel* no. 447.
15. Orphan Chamber, *boedel* no. 1197 I.
16. Records of Notary Frans Boogert, no. 2001, 20 April 1657.
17. Ibid., no. 2000, 14 May 1655.
18. Orphan Chamber, *boedel* no. 1865 I.
19. Ibid., *boedel* no. 1010.
20. Ibid., *boedel* no. 334.
21. Records of notary Johan van Beest, no. 1669, 17 January 1641.
22. Records of notary Testart van Hasselt, no. 2155, 2 May 1667.

NOTES TO CHAPTER 6

1. The inventory is given in the records of Notary Herman Jansz. van der Ceel, no. 1636, 21 December 1621. It is cited in Abraham Bredius, *Künstler-inventare; Urkunden zur Geschichte der Holländischen Kunst des XVI^{ten}, XVII^{ten}, XVIII^{ten} Jahrhunderts*, 7 vols. (The Hague: Martinus Nijhoff, 1915-1921), 5:1, 753 and ff.

2. The payment for painting the doors of privies is recorded in Delft, Municipal Archives, First Division, "Reckening; Meester Jan Hogenhouck Tesoryer der Stadt Delft," 1608, fol. 303. On Jan Molijn's copy, see Chapter 10, note h.

3. Ake Bengtsson, *Studies on the Rise of Realistic Painting in Holland*, 1610-1625, (Stockholm: Institute of Art History of Uppsala, 1952), pp. 34-35.

4. Delft, Municipal Archives, Reformed Community, "Lidtmaten registers," no. 203 (1598 to 1604).

5. Briefly summarized in Bredius, *Künstler-inventare*, 5:1,758. The original source from which I have drawn my account of the dispute is the records of Notary Henrick Vockestaert, no. 1581, 9 July 1617.

6. Records of Notary Cornelis Pietersz. Bleiswijck, no. 1901, 20 October 1659.

7. P. T. A. Swillens, "R. K. Kunstenaars in de 17de Eeuw, "*Katholiek Cultureel Tijdschrift*, 15 January 1946, pp. 416-19.

8. Records of Notary Nicholaes Vrienbergh, no. 2052, 20 June 1654.

9. Records of Notary Adriaen Rijshouck, no. 1814, 18 June 1622.

10. See the discussion in Albert Blankert, *Vermeer of Delft: Complete Edition of the Paintings* (Oxford: Phaidon, 1978), p. 88.

11. Orphan Chamber, *boedel* of the Verboom family, no. 1760 II.

12. Records of Notary Cornelis Ingelo, no. 1634c.

13. Records of Notary Johan van Beest, no. 1664.

14. Records of Notary Willem van Assendelft, no. 1855.

15. Orphan Chamber, *boedel* of Jan Joppens van Waterwijck, no. 1884.

16. Records of Notary Herman Jansz. van der Ceel, no. 1639, 28 May 1623; cited in Bredius, *Künstler inventare*, 1:120.

17. Records of Notary Govert Rota, no. 1978, 27 May 1645.

18. Bredius, *Künstler-inventare* 6:1,927-28.

19. Records of Notary Johan van Ruiven, no. 1958.

20. Records of Notary Frans Boogert, no. 2000, May 1655.

21. Orphan Chamber, *boedel* no. 1126.

22. Records of Notary Frans Boogert, no. 2000, 19 December 1655, cited in Bredius, *Künstler-inventare*, 2:687.

23. Records of Notary Herman Jansz. van der Ceel, no. 1639, 13 April 1625 and Camer van Charitate, "Reckeningen van de deuijt op de gulden," no. 52, fol. 38v.

24. Orphan Chamber, *boedel* of Pieter Dircksz. van Roon, delivered 11 May 1621.

25. Orphan Chamber, *boedel* no. 1324 I, cited in J. M. Montias, "New Documents on Vermeer and His Family," *Oud-Holland* 91(1977):287.

26. Records of Notary Cornelis Pietersz. Bleiswijck, no. 1899, 11 March 1642.

27. Records of Notary Govert Rota, no. 1978, 22 October 1646; and Notary Adriaen van der Wiel, no. 1826, 5 April 1646.

28. Hanns Floerke, *Die Formen des Kunsthandels, das Atelier und die Sammler in den Niederlanden vom 15-18 Jahrhundert*, Studien zur Niederländischen Kunst- und Kulturgeschichte (1905; reprint ed., Soest, Holland: Davaco Publishers, 1972), pp. 132-33.

29. Egbert Haverkamp-Begemann, Introduction to *Rembrandt after Three Hundred Years: An Exhibition of Rembrandt and His Followers* (Chicago: Art Institute of Chicago, 1969), p. 21.

30. Records of Notary Frans Boogert, no. 1993, 7 February 1646.

31. Records of Notary Simon Mesch, no. 2048, 12 December 1651.

32. Records of Notary Henrick Vockestaert, no. 1586, 3 March 1622.

33. Cf. Max Eisler, *Alt-Delft: Kultur und Kunst* (Amsterdam: Elsevier, 1923), pp. 146-50.

NOTES TO CHAPTER 7

1. Cf. Peter Burke, *Tradition and Innovation in Renaissance Italy: A Sociological Approach* (London: William Collins and Sons, Fontana Books, 1974), pp. 97-98, 131-37.

2. J. Soutendam, "Eenige aanteekeningen betreffende Delfsche kunstenaars," *Nederlandsche Spectator* (1870):2.

3. Delft, Municipal Archives, First Division, "Chirurgyns gilde-boek," fol. 43.

4. Soutendam, "Eenige aanteekeningen," p. 11 and Chapter 3 above.

5. Records of Notary Jacob Spoors, no. 1676, 28 August 1655.

6. Hanns Floerke, *Die Formen des Kunsthandels, das Atelier und die Sammler in den Niederlanden vom 15-18 Jahrhundert*, Studien zur Niederländischen Kunst- und Kulturgeschichte (1905; reprint ed., Soest, Holland: Davaco Publishers, 1972), pp. 36-37.

7. Records of Notary Willem de Langue, no. 1695, 4 February 1653, cited in Heinrich Wichmann, *Leonaert Bramer: Sein Leben und Sein Kunst; ein Beitrag zur Geschichte der Holländische Malerei* (Leipzig: W. Hiersemann, 1923), p. 6.

8. Hoogstraten, *Inleyding tot de Hooge schoole der schilder-konst anders de Zichtbaere Werelt* (Rotterdam, 1678), p. 276.

9. Contracts signed 4 and 15 October 1659, and 6 September 1661 (Records of Notary Nicholaes Vrienbergh, nos. 2056, 2058, 2062).

10. Ibid., 4 February 1665.

11. Records of Notary Adriaen Rijshouck, no. 1764, 6 December 1612.

The entire document is transcribed and translated in Abraham Bredius, *Künstler-inventare: Urkunden zur Geschichte der Holländischen Kunst des XVI^{ten}, XVII^{ten}, und XVIII^{ten} Jahrhunderts*, 7 vols. (The Hague: Martinus Nijhoff, 1915-1921) 5:1,756-57.

12. Records of Notary Frans Boogert, no. 2008, 30 January 1671.

13. Records of Notary Cornelis Pietersz. Bleiswijck, no. 1909, 21 October 1656.

14. Records of Notary Abraham van der Velde, no. 2173, 6 April 1674.

15. Orphan Chamber, *boedel* no. 1352.

16. Henry Havard, *L'Art et les Artistes Hollandais* (Paris, 1879), pp. 45-46.

17. Records of Notary Gerrit Adriaensz. van der Wel, no. 1926, 24 August 1638.

18. Orphan Chamber, *boedel* no. 301, 8 August 1628; Bredius, "Wat Anthony Palamedes aan een portrait verdiende," *Oud-Holland* 34 (1916):131.

19. Records of Notary Guillaume de Graeff, no. 1707, 31 December 1638.

20. Records of Notary Abraham van der Velde, no. 2172, 15 December 1669.

21. Records of Notary Johan van Steeland, no. 1831, 11 December 1639.

22. Records of Notary Henrick Vockestaert, no. 1580, 11 October 1617; and of Notary Jan Jorisz. van Ophoven, no. 1956, 27 November 1673.

23. Records of Notary Govert Rota, no. 1984, 9 August 1653.

24. Bredius, "Drie delftsche schilders," *Oud-Holland* 6 (1888):291.

25. Records of Notary Henrick Vockestaert, no. 1581, 16 October 1617.

26. Records of Notary Jacob van Santen, no. 2017, 1 October 1651.

27. P. Haverkorn van Rijswijck, "Eenige aanteekeningen betreffende schilders wonende buiten Rotterdam uit het Archief te Rotterdam," *Oud-Holland* 8 (1890):214.

28. Bredius, "De delftsche schilders Jan Willemsz. Decker en Willem Jansz. Decker," *Oud-Holland* 10 (1892):195. The estate papers of Willem Jansz. Decker are in the records of Notary Adriaen Rijshouck, no. 1817.

29. Records of Notary Nicholaes Vrienbergh, no. 2052, 7 February 1653.

30. Records of Notary Cornelis Pietersz. Bleiswijck, no. 1903, 13 July 1666; and Bredius, *Künstler-inventare*, 4:1,438.

31. J. M. Montias, "Vermeer and His Milieu: Conclusion of an Archival Study," *Oud-Holland* 94 (1980):50-51 and Albert Blankert, *Vermeer of Delft: Complete Edition of the Paintings* (Oxford: Phaidon, 1978), p. 147.

32. The *contracedulle* of Boudewijn de Man's collection, one of the finest auctioned in Delft in the first eighty years of the seventeenth century, is in the records of Notary Willem van Assendelft, no. 1861, 15 March 1644.

33. Soutendam, "Eenige aanteekeningen," pp. 3-4.

34. Records of notary Adriaen Rijshouck, no. 1814, 25 April 1622 and 15 October 1622 and no. 1816, 30 May 1624.

35. Schiedam. Municipal Archives. Records of Notary A. Mulswyck, 9 July 1625, fols. 881-882.

36. Records of Notary Roelandus van Edenburgh, no. 2256, 26 April 1673, deposition by Versteegh.

37. Records of notary Willem van Assendelft, no. 1855, cited in Bredius, *Künstler-inventare*, 6:2,157-58.

38. Orphan Chamber, *boedel* no. 1269 I of Boudewyn van Ortegem, *contracedulle* of 23 March 1618.

39. Orphan Chamber, *boedel* no. 1470, *contracedulle* of Fredrick van Ruyven, brewer, 21 May 1622.

40. Orphan Chamber, *boedel* no. 347 IV.

41. Orphan Chamber, *boedel* of Jan Joppe Waeterwijck, no. 1884.

42. Records of Notary Henrick Vockestaert, no. 1582, 28 March 1618.

43. Records of Notary Henrick Vockestaert, no. 1579, 26 March 1615.

44. Records of Notary Henrick Vockestaert, no. 1582, 9 March 1618.

45. Orphan Chamber, *boedel* no. 500.

46. Records of Notary Willem van Assendelft, no. 1858, 25 April 1635.

47. Records of Notary Testart van Hasselt, no. 2157, 1 March 1672. See also Chapter 7, note u.

48. Records of Notary Jan de Molijn, no. 1550, 16 January 1612.

49. Records of Notary Dirck Rees, no. 2135, 12 July 1660.

50. On his residence in Rotterdam, see records of Notary Pieter Adriaensz. de Roon, no. 1619, 14 and 19 January 1619. The two documents are in such poor shape they cannot be made out completely. Serange's inventory was published in Bredius, *Künstler-inventare*, 3:948 and 6:2,232-37.

51. Camer van Charitate. "Opperste Kleed Boeken," 26 May 1629.

52. Records of Notary Adriaan van Twelle, no. 1653, 7 December 1624; and records of Notary Johan van Beest, no. 1661, 20 September 1624.

53. Records of Notary Adriaan van Twelle, no. 1654, 12 April 1624.

54. Gorinchem, Municipal Archives, "Rechterlijk archief," no. 553, 14 April 1627. On Reynier Vermeer, see also Montias, "New Documents on Vermeer and His Family," *Oud-Holland* 91 (1977):274-84.

55. Floerke, *Die Formen des Kunsthandels*, p. 90.

56. Records of Notary Willem van Assendelft, no. 1859, 28 August and 8 September 1637; of Notary Willem de Langue, no. 1696, 22 January 1655; and of Notary Cornelis Georgin, no. 2084, 29 January 1655.

57. Records of Notary Willem de Langue, no. 1695, cited in Bredius, *Künstler-inventare* 7:39.

58. Erik Duverger, *Nieuwe gegevens betreffende de Kunsthandel van Matthijs Musson en Maria Fourmenois te Antwerpen tussen 1633 en 1681* (Gent: n.p., 1969), p. 79.

59. Bredius, "Het geboortejaar van Jacob van Ruisdael," *Oud-Holland* 6 (1888):22-24.

60. Bredius, *Künstler-inventare*, 8:156.

61. Records of Notary Jacob Spoors, no. 1678, 9 June and 10 July 1663.

62. F. D. O. Obreen, *Archief voor Nederlandsche Kunstgeschiedenis*, 7 vols. (Rotterdam, 1877–1890), 1:71.

63. Records of Notary Cornelis Pietersz. Bleiswijck, no. 1903, 12 and 13 July 1666, cited by Bredius in Obreen, *Archief* 5:168–69.

64. Bredius, *Künstler-inventare* 7:1,438.

65. Bredius, "Drie delftsche schilders," p. 295, citing records of Notary Jacobus van Berlecum, no. 2164, 28 September 1667.

66. Bredius, *Künstler-inventare*, 7:1,512.

67. Records of Notary Dirck Rees, no. 2147, 22 April 1672.

68. Records of Notary Roelandus van Edenburgh, no. 2257, 11 March 1674.

69. Bredius, *Künstler-inventare*, 1:110.

70. Records of Notary Roelandus van Edenburgh, no. 2257, 11 March 1674.

71. Montias, "Vermeer and His Milieu," pp. 50–51.

72. Bredius, "Nieuwe bijdragen over Johannes Vermeer," *Oud-Holland* 29 (1910):62.

73. Bredius, "Italiaansche schilderijen in 1672 door Haagsche en Delftsche schilders beoordeeld," *Oud-Holland* 34 (1916):88–93.

74. See Blankert, *Vermeer of Delft*, p. 9 and pp. 150–52.

75. Records of Notary Willem de Langue, no. 1688, 24 January 1636. The document is severely damaged by humidity.

76. Records of Notary Willem van Ruyven, no. 2278, 12 April 1675.

77. Bredius, *Künstler-inventare* 5:1,676.

78. Records of Notary Cornelis Pietersz. Bleiswijck, no. 1917.

NOTES TO CHAPTER 8

1. On these donations, see Chapter 5.

2. Records of Notary Cornelis Ingelo, no. 1634D, 8 February 1618.

3. Records of Notary Herman Jansz. van der Ceel, no. 1635, 12 September 1620.

4. Orphan Chamber, *boedel* no. 1045, 19 May 1637.

5. Orphan Chamber, *boedel* no. 1526 III, 13 December 1624.

6. Orphan Chamber, *boedel* of Lieven Pieckius, no. 1313 I, 27 April 1638.

7. Inventory of Maritge Willems van Noorden (Records of Notary Govert Rota, no. 1990, 30 August 1659).

8. Inventory of Dirck Cornelis van den Bijl (Orphan Chamber, *boedel* no. 285, 19 October 1650).

9. Inventory of Dr. Johan Hogenhouck (Orphan Chamber, *boedel* no. 810 I).

10. Inventory of the widow of H. M. van Gogh (Orphan Chamber, *boedel* no. 635 I, delivered 19 July 1661).

11. Records of Notary Testart van Hasselt, no. 2157, 1 March 1672.

12. Records of Notary Testart van Hasselt, no. 2156, 12 August 1668.

13. Records of Notary Frans Boogert, no. 2001, 16 August 1657.

14. Records of Notary Testart van Hasselt, no. 2158, 4 July 1673.

15. Inventory of Samuel La Roche, Orphan Champer, *boedel* no. 1955, 14 December 1667.

16. Records of Notary Henrick Vockestaert, no. 1585, 16 February 1621. On Grimani, see also Chapter 2.

17. Abraham Bredius, "Drie delftsche schilders," *Oud-Holland* 6 (1888):290-91. The summary here contains details of the original omitted by Bredius (Records of Notary Frans Boogert, no. 1995).

18. J. M. Montias, "New Documents on Vermeer and His Family," *Oud-Holland* 91 (1977):287.

19. Orphan Chamber, *boedel* no. 1863 of Jacob Corstiaensz. Goosens who died on 12 June 1669.

20. Orphan Chamber, *boedel* no. 1204 I, 20 April 1645.

21. Orphan Chamber, *boedel* no. 599 II, III.

22. Records of Notary Johan van Steeland, no. 1843, April 1646 (Marriage contract, Anna van der Made and Michiel van der Hoef).

23. Records of Notary Gerrit Adriaensz. van der Wel, no. 1928, 9 October 1648.

24. Records of Notary Govert Rota, no. 1977, 13 August 1648.

25. Orphan Chamber, *boedel* no. 840, 12 September 1676.

26. Jan Emmens, "Einst aber ist nötig: Inhalt und Bedeutung von Markt- und Küchenstücke des 16 Jahrhunderts," in *Album Amicorum J. G. van Gelder* (The Hague: M. Nijhoff, 1973), pp. 93-101.

27. Orphan Chamber, *boedel* no. 347 V.

28. Orphan Chamber, *boedel* no. 1182.

29. Orphan Chamber, *boedel* no. 761.

30. Orphan Chamber, *boedel* no. 294 II.

31. Montias, "Vermeer and His Milieu: Conclusion of an Archival Study," *Oud-Holland* 94 (1980):50-51.

32. Records of Notary Govert Rota, no. 1981, 31 May 1650.

33. Records of Notary Willem de Langue, no. 1691, 31 August 1643.

34. Records of Notary Johan van Beest, no. 1669, 18 January 1641.

35. Records of Notary Willem van Assendelft, no. 1861, 15 March 1644.

36. K. W. Swart, "Holland's Bourgeoisie and the Retarded Industrialization of the Netherlands," in *Failed Transitions to Modern Industrial Society: Renaissance Italy and Seventeenth Century Holland*, ed. F. Krant and P. M. Hohenberg (Montreal: Concordia University and Université du Quebec à Montréal, 1975), p. 47.

37. Cited in Hanns Floerke, *Die Formen des Kunsthandels, das Atelier und die Sammler in den Niederlanden vom 15-18 Jahrhundert*, Studien zur Niederländischen Kunst- und Kulturgeschichte (1905; reprint ed., Soest, Holland: Davaco Publishers, 1972.)

NOTES TO CHAPTER 9

1. Records of Notary Frans Boogert, no. 1994, 8 May 1647.

2. J. G. C. Briels, *Zuidnederlandse boekdrukkers en boekverkopers in de Republiek der Verenigden Nederlanden omstreeks* 1570-1630 (The Hague: Nieuwkoop and B. de Graaf, 1974) p. 24.

3. Ibid.

4. Records of Notary Adriaen Rijshouck, no. 1770, 13 February 1618.

5. Records of Notary Herman Jansz. van der Ceel, no. 1639.

6. Ibid.

7. The original of the contract for this sale, which has long been known, is in the records of Notary Adriaen Rijshouck, no. 1813, 21 June 1621.

8. Cited in Joseph Moxon, *Mechanick Exercises on the Whole Art of Printing 1683-1684,* ed. H. Davis and H. Carter (London: Oxford University Press, 1958), p. 372.

9. Records of Notary Cornelis Adriaansz. de Roon, no. 1698, 15 January 1627. This document, like most of those that survived from this notary's papers, is severely damaged by humidity.

10. Records of Notary Willem van Assendelft, no. 1856, 18 October 1631.

11. Ibid, 20 October 1631.

12. Records of Notary Arent Bogaard, no. 1874, 17 April 1631.

13. Records of Notary Willem van Assendelft, no. 1857, 17 January 1632.

14. Ibid., 19 May 1632.

15. Ibid., 22 September 1632.

16. Ibid., 14 April 1633.

17. Moxon, *Mechanick Exercises,* pp. xx, xxi.

18. Records of Notary Willem de Langue, no. 1687, 15 March 1633.

19. For his biography, see Briels, *Zuidnederlandse boekdrukkers,* pp. 192-93.

20. Records of Notary Gerrit Adriaensz. van der Wel, no. 1938, 27 November 1636.

21. Records of Notary Willem van Assendelft, no. 1859, 3 March 1637.

22. Moxon, *Meckanick Exercises,* p. xix.

23. Ibid, p. xx.

24. Records of Notary Govert Rota, no. 1976, 10 April 1641.

25. Records of Notary Cornelis Cornelisz. Brouwer, no. 1660, 31 August 1644.

26. Records of Notary A. C. Bogaard, no. 1880, 11 August 1651. Heuckelom was not a member of the Guild of St. Lucas in Delft.

27. Briels, *Zuidnederlandse boekdrukkers,* p. 192.

28. Records of Notary Cornelis Pietersz. Bleiswijck, no. 1909, 16 October 1649.

29. Briels, *Zuidnederlandse boekdrukkers,* pp. 191-92.

30. Records of Notary Adriaen Rijshouck, no. 1823, 16 November 1641.

31. Records of Notary Testart van Hasselt, no. 2152, 12 June 1661.

32. Records of Notary Jacob Spoors, no. 1675, 6 July 1653.

33. Albert Blankert, *Vermeer of Delft: Complete Edition of the Paintings* (Oxford: Phaidon, 1978), p. 153.

34. Records of Notary Johannes Ranck, no. 2114.

35. Records of Notary Jacob Spoors, no. 1676, 15 February 1656.

36. Records of Notary Johan van Ruiven, no. 1963, 28 November 1652.

37. On Van Buchell's visit to Delft, see above, Chapter 2.

38. Max Eisler, *Alt-Delft: Kultur und Kunst* (Amsterdam: Elsevier, 1923), p. 113.

39. *Resolutïen der Staten-Generaal (Nieuwe reeks)* (The Hague: M. Nijhoff, 1971), p. 89.

40. Eisler, *Alt-Delft,* p. 113; Bredius, "De tapijtfabriek van Karel van Mande de Jonge te Delft," *Oud-Holland* 3 (1885):2.

41. F. D. O. Obreen, *Archief voor Nederlandsche Kunstgeschiedenis,* 7 vols. (Rotterdam, 1877-1890), 1:294.

42. Bredius, "De tapijtfabriek," p. 8, citing a deposition of 12 February 1632 (Records of Notary Johan van Beest, no. 1666) describing the operation in some detail.

43. Records of Notary Herman Jansz. van der Ceel, no. 1639, 15 February 1624.

44. Bredius, "De tapijtfabriek," p. 11.

45. Ibid., p. 8.

46. Ibid., pp. 6-8.

47. Ibid., p. 13.

48. Ibid., p. 14.

49. Eisler, *Alt-Delft,* p. 120.

50. Ibid.

51. Bredius, "De tapijtfabriek," p. 8.

52. Ibid., p. 8.

53. Ibid., pp. 8-9.

54. Eisler, *Alt-Delft,* p. 117.

55. Ibid., p. 122.

56. Ibid., p. 124.

57. Ibid., p. 125.

58. Ibid., pp. 126-27.

59. Ibid., pp. 128-31.

60. Henry Havard, *Histoire des faïences de Delft, Haarlem, Rotterdam, Utrecht, etc. et des porcelaines de Weesp, Loosdrecht, Amsterdam et La Haye,* 2 vols. (Amsterdam: "Vivat," 1909); C. H. de Jonge, *Dutch Tiles* (London: Pall Mall Press, 1971); Ferrand W. Hudig, *Delfter Fayence; ein Handbuch für Sammler und Liebhaber* (Berlin: R. C. Smidt, 1929).

61. Dirck van Bleyswijck, *Beschryvinge der Stadt Delft* (Delft, 1667), p. 736.

62. Records of Notary Guillaume de Graeff, no. 1721, 4 November 1644.

63. Records of Notary Testart van Hasselt, no. 2154, 24 December 1663.

64. Ibid., no. 2159, 3 January 1676.

65. Records of Notary Dirck Rees, no. 2150, 2 March 1676.

66. Violet Barbour, *Capitalism in Amsterdam in the 17th Century* (Ann Arbor: University of Michigan Press, Ann Arbor Paper Books, 1963), p. 53.

67. Records of Notary Testart van Hasselt, no. 2159, 12 November 1676.

68. Hudig, *Delfter Fayence*, p. 278.

69. On such dispensations, see above Chapter 3.

70. Handwritten notes of A.H.H. van der Burgh, in the Delft Municipal Archives.

71. Records of Notary Cornelis Coeckebakker, no. 1609, 9 December 1613.

72. Camer van Charitate. "Reckeningen van de deuijt op de gulden," vol. 30, part 29, fol. 8.

73. A.H.H. van der Burgh, "Aanteekeningen betreffende de oudste Delfsche plateelbakkers," *Oud-Holland* 21 (1903):32-34.

74. Records of Notary Johan van Beest, no. 1668, 12 March 1640.

75. Ibid.

76. Ibid., no. 1671, 1 May 1647.

77. Records of Notary Frans Boogert, no. 2003, 20 May 1661.

78. Records of Notary Willem de Langue, no. 1687, 3 December 1631; of Notary Willem van Assendelft, no. 1848, 18 Dec. 1632; and of Notary Guillaume de Graaf, no. 1720, 25 March 1642.

79. On Cater, see Van der Burgh, "Aanteekeningen betreffende," p. 44.

80. Van der Burgh, "Delfsche Roode Theepotten," *Oud-Holland* 19 (1901):117.

81. Records of notary Johanne Ranck, no. 2118, 7 March 1662.

82. Obreen, *Archief* 1:69.

83. Van der Burgh, "Delfsche Roode Theepotten," p. 110.

84. Records of Notary Abraham van de Velde, no. 2117, 28 February 1671; and of Notary Frans Boogert, no. 2007, 9 April 1669.

85. The widow's estate papers are contained in the Records of Notary Testart van Hasselt, no. 2155, 2 May 1667.

86. Records of Notary Abraham van de Velde, no. 2176.

87. Ibid., 2 July 1670.

88. Records of Notaries Schalkius van der Walle, no. 1973, 25 July 1661; Dirck Rees, no. 2136, 29 July 1661; Melchior van der Borcht, no. 2042, 5, 8, and 12 December 1661; E. van der Vloet, no. 2070, 11 December 1661, January 2, 1662, and E. van der Vloet, no. 2070, 2 January 1662.

89. De Jonge, *Dutch Tiles*, p. 57.

90. J. Nieuwstraten, "Frederick van Frytom faience-tekenaar en landschap-schilder," *Bulletin Museum Boymans-van Beuningen* 20 (1969):6.

91. De Jonge, *Dutch Tiles*, p. 59-60; and Nieuwstraten, "Frederick van Frytom," p. 30.

92. Havard, *Histoire des faïences de Delft*, 2:99.

93. Illustrated in Hudig, *Delfter Fayence*, p. 102.

94. Records of Notary Johan van Beest, no. 1664, 3 April 1629.

95. Records of Notary Willem de Langue, no. 1685, 1 January 1627.

96. Records of Notary Johan van Beest, no. 1664, 15 July 1628.

97. Havard, *Histoire des faïences de Delft*, 2:61.

98. Records of Notary Roelandus van Edenburgh, no. 2246, 31 January 1676.

99. Records of Notaries Dirck Rees, no. 2148, 28 April 1673; and Obreen, *Archief*, 1:825.

100. Records of notary G. de Graaf, no. 1719, 25 February 1640.

101. Havard, *Histoire des faïences de Delft*, 2:64.

102. Delft, Municipal Archives., First Division. "Rekening; Meester Jan Hogenhouck Tesoryer der Stadt Delft," 1608, fol. 195v.; 1610, fols. 280v.

103. Van der Burgh, "Aanteekeningen betreffende," p. 33.

104. Records of Notaries Simon Mesch, no. 2046, 20 September 1649 and Adriaen van der Block, no. 1756, 23 June 1689.

NOTES TO CHAPTER 10

1. Max Eisler, *Alt-Delft: Kultur und Kunst* (Amsterdam: Elsevier, 1923), p. 147.

2. Ibid.

3. Ibid., pp. 24-25.

4. Dirck van Bleiswijck, *Beschryvinge der Stadt Delft* (Delft, 1667), p. 642.

5. A. C. Crena de Iongh, *G. C. van Santen's Lichte Wigger en Snappende Siitgen; zeventiende-eeuwse gesprekken in Delfts Dialect* (Assen: Van Gorcum, 1959), pp. 1-3.

6. Records of Notary Willem de Langue, no. 1686, 17 April 1628.

7. Ibid., no. 1690, 3 July 1642.

8. Records of Notary Herman Jansz. van der Ceel, no. 1639, 1 October 1623.

9. The apprenticeship contract is contained in the records of Notary Adriaan van Twelle, no. 1654, 27 July 1628.

10. Above, Chapter 2, note b.

11. Records of Notary Adriaen Rijshouck, no. 1760, 18 October 1618.

12. Records of Notary Joris van der Houve, no. 2023, 16 May 1650.

13. See above, Chapter 3 and Appendix 3.

14. Walter Liedtke, Review of *Perspective, Optics and Delft Artists around 1650*, by Arthur Wheelock, *Art Bulletin* 61 (1979):492.

NOTES TO APPENDIX B

1. Delft, Municipal Archives, First division (1ᵉ *afdeeling*), "Keurboek" 5, fols. 305-313v.
2. Ibid., fol. 388-388v.
3. Ibid., "Keurboek" 6, fol. 19-19.
4. Ibid., fol. 180-180v.
5. Ibid., "Keurboek" 7, fol. 184-184v.
6. Ibid., fol. 345-346v.
7. Ibid., "Keurboek" 8, fols. 75v.-76.
8. Ibid., fols. 130v.-131v.
9. Ibid., fols. 151v.-153.
10. Ibid., fols. 355v.-356.
11. Ibid., "Keurboek" 9 fols. 6-7.

Bibliography

MANUSCRIPT SOURCES

Belgium

Brussels. Algemeen Rijksarchief. "Quahier ofte registre van den hondersten penninck van die meuble gueden," (Delft, 1568). Audience 618/36. Handwritten copy in Delft Municipal Archives.

The Netherlands

The Hague. Algemeen Rijksarchief, Staten van Holland, 1572-1795. "Quoyier van de taxatie van alle huijsen staende binnen der stadt Delft" (1576). No. 1290 J. J.

The Hague. Rijksbureau voor kunsthistorische documentatie. Handwritten notes of Abraham Bredius. Photographic files.

Delft. Archives of the Hoogheemraadschap van Delfland. "Elfde reckening" no. 798.

Delft. Municipal Archives. First Division (1ᵉ *afdeeling*)

"Begrafboeken van de Oude en Nieuwe Kerck," 1593-1611 (Burial files).

"Chirurgyns gilde-boeck."

"Doopboeken" 1617-1680, (Baptism files).

"Haardsteden register," 1600.

"Keurboeken," nos. 5-9.

"Legger van de persoonen die haer begaven in den H. echten staat," 1593-1680 (Marriage files).

"Legger van der verpondingen op den huysen ende gronden," 1620.

"Legger van der verpondingen op den huysen ende gronden volgen uyt't redress general begonnen metten jare 1632."

"Porters der stede van Delft gemaect: Poyrter regyster," 1536-1649.

"Register van de doden begraven," 1612-1685 (Burial files).

"Regyster boek(en) van de getroude personen," 1590-1611.

"Reckening; Meester Jan Hogenhouck Tesoryer der stadt Delff van den jaere 1601, 1608, 1611."

"Rekeningboekje (van de deken) van het Sint Lucas gilde te Delft over de jaren 1537-1593" (also, unpublished transcription by J. L. van der Gouw).

"Rekkeningen van het St. Lukas gilde beginnende den jare 1723."

"Resolutie boucken van veertigen ende vroedschappen der stadt 1592-1625."

Delft. Municipal Archives. Camer van Charitate.

"Opperste Kleed Boeken," 1598-1680.

Bibliography

"Reckeningen van de deuijt op de gulden," 1598-1644.
"Register van Ambachtsjongens," 1597-1611, 1612-1630.
Delft. Municipal Archives. Justice Archives (O.R.A.).
  "Camerbouck" no. 168 (1596 to 15 April 1603).
  "Camerbouck" no. 169 (16 April 1603 to May 1613).
Delft. Municipal Archives. Orphan Chamber. *Weeskamer* Estate Settlements
  (*boedels*).
Delft. Municipal Archives. Reformed Community (Kerk voogdy).
  "Dit is alsulck uytgheef als die meesters der fabrike van die nieuwe kerck
    vuijtgegeven hebben" (not dated, c. 1536-1560).
  "Lidtmaten registers," 1598-1604.
  "Thienste reckeninge van de Oude Kerck," 1597-1598.
  "Twede generale reckening," 1608-1609.
Delft. Municipal Archives. Handwritten notes of A.H.H. van der Burgh.
Gorinchem. Municipal Archives. "Rechterlijk Archief."
Leyden. Municipal Archives. no. 849. "Deeken ende hooftmans boek vant
  gilde van St. Lucas Ordre."
Schiedam. Municipal Archives. Records of Notary A. Mulswyck.

RECORDS OF NOTARIES CONSULTED IN DELFT MUNICIPAL ARCHIVES

	Archive numbers	Dates
Cornelis Westerbaen	1522-1534	1589-1602
Vranck van Uytenbrouck	1525-1535	1592-1624
Jacob Dassegny	1536-1538	1592-1598
Herman Cornelis van Overgaeu	1539-1547	1596-1615
Jan de Molijn	1548-1569	1608-1618
Henrick Vockestaert	1577-1601	1613-1634
Cornelis Coeckebakker	1609-1617	1612-1652
Pieter Adriaensz. de Roon	1618-1619	1613-1619
Cornelis van Vliet	1621	1642-1650
Jan de Roon	1623-1630	1614-1634
Andries Schieveen	1631-1634	1621-1664
Cornelis Ingelo	1634a-1634f	1616-1628
Herman Jansz. van der Ceel	1635-1646	1618-1662
Dirck de Haen	1648-1649	1618-1629
Gerard Camerling	1650	1619-1623
Jan Adriaensz. van Hensbrouck	1652	1622-1624
Adriaan van Twelle	1653-1654	1622-1629
Cornelis Cornelisz. Brouwer	1655-1660	1622-1669
Johan van Beest	1661-1671	1624-1647
Jacob Spoors	1672-1681	1637-1676
Cornelis van Overgaeu	1683	1621-1623
Willem de Langue	1684-1696	1623-1655
Cornelis Adriaansz. de Roon	1698-1700	1623-1636
Guillaume de Graeff	1701-1723	1623-1648

	Archive numbers	Dates
Adriaen (Adriaensz.) van der Block	1724-1757	1625-1662
Adriaen Rijshouck	1758-1823	1606-1648
Adriaen (Pietersz.) van der Wiel	1825-1826	1627-1652
Johan van Steeland	1831-1846	1626-1650
Jacob (Jansz.) Bijl	1847	1632-1633
Willem van Assendelft	1848-1871	1626-1676
Zeger Bogaerdt	1873	1627-1632
Arent (Cornelisz.) Bogaard	1874-1881	1627-1664
Andries Bogaert	1882-1888	1627-1658
Cornelis Pietersz. Bleiswijck	1899-1917	1629-1676
Gerrit Adriaensz. van der Wel	1925-1944	1634-1668
Jan Jorisz. van Ophoven	1947-1956	1634-1677
Johan van Ruiven	1958-1969	1638-1670
Schalkius van der Walle	1971-1973	1644-1662
Govert Rota	1976-1991	1638-1660
Frans Boo?ert	1992-2012	1642-1676
Jacob van Santen	2015-2019	1645-1662
Joris (Frans) van der Houve	2022-2028	1644-1679
Christiaen van Vliet	2032-2038	1653-1677
Melchior van der Borcht	2040-2043	1648-1677
Simon Mesch	2044-2050	1644-1653
Nicholaes Vrienber?h	2051-2065	1649-1668
En?elbert van der Vloet	2066-2072	1649-1666
Simon van Steelant	2075-2081	1650-1675
Cornelis (Adriaensz.) Geor?in	2083-2089	1650-1678
Frans van Hurck	2090-2093	1650-1680
Johannes Ranck	2104-2125	1652-1677
Gerard van Assendelft	2128-2133	1660-1681
Dirck Rees	2135-2150	1658-1676
Testart van Hasselt	2151-2160	1658-1680
Adriaan van der Block	2161	1666-1668
Jacobus van Berlecum	2162-2167	1662-1678
Abraham van der Velde	2171-2179	1663-1677
Abraham Verkerck	2200-2205	1663-1676
Cornelis Ouwendijck	2208-2210	1668-1676
Johannes van Veen	2223-2224	1669-1676
Floris van der Werff	2228	1677-1679
Paulus Durven	2237	1668-1679
Roelandus van Edenbur?h	2244-2261	1669-1676
Willem van Ruyven	2276-2278	1670-1675
Jan Boo?ert	2306	1676-1678

PUBLISHED SOURCES

Alpers, Svetlana. "Is Art History?" *Daedalus* 106 (Summer 1977):1-13.
Barbour, Violet. *Capitalism in Amsterdam in the 17th Century.* Ann Arbor: University of Michi?an Press, Ann Arbor Paper Books, 1963.

Bengtsson, Åke. *Studies on the Rise of Realistic Painting in Holland,* 1610–1625. Stockholm: Institute of Art History of Uppsala, 1952.

Berichten van het Historisch Gezelschap te Utrecht, vol. 1/2 (1846).

Beydals, Petra. "Cornelis Jacobsz. uit Delft." *Oud-Holland* 69 (1951):69–72.

Blankert, Albert. *Vermeer of Delft; Complete Edition of the Paintings.* Oxford: Phaidon, 1978.

Bleyswijck, Dirck van. *Beschrijvinge der stadt Delft.* Delft, 1667.

Boîtet, R. *Beschrijvinge der stadt Delft.* Delft, 1729.

Bol, Laurens. J. *Holländische Maler des 17. Jahrhunderts nahe den grossen Meistern: Landschaften und Stilleben.* Braunschweig: Klinkhard and Bierman, 1969.

Boon, K.G. "De meester van de Virgo inter Virgines." In *Oud Delft: Een serie van Historische Publicaties,* edited by V. van't Hoff. Rotterdam and The Hague: Nijgh en van Ditmer, n.d.

Bredius, Abraham. *Künstler-inventare; Urkunden zur Geschichte der Holländischen Kunst des XVI^{ten}, XVII^{ten}, und XVIII^{ten} Jahrhunderts.* 7 vols. The Hague: Martinus Nijhoff, 1915–1921.

————. "De tapijtfabriek van Karel van Mander de Jonge te Delft." *Oud-Holland* 3 (1885):1–11.

————. "Het geboortejaar van Jacob van Ruisdael." *Oud-Holland* 6 (1888):22–24.

————. "Drie delftsche schilders." *Oud-Holland* 6 (1888):289–98.

————. "Kunstkritiek der XVIIᵉ eeuw." *Oud-Holland* 7 (1889):42–44.

————. "De delftsche schilders Jan Willemsz. Decker en Willem Jansz. Decker." *Oud-Holland* 10 (1892):193–96.

————. "Het schildersregister van Jan Sysmus." *Oud-Holland* 12 (1894):160–171.

————. "Nieuwe bijdragen over Johannes Vermeer." *Oud-Holland* 29 (1910):61–64.

————. "Wat Anthony Palamedes aan een portrait verdiende." *Oud-Holland* 34 (1916):131–32.

————. "Italiaansche schilderijen in 1672 door Haagsche en Delftsche schilders beoordeeld." *Oud-Holland* 34 (1916):88–93.

————. "Twee leerlingen van Jacob Delff die geen voet bij stuk hielden." *Oud-Holland* 47 (1930):189.

Briels, J.G.C. *Zuidnederlandse boekdrukkers en boekverkopers in de Republiek der Verenigden Nederlanden omstreeks* 1570–1630. The Hague: Nieuwkoop and B. de Graaf, 1974.

————. *De Zuidnederlandse immigratie* 1572–1630. Haarlem: Fibula-van Dishoeck, 1978.

Brom, G.; and Langeraad, L.A. *Diarium van Arend van Buchell* in *Werken,* Series 3, no. 2. Utrecht: Historisch Genootschap, 1907.

Broos, B.P.J. Review of *Frans Hals* by Seymour Slive. *Simiolus* 10 (1978–79):115–123.

Brown, Christopher, *Carel Fabritius.* Oxford: Phaidon, 1981.

Bibliography

Bruyn, Josua de. "Een onderzoek naar 17ᵉ eeuwse schilderijformaten, voornamelijk in Noordnederland." *Oud-Holland* 93 (1979):96-115.

Burgh, A.H.H. van der. "Delfsche Roode Theepotten." *Oud-Holland* 19 (1901):99-120.

_____. "Aanteekeningen betreffende de oudste Delfsche plateelbakkers." *Oud-Holland* 21 (1903):22-50.

Burke, Peter. *Tradition and Innovation in Renaissance Italy: A Sociological Approach.* London: William Collins and Sons, Fontana Books, 1974.

Campo-Weyermann, Jakob. *De levensbeschryvingen der Nederlandsche konst-schilders ende konstschilderessen.* 3 vols. The Hague, 1729.

Crena de Iongh, A. C. G. C. *van Santen's Lichte Wigger en Snappende Siitgen; zeventiende-eeuwse gesprekken in Delfts Dialect.* Assen: Van Gorcum, 1959.

Delenne, René-Louis. *Dictionnaire des marques de l'ancienne faïence de Delft.* Paris: Richard Masse, 1947.

Dijck, J. H. van. "Rekeningen betreffende het financieel aandeel van Delft aan den vrijheidsoorlog." *Bijdragen en mededeelingen van het Historisch Genootschap* 54 (1933):43-124.

Dillen, Johannes G. van. *Van rijkdom en regenten; handboek tot de economische en sociale geschiedenis van Nederland tijdens de Republiek.* The Hague: M. Nijhoff, 1970.

_____. "Summiere staat van de in 1622 in Provincie van Holland gehouden volkstelling." *Economisch-historisch Jaarboek* 21 (1940):175-78.

Duverger, Erik. *Nieuwe gegevens betreffende de kunsthandel van Matthijs Musson en Maria Fourmenois te Antwerpen tussen 1633 en 1681.* Ghent: n.p., 1969.

Eisler, Max. *Alt-Delft: Kultur und Kunst.* Amsterdam: Elsevier, 1923.

Emmens, Jan. "Einst aber ist nötig: Inhalt und Bedeutung von Markt-und Küchenstücke des 16 Jahrhundert," in *Album Amicorum J.G. van Gelder,* ed. J. Bruyn, J. A. Emmens, E. de Jongh, and D. P. Snoep, pp. 93-101. The Hague: M. Nijhoff, 1973.

Floerke, Hanns. *Die Formen des Kunsthandels, das Atelier und die Sammler in den Niederlanden vom 15-18 Jahrhundert.* Studien zur Niederländischen Kunst- und Kulturgeschichte. 1905; reprint ed., Soest, Holland: Davaco Publishers, 1972.

Gelder, J. G. van. "De schilders van de Oranje-zaal." *Nederlandsch Kunsthistorisch Jaarboek* 2 (1948-49):118-164.

Hauser, Arnold. *The Social History of Art,* 4 vols. London: Routledge and Kegan Paul, 1951.

Havard, Henry. *L'Art et les Artistes Hollandais.* 4 vols. Paris, 1879-1881.

_____. *Histoire des faïences de Delft, Haarlem, Rotterdam, Utrecht, etc. et des porcelaines de Weesp, Loosdrecht, Amsterdam et la Haye.* 2 vols. Amsterdam: "Vivat," 1909.

Haverkamp-Begemann, Egbert. Introduction to *Rembrandt after Three*

Hundred Years: An Exhibition of Rembrandt and His Followers. Chicago: Art Institute of Chicago, 1969.

Haverkorn van Rijswijck, P. "Eenige aanteekeningen betreffende schilders wonende buiten Rotterdam uit het Archief te Rotterdam," *Oud-Holland* 8 (1890):210-14.

———. "Rotterdamsche schilders, de schilders Volmarijn." *Oud-Holland* 12 (1894):136-59.

Hollstein, F. W. *Dutch and Flemish Etchings, Engravings and Woodcuts* 1450-1700. 18 vols. Amsterdam: M. Hertberger, 1949-1974.

Hoogenwerff, G. J. *De geschiedenis van de St. Lucasgilden in Nederland.* Amsterdam: P. N. van Kampen en Zoon, 1947.

———; and J. Q. Van Regteren Altena. *Arnoldus Buchelius "Res pictoriae."* Quellenstudien zur Holländische Kunstgeschichte, vol. 15. The Hague: M. Nijhoff, 1928.

Hoogstraten, Samuel. *Inleyding tot de hooge schoole der schilder-konst anders de Zichtbaere Werelt.* Rotterdam, 1678.

Houbraken, Arnold. *De Groote Schouburgh der Nederlandsche Konstschilders en Schilderessen.* Edited by P. T. Swillens. 3 vols. Maastricht: Leiter-Nypals, 1943.

Hudig, Ferrand W. *Delfter Fayence; ein Handbuch für Sammler und Liebhaber.* Berlin: R. C. Smidt, 1929.

Inventarissen van de inboedels in de verblijven van de Oranjes. The Hague: M. Nijhoff, 1974. (Rijksgeschiedkundige publicatiën.)

Jonge, C. H. de. *Dutch Ceramics.* New York: Praeger, 1970.

———. *Dutch Tiles.* London: Pall Mall Press, 1971.

Kernkamp, J. H. *De handel op den vijand* 1572-1690. 2 vols. Utrecht: Kemink en Zoon, n.d.

Kloot Meijburg, L. H. H. van der. *De Nieuwe Kerk te Delft.* Rotterdam: W. L. J. Brusse, 1941.

Ledeboer, A. M. *De boekdrukkers, boekverkoopers en uitgevers in Noord Nederland sedert de uitvinding van de Boekdrukkunst tot den aanvang der negentiende eeuw.* Deventer, 1872.

Liedtke, Walter, "Hendrick van Vliet and the Delft School." *Museum News* 21 (1979):41-52.

———. Review of *Perspective, Optics and Delft Artists around* 1650, by Arthur Wheelock. *Art Bulletin* 61 (1979):490-96.

Mander, Karel van. *Het Schilderboeck . . . der Edele Vrye Schilderkonst.* Haarlem, 1604.

Montias, J. M. "New Documents on Vermeer and His Family." *Oud-Holland* 91 (1977):267-87.

———. "Vermeer and His Milieu: Conclusion of an Archival Study." *Oud-Holland* 94 (1980):44-62.

Moxon, Joseph. *Mechanick Exercises on the Whole Art of Printing* 1683-1684. Edited by H. Davis and H. Carter. London: Oxford University Press, 1958.

National Gallery. *Art in Seventeenth-Century Holland*. Exhibition catalogue. London: National Gallery, 1976.

Naumann, Otto. *Frans van Mieris the Elder*. Doornspijk, Holland: Davaco Publishers, 1981.

Neumann, W. *Beschreibendes Verzeichnis der Gemälde der Vereinigten Sammlungen der Stadt Riga, des Rigaschen Kunstvereins und des Weil. Rigaschen Ratsherrn Fried. Wilh. Brederlo*. Riga: Rigaer Tageblatt, 1906.

Nieuwstraten, J. "Frederick van Frytom faience-tekenaar en landschapschilder." *Bulletin Museum Boymans-van Beuningen* 20 (1969):2-36.

Obreen, F. D. O. *Archief voor Nederlandsche Kunstgeschiedenis*. 7 vols. Rotterdam, 1877-1890.

Oosterbaan, D. P. "Kroniek van de Nieuwe Kerk te Delft; inleiding en aantekeningen." *Haarlemse Bijdragen* 65 (1958).

———. *De Oude Kerk te Delft gedurende de Middeleeuwen*. The Hague: J. N. Voorhoeve, 1973.

Oosterloo, Jan H. *De Meesters van Delft; Leven en werken van de Delftse schilders der zeventiende eeuw*. Amsterdam: A. J. G. Strenghold Uitgeverij, 1948.

Peer, A. J. J. M. van. "Rondom Jan Vermeer van Delft." *Oud-Holland* 74 (1959):240-45.

Posthumus, N. W. *De geschiedenis van de Leidsche lakenindustrie*. 3 vols. The Hague: M. Nijhoff, 1908-1939.

———. *Inquiry into the History of Prices in Holland*. 2 vols. Leyden: E. J. Briel, 1946.

Resolutiën der Staten-Generaal (Nieuwe reeks). The Hague: M. Nijhoff, 1971. (Rijksgeschiedkundige publicatiën.)

Rijksmuseum, Amsterdam. *Catalogue des tableaux, miniatures, pastels, dessins encadrés du Musée de l'Etat à Amsterdam*. Amsterdam: Roeloffzen-Hübner en van Santen, 1904.

———. *All the Paintings in the Rijksmuseum*. Maarssen: Gary Schwartz, 1979.

Rosenberg, Jacob; S. Slive; and E. H. ter Kuile. *Dutch Art and Architecture 1600-1800*. Pelican History of Art Series. Rev. ed. Baltimore: Penguin Books, 1972.

Scheller, R. W. "Nieuwe gegevens over het St. Lukasgilde te Delft in de zestiende eeuw." *Nederlandsch Kunsthistorisch Jaarboek* 26 (1972):41-48.

Scitovsky, Tibor. *The Joyless Economy: An Inquiry into Human Satisfaction and Consumer Dissatisfaction*. London: Oxford University Press, 1976.

Soutendam, J. "Eenige aanteekeningen betreffende Delfsche kunstenaars." *Nederlandsche Spectator* (1870):1-17. (separately bound reprint in Delft Archive)

———. "Beeldstormerij te Delft in Augustus en October 1655." *Bijdragen voor Vaderlandsche Geschiedenis en Oudheidkunde*, n.s., pt. 9 (1877):173–222.

Stedelijk Museum Het Prinsenhof. *De Stad Delft; Cultuur en Maatschappij tot 1572*. 2 vols. Delft: Stedelijk Museum, 1979.

Sutton, Peter. "Hendrick van der Burch." *The Burlington Magazine* 122 (1980):315–26.

———. *Pieter de Hooch; Complete Edition*. London: Phaidon, 1980.

Swart, K. W. "Holland's Bourgeoisie and the Retarded Industrialization of the Netherlands," in *Failed Transitions to Modern Industrial Society: Renaissance Italy and Seventeenth Century Holland*, ed. F. Krant and P. M. Hohenberg. Montreal: Concordia University and Université du Québec à Montréal, 1975.

Swillens, P. T. A. "R. K. Kunstenaars in de 17de Eeuw," *Katholiek Cultureel Tijdschrift*, 15 January 1946, pp. 416–19.

Thieme, V., and F. Becker. *Allgemeines Lexicon der Bildenden Künstler von der Antike bis zur Gegenwart*. 37 vols. Leipzig: W. Engelmann, 1907–1950.

Vermeeren, P. J. "Delftse verluchte handschriften ter Koninklijke Bibliotheek" in *Oud-Delft: Een Serie van Historische Publicaties*, ed. B. van't Hoff. Rotterdam and The Hague: Nijgh en van Ditmer, n.d.

Vries, Jan de. *The Dutch Rural Economy in the Golden Age*. New Haven: Yale University Press, 1974.

———. "Barges and Capitalism: Passenger Transportation in the Dutch Economy 1631–1839." in *Bijdragen*, Adfeling Agrarische Geschiedenis, Landbouwhogeschool, Wageningen, vol. 21 (1978), pp. 33–361.

Weisbrod, Burton A. "Toward a Theory of the Voluntary Non-Profit Sector in a Three-Sector Economy." in *Altruism, Morality, and Economic Theory*, ed. Edmund Phelps. New York: Russell Sage Foundation, 1972.

Wheelock, Arthur K. *Perspective, Optics and Delft Artists Around 1650*. New York: Garland Publications, 1977.

Wichmann, Heinrich. *Leonaert Bramer; Sein Leben und Sein Kunst: ein Beitrag zur Geschichte der Holländische Malerei*. Leipzig: W. Hiersemann, 1923.

———. "Mitteilungen über Delfter Künstler des XVII Jahrhunderts." *Oud-Holland* 42 (1925):60–71.

Index

Index

John Michael Montias is Professor of Economics at the Institution for
Social and Policy Studies, Yale University. His previous books include
*Central Planning in Poland, Economic Development in Communist
Romania,* and *The Structure of Economic Systems.*

Library of Congress Cataloging in Publication Data

Montias, John Michael, 1928–
   Artists and artisans in Delft.

   Bibliography: p.
   Includes index.
     1. Artists—Netherlands—Delft—Socio—
economic status. 2. Art, Modern—17th-18th
centuries—Netherlands—Delft. 3. Art
industries and trade—Netherlands—Delft—
History—17th century. I. Title.
N6946.M6   709'.493'3   81-11953
ISBN 0-691-03986-0   AACR2
ISBN 0-691-10129-9 (pbk.)